In Defense of American Higher Education

In Defense of American Higher Education

EDITED BY

Philip G. Altbach
Patricia J. Gumport
D. Bruce Johnstone

The Johns Hopkins University Press ∽ *Baltimore and London*

05   # 44972214

9 8 7 6 5 4 3 2 1

The Johns Hopkins University Press
2715 North Charles Street
Baltimore, Maryland 21218–4363
www.press.jhu.edu

ISBN 0-8018-6654-5
ISBN 0-8018-6655-3 (pbk.)

Library of Congress Cataloging-in-Publication Data
In defense of American higher education / edited by Philip G.
Altbach, Patricia J. Gumport, and D. Bruce Johnstone.
    p.   cm.
Includes bibliographical references and index.
    ISBN 0-8018-6654-5 (alk. paper) — ISBN 0-8018-6655-3 (pbk.:
alk. paper)
    1. Education, Higher—Aims and objectives—United States.   2.
Education, Higher—Social aspects—United States.   I. Altbach,
Philip G.   II. Gumport, Patricia J.   III. Johnstone, D. Bruce
(Donald Bruce), 1941–   IV. Title.
    LA227.4.I5   2001
    378.73—dc21

00-011291

A catalog record for this book is available from the British Library.

Contents ～

Part Two   Within the Academy

In Defense of American
Higher Education

Introduction ～

Contemporary criticisms of U.S. higher education tend to overlook valuable enduring legacies. In this volume we take a different approach, because we are committed to preserving the strengths as well as addressing the weaknesses of the higher education system. Thus, the contributors to this volume analyze universities and colleges from both critical and compassionate perspectives.

This approach stands in stark contrast to that of such critics as Peter Drucker, who recently claimed (1993) that the university would disappear under the pressure of technology and changing ideas about higher education, and Bill Readings, who suggests (1996) that nostalgia is fruitless. Hardly a day goes by without an attack on academic institutions for inefficiency, irresponsibility, and ungovernability.

Our premises are unabashedly idealistic. We cherish the best ideals of institutions of higher education: academic freedom, commitments to both inquiry and teaching, engagement with ideas and critiques, and preserving an independence of mind and spirit in the face of external pressure, which represents simultaneously a detachment from and an involvement with society.

At the same time, we aim to be realistic in reflecting upon the failings of universities and colleges. Clearly, not all legacies are worth preserving. Consider, for example, some of the obvious negatives in the historical record: racism, sexism, and anti-Semitism, as well as the liabilities associated with nuclear weapons research and scientific misconduct. Consider also the broader assessments that the institution is slow to change, inefficient, and hampered by cumbersome governance. In essence, we believe that not all legacies are meant to be handed down in their existing forms without scrutiny.

What, then, are the enduring legacies worthy of preservation and in what form? As a beginning, we affirm a fundamental affection for the enterprise similar to that of Daniel Webster, who, in his defense of Dartmouth College before the United States Supreme Court on March 10, 1818, said: "Sir, you may wish to destroy this little institution . . . , but if you do . . . you must extinguish, one after another, all those great lights of science, which, for more than a century, have thrown their radiance over the land! It is, sir, as I have said, a small college, and yet there are those that love it" (quoted in Rudolph, 1990, 209–10). We extend these sentiments to the full range of the institutions that constitute the U.S. higher education system. We believe that many criticisms are based on a misunderstanding or a lack of commitment to the diverse missions of these institutions. Moreover, we believe that many criticisms reflect an inadequate understanding of the magnitude of today's challenges: accountability demands, access demands, and expectations to contain costs and improve fiscal management, in addition to embracing new technologies in both internal management and the delivery of educational services. These demands constitute a tall order alongside the legacies of academic freedom, critical inquiry, and advanced education and training for future generations.

Even as U.S. universities and colleges have at times faltered in fulfilling their missions, in our view they, and particularly U.S. universities, are one of the success stories of the past century. The university as an institution has survived for most of the millennium. Indeed, if one looks historically at institutions that have survived as long as the university, one finds just a small number—the Roman Catholic Church, the British and Japanese monarchies, and perhaps a dozen universities! The American university—combining as it does undergraduate instruction from the English colleges, the research ideal of the nineteenth-century German universities, and the home-grown concept of service to society—is, at the beginning of the twenty-first century, the most influential academic model in the world.

This book is committed to the continued prosperity of the American university alongside the institutional diversity achieved by the entire U.S. higher education system. We think it is essential to look critically in order to best understand and preserve its strengths and at the same time change those elements to better align with circumstances of the twenty-first century.

The Premises of This Book

In these chapters we look mainly at the research university, which is what most critics seem to have in their minds when they criticize "higher education." We did not want to write or edit a simple apologia, nor to deny the validity of many of the observations underlying the conventional criticisms of higher education. Rather we wanted contributions that would go beyond mere critical observation (e.g., of the research orientation of many faculty) to an examination of the forces that cause or maintain that behavior and an accurate portrayal of its occurrence, and a weighing of the benefits and the costs (e.g., of a dominant scholarly orientation among university faculty).

Although the chapters each focus on different themes and domains within higher education, there are some criticisms that cut across those topics. The criticisms of university faculty include claims that some of them do too little work, that some who work hard spend too little time on the things they are mainly (at least in the minds of their critics) paid to do, or that they may work hard on the right things but do so ineffectively. Conventional criticism is also aimed at administrators and the various positions of institutional management: presidents, deans, department chairs, multicampus system heads, or governing boards. Depending upon the source and the object of the criticism, the charge may be that governing boards and university management have sold out to corporate or political influences and have thereby betrayed fundamental and presumably noble academic values. Or, the criticism may be the mirror opposite: that academic management (presidents, provosts, and deans) is in virtual thrall to faculty interests, which may not necessarily be congruent with the interests of the taxpayers, parents, and students who pay the bills.

This state of affairs is presumed to exist either because the presidents, vice presidents, and deans genuinely believe that most of the faculty are behaving appropriately (as they themselves intend to behave when they return to the classroom or laboratory) or because they are too weak or otherwise managerially ineffectual to get the faculty to behave as they should. And to complete the almost conspiratorial loop, this allegedly dysfunctional managerial behavior, which is unable to cure the allegedly dysfunctional faculty behavior, is presumed to be almost uncorrectable as a result of the traditions of faculty participation in (and virtual veto over) the selection of the president, and the tradition that he or she be first a scholar and only secondarily, if at all, a proven manager.

Sometimes the alleged inadequacies are laid at the door of something more conceptual, or at least impersonal. Thus, the reward system is to blame (for alleged deficiencies in teaching). Or the market (for the alleged overemphasis on vocational skills and subservience to student demand, to the denigration of more fundamental intellectual values). Or the high schools, or television and video games (for giving us 18-year-olds who are neither prepared for, nor interested in, genuine learning). Or capitalism (for enshrining values of competition, materialism, and exploitation to the alleged exclusion or diminution of cooperation, sharing, compassion, and economic justice). Or liberalism (for its notions of cultural relativism, victimization, and egalitarianism to the exclusion of fundamental values, scientific truths, and individual responsibility).

Wherever blame is thought to lie, the criticisms may range from criteria for entry (especially those that recognize racial preferences), standards for entry (allowing in too many with inadequate academic preparation), the curriculum (either too rigid and traditional or too loose and insufficiently appreciative of the Western literary and historical canon), and the cost of college (criticizing either the underlying per-student cost of instruction or the price, meaning tuition).

The Critiques

Many of the criticisms have a political or ideological cast. Most of the criticisms of the 1980s and 1990s were from the ideological right (Allan Bloom, William Bennett, Martin Anderson, Dinesh D'Souza), although many of them have been echoed by people who would reject the label of political conservatism. But there remains a vestige of criticism that is more traditionally liberal or leftist by those who criticize the higher education establishment for insufficient effort (and vastly insufficient success) in overcoming the class, race, and gender biases that still exist. Recent critics from the left also decry the universities for their ever closer ties to corporate interests, proprietary research in biotechnology, and the general trend toward university-industry linkages (Slaughter and Leslie 1997). And both sides of the conventional political spectrum tend to decry what is perceived as higher education's overeager embrace of market mechanisms for the allocation of resources both to and within the college or university.

A central line of criticism since the 1970s has argued that the core of the undergraduate curriculum has been lost in a rush toward vocationalism, multiculuralism, ethnic and gender studies, and the like. Critics claim that the university has simply let forces within and outside of academe determine the direction of academic programs. Nannerl O. Keohane, in this volume, makes a strong argument for the liberal arts and general education. In fact, general education, perhaps with a somewhat expanded definition, is alive and well in U.S. colleges and universities. After permitting the liberal arts curriculum to deteriorate in the aftermath of the student protests of the 1960s and the vocationalism of the 1970s, the faculty reasserted its control over the curriculum and reestablished a core curriculum at many institutions.

Changes in the curriculum have taken place, reflecting the ability of American higher education to respond to new realities. Entirely new fields, such as computer science, some of the new biotechnology disciplines, and others have been added. New interdisciplinary fields such as gender and ethnic studies have joined traditional disciplines. We do not see these changes as a cause for criticism of academe. On the contrary, the ability to respond to changing needs while retaining the core values of the curriculum and the university is, to us, one of the abiding strengths of the university. There has been struggle, for example, concerning the control of the curriculum or over "political correctness," when one point of view sought to impose its will on departments or disciplines. But, in general, the result has been the addition of new ideas and fields to the curriculum while maintaining traditional values and orientations (Wilson 1995). The "curriculum wars" of the 1980s and beyond show that eternal vigilance is indeed the price of maintaining the best values in higher education.

Some of the criticism is shrill and overreaching, reflecting political or ideological agendas extending beyond the academy: attacks on multiculturalism or affirmative action or public-sector unions, or the promotion of particular religious or spiritual values. The criticisms may be based on anecdotes, reflecting the variation that may be found in any enterprise or profession and that represent mainly the inevitable extremes or outliers. Some of the criticism is ahistorical, overlooking many developments in higher education's rich past. Some criticism is mistaken or careless in its aim or not really aimed at all: for example, extending the quite legitimate criticisms of research universities (say, the use of clearly unqualified graduate students as teaching assistants or the preoccupation with research to the exclusion of involvement with undergraduate teaching) to undergraduate colleges, where such practices simply would not exist. And some criticisms are simply demonstrably incorrect: for example, the charge that private tuitions are so high because of federal Pell grants (the Pell grants are and have always been tuition neutral) or that costs (or prices) are forcing the middle class out of higher education (not so), or that *The Color Purple,* by Alice Walker, is now taught more than the works of Shakespeare (one of those unfounded charges that gets picked up by the press and acquires authority by repetition).

U.S. higher education, for all its seeming success (as measured, for example, by its phenomenal growth, international prominence, much vaunted connection to technology and economic expansion, and increasing importance to individual economic and social mobility) continues to be subject to heavy criticism. Moreover, this criticism, and the higher education reform agenda it spawned, resembles the criticism and reform agenda that emerged a generation ago from the Carnegie Commission and Council on Policy Studies and their rich 12-year output of 36 policy recommendation reports and more than 120 sponsored studies and technical reports. And if one goes back, for example, to Nisbet's *The Degradation of the Academic Dogma* (1971) or Jencks and Riesman's *Academic Revolution* (1968), or farther, to Hutchins's *Higher Learning in America* (1936), or even farther, to Veblen's *Higher Learning in America* (1918) or James's "The Ph.D. Octopus" (1903), one finds a remarkable continuity of criticism and reform agenda.

Does this mean that higher education really hasn't changed that much—or at least, not in fundamental ways? Is the enormous growth of community colleges or the expansion of participation to include so many more older, part-time, low-income, and minority students (not to mention females, who are now a majority of first-time college students) diminished because most of our learning still takes place in traditional classrooms, taught in modules of three- or four-credit semester courses? Is the explosive growth of new knowledge and new fields of study, including interdisciplinary programs of study and research, diminished by the fact that most faculty and students are engaged not in molecular and subcellular biology or physical biochemistry but in undergraduate courses in mathematics and English and history, where any changes in content and pedagogy are modest?

Have campuses failed to reform because they have been shielded from market forces by growth or by public subsidies or by their own self-serving myths? Or is that folly, such as it may be, best evidenced (as it always has been) by an overattention to the market—to the detriment of the core liberal arts and to higher education's responsibility as guardians of a historical and literary canon?

Are we in higher education, as at least some of our critics would have it, obtuse and defensive? Or, is it our critics who fail to acknowledge our profound changes and improvements, and who insist on dwelling instead on aspects of the academy that are either anecdotal, unrepresentative, or trivial or properly resistant to change (especially to changes pressed by political and commercial interests)?

The Case of the Professoriate

We acknowledge that there is much that is both true and useful in the conventional criticisms of the U.S. university, particularly if the criticism be sharpened, clarified, and aimed more accurately. For example, some faculty in some colleges and universities have undoubtedly "retired on the job." And tenure surely has something to do with the phenomenon, or at least with its persistence. But to the degree that the criticism is valid—as well as the degree to which the phenomenon is potentially avoidable or at least reducible—it is necessary to address the following kinds of questions:

—What is the extent and pattern of its occurrence (that is, of the demonstrably unproductive faculty member)?
—To what degree, and in what kinds of institutions, is the alleged deficit of academic productivity manifested in, for example, an insufficient amount of teaching (too few classes or too few students per class), inadequate or ineffective teaching, or quantitatively or qualitatively insufficient scholarship?
—To what degree, and in what pattern, is this phenomenon (unproductive faculty) occurring more than might naturally be expected? That is, is it more prevalent than in other organizations or enterprises, in which there is also an inevitable range of measurable productivity among members? (In other words, is there a defense in the fact that in any assemblage there will always be a least productive and a most productive?)
—If "fault" is to be found in the case of the insufficiently productive or ineffective faculty member, then it seems reasonable to blame not just the faculty member but, more importantly, management as well for inadequate policies and practices that have allowed the problems to occur and to persist. So, one must ask, what is the record of managerial (department chair, dean, or academic vice president) complicity in the situation—in the initial ap-

pointment and awarding of tenure, as well as in efforts to help the allegedly unproductive faculty member improve and, if necessary, to bring to bear the available procedures for discipline?

This is the spirit of our book. We, and our contributors, are engaged in a constructive analysis of contemporary U.S. higher education with its enduring legacies in mind. We are committed to understanding and improving an amazingly successful set of institutions. We have every expectation that U.S. higher education will survive this new millennium, just as it grew and flourished in the past. Yet, the challenges are significant. As such, careful analysis of what we have inherited, along with a critical eye for constructive reform, is necessary if U.S. higher education is to continue to thrive.

References

Bloom, A. 1987. *The closing of the American mind: How higher education has failed democracy and impoverished the souls of today's students.* New York: Simon & Schuster.

Carnegie Council on Policy Studies in Higher Education. 1980. *A summary of reports and recommendations.* San Francisco: Jossey-Bass.

D'Souza, D. 1991. *Illiberal education: The politics of race and sex on campus.* New York: Free Press.

Drucker, P. F. 1993. *Postcapitalist society.* New York: HarperCollins.

Hutchins, R. M. [1936] 1979. *The higher learning in America.* Reprint, Westport, Conn.: Greenwood.

James, W. 1903. The Ph.D. octopus. *Harvard Monthly* 36, no. 1.

Jencks, C., and D. Riesman. 1968. *The academic revolution.* Garden City, N.Y.: Doubleday.

Nisbet, R. 1971. *The degradation of the academic dogma: The university in America, 1945–1970.* New York: Basic Books.

Readings, B. 1996. *The university in ruins.* Cambridge: Harvard University Press.

Rudolph, F. C. 1990. *The American college and university: A history.* Athens: University of Georgia Press.

Slaughter, S., and L. L. Leslie. 1997. *Academic capitalism: Politics, policies, and the entrepreneurial university.* Baltimore: Johns Hopkins University Press.

Veblen, T. 1918. *The higher learning in America: A memorandum on the conduct of universities by business men.* New York: B. W. Huebsch.

Wilson, J. K. 1995. *The myth of political correctness: The conservative attack on higher education.* Durham, N.C.: Duke University Press.

Part One ∾

The University in Society

Chapter One

The American Academic Model in Comparative Perspective

Philip G. Altbach

In a curious paradox, at the same time that American academe has come in for unprecedented criticism at home, it is widely emulated abroad. Indeed, the American higher education system has become the worldwide "gold standard" for higher education, respected for its leadership in research and scholarship and for providing access to large numbers of students. Foreign delegations tour American campuses seeking to glean useful insights. Entire academic systems are reengineered to reflect such U.S. practices as the course credit system, competition among academic institutions, the coexistence of public and private universities and colleges, diversity in institutional missions and goals, accountability within and among academic institutions, and the organization of public universities and colleges into state systems. Unique American innovations such as the community college are carefully studied by foreign experts. American universities and colleges are widely viewed as having dealt constructively with many of the challenges facing higher education throughout the world.

This chapter explores just what makes the American academic system so attractive. Here, a comparative perspective can provide useful insights, and the mirror of foreign experience can show Americans just what is valuable about their own system. A comparative approach that examines how other societies have attempted to solve their problems allows issues and solutions to be critically evaluated (Altbach 1998). This approach exposes policymakers to a broader range of possibilities and warns of potential problems. A comparative perspective provides an opportunity to examine alternatives. Yet, it is seldom possible to apply an institutional model or a specific policy from abroad directly, without considerable modification and adaptation. Thus, a comparative approach may raise consciousness and indicate a direction, but it cannot deliver external solutions to a domestic problem. Where this has been tried—in the export of the American land-grant concept to Nigeria, India, and other countries, for example—the results have been mixed and, in many instances, quite different from what the planners had anticipated.

The reasons for American academic preeminence at the beginning of the twenty-first century are no secret, nor are they entirely due to the creativity of those responsible for organizing American higher education. Because the United States was the first nation to commit itself to mass higher education, and later to universal access, Americans had to design an academic system early on to deal with large numbers of students. This led to such innovations as diversity of mission among academic institutions, the organization of public systems of higher education, and a hierarchy of quality and selectivity among institutions.

The very size and wealth of the American academic system means that it commands interest overseas. With more than 14 million students in postsecondary education, the United States educates perhaps 20 percent of the world's students. More important, the United States accounts for almost half of the world's research-and-development expenditures, a significant share of which goes to academic institutions. A large majority of the most prominent academic journals are edited in the United States, where many of the databases and other elements of the new information technology network are also based. The country is also host to close to a half million students from other countries—about a third of the world's total of students who study abroad—another indication of the importance of the American academic system.

Historical Perspectives

The American university developed out of specific historical realities, which shaped the nature of the system. It may be useful to examine some of the factors in the history of American higher education (Vey-sey 1965; Ben-David 1972). All university systems are a combination of national and international traditions. The basic university model is European and goes back to the medieval universities of Paris and Bologna. These are the antecedents not only for the universities in North America and Europe, but also in Asia and Africa. In the American case, the earliest models, such as Harvard and Yale, were English and patterned after Oxford and Cambridge as these universities were when they were concerned with the education of Protestant clergymen. Educational ideas from Scotland of a more democratic nature were also influential. The early American colleges were religiously oriented for the most part and aimed at training a small elite. With a few exceptions, such as Thomas Jefferson's University of Virginia, the curriculum was narrow and strictly followed English patterns.

At the end of the eighteenth and the beginning of the nineteenth centuries, American higher education expanded impressively, while not changing its basic curricular orientation. The colleges provided a fairly narrow curriculum, steeped in classical studies and languages. Many of these new institutions were established in the newly settled parts of the nation and were products of the growing egalitarianism of American society. No longer was higher education a preserve of the urban elite; the middle classes in the new towns and in rural areas gained access to a college education. They did this largely by establishing their own colleges. The new institutions on the frontier copied the established curricula of Harvard and Yale. Most were established by religious denominations concerned not only with general education but also with the inculcation of Christian values. As the number and variety of Protestant denominations grew in America, their educational institutions also proliferated. Even today, the American heartland of Ohio, Indiana, Illinois, and even New York and Pennsylvania, is dotted with undergraduate colleges established by Protestant denominations and, in some cases, still affiliated to them. Some of these schools—Oberlin, Swarthmore, Knox, and Grinnell, among many others—are of very high standard. These colleges are oriented toward liberal education in the arts and sciences and have maintained a commitment to educational excellence over the years. An English academic tradition, changed and democratized by the American experience, is one of the key historical elements of the American academic system. The Roman Catholic Church has also been active in establishing colleges and universities—more than 200 academic institutions are Catholic in origin and tradition.

A second, and in many ways more complicated, historical tradition involves the emergence of graduate education in the decades following the Civil War (Veysey 1965). This development accompanied the rise of the public universities, the ethos of public service, and the linking of research to agricultural and industrial development. Facilitated by the Morrill Act of 1862 that provided large amounts of government land to each of the states for the support of public higher education, the great land-grant universities of the Middle West grew and took a key position in the academic system. The land-grant concept, exemplified by the Wisconsin Idea, argued that the boundaries of the universities are the boundaries of the state and that a state university has the responsibility of serving the entire population, not only with traditional education, but also with applied research that would promote emerging industry and agriculture (Curti and Carstensen 1949). The University of Wisconsin along with the state universities in Michigan, Illinois, Indiana, Minnesota, and several other states exemplified this new tradition. They grew rapidly and became America's first "multiversities," offering traditional undergraduate education as well as extension courses, informal advice and consulting, and other services. The land-grant institutions combined several key ideas in American higher education: the concept of direct service to society, the traditional idea of liberal arts studies as the cornerstone of undergraduate education, and the emphasis on research as part of the academic enterprise. These ideas spread from the great state universities to the established private institutions such as Harvard and Yale and had significant impact on the smaller institutions.

The gradual establishment of research as part of American higher education was an important development of the early twentieth century. In this, the American academic system looked to Germany for its model, importing the German concept of academic research and expanding the German ideal of academic freedom. German universities did not stress "pure" research but rather strove to make their research relevant to the emergence of Germany as a major industrial and scientific power. Americans traveled to Germany in the latter nineteenth century to obtain doctoral degrees, returning to the United States imbued with the importance of research as an integral part of the university. In this regard, Americans returned from their academic "Mecca" in Germany, much as students from the Third World now return from Western universities, fired with enthusiasm for the academic traditions and ideas they experienced during their formative student days (Geiger 1986). The aspects of American higher education most valued abroad are the powerful combination of service to society with research and the ability of the American research universities to foster both basic and applied research.

The contemporary American university was shaped by these three influences, two of which were foreign: the English liberal arts tradition, the German research concept, and the idea of service to the state as embodied by the public land-grant universities. Today's leading U.S. academic institutions combine these elements effectively. Yet it should be noted that the American university was shaped in part by foreign ideas. A key generation of American scholars—including leaders such as William Rainey Harper, who transformed higher education in the early years of the twentieth century—received their graduate education abroad. The changes took place over time, and they were opposed by important segments of the academic community. It is significant that Harvard became a research-oriented university rather late—only after this new model had proved its success at institutions such as the newly established universities of Chicago, Johns Hopkins, and Stanford. In some ways, it was easier for academic innovators to establish new institutions than to attempt to reform existing universities (Hawkins 1972). Only when the power of the new academic ideas had proven their worth did the established institutions adopt them.

By 1910, the basic structure of the research-oriented American university was well entrenched. While it is true that the large multiversities underwent their most dramatic expansion between 1950 and 1970, their orientation and structure date from the early years of the twentieth century. Another important early-twentieth-century structural innovation was the community colleges, which by the 1990s enrolled close to 40 percent of all postsecondary students (Cohen and Brawer 1996).

The historical development of the American academic system illustrates several important points. The American system is the creation of a number of foreign influences that melded together in the American context over a period of time. English and German influences were combined with forcefully articulated public policy and substantial financial support. The process of reform and development was a slow and often uneven one. As an increasing proportion of the population, particularly the articulate middle classes, became involved with colleges and universities and saw higher education as a means of social mobility, public support for higher education increased.

American higher education has historically shown remarkable adaptability (Geiger 1999). It has been able to take on new functions—from military training at the time of the Civil War to the community colleges in the twentieth century—in order to meet societal demands. The complex array of institutions that now constitute American postsecondary education is a tribute to the adaptability of the system.

Society and the University

Universities, after all, are embedded in the political, social, economic, and historical realities of their societies. The American tradition of private initiative influenced higher education from the beginning. The earliest colleges were private institutions, although it should be remembered that many of them had public support from the start. Harvard, for example, received some public funds (Rudolph 1990). Today, public funds go to private institutions for research through many government-supported loan and grant programs and in other ways. The religious impulse was also responsible for much of the early development of American higher education—and for the expansion of colleges westward in the late eighteenth and early nineteenth centuries. As already noted, many of the great American universities, including Harvard, Yale, Chicago, Georgetown, and others, were established with religious inspiration (Marsden 1994).

From the beginning, tuition was charged for higher education. Because of the private roots of the U.S. system, students and their families are used to paying for higher education. This contrasts with the situation in many countries, where public higher education is financed entirely by the state. Although the state has traditionally paid the bulk of the cost of education in the public institutions in this country, American colleges and universities, both public and private, have always charged tuition.

The U.S. Constitution gave basic responsibility for education to the states, and this has created a closer link between the colleges and universities and the government. While there are variations in state policies concerning postsecondary education, state control of higher education has been an advantage in that policymakers can accommodate the needs of specific regions. Because both policy and funding are decentralized, policymakers can respond quickly to regional and local needs and implement changes in the universities and colleges. Many other countries have highly centralized and bureaucratic academic systems that are difficult to change and rather inflexible in the face of new circumstances.

The Nonsystem of American Higher Education

Americans often take for granted the size, diversity, and complexity of the academic system. While there is considerable truth to David Riesman's observation that American academe is a kind of meandering procession, with everyone following after and seeking to emulate the prestigious research universities (1958), the system is tremendously diverse. A more accurate characterization of American higher education may be Ezra Cornell's stated goal in establishing what came to be Cornell University, "I would found an institution where any person can find instruction in any study" (Ashby 1971, ix). The United States pioneered the revolutionary idea that postsecondary education could, and should, provide education and training in virtually all fields. The academic system has been a beacon of quality, while at the same time striving to provide the widest possible range of academic preparation. American higher education has often been criticized for its lack of direction and focus, yet diversity and differentiation have been central organizing principles of the system (Flexner 1930).

Sponsorship, governance, and funding of American higher education come from a wide variety of sources. While critics fault the system for duplication and lack of coordination, in a sense, these features may constitute a strength, especially when compared to the often highly centralized and bureaucratic arrangements in many other countries. The worldwide trend is toward thinking about higher education as an integrated system that will provide the most efficient delivery of academic programs and maximize accountability. American academe is part of this trend, especially in states such as California and New York that have master plans regulating institutional specialization and functions for their public higher education systems (Smelser and Almond 1974). A state of creative confusion, however, characterizes most of the U.S. system. Private institutions, which educate 20 percent of students, range from some of the most prestigious universities to the many small schools struggling to survive in the educational marketplace. Government funds help to support private institutions through student loan programs, research grants, and the like. Government research support is, in general, given for specific projects on a competitive basis rather than provided directly as an entitlement to departments or universities. Among state universities, the new emphasis is on obtaining funds from private donors, links with private firms, and other public-private partnerships. In some ways, there are fewer distinctions between public and private institutions, a trend that can also be observed in other countries (Altbach 2000).

Despite its diversity, a clear hierarchy exists in American higher education, with the research universities on the top. These are the "multiversities" that Clark Kerr discussed in his 1963 book *The Uses of the University*. The evolution of these institutions since the end of the nineteenth century is another example of the genius of American higher education. Universities such as Harvard, the University of California at Berkeley, and the University of Chicago are recognized as being world-class academic institutions. They provide leadership in research and have been creative in developing models to deliver the educational and research services demanded by society.

The organized research unit, for example, has permitted universities to focus on new and often interdisciplinary research ideas (as well as funding possibilities) while at the same time retaining the core discipline-based department structure. The research universities have managed to combine basic and applied research. This American organizational innovation has been key to fostering interdisciplinary research while at the same time protecting the traditional academic disciplines. It is an excellent example of the American penchant for reform in the context of conservative academic structures.

Despite the lecture-based traditional teaching methods, large classes, and an overreliance on graduate teaching assistants, for which they have been justly criticized, the research universities have managed to provide an acceptable quality of teaching and a comprehensive curriculum for both undergraduate and graduate students.

In the 1990s many of the top research universities have reexamined the quality of their teaching and focused more attention in this area. Some have argued that the research university model now dominates American higher education. Even colleges and universities that are not primarily research institutions are focusing too much on research, and promotion policies at schools largely involved in teaching stress research too much (Boyer 1990). This emphasis is a recognition that the research universities constitute the gold standard of American higher education. Some segments of the system, such as the elite liberal arts colleges, have managed to combine a research orientation with a primary commitment to undergraduate teaching. Other parts of the system—for example, universities that started out as teachers colleges and attempted to transform themselves into research universities—have been less successful, in many cases losing sight of their original missions while failing to break into the top ranks of research schools. The fact is that most American colleges and universities are largely devoted to teaching, with research as a modest part of their mission.

A second major category of institutions is the undergraduate arts and sciences colleges. These range from some of the most prestigious and competitive academic institutions in the nation to the many four-year colleges in both the public and private sectors that educate large numbers of students but have no pretensions to greatness. They offer a basic education in the liberal arts, with some specialization in an academic or vocationally oriented field toward the end of the four-year curriculum. Some of these colleges, particularly in the public sector, also offer limited graduate programs, typically at the master's level. The more prestigious of these liberal arts colleges are the inheritors of the liberal tradition in American higher education. Despite considerable differences in prestige, quality, and sponsorship, they share a considerable unity in their orientation toward general education, emphasis on teaching, and provision of an attractive extracurricular environment.

While most of these colleges are able to maintain their enrollment levels, long-term demographic and financial trends mean that a significant number of the less prestigious of the liberal arts colleges will face severe problems in the future. Much of American higher education is dependent on government guaranteed and subsidized student loan programs. These loans are "portable": they can be used at any accredited institution and are not dependent on academic merit but only on the borrower's ability to obtain admission and maintain an acceptable academic record.

The third major segment of the academic system is the community college, an institution that stems directly from the American commitment to "open access" to higher education. The community college sector enrolls one-third of all American students in postsecondary education. Its curriculum is varied, emphasizing applied and vocational training in fields such as data processing, restaurant management, metalworking, and automobile mechanics that lead directly to employment. Most community colleges also provide some liberal arts courses that are intended in part to expose vocational students to general education and in part as a "transfer" curriculum for students who wish to go on to obtain a baccalaureate degree from a four-year liberal arts college or a university. This transfer function, which was part of the original vision of the community college early in the twentieth century, has been reemphasized in recent years as a means of providing the first two years of undergraduate study at lower cost to expanding numbers of students.

The community college provides virtually open access to anyone who has completed secondary education. In general, entrance examinations are not given and, with the exception of some high-demand fields, there is little competition for entry. One of the major purposes of the community college is to provide a means for social and occupational mobility to segments of the population that have been disadvantaged. Community colleges are available for individuals of varied age groups as well. As Burton Clark has indicated, the community college is intended as an "open door" institution (Clark 1960). There has been considerable criticism of community colleges for, among other things, lack of clarity of mission and changing priorities (Brint and Karabel 1989).

A segment of American higher education that has traditionally received little attention but that has recently come into prominence in the United States and abroad is the "for-profit" sector—institutions designed to earn a profit for owners. The new prominence of this sector is related to the "privatization" of higher education generally, and the "marketization" and commodification of higher education in society. While for-profit institutions have long existed, the prominence of the University of Phoenix, with its innovative marketing and course-delivery strategies, has heightened interest in them. Traditionally, the for-profit sector has been dominated by vocational schools that had few links with and little impact on the rest of postsecondary education. With the for-profit sector expanding rapidly in other countries, the American experience with this sector may provide some instructive background.

American higher education is quite diverse. In states such as California and New York that have carefully planned public postsecondary education systems, there are planning and accountability mechanisms. Yet, even in the public sector, there is considerable competition among institutions. The private institutions are free to develop independently. Institutions have shown considerable skill in adapting to new opportunities—and in surviving difficult times. While there is pressure for more accountability and uniformity in public higher education and a clear hierarchy among institutions and sectors, the American "nonsystem" has been able to adapt to new circumstances.

The Relevance of the American Model

It is worth stepping outside a parochial American perspective to examine the U.S. academic system as others view it. At the beginning of the twenty-first century, the American system of higher education is the most widely admired and emulated model in the world. The purpose of this discussion is to outline some of the more creative American organizational and curricular models that have helped the U.S. university develop and cope with rapid expansion. This discussion will not encompass all aspects of American higher education that may have international relevance; rather our purpose is to provide a new way of thinking about familiar realities.

The Community of Scholars and Governance

The internal organization of American colleges and universities is based on the idea of a community of scholars and shared governance. The basic building block of governance is the department. This unique organizational model was adapted from the European "chair" system, in which one senior professor dominates a discipline or field of study. The department, in contrast, is based on the premise that all members of the academic staff within a discipline are equal. All votes on academic programs, curriculum, staffing, and other matters are open to every member of the department. In many universities, the department chair is elected by a vote of the academic staff, and he or she serves for a limited term—usually not more than five years (McHenry 1977; Tucker 1981). The department structure builds a basic level of participation into the governance structure and does not permit domination either of the curriculum or of a discipline by a single individual. This fairly democratic decision-making structure ensures that junior members of the department have a voice in departmental affairs and thus can inject new ideas into the disciplines. For the most part, however, the American departmental structure has not permitted more than token student involvement in governance—in some cases a token student representative participates in departmental discussions and votes on most matters.

While American academic departments have their share of disputes and acrimony, the structure does promote relatively broad participation in academic decision making. The democratic structure of the department has influenced other governance bodies (senates, faculty councils, and the like), at least in the better American universities. Compared to the system in most other countries, the American academic department permits an unusual degree of democratic participation among faculty of all ranks.

The department has, however, been criticized on a number of grounds. Especially during the 1960s, many argued that the discipline-based department was too rigid a structure and that it hindered interdisciplinary teaching and research. It is certainly the case that the individual member of the academic staff must look to the department for promotion, and if the department does not encourage interdisciplinary work, it is sometimes risky for faculty to engage in it. It has also been argued that the department rigidifies the academic disciplines by giving them an organizational base that is hard to alter. Finally, many critics point out that departments tend to see decisions in the context only of their own narrow interests and not in that of the total university. These criticisms all have some validity, but the structure of the department is sufficiently ingrained in the American university that it is unlikely to be dislodged.

An alternative organizational arrangement has emerged that provides flexibility and stimulates interdisciplinary work at many research universities. The organized research unit (ORU) is typically organized around a research area (i.e., environmental studies or information technology) that is of interest to faculty and to the institution. The ORU draws faculty and other researchers from different departments to address a central topic. It is not considered a permanent part of the university and can be dismantled should the interests of the academic community change or funding cease. The ORU is a typical American innovation, ensuring stability in the basic organizational structure of the university while at the same time permitting innovative and entrepreneurial work.

The organization of the American academic profession has served higher education well. It is considerably more flexible than that of many other countries. There is a fluidity among the ranks, and an academic can be promoted from rank to rank generally without rigid quotas, although some universities have been worried about an "overtenured" faculty and have imposed informal restrictions. Compared to many other countries, the probationary period for American professors is long and the evaluation unusually rigorous. The "six-year-up-or-out" policy for assistant professors—the norm in the United States for almost a century—is more extensive and thorough than the promotion policy in most other countries. A rigorous evaluation at the time of promotion to tenure and later evaluations for promotion to full professor provide accountability in the U.S. system. Current calls for posttenure review, if implemented, will further strengthen accountability in the context of the tenure system (Altbach 1999).

In the past few years, there have been demands for an end to the tenure system. Criticisms of tenure arise in the United States at times of economic constraints in higher education, and it is not surprising that they grew in vehemence at the end of the 1980s. In 2000, despite fewer financial problems for most of higher education, tenure remains controversial because of pressure for more flexible and "efficient" management. Tenure, it is claimed, does not provide sufficient accountability for academic performance over a career and hampers the flexibility of universities to shift staffing patterns to meet new priorities or changing economic circumstances. The current pattern is to hire more part-time teaching staff, who now constitute about 40 percent of the academic profession, and more full-time, non-tenure-track faculty. On the other side, many fear that the academic community, which was built on the basis of a full-time tenure-eligible faculty, may be seriously eroded by these changes (Finkelstein, Seal, and Schuster 1998).

In the traditional European pattern, which is gradually undergoing significant change, a junior academic is hired with the assumption that after a few years of a "probationary appointment," promotion to permanent status will be fairly automatic. Likewise, in Japan, everyone hired at the most junior level has the expectation of a permanent job. These practices are considerably less flexible than the traditional U.S. system. There are many patterns of academic appointment worldwide, including the German-style chair system— still in place in Japan and to some extent in a number of European countries—which places a single full professor permanently at the top of an academic hierarchy, thus blocking other faculty from promotions to professorial rank. In Argentina and some other Latin American countries, professors are expected to "contest" for their jobs every five years or so in a system that neither works well nor provides much security for academic staff. Many other countries have looked to the United States as a model for the reorganization of the professoriate.

An Administrative Cadre

To administer very large academic institutions, a professional administrative cadre with responsibility for the day-to-day operation of the university has developed. This cadre has divided into a number of subspecialties that serve particular needs. These business officers, legal experts, student affairs staff, and international education administrators have created their own professional associations. It is possible in most American colleges and universities to have a career entirely in the administrative field, and many universities have graduate programs to train academic administrators as well as to produce researchers and scholars in the field of higher education (Dressel and Mayhew 1974).

American universities were the first to establish the profession of academic administration. While the emergence of the profession has been controversial, it is by now well established, and it is necessary for the efficient operation of large academic institutions and systems. Large universities employ as many as four thousand or more individuals, including faculty and support staff, and have budgets of more than $1 billion that require a sophisticated administrative apparatus. The administrative cadre has been the fastest-growing segment of academe in recent decades. This is not surprising, given the expansion of universities and the growing complexity of institutions.

Entirely new categories have been added, from legal specialists to information technologists to affirmative action officers. The administrative cadre has permitted American academic institutions to be managed effectively in an environment of accountability.

It is important to differentiate between two levels of administrators in American higher education. Senior administration remains dominated by professors trained in one of the academic disciplines who often take administrative posts on temporary assignment, obtaining their training "on the job." Although some senior administrators do have their academic training in the field of higher education, the tradition of appointing discipline-based academics to leadership positions from the level of the department chairperson, to dean, to president remains strong. The new career-based higher education administrators function in the middle-rank service functions of the university. For example, the dean of the graduate school is likely to be a professor from an academic discipline, while the associate dean is increasingly likely to hold a doctorate in higher education and to have spent an entire career in administrative positions. The vice president for academic affairs (responsible for faculty and curriculum) is usually a professor, but the vice president for business affairs is increasingly likely to be a career administrator.

An academic field has grown up to serve this new career line—the field of higher education. It is now possible to earn the doctoral degree in higher education at about a hundred American universities. Those trained in the emerging field of higher education learn about the theories and practice of administration and also study the nature and traditions of the university. Practical training in specialized areas of academic administration, from financial management of universities to student affairs, is a part of higher education degree programs. A considerable literature, several research journals, and a professional organization serve this field of study and research.

It has been argued that the balance of power in many academic institutions has shifted from the faculty to administrators. While this generalization has considerable truth, the situation varies according to the status and tradition of the institution, with high-prestige universities and colleges retaining much more "faculty power" than schools lower in the hierarchy. There is no question that the administrative cadre has come into its own as a central element in the management of higher education regardless of the type of institution.

Curricular Expansion

The traditional European university had a narrowly circumscribed curriculum and an ideology that defined a fairly narrow role for academic institutions. Even with the expansion of higher education in Europe and the increasing involvement of the university in societal affairs, the curriculum has remained fairly traditional. During the twentieth century, American colleges and universities, in response to changing societal needs, added new specializations, curricular offerings, and research directions. Even such prestigious institutions as the University of Wisconsin offer academic degrees in poultry science, mass communications, and recreational education. American universities adapted quickly to the information age by developing specialties in computer science, information technology, and related fields. An example of the linking of curriculum, entrepreneurialism, and research is the Massachusetts Institute of Technology's world-famous media laboratory, where a concern with the technology of communication drives a multidisciplinary research and teaching program.

Some have argued that higher education has gone much too far in responding to external demands at the cost of a liberal education (Nisbet 1997; Bloom 1987). The struggle between the traditional liberal arts curriculum and applied specialization has been a central feature of academe over the past century. At the beginning of the twenty-first century, both elements exist in uneasy balance in many colleges and universities. The multifaceted functions of the university once led Clark Kerr to define the American multiversity as a series of academic buildings connected by a common heating system (Kerr 1995).

Research and the Academic Profession

Research has been a hallmark of the American academic system for more than a century. The way in which American universities have promoted research is central to the creativity of American academe over the last century (Ben-David 1968; Clark 1983; Graham and Diamond 1997). Not all American universities and colleges are directly involved in the research enterprise. Many professors do not produce much research. Studies show that a small minority of the professoriate working at the top research-oriented universities produces the bulk of research. These faculty also obtain the large majority of external funding for research (Haas 1996). Liberal arts colleges, except for a handful of the most prestigious, do not expect their academic staff to produce much research. The majority of the public universities and colleges in the midrange of the American academic system also produce relatively little research.

It is worth considering the role of research among the "research cadre": the minority of highly productive scholars who are responsible for most of the publications and receive most of the external funding. Using data from the Carnegie Foundation, Gene Haas estimates that 19 percent of American academics are in the research cadre—they identify strongly with the research mission of the university, and they are actively engaged in research. In research universities, this group constitutes 37 percent of the total; in other institutions they are 12 percent of the faculty (Haas 1996, 358). These faculty can be identified as "cosmopolitan": they are involved in international professional meetings, change jobs more frequently than others, and tend to identify more with their disciplines than with the institution at which they are employed (Gouldner 1957). Professors who are productive in terms of research and publication tend to be more highly paid than others and are more frequently clustered at the top ranks of the profession. The prestige hierarchy of American academe favors research and publication even though the large majority of the professoriate are not heavily engaged in these activities.

There is currently much debate about the role of research in American higher education, stimulated by a perception that research has come to dominate the ethos of the academic system. Ernest Boyer's influential book *Scholarship Reconsidered* (1990) gave voice to this criticism and advocated a broader definition of scholarship along with greater emphasis on teaching. The American academic system is in the process of placing greater emphasis on the teaching role. Research will remain a central function, and it will probably retain its primacy in the prestige hierarchy, but teaching, which is after all the main role of the large majority of academics, is receiving greater respect.

Autonomy and Accountability

Establishing the appropriate mix of autonomy and accountability in higher education is of crucial importance in the United States and abroad. It is also a point of contention (Berdahl and McConnell 1999). Academic institutions must have a large measure of autonomy if they are to provide creative teaching and useful research. The demands of the society for accountability, especially for financial expenditures, expressed through government, are also legitimate, especially when the bulk of financial support for higher education comes from public funds. At issue is the balance between these two interests. Faculty must be free to teach, without political or ideological fetters, in their classrooms. The university community must be free to push forward the frontiers of knowledge even if this is sometimes of potential embarrassment to governments. Knowledge is not a commodity that can be controlled without hindering creativity. At the same time, universities are not ivory towers. They function as integral parts of society and have responsibilities for teaching, research, and service to agencies that provide their financial sustenance. The American experience shows that the universities flourish intellectually and financially when they have links with society but at the same time have freedom to pursue new ideas in classroom and laboratory.

There is no formula that can be used to define appropriate autonomy. The current debate in the United States is proof that even in an established academic system, this question remains very much at issue. At present academic institutions still have a considerable measure of autonomy, with the more prestigious, research-oriented universities having more autonomy than the others. The last decade, however, has seen a slow but steady intrusion of government authority into the affairs of higher education regardless of the political ideology of the states involved or of the federal administration in Washington (Shils 1997).

Service

The university's role in providing direct service to society—to government, industry, agriculture, and special interests such as labor unions and public interest organizations—is central to American higher education (Crosson 1983). This tradition dates from the establishment in the nineteenth century of the state universities, with their strong and direct commitment to aiding the development of their regions. The previously mentioned land-grant act provided federal support for the concept of practical service by academe. Indeed, such state universities as those in Wisconsin, California, and Illinois were very important in the development of agriculture, and later of industry. These institutions engaged in research with direct practical applications and then ensured that research results were disseminated widely through extension agents and other efforts, such as noncredit courses. In Wisconsin, the university still employs staff in each of the state's counties who are responsible for bringing knowledge created at the university to agriculture and industry. The university also owns a radio and television network reaching most parts of the state, again as a means of providing educational and other services (Nichols 1999).

Universities actively solicit research contracts with government agencies and the private sector for both pure and applied research. Increasingly, academic institutions have entered into long-term agreements with industrial firms that fund university-based research. The schools guarantee these funding sources initial control over any commercially useful results. Individual professors also engage in a range of service activities to the community—in some cases, paid private consulting for industry or for governmental and nongovernmental agencies. These ventures have some critics arguing that universities have become commercialized and have strayed too far from their mission of teaching and research (Slaughter and Leslie 1997).

University policies promote service activities in a number of ways. Individual academic staff are permitted to spend a portion of their time on remunerative consulting activities and are encouraged to perform unpaid service. Evaluation procedures for promotion and tenure include service as a component, although it is generally valued below the other two elements: teaching and research. University fiscal policy encourages individual professors as well as departments and institutes to obtain external grants and allows them to engage in relationships with outside agencies for research and service under rather broad guidelines. Service has become a central part of the responsibility of the American university.

Student Services

American colleges and universities not only educate students but also provide them with a variety of services, from health and recreational facilities to religious services in some private schools. The European tradition, in contrast, assumes that students are adults, and academic institutions have not been involved in providing such services. The concept of in loco parentis (the university acting in place of the parent), central to American higher education from the beginning, which gave universities responsibility for the extracurricular lives of students as well as key aspects of their behavior, contributed to a tradition of providing such programs to undergraduate students. The tradition of in loco parentis was substantially weakened in the aftermath of the student uprisings of the 1960s and by the abdication of responsibility on the part of the professoriate. Nevertheless, American colleges and universities still provide recreational facilities, counseling services, intramural sports and athletic facilities (and in some cases intercollegiate sports programs as well), career placement offices and vocational guidance, and many extracurricular activities. Many colleges provide residence hall facilities for their students, which involves not only the responsibility for the management of these buildings but also for hiring staff to help the students who reside in the dormitories.

The student services apparatus of most American academic institutions is large and complex. Staff with special training in many areas are employed by the institution. It is possible to obtain advanced degrees in such fields as student counseling. In many institutions the cost of such services is borne by the students through their tuition fees or through specifically earmarked fees for services. Residence halls and food services are usually self-supporting and paid for by specific student fees.

Stability and Change

Over the last century, the American academic system has evolved a fairly unique combination of considerable institutional stability, even conservatism, while retaining an ability to adjust to new demands and directions. This state of affairs is not the result of careful planning but rather of evolution. The basic organizational structure of American higher education has not changed for almost a century. When faced with new situations, the traditional institutions either adjust by adding functions without changing their basic character or create entirely new divisions or institutes.

Established universities have been most resistant to basic change, but they have nonetheless been able to add new specializations fairly easily and accommodate to changing functions. Large-scale institutional reforms have been quite rare, but there has been a great deal of change at the periphery. The basic models have been growth by accretion, involving existing institutions, departments, or programs. In this way, the institution operates without major disruption but is able to accommodate, often at relatively low cost, new demands.

Academic institutions may create new departments as new disciplines and multidisciplinary fields develop. Or existing departments may split, with their faculty dividing into several entities. A common approach is to establish interdisciplinary institutes or centers, using academic staff from several different departments. Such arrangements permit the departments to remain intact while at the same time providing stimulus for innovative research and teaching. As noted earlier, at times entirely new institutions have been established to meet new needs. When the German-trained scholars returned from their studies abroad in the late nineteenth century and found that they could not change Harvard or Yale, they started new institutions, and eventually the old elite universities did adapt to the ideas embodied in the new schools.

Although there has been periodic updating, colleges and universities have maintained their traditional undergraduate curriculum with its stress on the liberal arts and general education for more than a century. During the 1960s, many universities permitted more student choice in the curriculum, responding to the student activism of the period. In the 1980s, students showed an increasing interest in vocational training to which universities responded. The trend in the 1990s was to reestablish the traditional undergraduate liberal arts curriculum, ensuring that students are exposed to a range of disciplines and perspectives as part of their undergraduate education (Kanter, Gamson, and London 1997).

Because there is no national master plan for higher education and institutions have a considerable degree of autonomy, change has occurred in varying ways in different institutions. This has helped to maintain considerable diversity in the academic system. Even in states that have implemented systemwide planning for higher education, there is generally scope for considerable variation among the institutions. The existence of a large and active private sector also contributes to diversity in the overall system. In the American pattern, academic change takes place without central planning, but not without direction.

Adversity and Recovery

American higher education, which faced multiple problems in the 1980s and early 1990s, entered more prosperous times at the end of the decade. It is useful to see how academe dealt first with adversity and then with recovery. In the 1980s, financial problems caused first by inflation combined with economic downturn and then by changes in thinking about public expenditure created severe problems for higher education. As noted earlier, policymakers at the state and federal levels came to believe that students and their families should pay for a larger share of the cost of public higher education. Enrollment growth, which had characterized higher education since the 1960s, slowed or stopped, due in part to demographic shifts that resulted in smaller age cohorts. Fiscal difficulties caused severe problems for many universities and colleges.

How did academe deal with these problems? As state governments cut back on funds for higher education, institutions raised tuition. The cost of attending college increased in both the public and private sectors. In part, tuition in the public sector increased simply to provide the needed funds. But there was also a change in government's longstanding commitment to providing access to postsecondary education at the lowest possible cost.

Academic institutions saw their budgets cut and had to reduce their expenses. In most cases, cuts were made at the edges of academic programs. Rarely did institutions drastically alter programs or priorities in order to save money. Instead, support staff were eliminated and maintenance was deferred. A hiring freeze was put into place, salaries were frozen, and part-time teachers replaced full-time faculty. Libraries were unable to buy books, and journal collections were cut. Yet, only a handful of colleges or universities violated the tenure of senior faculty. Departments were seldom eliminated, even where enrollments were low. Administrators tried to "protect the faculty," even at the expense of rational planning or institutional development. A few of the weakest private colleges merged or closed. Virtually no public institutions were closed, even where campus closings or mergers would have been in the best interests of the statewide system.

The American academic system as a whole decided, without planning or deliberate policy, to weather the crisis and hope that more favorable conditions would return before the system was irreparably damaged. The gamble, for the most part, paid off. By the mid-1990s, the conditions for higher education had improved. The economy was in a period of unprecedented prosperity, with low inflation rates. The emergence of such economic powerhouses as biotechnology and information technology firms, which rely heavily on academe for both research and training, supported higher education. The long boom in the stock market increased the value of the endowment funds of many universities and made it easier to raise money from alumni and others. Even demographics assisted academe—a temporary bulge in the age cohort caused by the "baby boom echo" boosted enrollments. In the public sector, a number of states that had faced severe financial problems leading to budget cuts and shrinking allocations for higher education in the 1980s began to restore some of the lost funding.

While the end of the millennium found higher education in a relatively healthy condition, critical challenges remain that deserve careful attention. Among them are

—*Information technology.* The implications of the information revolution for higher education will inevitably be substantial but remain unclear. Teaching and learning will be affected, at least in some sectors of the academic system. There are already implications for information retrieval and dissemination. Distance education using the Internet and other electronic means is growing in importance. The internal management of academic institutions and systems has already been transformed and will continue to be affected.

—*For-profit higher education.* For close to a century, for-profit institutions have occupied a small and marginal place in American higher education, although it has been a significant sector in some other parts of the world. The success of the University of Phoenix may be an indication that for-profit higher education is emerging as a significant mainstream factor in the United States.

—*Higher education as a "mature industry."* As Arthur Levine argues in this book, universities have been in a growth mode for a half century or more. It is possible that demographic and economic factors are bringing this period of unprecedented growth to an end. Academe will need to adjust.

—*The demand for greater productivity.* A trend toward "reengineering" and "downsizing" in the economy along with continuing demands—especially in public higher education—for more accountability may mean that academe will have to provide evidence of greater productivity.

—*The problem of basic research.* As greater emphasis is placed on applied research and on providing accountability for research expenses, basic research is receiving less support. This may become a serious problem for research-oriented universities—and for American scientific leadership internationally.

These are some of the challenges facing American higher education in the new millennium. History shows that American academe is remarkably resilient and has met crises in the past. It is even possible to be optimistic that an academic system that prefers small pragmatic solutions achieved through many decentralized decisions rather than major systemwide restructuring can meet these challenges successfully.

Conclusion

This chapter has provided an overview of American higher education, looking at the strengths and weaknesses of the system. The American university is the model for the rest of the world. Foreign institutions admire American leadership in research, the ability to provide widespread access while maintaining high quality, the adaptability of American academic institutions, the vitality of the private sector, and the openness of American higher education to students and scholars from all over the world.

Americans can take much solace from the high esteem in which the rest of the world holds U.S. higher education. Indeed, holding a mirror to our own system can be quite useful. At the same time, the American tendency to ignore the rest of the world does not serve us well in a globalized society. There may well be lessons to be learned from new approaches to teaching and research assessment in Britain, the reform of governance in the Netherlands, or the efforts to free the Japanese national universities from the Ministry of Education. It may be useful to study academic systems that are largely private, such as those in Korea, the Philippines, or Japan. In short, while there is much that American higher education can teach the rest of the world, there are also useful lessons that we can learn from abroad.

References

Altbach, P. G. 1998. *Comparative higher education: Knowledge, the university, and development.* Greenwich, Conn.: Ablex.

————. 1999. Harsh realities: The professoriate faces a new century. In *American higher education in the 21st century,* edited by P. G. Altbach, R. O. Berdahl, and P. J. Gumport. Baltimore: Johns Hopkins University Press.

Altbach, P. G., ed. 2000. *Private Prometheus: Private higher education and development in the 21st century.* Westport, Conn.: Greenwood.

Ashby, E. 1971. *Any person, any study: An essay on higher education in the United States.* New York: McGraw-Hill.

Ben-David, J. 1968. *Fundamental research and the universities: Some comments on international differences.* Paris: Organisation for Economic Co-operation and Development.

————. 1972. *American higher education: Directions old and new.* New York: McGraw-Hill.

Berdahl, R. O., and T. R. McConnell. 1999. Autonomy and accountability: Who controls academe? In *American higher education in the 21st century,* edited by P. G. Altbach, R. O. Berdahl, and P. J. Gumport. Baltimore: Johns Hopkins University Press.

Bloom, A. 1987. *The closing of the American mind.* New York: Simon & Schuster.

Boyer, E. L. 1990. *Scholarship reconsidered: Priorities of the professoriate.* Princeton, N.J.: Carnegie Foundation for the Advancement of Teaching.

Brint, S., and J. Karabel. 1989. *The diverted dream: Community colleges and the promise of educational opportunity in America, 1900–1985.* New York: Oxford University Press.

Clark, B. R. 1960. *The open door college.* New York: McGraw-Hill.

————. 1983. *The higher education system.* Berkeley: University of California Press.

Cohen, A. M., and F. B. Brawer. 1996. *The American community college.* San Francisco: Jossey-Bass.

Crosson, P. H. 1983. *Public service in higher education: Practices and priorities.* Washington, D.C.: Association for the Study of Higher Education.

Curti, M., and V. Carstensen. 1949. *The University of Wisconsin: A history, 1848–1925.* 2 vols. Madison: University of Wisconsin Press.

Dressel, P., and L. Mayhew. 1974. *Higher education as a field of study.* San Francisco: Jossey-Bass.

Finkelstein, M., R. K. Seal, and J. H. Schuster. 1998. *The new academic generation: A profession in transformation.* Baltimore: Johns Hopkins University Press.

Flexner, A. 1930. *Universities: American, English, German.* New York: Oxford University Press.

Geiger, R. 1986. *To advance knowledge: The growth of American research universities, 1900–1940.* New York: Oxford University Press.

———. 1999. Ten generations of American higher education. In *American higher education in the 21st century,* edited by P. G. Altbach, R. O. Berdahl, and P. J. Gumport. Baltimore: Johns Hopkins University Press.

Gouldner, A. W. 1957. Cosmopolitans and locals: Toward an analysis of latent social roles. *Administrative Science Quarterly* 2 (December): 281–303.

Graham, H. D., and N. Diamond. 1997. *The Rise of American research universities: Elites and challengers in the postwar era.* Baltimore: Johns Hopkins University Press.

Haas, J. E. 1996. The American academic profession. In *The international academic profession: Portraits of fourteen countries,* edited by P. G. Altbach. Princeton, N.J.: Carnegie Foundation for the Advancement of Teaching.

Hawkins, H. 1972. *Between Harvard and America: The educational leadership of Charles W. Eliot.* New York: Oxford University Press.

Kanter, S., Z. Gamson, and H. London. 1997. *General education in a time of scarcity.* Boston: Allyn & Bacon.

Kerr, C. [1963] 1995. *The uses of the university.* Reprint, Cambridge: Harvard University Press.

Marsden, G. M. 1994. *The soul of the American university: From Protestant establishment to established nonbelief.* New York: Oxford University Press.

McHenry, D., ed. 1977. *Academic departments.* San Francisco: Jossey-Bass.

Mingle, J. R., ed. 1981. *Challenges of retrenchment.* San Francisco: Jossey-Bass.

Mortimer, K. P., and M. L. Tierney. 1979. *The three R's of the eighties: Reduction, reallocation and retrenchment.* Washington, D.C.: American Association for Higher Education.

Nichols, D. A. 1999. Public access to university expertise. In *Proud traditions and future challenges,* edited by D. Ward. Madison: Office of University Publications, University of Wisconsin–Madison.

Nisbet, R. 1997. *The degradation of the academic dogma: The university in America, 1945–70.* New Brunswick, N.J.: Transaction.

Riesman, D. 1958. The academic procession. In *Constraint and variety in American education.* Garden City, N.Y.: Doubleday.

Rudolph, F. 1990. *The American college and university: A history.* Athens: University of Georgia Press.

Shils, E. 1997. *The calling of education: The academic ethic and other essays on higher education.* Chicago: University of Chicago Press.

Slaughter, S., and L. L. Leslie. 1997. *Academic capitalism: Politics, policies, and the entrepreneurial university.* Baltimore: Johns Hopkins University Press.

Smelser, N., and G. Almond, eds. 1974. *Public higher education in California.* Berkeley: University of California Press.

Tucker, A. 1981. *Changing the academic department: Leadership among peers.* Washington, D.C.: American Council on Education.

Veysey, L. 1965. *The emergence of the American university.* Chicago: University of Chicago Press.

Chapter Two ～

Higher Education as a Mature Industry

Arthur Levine

This chapter examines the changing status of America's colleges and universities. Higher education has evolved from a growth industry to a mature industry. This represents a dramatic change in both the perception of the nation's colleges and the demands made upon them by the public and their largest patron, government. Higher education has responded slowly—too slowly—to these demands for change. As a result, new competitors, such as Harcourt General or the University of Phoenix, are springing up in the private sector and among such nonprofit knowledge organizations as museums, libraries, and public television. They believe they can do the job that is being demanded of higher education better than traditional colleges and universities. This raises large questions about the future directions of American higher education.

Becoming a Mature Industry

During the late 1980s and 1990s, government support for higher education declined, both financially and politically. Two rationales have generally been offered to explain the reductions. The first is that these are bad times for government; it simply has less money to give away. The assumption is that when government is flusher, higher education will receive additional support. The second explanation is that government priorities have changed. Higher education has had to give way in importance to prisons, health care, and highways. Even in the area of education, preference is now given to primary and secondary schools over colleges and children over adults. The thinking is that the change is temporary: higher education's priority will rise again in the future; what goes around comes around.

I would suggest a third rationale, which is likely to be far more permanent. American higher education has become a mature industry. More than 60 percent of all high school graduates now go on to some form of postsecondary education. This matriculation rate is viewed in state capitals as sufficient or even an overexpansion of traditional higher education. There is no enthusiasm on the part of government to expand the system to accommodate an attendance rate of 70 or 80 percent.

This attitude represents a dramatic change in the condition of American higher education. Throughout this century, colleges and universities have been a growth industry. Except for the world wars and two years of the Depression, enrollment has risen every year. In the decades following World War II, the primary and most persistent demand that government made on higher education was to increase capacity: provide a college education to more and more people. Rising government support was the norm. Public institutions of higher education multiplied. Government aid was targeted at private schools to promote expansion. Few questions were asked. This is the lot of growth industries in America.

Government treats mature industries very differently from growth industries. It seeks to regulate or control them. It asks hard questions about their cost, efficiency, productivity, and effectiveness. It attempts to limit their size and funding. It reduces their autonomy, increases their regulation, and demands greater accountability.

This is precisely what is happening to higher education today. Government is asking questions of colleges and universities that have never been asked before. The cost of the enterprise is being scrutinized. The price of higher education is being attacked loudly and continuously. Funding formulas are being reexamined. Financial aid is shifting from grants to loans. Questions of productivity and efficiency are being raised: How much should faculty teach? What is the appropriate balance between teaching and research? How much should it cost to educate a student? Can campuses be replaced by new technologies? Should there continue to be lifetime employment, or tenure, for faculty? Which programs should colleges offer? How much course and program redundancy is necessary? What is the proper balance between graduate and undergraduate education? Questions of effectiveness are also being asked: Why aren't graduation rates higher? Why should students take more than four years to graduate from college? Why do colleges offer remedial education?

Government is shifting the terms of the relationship between higher education and the public. The focus is moving from what faculty do in their classrooms (teaching) to what students get out of the classes (learning). The emphasis is moving from courses and credits, or process, to what students achieve as a result of a college education, or outcomes. In short, the state is demanding greater accountability from higher education.

The effects of these changes on higher education are profound. As a growth industry, colleges and universities could almost count on additional resources annually. Growth and progress were treated as synonyms. New developments were a matter of addition; the new was simply added to the old. Today, with resources stable or declining, this is no longer possible. Change occurs by substitution. If something new is added, something old must be eliminated.

The net result is likely to be a "boutiquing" of higher education. Most colleges and universities in the country are now fundamentally alike. They vary largely in terms of the number of professional programs offered and the relative size of their upper division and graduate programs. In this sense, most institutions are comprehensive. Today they are being forced to eliminate overlapping or redundant offerings, both internally and as relates to competing schools, and make themselves more specialized and individual. They are moving from something akin to full-service department stores to specialty boutiques. The common wisdom today is that higher education must do more with less. The reality is that institutions will have to do less with less.

These changes are likely to be permanent. They will not go away when government has more money or higher education's relative priority in the public agenda rises. The problems higher education faces are threefold. First, higher education is, for the most part, unaware of its new condition as a mature industry. We are ineffectively fighting the change rather than attempting to adapt to our new reality. If we do not change our posture, government will take the lead and, out of frustration and anger, restructure higher education without our assistance in ways that are likely to be very damaging to the enterprise.

Second, higher education is doing a miserable job of answering the basic questions that are now being raised by government. In the past, we were asked principally whether higher education could increase capacity. Now we are unable and, on many campuses, unwilling to answer the hard questions that government should always have been asking colleges. Moreover, we speak in a rhetoric the public does not understand or believe. Once it was adequate to say American higher education was the best in the world and cheap as well, given the returns on investment—an entire undergraduate degree costing no more than a new Ford. This is no longer sufficient. Not long ago I visited a state in which the legislature was considering a bill tying faculty salaries entirely to time spent in the classroom. I asked the faculty at a major research institution in that state what they thought of the bill. Their response was "intellectual McCarthyism." I wondered how such bright people could be so out of touch with reality. It is imperative that teaching staff and administrators in higher education learn to speak to government and the public in ways that are comprehensible and compelling. The questioning won't stop if we continue to drag our feet. That will only bring further regulation by the state or competition from the business community or other nonprofits. One way or another, higher education is now ripe for a takeover by public or private forces.

Third and finally, higher education must learn to function as a mature industry. We have done poorly in this regard. Faced with declining resources, higher education's first response was to attempt to raise more money. Tuition increases outpaced the inflation rate. More admissions officers were hired to attract more students. More development staff were hired to raise more money. More student affairs professionals were hired to reduce attrition. And more finance staff were hired to control spending. Higher education quickly found that this course of action only increased costs. It didn't produce more revenue.

The second response was to cut costs around the edges—that is, make across-the-board budget cuts, impose hiring freezes, and defer maintenance. The stated goal for these actions was to preserve institutional quality, staff morale, and student access. In reality preserving quality meant maintaining every program and every faculty member on campus, and thus was a synonym for preserving morale. At bottom, this strategy sacrificed quality to avoid rocking the boat. Strong and weak programs were cut equally. Staff reductions followed random attrition patterns rather than institutionally determined priorities. Only the commitment to access was allowed to wither. It has been preserved rhetorically and abandoned financially on many campuses.

All in all, higher education's response has been akin to the captain of a boat that has hit an iceberg announcing that his highest priority, as the boat sinks, is saving the crew. The next priority is avoiding any inconvenience as the boat goes down by continuing all activities (the midnight buffet, the bingo game, and the shuffleboard tournament). The third priority is repairing the boat. And the fourth and final priority, should time permit, is saving the passengers. Aside from penalizing the students and diminishing academic quality, this approach has another problem: it doesn't save enough money.

This realization has caused institutions of higher education to attempt a third response: choosing priorities—defining areas central to an institution's mission and then identifying more marginal activities that could be reduced or eliminated. The usual mechanism has been to create an 87-member strategic planning committee that after two years of weekly meetings manages to select for cutting one program, one with no new students in three years. This recommendation triggers a faculty no-confidence vote in the president. A new president is hired, who says the institution can get out of this situation by raising more money. And the cycle starts again.

This is, of course, a parody of how higher education has responded to its new status as a mature industry. But it is true that colleges and universities have been unable to accept their new situation or to develop successful methods for responding to it. It is not an exaggeration to say that government is angrier today with higher education than it ever was with primary and secondary schools. Words like *arrogant* and *self-serving* are commonly used in statehouses to describe colleges and universities.

Higher Education's New Competitors

Industries become mature for one of two reasons. Either they are meeting or largely meeting market demand for their product, or the market is demanding forms of the product that they are unable or unwilling to provide. American colleges and universities are facing the latter challenge. Modern society in the United States needs more higher education, rather than less or even the existing amount. The problem is that traditional higher education no longer meets the full needs of our society. At bottom, government and the public are demanding not a limit on higher education's expansion but rather a readjustment and redesign of the enterprise. This is being driven by several critical societal changes.

The Rise of an Information Economy

Our nation has shifted from an industrial to an information economy. We live in an era in which the new sources of wealth are found in knowledge and communication rather than in the natural resources and physical labor that characterized the United States as an industrial society. Industrial societies have historically been national in focus and put a premium on physical capital: plants, machinery, and the like. In contrast, an information society is global and puts a premium on intellectual capital: knowledge and the people who produce it. As a result, education is fundamental to an information society, which demands higher levels of skills and knowledge of its workforce and its citizenry than an industrial economy.

The best jobs in our society increasingly require more advanced educational credentials than in the past. A recent report of Nations-Banc Montgomery Securities shows that by the year 2000, 85 percent of U.S. jobs will require education beyond high school, up from 65 percent in 1991. Moreover, 18 of the 25 fastest-growing, highest-paying occupations in the country through the year 2006 will require at least a baccalaureate degree (Gay 1998, 60). In this environment, the value of educational credentials is similarly increasing. For example, in 1980 the weekly salary of someone with at least a college degree was 40 percent higher than that of a high school graduate. By 1997, the gap had risen to 73 percent (*Wall Street Journal Almanac* 1998, 612).

Hand in hand with the demand for increased levels of education comes the need for more frequent education in an information society. The half-life of knowledge is shorter in the current environment, and there is increased pressure for people to remain at the forefront of knowledge use and production. This requires continuing education throughout one's career and greater use of continuing education or professional development programs. James Duderstadt, former president of the University of Michigan, says the emphasis in an information society shifts from "just in case" education to "just in time" education.

The bottom line is that an information society means more higher education, more advanced degrees, more continuing education, and a global marketplace for higher education. It means more and more students coming to college throughout their lives. What is new is the need to tailor education, not to the wishes of the professoriate, but to the demands of the workplace. What has changed is the demand for education not structured around the 15-week semester and four-year degrees, but around the schedules of those to be educated. Education will be needed around the clock in amounts varying from hours to years.

Changing Students

Perhaps the largest change in higher education in recent years is in the students themselves. During the 1980s and early 1990s, the lion's share of college enrollment growth came from students who might be described as nontraditional. By 1993, 38 percent of all college students were over 25 years of age; 61 percent were working; 56 percent were females, and 42 percent were attending part time. Less than a fifth of all undergraduates fit the traditional stereotype of the American college student—between 18 and 22 years of age, enrolled full time, and living on campus.

What this means is that higher education is not as central to the lives of many of today's undergraduates as it was to previous generations. Increasingly, it is just one of a multiplicity of activities in which they are engaged every day. For many, college is not even the most important of these activities. Work and family often overshadow it.

In a national study I conducted of undergraduate attitudes and experiences between 1992 and 1997, older, part-time, and working students, especially those with children, often said that they wanted a new type of relationship with their colleges, different from what students historically have had. They preferred relationships like those they already enjoyed with their bank, the gas company, and the supermarket. They wanted their colleges nearby and operating at the hours most useful to them—preferably, around the clock. They wanted convenience: easy, accessible parking, no lines, and polite, helpful, and efficient staff. They also wanted high-quality education but were eager for low costs. For the most part, they were very willing to comparison shop, placing a premium on time and money. They did not want to pay for activities and programs they would not use.

Students today increasingly bring to higher education exactly the same consumer expectations they have for every other commercial enterprise with which they deal. Their focus is on convenience, service, quality, and low cost. They believe that since they are paying for their education, colleges should give them the education they want. They are likely to find distance education appealing because it offers the convenience of instruction at home or the office. They are prime candidates for stripped-down versions of college, located in the suburbs and business districts of our cities, that offer low-cost instruction, high faculty teaching loads, a primarily part-time faculty, limited numbers of majors, and few electives. Proprietary institutions of this type are starting to spring up around the country.

In this regard, the University of Phoenix is instructive. It is now one of the largest private colleges in America, enrolling more than seventy thousand students. Traded on the NASDAQ exchange, this profit-making college is regionally accredited, offering degrees from the associate through the master's and soon the doctorate. The faculty, who boast traditional academic credentials, are largely part time, having other forms of primary employment in the fields in which they teach. Class syllabi are uniform, prepared every three years by professionals and practitioners in the subject area. In other words, faculty teach the courses; they do not prepare or design them. Students attend school as a cohort at convenient hours, taking precisely the same courses in sequence. There are no electives. The University of Phoenix, which puts an emphasis on assessment of student learning and faculty teaching, has plans to expand enrollments to 200,000 students over the next decade.

While the University of Phoenix is the largest example of proprietary higher education, it is not unique, and its example is being watched not only by other entrepreneurs but also by Wall Street and venture capital firms. We will see more institutions like it in the future. The University of Phoenix is more expensive than its primary competitors in the city of Phoenix—Maricopa Community College and Arizona State University. It competes by being more customer oriented—offering exceptional service and convenience.

Traditional undergraduates are also changing. They are coming to college more poorly prepared than their predecessors. As a result, there is a growing need for remediation. According to a national survey of student affairs officers I conducted in 1997, nearly three-fourths (74%) of all colleges and universities experienced an increase within the previous decade in the proportion of students requiring remedial or development education at two-year (81%) and four-year (64%) colleges. Today, nearly one-third (32%) of all undergraduates report having taken a basic skills or remedial course in reading, writing, or math. Colleges and universities have a poor reputation in providing effective remediation. This has attracted profit-making organizations such as Sylvan and Kaplan, which have built brand names on their reputations in this area.

There is another hurdle even more daunting than remediation: the widening gap between the ways in which students learn best and the ways in which faculty teach. According to research by Charles Schroeder of the University of Missouri-Columbia (1993, 21–26), more than half of today's students perform best in a learning situation characterized by "direct, concrete experience, moderate-to-high degrees of structure, and a linear approach to learning. They value the practical and the immediate, and the focus of their perception is primarily on the physical world." Three-quarters of faculty, on the other hand, "prefer the global to the particular, are stimulated by the realm of concepts, ideas, and abstractions, and assume that students, like themselves, need a high degree of autonomy in their work." In short, students are more likely to prefer concrete subjects and active methods of learning. By contrast, faculty are predisposed to abstract subjects and passive learning. The result, says Schroeder, is frustration on both sides and a tendency for faculty to interpret as deficiencies what may simply be natural differences in student learning patterns. This mismatch, and the unwillingness of higher education to address it, are an invitation to other providers to enter higher education and try to do better.

Demographics is also an issue. The number of 18-year-olds is growing at the rate of more than 1 percent a year nationally, with the growth disproportionately focused in the west and south of the United States. In addition, an increasing proportion of 18-year-olds are attending college: 65 percent of all high school graduates are now attending postsecondary education, up from 42 percent in 1970. The result is that California, for example, is bracing for a tidal wave of a half million additional college students within the next decade. The state lacks the capacity to accommodate the increase on existing campuses, yet it has no desire to spend substantial additional resources on higher education or to expand the number of new campuses. The state has considered meeting this onslaught of new students by creating a new breed of higher education: the California Virtual University, an on-line institution with the goal of increasing productivity and access to higher education while reducing the cost.

In this situation, international students are the wild card. They are very appealing as a new market for proprietary education in the United States. There is a growing demand for higher education around the world. The American university is thought of as a high-quality source of that education. English is increasingly the world's second language. The British Open University's remarkable success in developing an international market—it currently administers tests in more than 100 countries—has made the possibility of global education seem more achievable to both profit-making and nontraditional colleges.

The Cost of Higher Education

Between 1980 and 1997, the average price of college tuition, room, and board rose by well over 300 percent (*Wall Street Journal Almanac* 1998, 607). Today, the common wisdom among admissions officers is that fewer than 5 percent of American families can afford the full cost of a private college education. This is of concern to both the government and the public. There is a growing belief in state capitals that the costs of higher education are too high, owing to program redundancy, the proliferation of remedial programs, administrative overhead, the added costs of research, low teaching productivity, and physical plant upkeep.

Perhaps the most visible effort in recent years to respond to these perceived difficulties has been the creation by 17 of the nation's governors of an alternative to traditional higher education, called the Western Governors University. The university is being developed in partnership with 14 businesses—including IBM, AT&T, Sun, KPMG, Cisco Systems, 3Com, and Microsoft. The emphasis is on learning, but the new university will not employ faculty or design courses. Instead, it is planning a competency-based, on-line program developed from the offerings of colleges and businesses, domestically and internationally (Marchese 1998). Toward this end, Western Governors recently developed a partnership with the British Open University, the international pioneer in distance education. In this sense, states are actually attempting to develop higher education at a lower cost. Believing that "traditional" higher education is unwilling to respond, the states are creating new kinds of institutions.

New Technologies

Another force, which may have the greatest capacity to change higher education, is new technologies. Several years ago, the editor of a metropolitan daily newspaper told me his newspaper would be out of the paper business within the next several decades. Instead, the news would be delivered electronically. Subscribers would be able to design the newspaper they received. If they decided they wanted to begin the day with sports, the headlines and front-page news of their daily paper would, accordingly, focus on athletics. Subscribers with young children could ask that political news be excised. The new technologies have enormous import for colleges. They mean the age of textbooks is ending. The days of teaching from yellowing, old lecture notes are coming to an abrupt conclusion. Already private-sector companies are developing products, from publishers such as McGraw-Hill to new software companies like Blackboard.

In the same vein, an article I recently read described the travel agency of the future. Through virtual reality, travelers considering different vacation venues would be able to smell, hear, feel, and see the different locales. They could walk the beaches, climb the mountains, enter the local landmarks, and inspect the restaurants, hotels, and shops. The same might be done with historic locales. One could visit fifth-century Rome, eighteenth-century America, or fifteenth-century Paris. Imagine smelling the smells of fifteenth-century Paris (they must have been putrid), walking the cobblestones, entering the great and not so great buildings, and seeing the people on the street. This raises huge questions about pedagogy. How will a stand-up lecture on fifteenth-century Paris compare with the virtual experience of actually being there? As technology advances, we can anticipate dramatic, even revolutionary, changes in the nature of instruction.

For instance, the technology currently exists for a professor to offer a course at Teachers College of Columbia University in New York and for students to take that course in Los Angeles and Tokyo. It is possible for all of them to perceive they are sitting in the same classroom. The student in Los Angeles can electronically nudge her Japanese-speaking classmate, say she missed the professor's last comment, and get the appropriate answer. The professor can ask the two students to prepare a project together for the next class. The two students can agree to have tea together after class. If all of this can be accomplished electronically, why do we need the physical plant called a college, particularly given the changing demographics of higher education?

The American system of higher education was built on the principle of propinquity. The goal was to put a campus in reach of every citizen, to overcome the barrier of geography. Today this has been accomplished for more than 90 percent of the population. Technology makes physical proximity less important than it was in the past; it minimizes the barrier of geography. It also reduces the need to build physical plants. This invites the states to reconsider the design of their higher education systems. Why does New York need 64 campuses? Why does California need 9 public research universities?

The new technologies have the potential to revolutionize higher education. At present, institutions of higher education have had less experience in this area than profit-making, high-technology industry. The private sector has greater resources to invest in technology and new approaches to higher education. Moreover, the private sector is likely to move into this area with greater alacrity than existing colleges and universities. States are also finding taking advantage of new technologies an increasingly appealing way to go.

Changing Public Attitudes

Throughout much of this century, higher education was one of America's sacred institutions, deeply respected and placed on a national pedestal high above the profane aspects of daily life. By the mid-1980s this had changed. Beginning with a 1984 report by former secretary of education William Bennett entitled *To Reclaim a Legacy,* there has been a barrage of publications critical of higher education—books with such titles as *Illiberal Education, Profscam, Tenured Radicals, Killing the Spirit, How Professors Play the Game of the Cat Guarding the Cream, The Closing of the American Mind,* and *Integrity in the College Curriculum.* Several of these volumes made the national bestsellers' list. They inspired front-page newspaper articles, cover stories in weekly newsmagazines, and segments of television shows and radio broadcasts. They criticized higher education for rising costs, diminishing quality, low productivity, inefficiency, and ineffectiveness. In the aftermath of the private-sector transformation of healthcare, these perceived weaknesses make higher education a very appealing target for criticism and perhaps for participation by the corporate sector.

The bottom line is that the information economy is driving the demands for new forms of higher education. That demand is being reinforced by the changing demographics of higher education. Current weaknesses (the poor quality of remediation, high cost, and the institutional mismatch between faculty and students) and new opportunities in higher education (international markets and new technologies) are encouraging the private sector to enter the higher education market.

The Major Actors

There are three major actors in the higher education market today: existing colleges and universities, the business sector, and other knowledge-producing organizations. They have responded in very different fashions to the pressures for change.

Colleges and universities have been slow to act. The use of new technologies and the option of distance learning are good examples. A 1998 report by the U.S Department of Education found that only a third of all institutions were currently offering distance courses and another quarter were planning to begin offering distance instruction in the next three years. The scale of collegiate distance programs has been small. In fact, only 26 percent of colleges and universities with such programs offer more than 25 courses. The focus of distance programs has been narrowly targeted; they are mostly aimed at undergraduates (81% of institutions). Most schools involved in distance education are offering less than the equivalent of a full undergraduate degree program. They are also far less involved in other areas of education that would seem important in an information society: graduate education (34%), professional continuing education (13%), other forms of continuing education (6%), and adult literacy (2%). Additionally, the technology employed by colleges and universities is not as up-to-date as it might be; only a little more than half (57%) are using two-way interactive video. The rest are using the older technology of one-way prerecorded video (National Center for Education Statistics 1998).

Yet interest, even urgency, regarding the topic is building in higher education. A number of institutions, more public than private and more universities than colleges, have made a serious commitment to distance learning. New York University, for instance, made headlines when it announced the creation of "NYU On-Line, Inc.," a profit-making subsidiary designed to produce and market on-line courses and provide client consulting services. In a partnership with the Lotus Corp., the University of Wisconsin system has created a dual for-profit and nonprofit Learning Innovation Center to offer the university's courses and degrees globally. Already 565 courses are available. The University of Nebraska is creating global courses and a degree-vending operation as well. The University of Hawaii is using two-way video, cable, satellite, and the Internet to offer 13 degree programs across the state (Marchese 1998).

However, it is not yet clear to what degree higher education will be a leader in distance learning. What mitigates against it is tradition, cost, the glacial pace of action by higher education governance systems, and generally indifferent-to-hostile faculty attitudes. In contrast, the most aggressive and creative actor in higher education today is the private sector or business community. The motivation is profits. The private sector sees higher education as a very lucrative and poorly run industry.

As Michael Milken explained to me, higher education is a $225 billion industry with a reputation for low productivity, poor management, high cost, and low use of technology. He said, "higher education is going to be the next healthcare," in reference to the similar problems in both industries and the consequent opportunities for the business community. He went on to say, "we are going to eat your lunch." He reminded me that education was not new to business. There are more than 1,000 corporate universities, which are engaged in training company work forces. In these settings, he believed, the instruction was superior and better assessed than in the typical college. Also, higher education is seen as a countercyclical industry, meaning college enrollments and revenues increase when the economy is poor. That is, students are more likely to go to college when there are fewer jobs available and more likely to drop out when the job market improves. Countercyclical industries are relatively rare and very attractive investments.

Furthermore, higher education has a dependable revenue stream with a good cash flow. Enrollment growth is the norm, and half the customer base makes a two-to-four-year or longer commitment to the product. Customers pay a lot for the product, but it is also a subsidized industry, supported by enormous financial aid programs financed by the state and federal governments. Moreover, the federal program, through recent legislation, has become more open to distance learning and nontraditional students. Add to all this one more stunning fact: education and technology stocks have an incredible record, overwhelmingly outpacing traditional indicators such as the Standard and Poor's index. The story of the University of Phoenix has been everywhere—in newspapers and magazines and on radio and television. So both the press and the numbers look wonderful.

The rush to higher education is on in the private sector. Business brings to higher education money, imagination unimpeded by current practice, and speed in entering the field. It lacks the reputation, accreditation, and certification-granting ability of American colleges and universities. Venture capital firms such as Warburg, Pincus and Co. are studying the education market. Investment houses—including Legg, Mason; NationsBanc Montgomery Securities; and Merrill Lynch—have developed educational practices. One recent unpublished study found 72 significant private-sector firms had already entered the on-line postsecondary market. For example, Michael Milken and Larry Ellison of Oracle are creating a for-profit on-line university involving Columbia, Stanford, Chicago, the London School of Economics, and Carnegie Mellon. The Caliber Learning Network is offering graduate education with Johns Hopkins, the University of Pennsylvania, and Teachers College of Columbia University in health, business, and education. Jones Education Co., which recently received regional accreditation, put together an electronic catalogue offering certificate and degree programs of partnering universities through America Online. The company has developed what it hopes will be a worldwide electronic university. University Access is developing distance courses in core business subjects taught by renowned names in the field.

There is one more group of actors in education worth noting: the knowledge organizations: media, publishing houses, museums, libraries, professional associations, arts organizations, and grassroots neighborhood associations, often collaborating with universities. The activities of all these organizations are converging. Increasingly, all are in the business of producing and disseminating knowledge. All are in the field of education. Museums, YMCAs, and libraries are increasingly offering courses. The same groups are entering the publishing business—creating books, monographs, and other educational materials.

Not long ago, I visited with the technology division of Simon & Schuster, which I had thought of as a book publisher. They told me they were no longer exclusively in the book business; they were now in the knowledge and information business. They were focusing strongly on teacher education and the professional development of teachers and were involved with thousands of schools via television and computers. Their ultimate goal was to put the Simon & Schuster brand name on professional development products for teachers. This did not seem like a crazy possibility in that they are working in more schools than any education school in the country. But I was shocked. I had thought this was the work of schools like Teachers College. I had never considered a book publisher a competitor.

I asked where Simon & Schuster obtained the content for the materials it produced for teachers. The answer was they hire "content specialists." I had hoped they would say they worked with university faculty. The only obstacle they faced in doing exactly what colleges and universities do in terms of professional development was accreditation and certification.

Simon & Schuster is unusual in the scale of its activities but not in their direction. For instance, with support from the U.S. Department of Education, PBS (the Public Broadcasting System) has created "Mathline," the largest technology-based professional development program for math teachers. It now enrolls more than five thousand teachers. New York's public broadcasting station, WNET, is engaged in similar activities, through on-line courses for schools and professional development programs for teachers.

In sum, we are now entering a new world for higher education in which providers will be expanded to include not only traditional colleges and universities but also for-profit universities, technology companies, publishers, television stations, education conglomerates, training and consulting firms, professional associations, grassroots organizations, and foundations (Wikler 1999). This is not a pleasant prospect for traditional colleges and universities.

Table 2.1
New Providers of Higher Education

Category	Examples
Virtual universities	Western Governors University, California Virtual University, SUNY Learning Network
Foreign colleges and universities	McGill, Open University, University of Oxford
Technology companies	Courseware packagers and distributors (e.g., AT&T, Caliber, RealEducation, ISI, OnlineLearning.net., UOL Publishing, America Online, Jones Education Co.), authoring software and technology service companies (e.g., IBM, Lotus, Oracle, Collegis)
Publishers	Pearson, Houghton Mifflin, Harcourt General
Television companies	PBS, Thirteen/WNET, NBC
Education conglomerates	Sylvan Learning Systems, Knowledge Universe
Training and consulting firms	Times Mirror, Kaplan
Professional associations	National Association of Secondary School Principals, National Council of Teachers of English
Grassroots teacher groups	Global Schoolhouse, Tapped In
Foundations	Alfred P. Sloan Foundation

Source: Wikler 1999.

The Implications for Higher Education

Last summer I met with a business leader who was entering the education market. He told me about his plans to create a for-profit virtual university. He said the train was leaving the station and Teachers College needed to get onboard. We agreed that the train was indeed leaving the station. The only real difference in our thinking was that I believed the higher education community was driving the train.

American institutions of higher education have three critical characteristics. The first is reputation or, in business terms, a brand name in the field of education. The second is authorization to provide education—accreditation, certification, and licensure. The third element is content. Colleges and universities are in the business of discovering and disseminating content—information and knowledge—and today content is king. Digital technology gives television, telephone, and cable stations the capacity to distribute more and more content, and today there are more channels available to distribute content than there is content to fill them. The fellow I spoke with this summer was just another channel hungry for content.

These attributes may be only temporary advantages of higher education. With regard to reputation, Amazon.com, the on-line bookseller, showed the fragility of well-established brand names. In the space of just a few years, it managed to eclipse powerhouse booksellers such as Barnes & Noble and establish a brand name in a new business, on-line book sales. In the same way, on-line educators may well have the capacity to establish brand names in distance education, distinguishing them from prestigious campus-based colleges and universities.

With regard to authorization, at a meeting of representatives from investment houses and venture capital firms, the consensus was that degrees, credits, and accreditation were obstacles, but perhaps only in the short run. The conclusion was that it would take between one and five years to develop strategies to deal with these elements in most states. The University of Phoenix was regularly cited as the model of what a tenacious institution can accomplish in overcoming these barriers, even in the face of powerful opposition.

As for content, the story of Microsoft and Encyclopaedia Britannica is instructive. Bill Gates invited the most eminent of encyclopedias to develop a CD-ROM edition. Britannica turned him down, worried about losing the market for its traditional hard-copy edition. So Microsoft bought Funk & Wagnalls and turned their encyclopedia into the digital encyclopedia, *Encarta*. In less than two years, *Encarta* was the best-selling encyclopedia in the world. Britannica's sales plummeted. Britannica went back to Microsoft and was told it would now have to pay to put its encyclopedia on-line. The lesson is that if distributors like Microsoft are unable to get content providers to join them, they may buy the content or develop the capacity to create content themselves. This is the approach that Simon & Schuster has taken.

The lesson is that colleges and universities have a limited amount of time to decide what role they will play in designing higher education for a new era. In fall 1998 I participated in a teleconference sponsored by the College Board and PBS. My fellow panelists included the president of the University of Phoenix, the executive vice president of DeVry, Inc., and a senior administrator at Kaplan, which recently launched an on-line, for-profit law school. These are not people I have spent time with in the past. They were not considered part of the higher education community.

For the past year or two, I have had a new breed of visitor coming to my office. These visitors work at television networks, cable services, telephone companies, software firms, venture capital groups, investment houses, and start-up educational ventures. The topic we discuss is generally the same—prospects for a profit-making partnership between Teachers College and the visitor's organization.

In the current environment, colleges and universities have three choices. First, higher education can reject the entreaties of the business community. It might do this on the grounds that it currently has a near monopoly on educational content. It could base its resistance on principle, saying a profit motive is incompatible with higher education. Or it could do so for reasons of quality, believing that the educational ideas being advocated by the private sector diminish educational excellence.

Such a rejection would force the business community to confront higher education head on, as the University of Phoenix has done. Under these circumstances, the private sector can be expected to create its own content by hiring the expertise currently found in universities. Businesses would be able to do this at lower cost than institutions of higher education and would seek to reach larger audiences. For instance, a recent proposal I read from a venture capital firm suggested creating a distance learning university that would hire the nation's most eminent faculty at lucrative salaries for short periods of time to create curriculum materials and offer electronic courses intended to reach thousands. In short, the proposal sought to create the equivalent of an academic all-star team found at no other university. While the salaries paid would be high, they would be far less than the full-time salary of a distinguished tenured full professor. And the enrollments would be many times greater than those found in any college or university course. This is a potentially devastating alternative for higher education financially, especially given the changing expectations of current students.

Second, higher education could attempt to preempt the private sector by developing the technologies, service-delivery capacities, and economies businesses now offer or at least promise. This seems the least likely alternative. Particularly now, with declining government support, colleges lack the substantial capital that such development would require; they also lack the private sector's ability to act speedily.

The third and only reasonable alternative is for higher education to judiciously form partnerships with the private sector. This could be a wonderful opportunity for the nation's colleges and universities. Throughout its history, American higher education has always had a patron—first the church and then government. Government is currently withdrawing from the relationship. The business community is coming to higher education at exactly the same time and asking to join with it. This could be an excellent partnership for higher education, better than any in the past. The reason is that higher education entered its previous relationships, with the church and government, as the supplicant. It comes to the business community with very real assets. It entered its past relationships casually and often gave up too much for the dollars its patron offered. This is not necessary today. The imperative for higher education is to determine the ground rules by which partnerships with the private sector might be accomplished. This entails defining quality—rather than simply doing things as they have always been done. This definition requires a clear statement of essential purposes and core values. This juncture presents an enormous opportunity for American higher education.

This is also a time of danger. It is not clear that higher education as it has evolved to the present day can survive unchanged into the future, though this will vary dramatically by sector. Higher education's present design and structure may not be sustained. It faces a radically different environment than in the past, a product of the nation's transition from an industrial to an information society, dramatically different demographics, pressure to reduce the cost of higher education, burgeoning new technologies, and a legion of new competitors. Higher education faces the choice between reform and revolution. Reform means that professors and administrators will have to rethink how their institutions carry out their historic purposes in light of this new environment. Revolution, a shift in the power of who controls higher education, is likely to occur if these educators do not act.

References

Gay, K. 1998. *The age of knowledge.* A study presented at an education forum co-sponsored by NationsBanc Montgomery Securities and the Stanford Institute for Economic Policy Research. November, San Francisco.

Marchese, T. 1998. Not-so-distant competitors: How new providers are re-making the postsecondary marketplace. *AAHE Bulletin* 50, no. 9: 3–7.

National Center for Education Statistics. 1998. *Distance education in higher education institutions: Incidence, audience, and plans to expand.* Washington, D.C.: U.S. Department of Education.

Schroeder, C. 1993. New students—New learning styles. *Change* 25, no. 4 (October): 21–26.

The Wall Street Journal Almanac. 1998. New York: Ballantine Books.

Wikler, J. 1999. Teachers College. Population, opportunities, and prospective partners for computer-mediated instruction. Unpublished report.

Chapter Three ∽

The "Crisis" Crisis in Higher Education

Is that a Wolf or a Pussycat at the Academy's Door?

Robert Birnbaum and Frank Shushok Jr.

Cri·sis noun; plural **cri·ses**. **a.** A crucial or decisive point or situation; a turning point. **b.** An unstable condition, as in political, social, or economic affairs, involving an impending abrupt or decisive change.
—*The American Heritage Dictionary of the English Language*

Judging by the number of study groups and publications over the past several years that have identified higher education as being in crisis, college and university educators today appear to be living in the most perilous of times (the boldface in the following examples is ours). The National Association of State Universities and Land-Grant Colleges established a commission in 1994 to study the "**crisis** in higher education." In 1996 the Association of Governing Boards released its study of the academic presidency while warning of "a pending **crisis** in higher education unless bold steps are taken." In 1997, the Commission on National Investment in Higher Education published its report *Breaking the Social Contract: The Fiscal **Crisis** in Higher Education.*

In 1998, a report of a commission sponsored by the Carnegie Foundation for the Advancement of Teaching found the state of undergraduate education at research universities to be a "**crisis**."

At the same time, there has been a bumper crop of recent books whose titles refer explicitly to crisis, including *Will Teach for Food: Academic Labor in Crisis* (Nelson 1997), *Crisis in the Academy* (Lucas 1996), *Higher Education in Crisis* (Barba 1995), *The Academy in Crisis* (Sommer 1995), and *Higher Education under Fire: Politics, Economics, and the Crisis of the Humanities* (Berube and Nelson 1995). An even larger number of journal articles, conference presentations, and newspaper stories have decried, described, or advocated solutions for perceived academic crises of one or another kind.

Crises manifest themselves differently in different social institutions. A partial list of areas for which crises in higher education have recently been claimed include leadership (Fisher 1997); stagnation in the face of social change (Gingrich 1995); technology (Wood and Smellie 1991); teaching, learning, and assessment (Nettles 1995); confidence (Leslie and Fretwell 1996); access (National Commission on the Cost of Higher Education 1998); curriculum (Carnochan 1993); intercollegiate athletics (The crisis in intercollegiate athletics 1990); accreditation (Haaland 1995); governance (Association of Governing Boards 1996); values (Wingspread Group 1993); and minority enrollments (Rodriguez 1994). Some analysts focus on the effects of the crisis on students, faculty, or individual institutions; others present an apocalyptic vision questioning the very survival of the higher education system itself (Wood and Valenzuela 1996).

Crises in Higher Education

Within the past twenty or thirty years, our long-tested and successful system of collegiate instruction has . . . been so persistently decried and so seriously menaced as to fill the friends of sound education throughout the country with alarm and compel them to discuss the whole theory and practice of our higher education (Frederick Barnard, 1865 Inaugural Address [Caffrey 1969, 9]).

Higher education in the United States and elsewhere is beset by crises: crises of public confidence, questions of continuing relevance, doubts about continuing the emphasis on doctoral instruction, and a very real financial crisis (Balderston and Weathersby 1972, ii).

The present crisis has both deeper and broader implications for the future than the repeated periods of stress facing colleges and universities since about 1970. It is a common refrain with those we have consulted to suggest that things are not going to be the same this time, or ever again (Leslie and Fretwell 1996, xii).

These three statements—made in 1865, 1972, and 1996—are representative of a long-standing tendency to claim that higher education is in crisis. The language has changed: from about 1970, the word *crisis* has been substituted for the more euphemistic rhetoric of a gentler era. However, the statements are similar in suggesting that higher education is in grave difficulty, far greater now than in the past, and that the consequences will be dire unless Something Is Done. Alice Rivlin, looking back over 20 years of policy-making, commented that "in the 1960s, the crisis in higher education related to the prospect of absorbing rapid increases in enrollment. In the 1970s, it related to the prospect of declining enrollment. At various times the crisismongers have invoked the imminent demise of some type of institution: the death of the liberal arts college; the vanishing private higher education sector; or even, believe it or not, the special plight of the research university. When all else fails, the quality of higher education can always be deplored" (1988, 7).

What is a crisis? C. T. Kerchner and J. H. Schuster identify the Greek origin of the word, meaning "a point of culmination and separation, an instant when change one way or another is impending" (1982, 122). From an organizational perspective, Hermann considers a crisis to be something unexpected or unanticipated that threatens high-priority organizational values and requires a response in a restricted amount of time (1963). We offer our own definition of higher educational crisis as a situation that fulfills three criteria: it threatens values critical to one or more constituencies, existing channels of influence and modes of rhetoric are inadequate to address it, and it is claimed to require immediate action including the allocation of additional resources.

Higher education is integrated into the social, political, and economic fabric of American society, and so it should come as no surprise that many claims of academic crisis are linked to dramatic historic events. Over the decades, college presidents have identified university crises as related to the Great Depression, the loss of students at the start of World War II and the flood of new enrollees at war's end, and the military and scientific climate caused by the Cold War (Baldridge 1981). The university was in crisis again during the Vietnam War era "because society is in crisis" (Abram 1969, 7). Crisis was seen in the demographic trends of the 1980s, which were predicted to lead to a 15 percent enrollment decline (Breneman 1982) and the closing of 10 to 30 percent of American campuses (Keller 1983). One educator commented at a meeting that "the word crisis has been used here 4,913 times in three days, and the predicted enrollment crisis hasn't even begun yet. You ain't seen nothin' yet, boys and girls, wait until 1995" (Baldridge 1981, 3). It should be noted that the enrollment crisis was one of the few for which consequences were quantitatively predicted. According to the *1997 Digest of Educational Statistics,* FTE enrollment did not decline, but actually increased 17 percent between 1980 and 1995 (Snyder, Hoffman, and Geddes 1997). More recent crises have been related to the spread of new management systems in business and government, the culture wars, and advances in technology that will, in the words of Peter Drucker, eliminate the residential college and leave the large university campus as nothing but a "relic" (Lenzner and Johnson 1997, 127).

This listing of crises related to external forces is meant to be illustrative, not exhaustive. When there is war (hot or cold), depression, social upheaval, major demographic discontinuities, or the dramatic introduction of new technology such as Sputnik or the World Wide Web, all social institutions including higher education are affected.

Kinds of Crisis

In an effort to better understand the crisis phenomenon, we conducted a brief analysis of the periodical literature of higher education during the 25-year period between 1970 and 1994. A search of ERIC (*ERIC on CD-ROM* 1995) yielded 593 citations containing 797 references to specific crises. To clarify some of the trends in institutional crises, we identified crises that were named in at least 5 percent of the references in each five-year period from 1970 to 1994. These crises, listed by rank order based on frequency of mention, are shown in table 3.1.

We suggest that institutional crises in higher education may fall into four categories: pandemic, chronic, sporadic, or idiosyncratic.

Table 3.1
Higher Education Crisis, Cited by at Least 5 Percent of References, 1970–1994

Rank	1970–1974	1975–1979	1980–1984	1985–1989	1990–1994	All Years
1	Finance 33%	Finance 29%	Finance 27%	Finance 16%	Finance 28%	Finance 27%
2	Student Unrest 11%	Confidence 7%	Enrollment 8%	Curriculum 10%	Diversity, Equity 10%	Confidence 6%
3	Stagnation 8%	Leadership, Governance, Management 7%	Confidence 6%	Diversity, Equity 10%	Confidence 8%	Curriculum 6%
4	Confidence 8%	Stagnation 7%	Curriculum 6%	Stagnation 6%	Stagnation 6%	Stagnation 6%
5	Leadership, Governance, Management 8%	Diversity, Equity 5%	Literacy, Writing 6%	N.A.	Curriculum 6%	Diversity, Equity 6%
6	Curriculum 5%	Literacy, Writing 5%	N.A.	N.A.	Values, Morals 6%	Leadership, Governance, Management 5%
Other	27%	40%	47%	58%	36%	44%
N	168	191	146	115	179	797

N.A.: No category with over 5 percent of citations.

Pandemic crisis. A pandemic crisis is one that is claimed continually and with great frequency. Over the 25-year period, finance was the only pandemic crisis in higher education. It accounted for 27 percent of all references to crisis and was the most frequently identified crisis in each 5-year period.

Chronic crisis. A chronic crisis is one that appears with moderate continuity and frequency. We have operationalized chronic crises as being represented by at least 5 percent of all crisis citations for either the entire 25-year period, or at least three different 5-year periods. There were five chronic crises: confidence, curriculum, stagnation (our name for claims that higher education is not responsive to changing needs), diversity/equity, and leadership/governance/management. Although the frequency and intensity with which they were mentioned were considerably below the pandemic level, chronic crises have been and, we predict, will continue to be consistent themes on the higher education policy agenda.

Sporadic crisis. There were four crises that were identified in at least 5 percent of the citations in only one or two of the five-year periods. These included student unrest, literacy/writing, values/morals, and enrollment. We believe these represent responses to transient social conditions, and we do not expect to see them cited as major concerns in the future with any degree of frequency.

Idiosyncratic crisis. Forty-four percent of all mentions of crisis during the 25-year period were to issues categorized in table 3.1 as "other." We identify these as idiosyncratic because no individual crisis is identified more than five times over the 25 years, nor more than three times in any five-year period. Examples include claims of crises in accreditation, parking, or collective bargaining. These crises represent the views of small and specialized constituencies on issues seen by others as relatively unimportant.

Three Crises in Higher Education

In order to examine the elements of crisis in more detail, we have developed brief analyses of claims of three different crises. They include

the pandemic crisis of finance and the chronic crises of confidence
and of stagnation in the midst of rapid change.

The Pandemic Crisis of Finance

Claims of a fiscal crisis in higher education have a long and honorable
tradition. Fiscal solvency was generally precarious in institutions
during the nineteenth century (Jencks and Riesman 1968); Henry
Tappan, comparing the problems of new institutions to those of older
ones almost 150 years ago, said "we get under the same pressure of
debt and make the same appeals to the public to get us out of it" (Caffrey 1969, 10). More recently, there have been predictions that projected enrollment growth would create a fiscal crisis (Campbell and
Eckerman 1964) and threaten the very survival of private higher
education (Abram 1969). Fears of fiscal crisis caused by enrollment
growth were succeeded shortly thereafter by fears of fiscal crisis
caused by enrollment declines (Hauptman 1993). The year 1969 saw
an "increase in the news stories of financial crises" in all sectors of
higher education (Benezet 1969, 15), and the declaration of a "new depression in higher education" (Cheit 1971). By 1975, the higher education discourse of the day was "couched in terms of survival" (Carnegie Foundation for the Advancement of Teaching 1975, 4), and still
worsening financial conditions were predicted for the future (Keller
1983). More recently, the president of the American Council on Education declared that "higher education is in its most dire financial condition since World War II" and that things are unlikely to improve until after the year 2010 (Atwell 1992, 5B). "Skyrocketing" costs and
warnings of increasing college costs "beyond the average family's ability to pay" (Cox 1964, 3) were regularly reiterated (Lenning 1974) and
repeated again in 1996 with claims that "if appropriate steps are not
taken, higher education could become so expensive that millions of
students will be denied access" (National Commission on the Cost of
Higher Education 1998).

What are we to make of all this? Are college costs rising faster than
family income or inflation (National Commission on the Cost of Higher
Education 1998)? Nonsense, says economist J. L. Doti: "That view is
based on irrelevant data and faulty statistical methodologies" (1998,
B7). Is "American higher education a bargain" as stated in the draft
report of a national commission (Burd 1997a, A33), or must colleges
"take more seriously public concern over rising costs" as stated in the

final version revised after political pressure? (Burd 1997b, A31). Are colleges charging too much? A majority of the public believes college is worth its cost (Public attitudes 1998, A39). Do costs go up because colleges are providing more services desired by their "customers" and improving their quality (O'Keefe 1987), because higher education is labor intensive and thus unable to use technology to the degree seen in industry, or because the self-serving goals of insensitive faculty and administrators create inefficiency as well as ineffectiveness? There are no agreed-on answers to these questions.

The fiscal crisis claims of today seem remarkably like those of yesterday. Concerns that colleges and universities are in danger of failing are clearly misplaced, and claims that we are pricing ourselves out of the market are patently false. The failure rate of four-year colleges was lower from 1990 to 1994 than from 1969 to 1973 (Snyder, Hoffman, and Geddes 1997). Total higher education enrollment is increasing, applications to expensive institutions also known for their quality are not declining, and low-cost alternatives are available for almost anyone. Reflecting in 1969 on the apparent discrepancies between crisis claims on one hand and successful functioning on the other, Howard Bowen put the situation in context: "I agree that financial problems loom ahead, and that new financial solutions are called for. I think that 'crisis' is not the apt word to describe the situation. I doubt if there was ever a time in the history of higher education when educators could project past cost trends into the future and count confidently on finding the necessary funds. 'Crisis' in this sense is a normal situation for higher education; we are always faced with the necessity of securing a progressively increasing share of the national income" (1969, 206).

This suggests that higher education has, does, and probably will always have to deal with fiscal stress but that claims of crisis suggesting the need for major policy discontinuities are clearly overstated. Even if they were true, it is unlikely that colleges could do anything about it. Resources available to colleges and universities in the future will probably have more to do with overall economic growth than with public confidence or any specific reform activities or programs that institutions might develop (Hauptman 1993).

The Chronic Crisis of Confidence

Many sources tell us that "public esteem and support for higher education appear to be declining" (Association of Governing Boards

1996, ix, x). The loss of confidence in higher education is now conventional wisdom, despite the fact that most of the evidence is anecdotal rather than systematic, and what systematic evidence there is does not appear to support the claim (Prewitt 1993). Confidence was declared to be eroding in 1969 as part of a triple crisis (Ward 1969) and to be at a low ebb in 1970 (Sherriffs 1970). In 1970 just about everything was causing public anger, including "student alienation, irrelevant curricula, uninspired teaching, ironclad adherence to what may be outdated traditions, absentee professors, extravagantly high costs of research and graduate education" (Dunham 1970, 1). Educators could point to "a serious erosion of public confidence" in colleges and universities that were once "the pride of America and the envy of other nations" (Brubacher 1972, 9). National surveys showed the percentage of respondents indicating a great deal of confidence in educational leaders dropped from 61 percent in 1966 to 33 percent in 1972 (Lahti 1973, 1). In 1992 a confidence crisis was seen as "a storm breaking upon the university again" (Pelikan 1992, 12).

But what the pundits say may not always reflect what the public believes. A 1982 nationwide survey reported that over 72 percent of Americans thought that the quality of higher education was excellent or good (Group Attitudes Corporation 1984). In 1989, college or university president was the third most prestigious occupation in the United States, and college professors were seen as the tenth most prestigious on a list of 736 occupations (Prewitt 1993). A 1994 national Gallup Poll found that colleges and universities were highly regarded by the public; two-thirds of the respondents who had attended college said they were satisfied or extremely satisfied, while only 8 percent were dissatisfied (Gose 1994, A63).

There is no doubt that levels of public confidence in higher education have declined, but this is part of a national trend to view all societal institutions more critically. Between 1964 and 1992, those having high confidence in college presidents declined from 61 to 25 percent. Still, only the military (39%) and the U.S. Supreme Court (31%) had higher confidence ratings than higher education (Poll 1992; Harris 1994). A 1996 poll in Colorado showed that more respondents had confidence in colleges than in any other statewide institution (Poll 1996), and a comparable 1997 poll in California ranked public confidence in universities and colleges fourth highest among 34 different institutions (Field Institute 1997). A 1996 national survey found higher education rated either first or second in confidence among all public and private nonprofit institutions (Independent Sector 1996). In summary, although confidence in all social institutions has declined in recent years, public confidence in higher education remains higher than for other institutions. And there is a disconnect between the views of the elite and those of the general public. "A glance at the journals and newspapers covering higher education, or at the reading lists and journals of opinion makers, suggests that higher education is troubled" (Harvey et al. 1994, 1). At the same time, a survey of public opinion polls found that "the American people like almost everything about higher education" (Harvey and Immerwahr 1995, 3). Certainly the public is concerned about higher education costs, and this concern is generating increased public scrutiny. But there is little evidence to support the claim that the general public is losing confidence in higher education, despite consistent claims by a small group of academic and other opinion leaders to that effect. "If we take the early 1970s as the base point, the level of public confidence in higher education has not measurably declined [as of 1993]" (Prewitt 1993, 215). As a report issued by Columbia University stated it, "students keep enrolling, employers keep rewarding advanced studies, researchers keep making discoveries, and donors continue giving. Obviously the public believes that higher education has significant benefits" (Graham, Lyman, and Trow 1995).

The Chronic Crisis of Stagnation

There has probably never been a time in the recent past in which higher education has not been criticized for the slowness with which it changed. In 1969 J. Axelrod and his colleagues stated that higher education could not cope with the rapid changes of modern life (1969): "The social institutions serving our times are aging and have developed an unhappy rigidity that resists such examinations [of whether they are right for the times]; even the colleges and universities stiffen before the winds of change" (James 1969, 221). The same sentiments are echoed today when Newt Gingrich reminds us that colleges and universities don't change, campuses are run for the benefit of faculty, the faculty are out of touch with America, and the administrators are ineffective (1995).

But other voices refute the claim. An inventory of academic innovations in 1974 led the Carnegie Commission to say "the idea that colleges and universities have resisted experimentation with new structures and procedures is rendered almost obsolete" (Carnegie Commission on Higher Education 1975, 105). More recently, "sustained reform on college and university campuses is becoming prevalent and purposeful. Change is everywhere—in the classroom, across the curriculum, and in the ways that faculty define their roles and approach their tasks" (Finding proof in the pudding 1997, 57). Change in higher education, although usually neither quick or dramatic, is constant. Course materials change annually with the development of new knowledge and technology (Green 1997). Individual institutions respond to environmental pressures by developing new programs and services (O'Keefe 1987). The degree of change is difficult to quantify reliably, particularly when looked at over short intervals, but campus surveys indicate that it is widespread (El-Khawas 1996). While most changes are incremental, the cumulative effect over decades can be dramatic. As one example, because of continuing change and responsiveness to society's needs, the university is "no longer the site of homogeneity in class, gender, ethnicity, and race" (Levine 1996, xvii).

It is difficult to support the critics' argument that higher education doesn't change, although whether it is changing quickly enough and, more to the point, whether it is changing in the directions desired by the critic are other matters. Some crises are claimed when "the self-appointed guardians of the public good, those who know best, are always just a little nervous about markets when they *do* work, because, in fact, we don't like the results very much." (Rivlin 1988, 9). The problem is illustrated in the recent culture wars. One camp has argued that the curriculum hasn't changed quickly or widely enough to reflect the needs of students and an increasingly diverse society, while the other has argued that it has changed too quickly, eradicating the best of what has been thought in the past. In curriculum development, as in policy-making, where you stand depends on where you sit.

Crises and Attention

The strong rhetoric and vivid images of crisis are useful tools with which to gain attention, power, and control of organizational and symbolic processes in a noisy world. The rhetoric of crisis does not seek to further analysis, but to promote action and advance the priority of an issue on the always-overcrowded public policy agenda (Eccles and Nohria 1992; Birnbaum 1988). Statements such as a "rising tide of mediocrity" (National Commission on Excellence in Education 1983), a "disturbing and dangerous mismatch" between what higher education is providing and what society needs (Wingspread Group 1993), or "a time bomb ticking under the nation's social and economic foundations" (Commission on National Investment in Higher Education 1997) may carry more weight than rational discourse, particularly when the general public knows little about higher education (Immerwahr and Harvey 1995), and data to support the crisis rhetoric are either selectively cited, or nonexistent.

Claims of crisis can focus attention on the particular ideological interests of the claimant, as when a prominent politician connects "The Coming Crisis in Higher Education" to a host of conservative initiatives (Gingrich 1995, 217–22). Or they can certify the status of the claimant as a prescient seer in warning that time is running out—a reflection of what Richard Hofstadter has called the paranoid style (1965). Leaders may proclaim a crisis as justification for increasing their authority, for making changes that might not otherwise be palatable to constituents (Tucker 1981), and for coping strategically with shrinking resources (Kerchner and Schuster 1982, 121). A crisis claim may be constructed in such a way as to favor one kind of outcome over another as solutions search for problems to which they might be applied (Cohen and March 1974). Studying a problem and proclaiming it a crisis (as did the congressionally created National Commission on the Cost of Higher Education) may serve as a form of socially acceptable symbolic action and as a substitute for the more difficult task of initiating instrumental activities. But while crises may be claimed to gain political advantage, it would be a mistake to think that such claims are solely Machiavellian or manipulative in nature. Many—perhaps most—claims of crisis are part of good-faith efforts to improve society. Crises are social constructions, so that belief in the existence of a crisis is related to the ideology of the viewer. At the same time, there are natural cognitive processes of nostalgia, selective memory, and the vividness and intensity with which we experience current events that may facilitate the perception of crisis, regardless of the nature of the ideological issues involved.

In all spheres of social life, there may be a tendency for the past "to recede into a benevolent haze . . . The dirty business is swept under the Carpet of Oblivion . . . If we compare this purported Arcadia with our own days we cannot but feel a jarring discontent, a sense of despair that fate has dropped us into the worst of all possible worlds. And the future, once the resort of hopeful dreams, is envisioned as an abyss filled with apocalyptic nightmares" (Bettmann 1974, xi, xii–xiii). A college president commenting on the good old days said "we who lived through them find them good because we conveniently forget what we do not care to remember—and you, because you never lived through them, can find in the unknown the things the known has denied you" (Hilberry 1943, 11). Those who see crises in higher education may be seduced by the ahistorical "myth of the Golden Era" (Millard 1991, 21) in which the present situation is unfavorably contrasted with the false memory of a fabled past.

Past problems, having been resolved, fade from memory; current problems seem even more intense because of the cognitive tendency to give prominence to more recent events. When American higher education was enjoying prosperity in the mid-1980s, for example, "the funding 'recession' that had occurred in the early 1980s largely had been forgotten, and the hard times at the beginning of the decade were little more than a memory" (Breneman, Leslie, and Anderson 1993, xi). In contrast, contemporary problems are deeply etched and easily brought to mind. No wonder the problems of today appear more vivid and intense than the half-forgotten terrors of yesterday. The nature of today's circumstances can be given even greater emphasis because of the natural cognitive tendency to "project short-term circumstances into long-run laws of development" (Kerr 1975, 273). In 1997, for example, the Commission on National Investment in Higher Education supported its claims of a catastrophic shortfall of funding by the year 2015 on just such projections of current trends that suggested that state tax funds for higher education could drop to zero in the year 2036 (Still headed for zero 1997).

Crisis is related to change, and change always seems to be more rapid in the contemporary era than in our memories of the past. But the immediacy of the present always leads us to feel under pressure from what we believed to be an increased pace of change. In the 1950s business managers expressed the same perceptions of rapid change that we assume is unique to our present situation. "When one examines the historical literature, one is surprised to find that change

—indeed, transformative change—has *always* been a common theme" (Eccles and Nohria 1992, 20), and "every leader or manager views his or her era as especially provocative" (Secor 1995, 86). Why is this so? H. Mintzberg has argued that we are no more in crisis now than in the past half century, but that "we glorify ourselves by describing our own age as turbulent. We live where it's at, as the saying goes, or at least we like to think we do (because that makes us feel important) . . . In other words, what we really face are not turbulent times but overinflated egos" (1994, 207).

The Pandemic Crisis and Attention to Resources

The primary purpose of a crisis is to justify claims for the allocation of scarce social resources. Claims of crises can be used politically to advance an argument for the internal allocation of resources, as when a university information system administrator states that "25 percent of higher education institutions in this country will be out of business 20 years from now" because they won't be able to adapt to technology (Young 1997, A29). They can also be used to bolster claims for increased external support, as when a commission calls on the nation to address the fiscal crisis by allocating additional public resources to higher education (Commission on National Investment in Higher Education 1997).

The scramble for external resources increases as new and competing social priorities emerge, each with its own claims of crisis. The situation in higher education is made to appear even more desperate because, like many other nonprofit organizations, colleges and universities are engaged in an unbounded quest for prestige, excellence, and influence, and no institution ever has enough to do everything it wishes. As Bowen's law of higher education states, "no college or university ever admits to having enough money and all try to increase their resources without limit" (Bowen 1981, 20).

Chronic Crises and Attention to Narrative

The chronic crises of higher education are created by disagreements over the core questions of higher education's purposes, relationship to society, and decision processes. Different constituencies construct stories, or narratives, about who should go to college, what should be taught, the social obligation of institutions, and the proper way to make decisions. Since these are questions of values rather than facts, perceptions of public confidence and judgments of institutional success are influenced more by ideology than data. As the stories of some groups become dominant, the stories of other groups become marginalized. These narratives "are stories with a beginning, a middle, and an end, involving some change or transformation. They have heroes and villains and innocent victims, and they pit the forces of evil against the forces of good." One of the stories is "the story of decline, not unlike the biblical story of the expulsion from paradise . . . The story usually ends with a prediction of crisis" (Stone 1988, 109). Stories of the adulteration of the canon, threats to quality, or the fading of collegiality are examples of claims of crises in higher education based on the narrative of loss. Because there are so many possible narratives, "it is difficult to predict which national problem will be successfully turned into a major national educational crisis and which will not" (Meyer 1986, 50).

The social construction of a crisis is part of an interpretive process in which contending ideologies vie for supremacy through the offering of competing narratives. Merely presenting arguments or data refuting dominant narratives cannot displace them. This can only be done by providing a different narrative that tells a better and more compelling story (Roe 1994). One way of making a story compelling is to exaggerate it, connect it to important social values and symbols, and propose solutions that "appear to be in the public interest, or natural, or necessary, or morally correct" (Stone 1988, 122). A crisis may be, in David Berliner and Bruce Biddle's memorable phrase, a "manufactured crisis" (1995), but all claims of crisis, being constructions, are manufactured. Problems that may lead to crises are "not given, out there waiting in the world for smart analysts to come along and define them correctly. They are created in the minds of citizens by other citizens, leaders, organizations, and government agencies, as an essential part of political maneuvering" (Stone 1988, 122). Different groups have different narratives. When a group identifies something as a crisis, it is attempting to gain acceptance of its narrative in competition with other narratives. A crisis exists for us when the other's narrative gains ascendance; the crisis can be resolved if our own narrative gains ascendance, but this at the same time creates crisis for the other. This iterative cycle of claimed crisis based on competing narratives is a natural consequence of the policy process in a pluralistic and diverse society.

Crying Crisis: Are the Problems Real?
Does It Do Any Good?

Our historic faith in the effectiveness of education leads us to "turn perceived national problems into educational crises and reforms" even when "the crises may seem spurious to the observer, and the educational remedies far-fetched" (Meyer 1986, 47). The goals of higher education are ambitious, and while its achievements and contributions to the development of individuals and to society as a whole have been amply documented in general (see, for example, Bowen 1969), there is no agreement on how they can be assessed in specific cases. Educational institutions "cannot achieve all the things we want from them, and they cannot satisfy all the expectations we have of them. And the more important our goals for the schools are, the more intense the criticism is likely to be" (Levin 1998).

There is little evidence for contemporary claims of unusual crises in higher education, and those that claim them tend to rely on "facts" that are "typically anecdotal, often referring to contemporary events that are the focus of a great deal of interest and uncertainty. The empirical evidence, when collectable, is rather slippery. For every graph that can be used to suggest that we are in a unique moment of total upheaval, there is another, equally persuasive one that suggests the world is practically steady-state" (Eccles and Nohria 1992, 27). To say that colleges and universities today are in crisis is to simplify to the point of absurdity an extremely complex and dynamic relationship between higher education and society. The claimed existence of such a crisis is a myth that has been sustained as "the unproved assertion becomes 'documented' through the sheer force of repetition" (Levine 1996, 24). Ideology, tricks of memory, and an ahistorical view create claims of crisis. The Carnegie Commission's 1967 statement that "a crisis is approaching" in higher education (2) itself echoed statements of a hundred years earlier, and repeated regularly since then. J. B. Edmonson in his 1932 presidential address "The Newest Crisis in Education" suggested that while every few years seems to bring higher education to a critical situation, "that we are not facing the first crisis is an important fact to be kept in mind" (16). The stability in the number of claims of crisis shown in table 3.1 demonstrates the validity of Edmonson's view, and suggests that crises come and go in partially predictable cycles.

Even though claims of crisis may come from outside the academy, we inside the academy often sow the seeds of crisis ourselves. Noting the mass of critical literature in the 1980s, Kenneth Prewitt reminds us that much of it comes from academics: "it is often members of the university community who are confessing to all who will listen that the university stands guilty of fraud and failure" (1993, 207). Small numbers of critical faculty members write articulate, and in many cases newsworthy, critiques, possibly in response to "the masochistic need that is perhaps [academia's] most prominent common personality trait" (Kerr 1975, 273). These are transmitted to opinion leaders, whose views ultimately influence those of the general citizenry. Thus we have a curious paradox. The elite are critical, while the general public strongly supports higher education. Higher education pays a price for the "negative tendency of some academics when they comment on the situation of higher education . . . to see only the worst aspects." The solution? "Their views need to be discounted" (Carnegie Council on Policy Studies in Higher Education 1980, 13).

Declarations of crisis can have both positive and negative consequences. From a positive perspective, it has been said, "the first characteristic of policy-making is the need for a crisis. In higher education, as in other areas of public policy, the American political system seems unable to engage in a serious debate about policy change—let alone to undertake action—unless some form of doom is widely felt to be impending" (Rivlin 1988, 7) Thus "sporadic reform by major crisis" (Hefferlin 1969, 3) may be an expected and essential element in overcoming the inertia of institutionalized organizations and fostering adaptive change in complex, self-correcting systems. At the same time, what are the costs? Can calling out "crisis" in a crowded postsecondary world have negative consequences? Have the continuing claims of crises themselves reached a crisis point?

Focusing on a fatally flawed present and an apocalyptic future makes it increasingly difficult to consider the possibility that "the American academic world is doing a more thorough and cosmopolitan job of educating a greater diversity of students in a broader and sounder array of courses covering the past and present of the worlds they inhabit than ever before in its history" (Levine 1996, 17). If something is labeled a crisis, then everything connected with it may be seen from a negative perspective. The general public may be unduly alarmed and make personal decisions based on problems that don't really exist. Those who *think* that tuition is out of reach, even when it isn't, may be persuaded to alter their educational plans. Policies based on misinterpretations may be illogical and counterproductive (Jaschik 1988). Just as a crisis may serve as a call to arms and an invitation to action, it may also provide a counsel of despair and prove to be a self-fulfilling prophesy in which we become captives of our own rhetoric. Too frequent declarations of crisis may reduce the credibility of those who claim them (Kerchner and Schuster 1982), and the generalization of idiosyncratic crises (of parking, of accreditation, of academic freedom) tends to debase the word altogether. Claims of crisis and the actions that may follow from them may usually cause only minor mischief, but they have the potential for greater consequences as passion and ideology leave little room for measured analysis and strident advocacy contributes to growing cynicism and hopelessness.

To identify something as a crisis requiring special attention and resources may be functional when discrepancies between actual and desired performance reach intolerable and unstable levels, which place a system at risk. However, our review suggests that claims of crisis in higher education persist even when these discrepancies are absent (or at least not explicitly evident). On balance, we believe the problems we face now are not much different from the problems of the past, each of which has been overcome, and that no fundamental changes in processes, programs or structures are needed to deal with current problems. As Clark Kerr said almost a quarter century ago, "higher education has been and is going through a time of troubles, but it is more likely that it will survive and surmount the challenges it now faces than that it will decline and fall . . . To those who see only gloom and doom, we can say that much good is also occurring. To those who say everything fails, we can say that much is, in fact, succeeding. To those who see only problems, we can say there are possibilities for their alleviation" (Kerr 1975, 271, 275). Because of its unusual organizational properties, and the impossibility of clearly defining its processes and goals, higher education will always be in a state that some will refer to as crisis, even as it is "thriving and is perhaps stronger and more effective than ever before in its history" (Trow 1986, 171).

In his farewell speech upon stepping down in 1996 as president of the American Council on Education, Robert Atwell said, "this time the wolf is real. Unless we shift course and do it soon, many of us will be swept away" (Fisher 1997, 50). Is there really a crisis this time?

After all, even the economist who predicted eight of the past three recessions was sometimes right. Is the scratching sound we hear outside the academy's door a wolf waiting to devour Grandma? Or is it only the pussycat asking to come in from the cold for the night?

We lean toward the pussycat hypothesis, and we are concerned that unwarranted cries of "wolf" may eventually provoke yawns rather than attention and action. As both educators and the public become inured to claims of crisis, real signals of incipient threat may become indistinguishable from the background noise of the familiar crisis language. To call something a "crisis" may transform an important problem that might be ameliorated through thoughtful incremental improvements into a political jeremiad accompanied by the sort of fanciful and unfeasible recommendations that are a recipe for inaction (see, for example, the 1986 claim by the National Commission on the Role and Future of State Colleges and Universities that "nothing short of a creative state-by-state effort to strengthen education at all levels, comparable to the Marshall Plan in scope, cost, and dedication, can ensure the preservation of our democratic legacy for the twenty-first century"). As scholars of crises in elementary and secondary education have recognized, "the trouble with such messages is that they can lead to quick-fix or damaging 'solutions' for minor distresses and to ignoring the truly serious problems of education and American society that need long-term effort. People can become blasé when critics cry educational 'wolf' too often" (Berliner and Biddle 1995, 144).

In the past, critics have been loud and persistent, using vivid, if atypical, examples to argue that colleges and universities are self-serving, wasteful, and irrelevant. The responses of supporters have been sporadic, bland, and overly defensive. Since many critics insist on viewing us as just another "industry," perhaps we might be more assertive in the future in reminding the public—and ourselves—that as an industry we have experienced almost uninterrupted growth over the past 50 years. We are the acknowledged world leader in our field, we enjoy a positive balance of trade with the rest of the world, and we enjoy a higher level of trust than almost any other social institution in our country. We have been pioneers in such social movements as globalization, affirmative action, and collaborative labor-management relations. Our customers are highly satisfied, so much so that they voluntarily advertise our names on their car windshields and other personal belongings. Those who have done business with our industry recommend it to their children, and often donate money to it. We have such a strong and lasting impression on our customers that many choose to live nearby when they retire, and even to be buried on our sites. We create knowledge and give it away, we sell our services below cost, and we offer a high return on investment that generates wealth for our customers. We have relatively few scandals, our executives receive relatively low salaries, and our industry is relatively pollution-free. Our staff is highly trained and satisfied with relatively low wages. They work on average over 55 hours a week without overtime and are eager to participate in management. They continually retrain themselves, usually at their own expense. They design their own products, and they respond personally to their customers. No other industry can match higher education's achievements of the past. We predict that none will in the future.

Are there serious problems in higher education? Almost every observer would agree that there are, although there is no agreement on their nature. Is there a crisis in higher education? Probably no more so than there has ever been. Comparing critical assessments of the schools over the past decades, B. Levin suggests "the issues of 1957 are also the issues of 1997, suggesting that criticism is eternal—and perhaps by implication not very meaningful" (1998). As they say in the bayou country, *plus les choses changent, plus ça reste la même.* In times like these, it is good to remember there have always been times like these. Higher education is likely to continue on its unpredictable, bumpy road, using as its lodestone a utopian ideal that can never be achieved. This phenomenon is a natural and expected characteristic of the political process in a democratic society. Still, we shouldn't need crisis to improve. As Alice Rivlin said, "I don't perceive a crisis in higher education, but I don't think we need one to reassess periodically the strengths and weaknesses of our system, to readjust policy, to strengthen the weaker elements, and to carry on the whole enterprise. We should get over the need to feel that things are going to hell and we can't do anything to make them better" (1988).

References

Abram, M. B. 1969. The university in crisis, 1–9. College Entrance Examination Board Annual Meeting. New York: College Entrance Examination Board, 27 October.

Association of Governing Boards. 1996. *Renewing the academic presidency: Stronger leadership for tougher times.* Washington, D.C.: Association of Governing Boards.

Atwell, R. H. 1992. Financial prospects for higher education. *Policy Perspectives* 4, no. 3 (September): 5B.

Axelrod, J., M. B. Freedman, W. R. Hatch, J. Katz, and N. Sanford. 1969. *Search for relevance: The campus in crisis.* San Francisco: Jossey-Bass.

Balderston, F. E., and G. B. Weathersby. 1972. *PPBS in higher education planning and management: From PPBS to policy analysis.* Ford Foundation Sponsored Research Program. Berkeley: University of California Press.

Baldridge, J. V. 1981. Danger—Dinosaurs ahead. *AGB Reports* 23, no. 1 (January-February): 3–8.

Barba, W. C. 1995. *Higher education in crisis.* New York: Garland.

Benezet, L. T. 1969. Continuity and change: The need for both. In *The future academic community: Continuity and change,* edited by J. Caffrey. Washington, D.C.: American Council on Education.

Berliner, D. C., and B. Biddle. 1995. *The manufactured crisis: Myths, fraud, and the attack on America's public schools.* Reading, Mass.: Addison-Wesley.

Berube, M., and C. Nelson. 1995. *Higher education under fire: Politics, economics, and the crisis of the humanities.* New York: Routledge.

Bettmann, O. L. 1974. *The good old days: They were terrible.* New York: Random House.

Birnbaum, R. 1988. Administrative commitments and minority enrollments: College presidents' goals for quality and access. *Review of Higher Education* 11, no. 4: 435–57.

Bowen, H. R. 1969. The financing of higher education: Issues and prospects. In *The future academic community: Continuity and change,* edited by J. Caffrey. Washington, D.C.: American Council on Education.

Bowen, H. R. 1981. *The costs of higher education: How much do colleges and universities spend per student and how much should they spend?* San Francisco: Jossey-Bass.

Breneman, D. W. 1982. *The coming enrollment crisis: What every trustee must know.* Washington, D.C.: Association of Governing Boards.

Breneman, D. W., L. L. Leslie, and R. E. Anderson. 1993. Introduction. In *ASHE reader on finance in higher education,* edited by D. W. Breneman, L. L. Leslie, and R. E. Anderson. Needham Heights, Mass.: Simon & Schuster.

Brubacher, J. S. 1972. *The university and its identity crisis.* New Britain: Central Connecticut State College.

Burd, S. 1997a. Federal commission on the cost of college says it isn't so expensive after all. *Chronicle of Higher Education,* 28 November, A33–34.

————. 1997b. Republican pressure leads to shift in study of higher education costs. *Chronicle of Higher Education,* 12 December, A31–32.

Caffrey, J. 1969. *The future academic community: Continuity and change.* Washington, D.C.: American Council on Education.

Campbell, A., and W. C. Eckerman. 1964. *Public concepts of the values and costs of higher education.* Ann Arbor: University of Michigan Press.

Carnegie Commission on Higher Education. 1975. *Sponsored research of the Carnegie Commission on Higher Education.* New York: McGraw-Hill.

Carnegie Council on Policy Studies in Higher Education. 1980. *Three thousand futures.* San Francisco: Jossey-Bass.

Carnegie Foundation for the Advancement of Teaching. 1975. *More than survival: Prospects for higher education in a period of uncertainty.* San Francisco: Jossey-Bass.

Carnochan, W. B. 1993. *The battleground of the curriculum: Liberal education and the American experience.* Palo Alto: Stanford University Press.

Cheit, E. F. 1971. *The new depression in higher education: A study of financial conditions at 41 colleges and universities.* New York: McGraw-Hill.

Cohen, M. D., and J. G. March. 1974. *Leadership and ambiguity: The American college president.* New York: McGraw-Hill.

Commission on National Investment in Higher Education. 1997. Breaking the social contract: The fiscal crisis in higher education. <http://www.rand.org/publications/CAE/CAE100/#threat>

Cox, C. 1964. *How to beat the high cost of college.* New York: Bernard Geis Associates.

The crisis in intercollegiate athletics: A report by a panel of retired college presidents. 1990. *Chronicle of Higher Education,* 7 March, A38.

Doti, J. L. 1998. "Discounts" make colleges much more affordable for low-income students. *Chronicle of Higher Education,* 6 February, B7.

Dunham, E. A. 1970. *Rx for higher education: Doctor of arts degree.* Washington D.C.: George Washington University.

Eccles, R. G., and N. Nohria. 1992. *Beyond the hype: Rediscovering the essence of management.* Cambridge: Harvard Business School Press.

Edmonson, J. B. 1932. The newest crisis in education. *North Central Association Quarterly* 50, no. 2: 16–32, F75.

El-Khawas, E. 1996. *Campus trends 1996.* Washington, D.C.: American Council on Education.

ERIC on CD-ROM, 1966–1979, 1980–September 1996. 1995. Baltimore: National Information Services.

The Field Institute. 1997. *A digest describing the California public's confidence in institutions.* San Francisco: The Field Institute.

Finding proof in the pudding: The viability of reform in higher education. 1997. *Change* 29, no. 1 (January–February): 57–60.

Fisher, J. L. 1997. Who will lead higher education's transformation? *Planning for Higher Education* 26 (fall): 50–54.

Gingrich, N. 1995. *To renew America.* New York: HarperCollins.

Gose, B. 1994. Poll indicates that colleges are highly regarded by public, but that they shouldn't be complacent. *Chronicle of Higher Education,* 14 September, A63.

Graham, P. A., R. W. Lyman, and M. Trow. 1995. *Accountability of colleges and universities: An essay.* New York: Columbia University Office of the Provost.

Green, K. C. 1997. Money, technology and distance education. *On The Horizon.* <http://sunsite.unc.edu/horizon>

Group Attitudes Corporation. 1984. *American attitudes towards higher education: Results of a comprehensive nationwide survey.* New York: Group Attitudes.

Haaland, G. A. 1995. Scaling the depths of institutional evaluation. *Trusteeship* 3, no. 5 (September/October): 8–11.

Harris, L. 1994. Changing trends in American politics. <http://policy.gmu.edu/cif/whar.html>

Harvey, J., et al. 1994. *First impressions and second thoughts: Public support for higher education.* Washington, D.C.: American Council on Education.

Harvey, J., and J. Immerwahr. 1995. Public perceptions of higher education: On Main Street and in the boardroom. *Educational Record* 76 (fall): 51–55.

Hauptman, A. M. 1993. The economic prospects for American higher education. 1992. In *ASHE reader on finance in higher education,* edited by D. W. Breneman, L. L. Leslie, and R. E. Anderson. Needham Heights, Mass.: Simon & Schuster.

Hefferlin, J. L. 1969. *Dynamics of academic reform.* San Francisco: Jossey-Bass.

Hermann, C. F. 1963. Some consequences of crisis which limit the viability of organizations. *Administrative Science Quarterly* 8 (June): 61–82.

Hilberry, C. B. 1943. Yesterday, today, and tomorrow: A talk to the seniors of Wayne University on their class day. *Journal of Higher Education* 15, no. 1: 11–16.

Hofstadter, R. 1965. The paranoid style in American politics. In *The paranoid style in American politics and other essays,* edited by R. Hofstadter. New York: Knopf.

Immerwahr, J., and J. Harvey. 1995. What the public thinks of colleges. *Chronicle of Higher Education,* 12 May, B1–2.

Independent Sector. 1996. Levels of confidence in private charitable institutions: 1996. <http://www.indepsec.org/programs/research/charts/chart8.html>

James, H. T. 1969. Future costs and benefits. In *The future academic community: Continuity and change*, edited by J. Caffrey. Washington, D.C.: American Council on Education.

Jaschik, S. 1988. State-college officials call public's panic over fees needless. *Chronicle of Higher Education*, 18 May, A1, A22–23.

Jencks, C., and D. Riesman. 1968. *The academic revolution*. Chicago: University of Chicago Press.

Keller, G. 1983. *Academic strategy: The management revolution in American higher education*. Baltimore: Johns Hopkins University Press.

Kerchner, C. T., and J. H. Schuster. 1982. The uses of crisis: Taking the tide at the flood. *Review of Higher Education* 5, no. 3: 121–41.

Kerr, C. 1975. The moods of academia. In *Education and the State*, edited by J. F. Hughes. Washington, D.C.: American Council on Education.

Lahti, R. E. 1973. *Innovative college management*. San Francisco: Jossey-Bass.

Lenning, O. T. 1974. *The "benefits crisis" in higher education*. Washington, D.C.: George Washington University Press.

Lenzner, R., and A. Johnson. 1997. Seeing things as they really are. *Forbes*, 10 March, 122–28.

Leslie, D. W., and E. K. Fretwell. 1996. *Wise moves in hard times: Creating and managing resilient colleges and universities*. San Francisco: Jossey-Bass.

Levin, B. 1998. Criticizing the schools: Then and now. *Education Policy Analysis Archives* 6, no. 16 (20 August). <http://olam.ed.asu.edu/epaa/v6n16.html>

Levine, L. W. 1996. *The opening of the American mind: Canons, culture, and history*. Boston: Beacon Press.

Lucas, C. J. 1996. *Crisis in the academy: Rethinking American higher education*. New York: St. Martin's Press.

Meyer, J. W. 1986. The politics of educational crisis in the United States. In *Educational policies in crisis*, edited by W. K. Cummings, E. R. Beauchamp, S. Ichikawa, V. N. Kobayashi, and M. Ushiogi. New York: Praeger.

Millard, R. M. 1991. *Today's myths, tomorrow's realities: Overcoming obstacles to academic leadership in the 21st century*. San Francisco: Jossey-Bass.

Mintzberg, H. 1994. *The rise and fall of strategic planning: Reconceiving roles for planning, plans, planners*. New York: Free Press.

National Commission on Excellence in Education. 1983. *A nation at risk: The imperatives for educational reform*. Washington, D.C.: Government Printing Office.

National Commission on the Cost of Higher Education. 1998. Report of the National Commission on the Cost of Higher Education. <http://www.gwu.edu/~eriche/Library/ncche.html#appendixe>

National Commission on the Role and Future of State Colleges and Universities. 1986. *Report of the National Commission on the Role and Future of State Colleges and Universities.* Washington, D.C.: American Association of State Colleges and Universities.

Nelson, C. 1997. *Will teach for food: Academic labor in crisis.* Minneapolis: University of Minnesota Press.

Nettles, M. T. 1995. The emerging national policy agenda on higher education assessment: A wake-up call. *Review of Higher Education* 18, no. 3: 293–313.

O'Keefe, M. 1987. Where does the money really go? Case studies of six institutions. *Change* 19, no. 6 (November–December): 12–34.

Pelikan, J. 1992. *The idea of the university: A reexamination.* New Haven: Yale University Press.

Poll finds low confidence in college presidents. 1992. *Chronicle of Higher Education,* 15 April, A15.

Poll shows that Coloradans are confident of state universities. 1996. *Chronicle of Higher Education,* 29 March, A26.

Prewitt, K. 1993. America's research universities under public scrutiny. In *The research university in a time of discontent,* edited by J. R. Cole, E. G. Barber, and S. R. Graubard. Baltimore: Johns Hopkins University Press.

Public attitudes about paying for college. 1998. *Chronicle of Higher Education,* 28 May, A39.

Rivlin, A. 1988. Reflections on twenty years of higher education policy. In *Educational access and achievement in America.* Washington, D.C.: College Entrance Examination Board.

Rodriguez, R. 1994. Higher education crisis looms for Chicanos/Latinos. *Black Issues in Higher Education* 11, no. 3 (7 April): 20–23.

Roe, E. 1994. *Narrative policy analysis: Theory and practice.* Durham, N.C.: Duke University Press.

Secor, J. R. 1995. TGM: A flavor-of-the-month buzzword or step one to designing processes that deliver continuous value to the customer? In *Total quality management in academic libraries: Initial implementation efforts.* Washington, D.C.: Association of Research Libraries.

Sherriffs, A. C. 1970. Is the present anxiety about higher education justified? Paper presented at the Rational Debate Seminar, 6 May. Washington, D.C.: American Enterprise Institute for Public Policy Research.

Snyder, T. D., C. M. Hoffman, and C. M. Geddes. 1997. *Digest of educational statistics 1997.* Washington, D.C.: U.S. Department of Education, National Center for Educational Statistics.

Sommer, J. W. 1995. *The academy in crisis: The political economy of higher education.* New Brunswick, N.J.: Transaction.

Still headed for zero: Decline in state tax funds appropriations for higher education paused in FY1998. 1997. *Postsecondary Educational Opportunity,* 65 (November). Oskaloosa, Iowa: Mortenson Research Seminar on Public Policy Analysis of Opportunity for Postsecondary Education.

Stone, D. A. 1988. *Policy paradox and political reason.* Glenview, Ill.: Scott, Foresman.

Trow, M. 1986. The state of higher education in the United States. In *Educational policies in crisis,* edited by W. K. Cummings, E. R. Beauchamp, S. Ichikawa, V. N. Kobayashi, and M. Ushiogi. New York: Praeger.

Tucker, R. C. 1981. *Politics as leadership.* Columbia: University of Missouri Press.

Ward, R. C. 1969. Long-range planning. Paper presented at the Council for Business Officers Conference, 9–12 November, Association of State Universities and Land-Grant Colleges.

Wingspread Group. 1993. An American imperative: Higher expectations for higher education. <http://www.johnsonfdn.org/library/foundpub/amerimp/hiexp.html>.

Wood, J. L., and L. T. Valenzuela. 1996. The crisis of American higher education. *Thought and Action* 12, no. 2 (fall): 59–71.

Wood, K., and D. Smellie. 1991. *Educational technology: Initiative for change. Educational Media and Technology Yearbook,* vol. 17.

Young, J. R. 1997. EDUCOM notebook: Merger plans, high-tech colleges, and the death of the book. *Chronicle of Higher Education,* 7 November, A29.

Chapter Four

Built to Serve
The Enduring Legacy of Public Higher Education

Patricia J. Gumport

At the dawn of the twenty-first century, U.S. public higher education is under attack. Consider the lines of criticism and defense: at one extreme, critics rail against the enterprise for its organizational inefficiencies, its failure to meet the changing needs of employers and student populations, and its displays of complacency or at times outright resistance to change. In defense of the inability or unwillingness to adapt, advocates of public universities and colleges caution that they should not become beholden to any specific or immediate interests; rather they have a longer-range mandate to serve society by being insulated from the demands of the day. In the name of accountability, however, several antidotes to the alleged lack of responsiveness have been put forward by state governments as well as by some governing boards themselves. These include a mix of mechanisms and mandates for performance-based funding, academic restructuring, and outcome assessment initiatives.

At the other extreme, there are critics who suggest that public universities and colleges have been responding excessively, too ready to accommodate the changing agenda of commercial interests or the shifting mandates from federal and state government agencies, thereby distorting the enterprise into one serving short-term, utilitarian purposes (Press and Washburn 2000). Oft-cited contemporary evidence for this alleged selling-out ranges from diluting the curriculum with politically correct academic offerings, establishing academic-industry research agreements (e.g., the University of California, Berkeley, and Novartis), athletic teams sponsored by Nike or Reebok, exclusive "pouring rights" committed to Coca-Cola or PepsiCo, not to mention the decades of university science and engineering efforts to support national defense. A common line of defense against this set of criticisms is to cast these adaptations as entirely necessary alterations that enable the enterprise to progress and keep pace with changing environments.

Such a wide range of criticism suggests that there are competing interests at work in evaluating as well as choreographing how public higher education functions. Missing from such deliberations is a careful conceptual analysis of the legacies invoked for public higher education (Gumport 2000). On balance, as this chapter will suggest, U.S. public higher education has been remarkably adaptive to changing societal expectations. In a fundamental sense, public higher education was "built to serve," an expectation that was formalized in the late nineteenth century and has been reiterated ever since then by governmental agencies and public universities and colleges themselves. The thrust was a practical bent: that they would train future generations of citizens in worthwhile subjects and conduct research that could be beneficial to local, state, regional, and national needs. So the legacy of service, broadly construed, has been embedded in teaching and research, not only in those activities that were formally designated as "public service." As societal imperatives have changed over the past century, public universities and colleges have indeed responded, although at times not immediately or in the precise form expected.

It is the legacy of service that has anchored the dual societal mandate for public colleges and universities to respond as well as to protect, to evolve as well as to embody enduring values. In this light, much has been accomplished in the name of service to the wider society. The present era, however, is marked by a political-economic emphasis on academic consumerism and market forces that promotes an unprecedented enthusiasm to redefine public higher education as an industry. Those who advocate this redefinition invoke the legacy of service with demonstrated accountability. Thus, I think it is valuable to contrast the idea of higher education as an industry with that of higher education as a social institution and to show how the former more narrowly interprets the legacy of service, with possible negative consequences for the enterprise.

The Legitimating Idea of Higher Education

In this section, I propose that the dominant legitimating idea of public higher education has been moving away from the idea of higher education as a social institution and toward the idea of higher education as an industry.

A legitimating idea at the macrosocietal level suggests that there are taken-for-granted understandings that constitute parameters for what is legitimate—that is, what is expected, appropriate, and sacred, as well as the converse. In the realm of higher education, both of the legitimating ideas mentioned above have distinct premises regarding what is valued, problematic, and prescribed for improvement.

Simply stated, those who look at higher education as an industry, see public colleges and universities as a sector of the economy. The root metaphor is a corporate model: to produce and sell goods and services, train some of the workforce, advance economic development, and perform research. Harsh economic challenges and competitive market pressures warrant better management, which includes swift programmatic adjustment, maximum flexibility, and improved efficiency in the direction of greater accountability and, thus, customer satisfaction.

In contrast, those who look upon higher education as a social institution believe that public colleges and universities, by definition, must preserve a broader range of social functions that include such essential educational legacies as the cultivation of citizenship, the preservation of cultural heritage(s), and the formation of individual character and critical habits of mind, as well as economic development functions.

The tension between the two legitimating ideas is profound. The former perspective is dominated by a concern that higher education's inability or unwillingness to adapt will result in a loss of centrality and perhaps ultimately a loss of viability. Evidence to support this concern is found in widely cited proclamations that higher education has already lost the ability to judge itself in the United States (IRHE 1993a, 1993b, 1993c, and 1994; Zemsky and Massy 1990; Gumport and Pusser 1999) and in Europe (Neave and van Vught 1991). In contrast, the latter perspective is dominated by a concern that adaptation to market forces gives primacy to short-term economic demands at the expense of neglecting a wider range of societal responsibilities—including the concern that knowledge will become a privately held rather than a public good—and thereby jeopardize the long-term public interest. Further explication of the contrast is instructive, in order to show how the remaking of public higher education into an industry unduly narrows its social charter.

Higher Education as an Industry

Those who view higher education as an industry see public colleges and universities primarily as quasicorporate entities producing a wide range of goods and services in a competitive marketplace. A research university may be thought of as offering a very diverse product line, especially in the post–World War II era of Kerr's "multiversity" (Kerr [1963] 1995). Community colleges offer degrees or one course at a time, in many fields, to people of all ages, while the flagship university offers many courses and levels of degrees across hundreds of fields of study, professes to serve national, state, and local economic needs, and sells entertainment in sporting and cultural events to the local community.

Ideally, according to microeconomic theory, organizations are managed on the basis of assumptions of economic rationality. Public higher education supplies and prices its main services—teaching and research—to correspond to laws of supply and demand. Its customers are students, parents, state legislatures, employers, and research funders. Different customers have different tastes and preferences. The theory assumes that other people, such as faculty, employed by the organization participate out of calculated self-interest. For this reason, incentives and sanctions will motivate them to be more productive. Major obstacles to maintaining the organization's viability include fixed costs and inefficiencies, competition and oversupply, and uncertainty and imperfect information. It is important for the organization's managers to know its liabilities and assets, to anticipate costs and benefits, to enhance efficiency and flexibility, and—as the contemporary quality movement dictates—to increase customer satisfaction (Seymour 1992).

The industrial perspective focuses on the harsh realities of market forces and the urgency of doing something to stay competitive, be it planning strategically, scanning environments, attempting to contain or cut costs, correcting inefficiencies, or taking measures to maximize flexibility. Adjustments include changing product lines, substituting technology for labor, and reducing fixed costs through such means as outsourcing as well as increasing the proportion of part-time and temporary personnel. Doing nothing is not an option. The reengineering movement in the 1990s, catapulted by variations on Hammer and Champy (1993), popularized imperatives such as these.

Looking at higher education from this viewpoint, it is valuable to note that it does not have just one major marketplace, as determined by type of student served or geographic location or degrees granted. Instead, we can see several types of markets at work simultaneously, not only for obtaining students, but for placing graduates, hiring and retaining faculty, obtaining research funding, establishing collaboration with industry, maintaining endowments, sustaining and extending alumni giving and other fundraising sources, and so on.

A contemporary feature of higher education markets is the increased presence of nontraditional providers; facilitated by new telecommunications technologies, their emergence has recently been altering the competitive playing field by attracting students (Marchese 1998). In light of this, managers must read the barometer of market changes to assess the viability of their niches and adjust their offerings accordingly. If they can't compete in a given area, they should focus elsewhere; alternatively, if there is untapped demand for an educational product, they can supply it at a higher price. Those embracing the industrial perspective see the decision to add an academic program as a strategy to position the college or university to attract new customers and thereby increase revenue. Similarly, they see an increase in tuition as an appropriate response to increased demand or decreased supply of a particular educational product such as a professional degree in engineering, business, education, or law. Hence, programmatic changes can be seen as prudent market corrections.

All of this should sound quite familiar to observers of contemporary higher education management. The corporate metaphors of production in a competitive marketplace are omnipresent. Knowing one's resources, establishing a comparative advantage, and refining strategy have become standard in the United States and increasingly in Europe (Keller 1983; Chaffee 1985; Hearn 1988; Hardy 1990;

Massy 1996; Clark 1998). Of course, one might argue that these business principles are rendered irrelevant for public higher education, because the market is heavily regulated by state and federal government through several types of public subsidies, restrictions in pricing, regulated degree offerings, and admissions standards. Yet the industry perspective and its dominant corporate metaphor have nonetheless acquired a certain resilience, due in part to the parsimony they endorse, to today's uncritical acceptance of business and economic rhetoric, and to the very real complexity of today's campus operations. (See, e.g., Duderstadt's 1995 characterization of "the University of Michigan, Inc.," which with an annual budget of over $2.5 billion would have ranked roughly 200th on the list of Fortune 500 companies.) In many ways, adopting business rationales with strategic management principles has become de rigueur for repositioning higher education organizations to compete within new economic realities.

There are several consequences, of course, to this conception of higher education becoming the dominant legitimating idea that is used to make sense of and ultimately to redefine the parameters of higher education. It is worth noting that state policymakers and industry leaders expect public colleges and universities to demonstrate some willingness, if not enthusiasm, to consider market forces or else risk losing some legitimacy. The industrial model, however, pays no attention to what may be at stake in shortsighted adaptations to market forces, nor does it provide for a public agenda that may exceed the market's reach. In a fundamental sense, it is historically clear that the rationale that the market is imperfect and inappropriate as a sole operating logic has been one of the bases for public subsidy of public higher education. Contemporary discourse, however, is increasingly questioning, if not eroding, this premise.

Higher Education as a Social Institution

I turn now to the legitimating idea of higher education as a social institution, which I argue has been gradually displaced. A social institution may be seen as an organized activity that maintains, reproduces, or adapts itself to implement values that have been widely held and firmly structured by the society. According to Turner (1997), human history is characterized by the evolution of social institutions, relatively stable and conservative in norms, structures, and general standards of good/bad, appropriate/inappropriate, worthy/unworthy, and other evaluative criteria for behavior. Over time, as institutions change, they do so in relation to one another. Turner is among those who argue that social institutions have been in a process of ongoing differentiation with far-reaching consequences due to their interdependence with one another.

Thus, when one uses the lens of "social institution" to examine the institutional imperatives for public higher education, one sees educational organizations devoted to a wide array of social functions that have expanded over time: the development of individual learning and human capital, the socialization and cultivation of citizens and political loyalties, the preservation of knowledge, and the fostering of other legitimate pursuits for the nation-state. It is commonly acknowledged that the Morrill Acts establishing land grants for state colleges and the infusion of federal funds into public higher education in the decades following World War II not only expanded the enterprise but also dramatically diversified the activities regarded as its legitimate province. These included educating the masses, advancing knowledge through research, contributing to economic development by employing and producing workers, and developing industrial applications. In this sense, shifts in societal imperatives reshaped expectations for higher education and redefined what activities are or are not recognized as "higher education." Of course, such expectations and definitions continue to be reconstituted over time, at times signaling a major shift akin to the remaking of a social contract.

An additional dimension of the historical proposition warrants our consideration. As a social institution, higher education exists in an enduring interdependence with other social institutions—not only with other types and levels of education, but also with the family, government, industry, religion, and popular culture. Social institutions evolve in their interchanges with one another. As Turner argues, over time societal expectations for education have in part stemmed from broadened expectations that it take on human capital functions, political legitimation functions, and socialization functions:

Today, political leaders in industrial societies often view education as the key to economic development and political stability, since it performs such critical functions for political legitimation and for developing human capital. As education has differentiated and elaborated, many of the socialization and social-placement functions from kinship have been assumed by schools; and it has come to have increasingly far-reaching consequences for the economy (as a source of human capital and technology) and polity (as a source of political legitimation). (Turner 1997, 258–59)

The relevance of this proposition for higher education, particularly for contemporary public higher education, warrants further exploration. It is entirely possible that, with the decline of public trust in social (and particularly public) institutions, there is a corresponding redefinition of expectations for public higher education as a social institution; as a result, the expected Parsonian pattern-maintenance and socialization functions may be receding, while economic functions may come to dominate the foreground.

From this perspective, it is essential to acknowledge that the terms *institution* and *organization* do not have the same meaning, even though they are often used interchangeably. While colleges and universities are frequently referred to as organizations, the use of the term *institution* is more common—often used in its adjectival form and intended as a synonym, referring to organizationwide constructs such as institutional leadership, decisions, or policies. R. N. Bellah and colleagues (1991) have observed that this tendency has profound consequences in that it reflects reductionist thinking, where focusing on the organization reduces complexity to the point of oversimplifying what is problematic and neglecting historical patterns of rights and responsibilities that shape our lives. (Another possibility is that speakers are basically unaware of the sociological distinction and its import.)

In short, the language used to talk about higher education is important, for it not only reflects our thinking but also contributes to a construction of reality. While this observation has been noted by philosophers, linguists, and sociologists alike, Bellah et al. state it powerfully: "Institutions are very much dependent upon language: what we cannot imagine and express in language has little chance of becoming a sociological reality" (1991, 15). This observation carries with it even more weight when one considers the moral import. As the authors explain, in our thinking we often neglect "the power of institutions as well as their great possibilities for good and evil," the process of creating and recreating institutions "is never neutral, but always ethical and political" (1991, 11). For example, speaking of alternatives in a language of tradeoffs (such as tradeoffs between healthcare, prisons, higher education, or other public goods) "is inadequate for it suggests that the problems are merely technical, when we need a richer moral discourse with which to conduct public discussion." (26). Heeding the admonishment of Bellah et al., conceptualizing higher education as subject to a logic of "social institution" invokes normative considerations. Thus, in addition to the ways that their environments are reshaping contemporary public universities and colleges, the very discourse about those changes and challenges itself plays a significant role in such reshaping.

It is critical to identify a distinction regarding what may have changed: is it that the social functions of public higher education have changed, or is it that our talk and ideals about public higher education have changed? That is, has public higher education taken on principally economic functions, abandoning the more comprehensive institutional mandate of performing not only educational but also socialization and political functions? Or has it become commonplace to speak of higher education in industrial terms, reflecting by our parlance expectations that public colleges and universities are principally valued for their economic contributions (e.g., human capital, workforce training, and economic development)? Or is it both? The distinction between the two is critical as we consider the recent past as well as future prospects.

While changes in their social functions may signal a de facto shifting of the charter for public colleges and universities, the industrial discourse that has come to dominate reduces the scope and legitimacy of a wider range of organizational and individual academic commitments within public higher education. For example, the logic of managerial production renders irrelevant or unvalued the notion of higher education as a place for dissent and unpopular ideas, for creativity and the life of the mind, for caring and relationships except as inefficiencies that may be deemed wasteful or unaffordable. Of course, from a broader perspective, it is entirely possible to envision a mandate for service to society as multiple, involving each of these things as well as those more visibly and instrumentally valuable.

Converging Mechanisms

I propose that there are three interrelated mechanisms that have advanced the process of transforming the dominant legitimating idea of higher education (and especially public higher education) from that of a social institution to that of an industry. They are academic management, academic consumerism, and academic stratification.

Academic Management

The expansion in size, authority, and professionalization of academic managers in colleges and universities has drawn upon discourse from management science and organizational research for its ideology. The core premises are managerial; campus leaders and key administrators are managers who diagnose and prescribe organizational well-being. The rationale is simple: Organizations can and do adapt; and organizational survival is dependent upon the ability of the organization to respond to its environment, which is characterized as dynamic and therefore uncertain and potentially threatening. Thus, among other responsibilities, managers are expected to monitor the organization-environment interface, determine appropriate strategies, and develop effective bridging and buffering mechanisms.

When these premises are applied to the academic enterprise, campus leaders attend to both resources as well as resource relationships. The management of resources (their acquisition, maintenance, and internal allocation) and the management of resource relationships between the organization and its environment in themselves become major organizational practices to position organizations for survival. (See Gumport and Sporn [1999] for discussion of this adaptation dynamic.) Prominent examples include monitoring vulnerabilities that arise from resource dependence, trying to reduce existing dependencies, and meeting expectations for compliance. In the arena of public higher education, all three of these concepts have gained currency and are reflected in campus discourse and academic management rationales and are increasingly taken for granted.

First, with regard to monitoring vulnerabilities that come from environmental turbulence, campus managers give ongoing attention to forecasting enrollment changes and shifts in state appropriations and consider how such changes are handled by their peer institutions. It is essential to note that they must pay attention to multiple environments (e.g., local, state, regional, and national), especially when considering those resources on which the organization has had the greatest dependence.

Second, and extremely visible in the contemporary era, is the cultivation of new resources to reduce existing dependencies. For public universities and colleges, this primarily takes the form of adopting strategies that will generate revenue for the organization, whether it be seeking to improve public relations with the state legislature, seeking out new student markets, finding new sources for research funding, stepping up efforts for alumni giving, or cultivating new sources of private revenue. The cultivation of a plurality of resources to reduce existing dependencies has long been seen as a prudent course for organizations but has gained greater currency for public higher education in the contemporary era, where dependence on funding from state appropriations has created financial challenges.

A third ongoing function of managers is to ensure compliance with demands. They must establish various mechanisms—some of which are expensive for the organization—to ensure and then demonstrate that an academic organization is in compliance with demands from a number of different sources. Health and safety regulations abound, for example, as both public and private universities well know. With the most recent wave of accountability demands extending from operations to educational functions, mandates for satisfactory compliance are often tied to state and national funding (e.g., national funds for student financial aid, state general fund appropriations for institutions, etc.)—funding that is essential to organizational survival. These initiatives include asking public colleges and universities to demonstrate faculty productivity as well as student learning outcomes. One study documents that approximately half of the states in the United States have already instituted some type of performance-based funding, with 20 additional states anticipating it in the near future (Burke and Serban 1998).

The need to manage these challenges positions higher education administrators in the central mediating role of determining the potential costs and benefits of any course of action (or nonaction). In making such determinations, administrators who occupy the most visible leadership roles in public universities and colleges function as interpreters for the rest of the organization. They address such key concerns as, Who are the constituencies from whom the organization is seeking legitimacy and what do they want? What are successful peer institutions doing to manage contradictory demands? Can some demands be responded to symbolically, superficially, or minimally—as in a "satisficing" mode? Attending to these concerns, administrators can symbolically present the organization as responsive to a variety of external stakeholders as well as to organizational members internally. While a dissonance-free organization is unlikely to result, such efforts by managers can have powerful results in terms of securing a sense of stability as the organization navigates through times of environmental uncertainty and turbulence.

The above discussion characterizes higher education managers as positioned in an expanded role with authority over a broad domain of organizational decision-making as well as representing the organization's purposes and priorities to the external stakeholders. This characterization contains a key premise that warrants careful scrutiny: that these managers are appropriately and effectively positioned to act for the organization. This premise is of course questionable. Who should speak for the organization? Under what conditions and to what extent is it appropriate to reposition the organization to meet the demands of its changing environment? While the need to manage resources and resource relationships and the need to reduce resource dependence provide a compelling post hoc rationale for an expanded managerial domain, decision-makers should not overlook the role of faculty in academic governance, particularly when restructuring the academic landscape of programs offered.

This critical concern falls under the general category of "the politics of professional work." It is compatible with related critical analyses of "managerialism" (Enteman 1993) and "the emergence of technocracy" (Heydebrand 1990), a term that is intended to replace the simple bureaucracy-professionalism dualism previously used to characterize academic organizations. Building on the historical argument that research universities have become more entrepreneurial through increased academic capitalism, scholars have proposed that research universities have become more managerial in their governance and the division of labor (Rhoades and Slaughter 1997; Slaughter and Leslie 1997). Faculty have become "managed professionals," while middle-level administrators have become "managerial professionals" (Rhoades 1998). While changes in the power dynamics and their consequences remain topics for empirical study, the trend toward increased formalization and evaluation of faculty work is clear. Management has assumed more organizational space, visibility, and legitimacy in running the enterprise.

This notion has obvious relevance for the full range of U.S. public colleges and universities as well. A key rationale for this shift in authority to academic managers has been the need for flexibility to adapt swiftly and a concomitant need for discretion over resource reallocation and programmatic investment. The consequences for the organization are, of course, profound, as such centralized decisions determine where and how the organization will invest its academic resources and may ultimately change the very character of the enterprise. This includes such defining practices as selecting among academic priorities, eliminating or making the case to eliminate or downsize academic programs, and determining the academic workforce and its characteristics (e.g., full-time versus part-time course load, etc.). Critics of this expansion in managerial authority and its ensuing consequences have suggested that environmental conditions should not predetermine such academic restructuring. For example, in questioning the presumption that managerialism is a natural academic adaptation, Rhoades and Slaughter argue: "The structural patterns we describe are not just inexorable external developments to which colleges and universities are subject and doomed . . . The academy itself daily enacts and expresses social relations of capitalism and heightened managerial control grounded in a neoconservative discourse" (1997, 33). Thus, they make explicit a mechanism that has contributed to displacing organizational practices that advocated for preserving educational legacies where human development and citizenship were central imperatives alongside a full range of knowledge areas that were supported for reasons other than their anticipated human-capital or market value.

Academic Consumerism

A second mechanism that has contributed to the legitimating idea of public higher education as an industry is the sovereignty of the consumer. The rise of academic consumerism can be seen as a phenomenon that has emerged after the post–World War II decades of massification and its attendant democratic gains. The conceptual shift elevates consumer interests as paramount considerations in the restructuring of academic programs and the reengineering of academic services.

The needs and interests of several types of consumers (e.g., taxpayers, employers, research funders, students) come to mind, when considering who public universities and colleges serve. However, it is most commonly the student-as-consumer of public higher education and particularly the student-as-potential-or-current-employee who seeks workforce training or economic security. The fact that public universities and colleges are so functionally differentiated, offering such a wide range of programs, only reinforces the idea that students with different aspirations can find whatever they need to retrain right on through retirement.

The rise of academic consumerism in the contemporary era has been accelerated by four essential presumptions, although each is problematic in its own way. First, the student-consumer is presumed to be capable of informed choice and to have the ability to pay (Readings 1996). To view prospective students as prospective buyers conjures up the image of the smartest shoppers among them perusing *Consumer Reports,* as one would when considering the purchase of an automobile or major household appliance. The premise is that the intelligent consumer will select that which has the best value for the money. While in itself the spirit of this premise is not unsound, in practice the U.S. higher education system has no such organizational performance data available; in fact, campuses themselves have been vocal in their criticism of comparative data, such as that of the widely cited *U.S. News and World Report* rankings.

A second and related presumption is that the enrolled student-consumer chose to attend that particular college or university. This would be consistent with the economic theory of revealed preferences whereby behaviors are seen as matching desires. Thus, a student who has enrolled at a community college wanted to go there because it maximized his or her utility, rather than as a result of socialization, truncated aspirations, socioeconomic barriers, or a discriminatory culture.

Third, enrolled students-consumers are "encouraged to think of themselves as consumers of services rather than as members of a community," as Bill Readings (1996, 11) insightfully observed. Campus administrators and faculty may even be encouraged to think of students as consumers, too. The basis for exchange is the delivery of an academic service (e.g., lecture, course, piece of advice). This conception of students drastically reduces the potential richness of teaching and learning relationships, inclinations toward mentoring and sponsorship, and students forging meaningful bonds with their peers. In effect, it would place an emphasis on the campus as a business of academic transactions rather than as a community of inquirers, teachers, and learners.

Fourth, consumer taste and satisfaction can become elevated to new heights in the minds of those responsible for designing academic services and programs. The translation of this presumption into practice can be seen in the vocationalization of academic programs, which seem to be altered as easily as changing the time that courses are offered, or rushing to establish them on-line. It is also evident in the academic-quality movement, which places a premium on customer satisfaction. While attention to student needs and preferences is not by any means inherently misguided, it is the *reduction* of students to consumers and the supremacy attributed to presumed consumer interests in academic restructuring that may cumulatively do the educational enterprise a disservice.

Cumulatively, consumer taste rather than professional expertise may become the basis for legitimate change in public higher education. Academic consumerism would increasingly dictate the character of the academic enterprise, as public colleges and universities catered to the desires (short-sighted though they may be) of the individual, thereby further displacing faculty authority and perhaps ultimately the collective force of educational legacies.

Academic Stratification

The third mechanism advancing the conception of higher education as an industry is the restratification of academic subjects and academic personnel based upon the increased use value of particular knowledge in the wider society and its exchange value in certain markets. The increased use value of knowledge is evident in both the culture of ideas and the commerce of ideas, defining features of postindustrial society (Bartley 1990; Drucker 1993; Gibbons et al. 1994). The culture of ideas acknowledges an accumulated heritage of knowledge accepted by society. It is sometimes seen as a storehouse or stock of knowledge with shared understandings and values. From this perspective, public colleges and universities may be seen as social organizations of knowledge that contribute to society in the Durkheimian sense of integration. The commerce of ideas, on the other hand, casts a spotlight on the creation and distribution of ideas in the knowledge industry as well as on the growing exchange value of knowledge in specific markets. From this perspective, public colleges and universities—particularly research universities—may be seen as competitors in the commercial activities of publications,

copyrights, patents, and licenses, positioning themselves and the nation for global competitiveness. Such knowledge activities have, on
some campuses, come to be seen as essential—even, increasingly, as
core—pursuits of public universities. (This is quite compatible with
the revenue-generating aspirations of academic managers, as discussed above.)

In order to grasp the full import of this idea, one has to understand
higher education primarily as a knowledge-processing system. This
stands in contrast to the conventional view that characterizes higher
education as a people-processing system in which goals, structures,
and outcomes support students undergoing personality development,
learning skills, and acquiring credentials that may enable their upward mobility. In posing the alternative—that higher education has
central knowledge functions—knowledge is then seen as the defining core of academic work and academic workers. As Burton Clark
insightfully explains, knowledge is "the prime material around which
activity is organized . . . Knowledge materials, and advanced ones at
that, are at the core of any higher education system's purposes and
essence. This holds true throughout history and across societies as
well" (1983, 13). Following John Meyer (1977), Clark suggests that
knowledge is processed so as to have a wide array of intellectual, professional, economic, and social consequences.

As educational institutions evolve, they develop categories of
knowledge and thereby determine that certain types of knowledge
exist and are authoritative. They also define categories of persons
privileged to possess the bodies of knowledge and to exercise the authority that comes from knowledge. Educational structures, in effect,
are a theory of knowledge, in that they help define what currently
counts as knowledge" (1983, 26). Clark has since developed the conception even further by prescribing that universities, as "knowledge-
based institutions," should be more conscious of possibilities for risk-
taking investment in new fields along with recombinations of old
fields; with optimism regarding as-of-yet-unrealized potential, he
proposes that "certain ways of organizing knowledge offer the possibility of sustained insight, even to the point of a systematic claim on
wisdom" (1996, 429–30). Although gains in insight and wisdom have
indisputable significance for society, neither one has yet made it onto
the report card of organizational performance indicators. Nonetheless, we continue to see self-described strategic efforts to reorganize
academic areas in public universities and colleges.

An instrumental orientation toward academic knowledge also seems widespread in the contemporary era. The notion of knowledge as a public good seems increasingly unsustainable in a context where academic subjects and knowledge workers are not buffered from market forces and are increasingly privately held as intellectual property. Given the realities of complex organizations where resource acquisition and status considerations abound, these developments also have consequences for the stratified social order on campuses. In the contemporary era, academic knowledge areas require capital for fuel and the promise of future resources for sustained legitimacy. The resource requirements of knowledge areas and the likelihood of generating revenue have a salience that cannot be overstated. They are so important that today's knowledge creation and management may be interpreted as increasingly dominated by a proprietary ethic in the spirit of advanced capitalism. This characterization may be problematic for some, in that it uses a predominately managerial metaphor to talk about higher education in terms of entrepreneurial dynamics that can help a campus sustain its inventory and pursue its core competencies. However, in the present era, the resource requirements of creating, sustaining, and extending knowledge activities figure prominently in campus deliberations over what is academically worthy of support (Gumport 1993).

Selection processes are at work to determine what knowledge is considered most valuable and hence worthy of support. As an illustration, consider the ways in which state governments conceptualize public higher education as services to procure. Particularly in the past 15 years, we see signs that governments are willing to support (i.e., with financial resources to) public universities to procure teaching (and where applicable, research) services. This procurement orientation suggests an underlying production function approach, where higher education is valued for its instrumental contributions vis-à-vis the preparation and retraining of individuals for work and the application of useful knowledge to social and economic needs, rather than one in which all fields of study have inherent worth. In this sense, the context quite directly shapes what knowledge is selected as appropriate for instruction, research, or service. Conversely, the context neglects or perhaps actively dismantles those areas not valued. In this way, the context alters the academic landscape and its knowledge areas, and universities themselves come to advertise this conception of public higher education as yielding very high returns for every state dollar invested (NASULGC 1997).

Selection processes are also at work given external demands for managers to reshape the structure of the academic landscape. Evidence suggests that academic reorganization in times of resource constraint differs from the differentiation that accompanies expansion along with stratification of academic subjects and personnel (Blau 1970 and 1973; Clark 1983 and 1993; Gumport 1997; Metzger 1987; Rhoades and Slaughter 1997). Thus, what has come to count as knowledge did not simply unfold or evolve out of existing areas, but resulted in part from the differential valuing and resourcing of academic units competing for epistemological, organizational, and physical space. When additive solutions have not been possible, priorities are identified; particular units are constructed as failing to pull their weight and are targeted for downsizing and elimination.

For example, graduate-level programs and small humanities programs (such as foreign languages) have been losing resources and status within many campus settings. And at the state level, consolidation has, at times, been mandated. Examples of such state-level restructuring initiatives were seen in several states in the 1990s: over 80 academic programs were eliminated in Virginia; over 70 were eliminated in Massachusetts (Gumport and Pusser 1999). Significant costs savings can result: in Illinois public universities, 300 programs were eliminated, reduced or consolidated, for a savings of $181 million; and in Illinois community colleges, similar contraction in 335 programs accounted for a savings of $209 million. In each case, the savings were reallocated to salaries or new programs (IBHE 1998).

In the contemporary era, the rhetoric of selective reinvestment has gained ascendancy, while comprehensive field coverage is increasingly considered not viable for every campus—something that not every university can afford or aspire to—due to budget and management considerations. Restructuring for selective reinvestment on campuses is a marked departure from comprehensive field coverage, and the discourse of selective excellence that precedes it directly parallels the discussions about maximizing one's comparative advantage that dominate corporate approaches. In contrast, the histories of many of this country's public colleges and universities suggest that they were established with the ideal of openness to all knowledge, regardless of immediate applications and relevance.

Thus, it used to be assumed that access to the full range of knowledge is desirable and that higher education is the appropriate gateway to that reservoir. In the contemporary era, however, comprehensiveness is touted as unaffordable in light of current priorities and academic reorganization is cast as a set of budgetary issues and a management problem, albeit with educational implications. Such restructuring limits the scope of academic knowledge that students are offered on any given campus, with the longer-range potential of further stratifying who learns what. (An interesting irony of course is seen in the ascendancy of the Internet, which promises access to everything.)

At the same time, new forms of collaboration have been proposed as a partial antidote to the narrowing of subject matter. In one historical case study of academic planning in a state university system, an official from the university's systemwide office explained the need to depart from the practice of comprehensiveness in order to facilitate consolidation and urged the campuses to share resources with one another in an unprecedented cooperation:

> Despite the great need for economies in [our academic programs] and for directed applications of knowledge, the University and its publics should reaffirm the principle of the pursuit of knowledge irrespective of its immediate applications. Intrinsic to the idea of the university is that, in principle, no corner of knowledge should remain unexplored. It is equally clear, however, that this ideal, while remaining a principle for our University as a whole, is not viable as a principle for each campus. The idea of a general campus implies the capacity to cover those subjects necessary for a liberal arts education and to sustain subjects (such as mathematics and computer science) that are necessary to sustain different kinds of research. But it cannot imply that every campus develop every research and teaching program that the pursuit of knowledge and the impetus to excellence might suggest. Given that constraint, it is evident that each campus of the University should specialize in some ways, and that such specialization should be coordinated. Coordination would permit and encourage innovative and cutting-edge programs to develop, but would also control excess provision and unnecessary duplication in the interests of economy. Furthermore, access of students and faculty to highly specialized programs could be augmented by designing them on an intercampus or regional basis, by permitting students to move more freely through programs of campus interchange and by other institutional and technological inventions. (Gumport 1994)

It remains to be seen whether campuses that comprise a public system can be prodded into cooperation by such top-down pleas for "one-system thinking." At the very least, such academic resource-sharing runs directly counter to the competitive dynamic that has been ingrained in the academic socialization of some faculty and campus leaders.

It also remains to be seen whether campuses will become increasingly divided by contemporary initiatives, such as responsibility-centered budgeting and the pursuit of selective excellence where the paramount consideration is the revenue-generating capability of discrete academic units and their proximity to thriving industries, such as software and microelectronics. The longer-range consequences, of course, are not just organizational but institutional—that is, as the dominant institutional logic is reconstituted. As knowledge is seen as a source of wealth, it is increasingly constructed as a private good rather than a public good. The commodification of knowledge proceeds alongside negotiations over the ownership of knowledge and is refined in policies for intellectual property rights and responsibilities. Market consciousness of knowledge outputs and property rights is bound to constrain the sharing of ideas in teaching and research, and perhaps even thinking, in public higher education.

The Public Interest in Public Higher Education

For purposes of analytical contrast, the industry and social institution perspectives have each been characterized as a Weberian "ideal type." In practice, of course, there is much overlap and ambiguity between industrial and institutional functions. Yet the distinction between the perspectives is telling, for public higher education's institutional legacy has been one of service to society broadly defined. And as such, it has a historical record of grand achievement in meeting multiple and changing societal expectations over time. The problem with the industry perspective, then, is that it narrowly reshapes institutional purposes into an agenda that is too short-term and too utilitarian. Moreover, this discourse of contemporary adaptation displaces the public agenda and replaces it with an operating logic grounded in market forces. As such, it sets the enterprise on a more narrow trajectory.

In this light, we must consider a broader foundation for a legacy of service. The institution perspective includes a prominent mandate of service to society. This is an ethos of service to a multiplicity of interests, including those that might dictate nonresponsiveness. How could the legacy of service lead to this? The rationale is located in a higher set of values: protection, prudence, and insulation from the demands of the day. In this sense, not responding to an immediate demand is neither an entitlement nor a privilege, but it is a *necessary* condition for the pursuit of the longer-term societal mandate to advance knowledge, preserve heritage, and foster inquiry that may run against prevailing interests (be they of government, of industry, or of popular culture).

The problem with this principle in practice is that skeptics of this rationale tend to dismiss such acts of resistance as self-serving responses by those who lead and work in public universities and colleges. At this point, the rationale—the broader legacy of institutional service to society—tends to be abandoned rather than fortified on its own terms. And I think this is extremely unfortunate.

To salvage this legacy, higher education's leaders, planners, and stakeholders must reframe the issues as a wider public relations endeavor. This campaign must not only clarify the basic charter and rationale for a stable social investment beyond the here and now, but also respond to accountability concerns. Much of the attention to demonstrating accountability tends to focus on devising better measurements of selected inputs and outputs (e.g., dollars per full-time equivalent [FTE] student, test scores, credits per FTE faculty) rather than the additional complexities of obtaining consensus on the multiple dimensions of importance to the various actors.

Surprisingly, and somewhat ironically, I propose that we can learn a lesson from the cutting edge of industry in this regard. The legacy of service itself can be presented as other than a readiness to sell one's soul. Rather, it can be conceptualized, argued for, and supported for the ways in which it embodies enduring values. One such approach to reconcile competing imperatives for stability and change is found in *Built to Last,* in which James Collins and Jerry Porras (1994) argue that, taking a long-term perspective, successful companies have prospered through the ongoing support of particular core values as well as being market-savvy. This supports such contemporary prescriptions for higher education as those developed by Robert Zemsky (1999), where he advocates that institutions be "mission-centered and market smart." The challenge, of course, is to operationalize that vision in a way that continues to serve what is valued in the past, present, and future.

"Contrary to popular wisdom, the proper first response to a changing world is *not* to ask, 'How should we change?' but rather to ask 'What do we stand for and why do we exist?' This should never change. And *then* feel free to change everything else," write Collins and Porras (1994, xiv–xv). Visionary companies distinguish their timeless core values and enduring educational purposes from their operating practices and business strategies. In this way, they can distinguish between "core and noncore, between what should never change and what should be open for change, and between what is truly sacred and what is not."

In this light, the major dimensions of the prescription for public higher education become clearer. Talking past one another in a clashing of paradigms will not be a viable way to proceed. Moreover, in a battle between market and mission, the more idealistic among us will simply not win by maligning market realities. The way to chart a course for the future is to understand that embracing a legacy does not necessarily mean staying the same; nor does becoming more market-savvy mean pulling up anchor and letting loose in the currents.

Finally, higher education leaders, planners, and managers must keep in mind that demonstrating responsiveness to economic and political exigencies always entails potential costs: responsiveness to compelling economic pressures that dominate contemporary organizational imperatives in an attempt to gain legitimacy in one dimension may result in loss for another. For public higher education, this means that they have to determine what is to be *unchanging*—that is, what resides in their historical character, functions, and accumulated heritage as educational institutions—and to embrace that with pride for the decades of public investment that have already supported it.

We have yet to build a vocabulary that builds a bridge between what is most valued in our legacies and what is most needed to thrive today. In order to move forward, such diverse interests must not be cast as competing and contradictory. Instead, we need to elevate the discourse about the future of public colleges and universities to a new level where common ground may be shaped by a distinctive mix of educational legacies, democratic interests, and economic competitiveness. Meeting this challenge will undoubtedly entail greater imagination, perseverance, and dialogue than has been demonstrated to date. The enterprise is, of course, worthy of that collective effort.

References

Bartley, W. W. 1990. *Unfathomed knowledge, unmeasured wealth: On universities and the wealth of nations.* La Salle, Ill.: Open Court.

Bellah, R. N., R. Madsen, W. M. Sullivan, A. Swidler, and S. M. Tipton. 1991. *The good society.* New York: Random House.

Blau, P. 1970. A formal theory of differentiation in organizations. *American Sociological Review* 35: 201–18.

———. 1973. *The organization of academic work.* New York: John Wiley.

Burke, J. C., and A. Serban, eds. 1998. *Performance funding for public higher education.* New Directions for Institutional Research no. 97 (spring). San Francisco: Jossey-Bass.

Chaffee, E. E. 1985. The concept of strategy: From business to higher education. In *Higher Education: Handbook of Theory and Research,* edited by J. Smart. Vol. 1. New York: Agathon.

Clark, B. R. 1983. *The higher education system: Academic organization in cross-national perspective.* Berkeley: University of California Press.

———. 1993. The problem of complexity in modern higher education. In *The European and American university since 1800,* edited by S. Rothblatt and B. Wittrock. Cambridge: Cambridge University Press.

———. 1996. Substantive growth and innovative organization. *Higher Education* 32, no. 4: 417–30.

———. 1998. *Creating entrepreneurial universities: Organizational pathways of transformation.* Surrey, England: Pergamon.

Collins, J., and J. Porras. 1994. *Built to last: Successful habits of visionary companies.* New York: HarperCollins.

Drucker, P. F. 1993. *Post-capitalist society.* New York: HarperCollins.

Duderstadt, J. 1995. Academic renewal at Michigan. In *Revitalizing higher education,* edited by J. Meyerson and W. Massy. Princeton, N.J.: Peterson's.

Enteman, W. F. 1993. *Managerialism: The emergence of a new ideology.* Madison: University of Wisconsin Press.

Gibbons, M., C. Limoges, H. Nowotny, S. Schwartzman, P. Scott, and M. Trow. 1994. *The new production of knowledge: The dynamic of science and research in contemporary societies.* Thousand Oaks, Calif.: Sage.

Gumport, P. J. 1993. The contested terrain of academic program reduction. *Journal of Higher Education* 64, no. 3: 283–311.

———. 1994. *Academic restructuring in historical perspective: Shifting priorities in the University of California.* Paper presented at the Association for the Study of Higher Education Annual Meeting, Tucson, Ariz., November.

———. 1997. Public universities as academic workplaces. *Daedalus* 126, no. 4: 113–36.

———. 2000. Academic restructuring: Organizational change and institutional imperatives. *Higher Education* 39, no. 1: 67–91.

Gumport, P. J., and B. Pusser. 1999. University restructuring: The role of economic and political contexts. In *Higher education: Handbook of theory and research,* edited by J. Smart. Vol. 15. New York: Agathon.

Gumport, P. J., and B. Sporn. 1999. Institutional adaptation: Demands for management reform and university administration. In *Higher education: Handbook of theory and research,* edited by J. Smart. Vol. 15. New York: Agathon.

Hammer, M., and J. Champy. 1993. *Reengineering the corporation: A manifesto for business revolution.* New York: HarperCollins.

Hardy, C. 1990. 'Hard' decisions and 'tough' choices: The business approach to university decline. *Higher Education* 20: 301–21.

Hearn, J. C. 1988. Strategy and resources: Economic issues in strategic planning and management in higher education. In *Higher education: Handbook of theory and research,* edited by J. Smart. Vol. 4. New York: Agathon.

Heydebrand, W. 1990. The technocratic organization of academic work. In *Structures of power and constraint: Papers in honor of Peter M. Blau,* edited by C. Calhoun, M. W. Meyer, and W. R. Scott. Cambridge: Cambridge University Press.

IBHE (Illinois Board of Higher Education). 1998. *Results and benefits of PQP: Progress report.* March board report. Springfield, Ill.: IBHE.

IRHE (Institute for Research in Higher Education, University of Pennsylvania). 1993a. A call to meeting. *Policy Perspectives* 4, no. 4 (February).

———. 1993b. A transatlantic dialogue. *Policy Perspectives* 5, no. 1 (June).

———. 1993c. An uncertain terrain. *Policy Perspectives* 5, no. 2 (November).

———. 1994. To dance with change. *Policy Perspectives* 5, no. 3 (April).

Keller, G. 1983. *Academic strategy: The management revolution in American higher education.* Baltimore: Johns Hopkins University Press.

Kerr, C. [1963] 1995. *The uses of the university.* Reprint, 4th ed. Cambridge: Harvard University Press.

Marchese, T. 1998. Not-so-distant competitors: How new providers are remaking the postsecondary marketplace. *AAHE Bulletin* 50, no. 9 (May).

Massy, W., ed. 1996. *Resource allocation in higher education.* Ann Arbor: University of Michigan Press.

Metzger, W. P. 1987. The academic profession in the United States. In *The academic profession: National, disciplinary, and institutional settings,* edited by B. R. Clark. Berkeley: University of California Press.

Meyer, J. W. 1977. The effects of education as an institution. *American Journal of Sociology* 83: 55–77.

NASULGC (National Association of State Universities and Land-Grant Colleges). 1997. *Value added: The economic impact of public universities.* December board report. Washington, D.C.: NASULGC.

Neave G., and F. van Vught, eds. 1991. *Prometheus bound: The changing relationship between government and higher education in Western Europe.* Oxford, England: Pergamon.

Press, E., and J. Washburn. 2000. The kept university. *Atlantic Monthly,* March: 39–54.

Readings, B. 1996. *The university in ruins.* Cambridge: Harvard University Press.

Rhoades, G. L. 1998. *Managed professionals: Unionized faculty and restructuring academic labor.* Albany: State University of New York Press.

Rhoades, G. L., and S. Slaughter. 1997. Academic capitalism, managed professionals, and supply-side higher education. *Social Text* 15, no. 2: 11–38.

Seymour, D. T. 1992. *On Q: Causing quality in higher education.* New York: Macmillan.

Slaughter, S., and L. L. Leslie. 1997. *Academic capitalism: Politics, policies, and the entrepreneurial university.* Baltimore: Johns Hopkins University Press.

Turner, J. H. 1997. *The institutional order: Economy, kinship, religion, polity, law, and education in evolutionary and comparative perspective.* Menlo Park, Calif.: Addison Wesley Longman.

Zemsky, R. 1999. The third imperative. *Policy Perspectives* 9, no. 1.

Zemsky, R., and W. F. Massy. 1990. Cost containment: Committing to a new economic reality. *Change* 22, no. 6: 16–22.

Chapter Five

From Mass Higher Education to Universal Access

The American Advantage

Martin Trow

Expansion of access and its consequences have marked the history of higher education in both the United States and Europe since World War II. In Europe, the tiny numbers enrolled in a few European universities before the war have grown to the 30 to 40 percent of college-aged students currently enrolled in all forms of postsecondary education. This large and rapid expansion has come in part through increases in the size of the elite universities, in part through the creation of nonuniversity sectors and institutions. The increased demand for higher education that has driven both of these kinds of expansion reflects the growth in all modern societies of occupations requiring more than a secondary-school education, and the expansion has been marked, especially in recent decades, by a growth in the numbers of nontraditional students—mature, employed, studying part time, and aiming at employment in the rapidly growing semiprofessions and knowledge-based service industries. These students, defining by their origins and aspirations the emerging systems of mass higher education, are oriented chiefly toward gaining useful skills and knowledge rather than toward membership in a cultural elite marked by common bodies of arcane knowledge and cultivated ways of thinking and feeling.

The growth of mass higher education in Europe has been the subject of most of the commentary on higher education over the past half century. Increased numbers have occasioned a host of related problems: funding, organization, governance, and the challenge of teaching new kinds of students with diverse aspirations and academic talents. The focus on the enormous problems of creating systems of mass higher education to accommodate this growth, however, has not allowed much thinking about the next stage of postsecondary higher education: the extension of access beyond a third or a half of a population to universal access to some form of postsecondary education, education that is available throughout life and in homes and workplaces. The development of the new information technologies (IT) over the past few years creates new possibilities and problems for European systems of higher education even before they have fully solved those associated with the creation of mass systems—a process that is still under way.[1]

I reflect here on some of the main issues facing research universities as they strive simultaneously to complete the creation of systems of mass higher education and also move toward Internet-based universal access. Inevitably, I view these issues from an American perspective, but I look at them in a comparative context. Universities on both sides of the Atlantic face problems, but they take different (yet similar) forms and evoke different responses. These problems are part of a larger crisis in higher education in Western societies. They flow from the partial success of educational institutions over the past half century in creating and adapting systems of mass higher education, but this makes them no less threatening to the institutions that have achieved that success.

Among the major problems facing higher education in the twenty-first century is the impact of the new information technologies on traditional forms of higher education. I put this first, not only because it is the most destabilizing or transforming development in higher education but also because it is implicated in all the other problems higher education is facing. One effect of developments in IT is to put the survival of research universities at risk. Recently, three American university presidents expressed their anxiety about this in almost identical words: "We cannot even be certain whether the university as we know it will survive at all, nor, if so, in what form . . .

The existence of the university as it is now and as we know it is in doubt."[2] Leaders of European universities agree: "It is not an exaggeration to say that the issue of new information and communication technologies questions the basic functions of the university."[3]

Second, I would place the escalating costs of higher education combined with public fiscal stringency. This has resulted in significant underfunding almost everywhere but most dramatically in Europe. Despite the large increase in numbers of students, European governments resist the imposition of student tuition fees. With some exceptions, the funding arrangements for mass institutions and systems still resemble those central governments used to support universities 50 years ago, except that state support has not kept pace with the growth in the student population. The result throughout Europe is a marked underfunding of higher education in which productivity gains are claimed (if not demonstrated) on the grounds that more students are being educated for the same or less money. To put further pressure on education budgets, every advance in all fields of modern science is more expensive than the last—a serious problem for countries like the United Kingdom, where basic research is still carried out largely in universities.

The growth of the student body without a parallel increase in state support threatens the quality of instruction and research. As enrollments have grown, student-to-staff ratios have also increased in most European systems of higher education. The response of governments has been to demand greater productivity. The rationalization of university life and management, the pressures for "efficiency" in operation and outcome, the consequent loss of "slack" resources, and the imposition of the criteria and language of business and industry all threaten the autonomy of the university and the capacity of its scholars and scientists to pursue long-term studies that do not promise short-term results. In some countries, the growth of managerial control mechanisms by the central government works in the same direction.

Third, a variety of problems arise in adapting the governance structures of elite research universities to institutions of mass higher education or creating new structures. This problem is especially acute for European universities. A leading example—one of many— is the difficulty of establishing strong institutional leadership that can act quickly and decisively in the face of rapidly developing problems and initiatives. Another is establishing what role, if any, research universities can play in developing institutions that provide universal access and lifelong learning through the new information technologies.

Fourth—a problem for all advanced societies, but perhaps especially severe in the United States—is the decline in the cultural levels, shared knowledge, and literacy of students entering higher education. A "new" postlinear generation, immersed from early childhood in video and audio cultures, is less able or inclined to read. This phenomenon is visible everywhere. In the United States, the situation is made much worse by the near collapse of elementary and secondary school systems. It is widely held that the United States has the most successful system of higher education in the world and among the worst primary and secondary schools.[4] The two facts may well be related.

Fifth, over the past two decades, the globalization of economies and research systems, the intensification of international industrial competition, and the rise of IT have all accelerated the commercialization of research and teaching and increased the movement of both outside the institutions of higher education.[5] The short-term problem here is the maintenance of the integrity and autonomy of universities; the longer-term problem (i.e., over the next few decades) is the survival of research universities. One may welcome some of the developments behind these trends—for example, the closer relations between universities and private business in both Europe and the United States and the blurring of the distinction between pure and applied research.[6] Certainly the rapid movement of research findings into the market has many positive effects for consumers and for national economies. Similarly, the emerging transformation of continuing education through IT enormously extends access and gives new meaning to the notion of a "learning society." Both developments, however, pose significant problems for existing structures of teaching and research.

Sixth, there are important and disquieting changes in the culture of the university. In some countries there is a serious decline in morale among academics arising out of their increasing workloads and a general deprofessionalization of the university teacher and lecturer. Britain offers the clearest example here.[7] Elsewhere, we see a decline in the university as a community.[8] This is evidenced by the weakening of the identification of academic scientists and scholars with their institutions and their growing reluctance to serve on academic senates, faculty committees, and the like. Instead, professors are identifying more and more with communities of scholars in their disciplines and subdisciplines, while scientists turn to research teams, industrial partners, and consortia. This is accompanied by a loss of authority by the academic community and its committees. Control is shifting to increasingly powerful university administrators and state authorities and to the market through the commercialization of research and teaching. It is not a matter of administrators seizing power from academics; rather the size and complexity of universities, the variety of specialized problems that confront them, and above all the speed of change increase the necessity for central administration to act decisively and rapidly. Academic committees have many virtues: among them is the capacity to give legitimacy to decisions and policies and sometimes even to add wisdom to decisions and quality to policy. But decisiveness and speed are not among these virtues, and they are more and more required of academic administrators.

This is not an exhaustive inventory of problems facing modern research universities; others will have their own lists. It is a way of beginning an exploration of the modern crisis of the university in the United States and in other advanced societies.

The Emerging Crisis of Higher Education

The problems described above and others related to them add up to a crisis, in the sense of a major turning point, in the nature of our higher education institutions. In Europe, the crisis arises out of the incomplete transformation of systems of elite universities into systems of mass higher education; in the United States, it proceeds from strong pressures on higher education to expand further in order to provide universal access to some form of postsecondary education.

Crises of this order do not happen every day. The leading American universities experienced such a crisis after the Civil War when between about 1865 and 1890 they transformed themselves from liberal arts colleges into the research universities recognizable today. Similarly, European universities faced a crisis in the 1960s and 1970s under the impact of growth and democratization for which they were structurally unfitted. Moreover, while they are still adapting to the growth in enrollments of the past three decades, they have been, quite suddenly, overtaken by pressures for universal access and the transformation of the concept of a learning society. This concept, which was once a rhetorical flourish, may now be realizable thanks to the new information technologies. (Universal access to postsecondary education leading to a "learning society" is not the same as open access to university for those who earn an Abitur or baccalaureate.)

The development of IT, the third of the major forms of development that higher education continues to undergo in all advanced societies, requires that we rethink the nature of universal access. The distinctions among elite, mass, and universal access forms of higher education have become part of the ordinary discourse about education in rich societies.[9]

Just as forces outside higher education drove the expansion of elite universities into mass systems, so current developments are driving all national systems toward broader and broader access. The growing demand for lifelong learning is independent of the development of IT, which simply accelerates it. Rapid technological change (of which IT is a part) and international competition increase the value and importance of a well-educated citizenry and workforce to every country. Advanced economies now live and die by their educated labor forces and how they are employed.

The rapid development of IT makes possible what was once merely an educator's dream: that is, lifelong access to education for all in subjects and at times and places of individual convenience. It also requires a new conception of universal access—a change from my original conception of higher and higher levels of enrollment in colleges and universities by students of traditional college age to one of participation in lifelong learning on-line in homes and workplaces.

Freeing education and training from the constraints of time and place in ways hardly imaginable in the early 1970s enormously broadens the potential scope and range of lifelong learning. Of course this has long been possible on a limited scale through correspondence courses and latterly in several countries with the help of television. But IT changes the nature and potentialities of distance learning dramatically and qualitatively. The move toward universal participation in postsecondary education, already under way but not everywhere recognized, will surely have revolutionary consequences for existing institutions and systems of higher education as well as for the larger societies that sustain and depend on them.

Information technology is involved in each of the major problems mentioned above. Liberating learning from constraints of time and space opens teaching to the same forces for commercialization already seen in research as the distinction between pure and applied research has diminished.[10] Moreover, even before IT takes hold, the rapid expansion of enrollments, the diversification of student interests and talents, and the volatility of their academic preferences have led to an enormous expansion in part-time nontenured teachers on annual contract—a reserve army of workers who give university administrators the flexibility they need under the new conditions of constant uncertainty and change. In the United States, roughly 45 percent of teachers in postsecondary institutions are part-time nontenured staff, though the proportions are much smaller in research universities. Their numbers have grown in all countries with the expansion of enrollments. But these teachers cannot develop genuine mentoring relationships with students as they run between classes and even institutions; they may therefore be the first to be replaced by teaching over the Internet, especially since they have no security of employment. The role of these part-time instructors—and their vulnerability—is not changed by the fact that many of them prefer this status for personal and family reasons.

Increased enrollments, both on campus and at a distance, strain traditional forms of quality control and the confidence of governmental authorities in institution-based quality control procedures. This, in turn, leads to demands for external assessments and control—a trend carried to its greatest lengths in the United Kingdom.[11] The constraints on state support for higher education drive up student-staff ratios, while at the same time there is a broad consensus among teachers almost everywhere that students enter university more poorly prepared and less inclined to read than previously—a natural consequence of broadening access and of changes in secondary education and its graduation requirements that have made that broadening possible. Both these tendencies make traditional academic standards more problematic—especially in European systems that still assume governmental responsibility for a uniform level of university entry qualifications. And now education through the Internet poses special problems for quality control and for the accreditation of courses and programs.[12]

One could expand the links among these new problems. Behind them all lies the long secular trend seen in the fundamental democratization of modern life, marked by the weakening of elite hierarchies, values, and prerogatives. Universities inherently are to some degree elite institutions: they admit students of higher-than-average talent to study difficult subjects taught by teachers with academic qualifications gained through long and severe education and training. The growth of enrollments and the extension of the name and status of university to formerly less prestigious institutions have changed the relation of universities to governments, industry, and society. The spread of postsecondary education through IT, in some cases with the awarding of university-level qualifications and degrees, accelerates these democratizing tendencies and poses problems for all the arrangements—especially of governance and finance—traditionally associated with research universities.

These problems take very different forms in American and European universities, though they share many features. That is not surprising, since American universities had their origins in England, Scotland, and Germany and still show family resemblances. But behind these most visible, and in some respects substantial similarities, lie quite fundamental differences. While American higher education shows its origins in European models, it developed under different circumstances, in response to quite different historical, social, political, cultural, and economic forces. While there are lessons in that experience, they are limited; and there is a danger of learning the wrong lessons and drawing inappropriate conclusions from the American experience.[13]

The central principle of curricular organization in American colleges and universities is the modular course, the cumulation of unit credits earned therein, and the banking and transferability of these credits among most of the 3,700 colleges and universities in the United States. This arrangement, dominant in all but a handful of American institutions, introduces an extraordinary degree of flexibility within the system. Course credits, banked in each student's transcript, allow relatively easy transfer within an institution between major fields and between institutions. It enables students to "stop out" of formal education temporarily for work or travel and return to the same or a different institution, picking up his or her course of study without having to devote additional time toward earning a degree.

Of course, the few highly selective institutions will not always accept a transfer from a less selective institution or a student with a poor academic record. But most American colleges and universities are not highly selective—or selective at all—and transfer with acceptance by the new institution of all or most of the credits earned elsewhere is very common. The very ease of stopping out and credit transfer not only allows but encourages stopping out and transfer. It also greatly facilitates lifelong learning, both within institutions and at a distance. Students can combine credits earned in traditional courses in traditional institutions with credits earned miles away and years later in other institutions through on-line courses.

Distance learning raises special problems. Which distance courses will be awarded credit toward a degree by the institution offering the course? Who will accredit the institutions offering distance courses and assess the courses? What other institutions will accept credits earned this way as credits toward their own degrees? These are all questions currently under discussion in the United States, where there is no broad governmental authority to answer them. But they are fundamentally the same kinds of questions that attach to the transferability of credits earned in traditional institutions. While distance learning introduces special difficulties, these questions will doubtless be answered, with the answers varying among the relatively autonomous colleges and universities that make up the American system.

However, while the modular course and unit-credit system has many advantages for systems of mass higher education, and even more for emerging systems of universal access, these come at a price—chiefly to the coherence of the course of study. Especially affected is the general education that comprises the bulk of the study for most students during the first half of their work toward a degree. While most American institutions have "general education" requirements, these tend to be broad and easily fulfilled, placing little constraint on the preferences of students, who often choose courses for how they fit in with the demands of their work and leisure as much as for content. A few American institutions require courses comprising a small "core" of general studies; in other cases a major field, often in the sciences, imposes one or two introductory courses as preparation. On the whole, however, the range of elective courses is large; the constraint on the wholly free choice of the student may be no more than that he or she choose from the tens or hundreds of courses labeled "humanities" or "the social sciences"—a widely employed device known as "breadth requirements" to discourage premature specialization.

Even these mild constraints have been weakening rapidly. A recent study by the National Academy of Sciences of changes in the undergraduate curriculum in 50 leading American colleges and universities in this century finds that over this period there has been a steady de-emphasis on a common core of knowledge marked by a "precipitous drop in the number of basic courses that students are required to take. The average number of these mandatory courses fell from 9.9 in 1914, to 6.9 in 1964, to 2.5 in 1993."[14] "Moreover, the average percentage of the overall graduation requirement composed of required general education courses dropped from 55 percent in 1914, to 46 percent in 1964, to 33 percent in 1993."[15]

The result is that in the general education part of their studies it is rare that any two students at an American university will have taken the same array of courses or that at the beginning of a course any two students will have read any of the same books. A teacher, especially in a mass institution, cannot assume a common body of knowledge, or even of interest, among students in their introductory courses; every course before the specialized studies of the major starts from square one. The only common culture among beginning students, even in traditional institutions, is likely to be that of popular entertainment or sports or the shared fascination with their search for friends and mates and identity. The enormous flexibility and responsiveness of American higher education to student preferences and market demand are bought, in part, at the price of intellectual incoherence in the curriculum.

The radical voluntariness and self-selection of distance courses may compensate somewhat for the thinness of student cultures on the campuses of American mass institutions of education; that will surely vary with the nature of the course and subject. European educators, however, are wary about paying the price of incoherence that may come with moving toward American models. It is not just the inherent conservatism of academic institutions or the insensitivity of state-funded European universities to market pressures. There are also good pedagogical reasons for Europeans to be skeptical about the apparent virtues of American higher education—so visible and attractive in its leading liberal arts colleges and research universities and their graduate schools and departments.

Nevertheless, the flow of influence of forms and structures of higher education is today, as it has been since World War II, very much from the United States to Europe. Despite their deep-rooted distaste for American populism and for what they see as the commercialization of science and culture and the threat to universities posed by the domination of markets and their interests, European academics and leaders are fascinated by American colleges and universities. This intense interest is accompanied by a reluctance to surrender so much to markets and their mechanisms.

A fundamental difference is that in Europe higher education is a highly regulated industry, while in the United States it is much less so. Here, the market performs many of the functions that in Europe are performed by bureaucracies, laws, and regulations. Americans are, on the whole, far less worried by the dangers of commercialization in intellectual life; historically, in America the market preceded the society. While many European innovations are adaptations of American models, they operate under circumstances in which these elements come to serve quite different functions or function quite differently. While European countries can borrow many American institutional arrangements, such as the modular course and transferable academic credits, they have difficulty in reproducing the cluster of structural and cultural features that add up to a distinct American advantage in the move first to mass higher education and then to universal access.

The American Advantage

One could approach the American advantage from the perspective of other broad aspects of the economy and social structure. For example, in Silicon Valley and its counterparts, an entrepreneur with a new idea can find a broad support infrastructure nearby and can outsource design and production problems at low cost. Moreover, nearby there is an aggressive community of venture capitalists to get small firms started. There is also an abundance of educated people with various skills who combine their talents in multidisciplinary problem-solving groups outside universities, in what we have called the Mode 2 form of knowledge production.[16] But my focus here is on the American advantage arising more directly from the history and organization of its higher educational system.

American higher education today has quite different functions and structures from those elsewhere. In most countries, higher education trained and educated the ruling strata, selected and recruited people into government service and the learned professions, conferred status on those who earned degrees, and qualified them in various ways for the society's most challenging (and prestigious) jobs and occupations. In recent decades higher education has expanded those functions to provide education and training in a wide range of new and semiprofessions. In the United States, colleges and universities perform those functions, but also, and most importantly, they give substance to the idea that anything is possible to those with talent, energy, and motivation. This sense of a society with limitless possibilities for all, largely (though not exclusively) through higher education, is what is usually meant by "the American dream." The end of the American dream is continually proclaimed, usually by intellectuals who never believed in it to begin with and wished no one else would. But this faith, fundamental to the American political system, survives hostility and cynicism and underpins America's peculiar mixture of conservatism and radical populism. Through its role in fostering social mobility and the belief in a society open to talent, American higher education legitimates the social and political system and thus is a central element in this society as it is nowhere else.[17]

European models of higher education—the German, the French, the British, and others—reflect their elite origins and functions in their structures, even as they grow toward mass access. All characteristically are perched on top of an upper-secondary system that both prepares and qualifies students for university entry. Students have their general education in secondary school and in some systems, such as the English, will already have begun to narrow their studies there, basically choosing between the sciences and the humanities. Their university studies will not ordinarily include a period of general education, though there are exceptions and will be more in the future. Broadly speaking, a university education in European systems has been a preparation for a professional career in the civil service, the learned professions, and in upper-secondary and higher education. Only now is it expanding into the preparation of business managers and the semiprofessions. The first degree in a European university (B.A., B.Phil., Candidat, etc.), where it is offered, is ordinarily at a higher standard in their specialties than an American B.A. or B.S.—though such generalizations are increasingly problematic. European postgraduate studies, particularly the doctorate, are ordinarily linked directly and immediately to the dissertation, without the graduate course work required in American universities.

Much of what is done in American universities, especially but not only in the first two years, strikes Europeans as serving the function of their upper-secondary schools. Indeed, historically American universities and colleges did a lot of secondary school work because there was no developed system of public secondary education before the end of the nineteenth century. And while the principle of in loco parentis is formally dead in most American colleges and universities, the spirit of responsibility for the physical and spiritual welfare of students is still strong in a way that it is not in European universities. English universities are a halfway house in this respect, but my sense is that they are also moving toward Continental models. The change can be traced to the influence of the European Union and its educational schemes and also to the fact that the old nurturing relationship of teachers and students in British universities required a high teacher-student ratio that has been lost in recent decades. Elite American colleges and universities still have relatively rich teacher-student ratios; others employ armies of para-educators—professional counselors, deans of student life, remedial specialists, and the like—whom Europeans do not employ, certainly not in the same numbers. These para-academics preserve the pastoral function as the academics themselves increasingly surrender that function in response to the increased emphasis on research and publication.

The enormous diversity of American higher education and the rapid growth and increasing diversity of European higher education systems, however, make all such generalizations less true than they were even a decade ago. European systems are moving toward American models. This is not because the United States is rich and a superpower or because of the power of American popular culture—elements in the Americanization of so many other institutions in other countries—but because American higher education as a system is simply better adapted, normatively and structurally, to the requirements of a postindustrial age, which puts a great premium on the creation and wide distribution of knowledge and skill and is marked by such rapid social and technological change that decisionmakers in all countries begin to see (or at least believe in) the necessity for broader access to postsecondary education.

So the new crisis of universal access arises, I suggest, while European universities are still trying to adapt their organizational, governance, and funding arrangements to their relatively new mass numbers. The United States, by contrast, had the structures for mass higher education in place long before they actually had mass higher education, which came with the GI Bill just after World War II and never went away.

The First System of Mass Higher Education

Why is it that the United States developed a system of mass higher education so much earlier than anyone else? What have been the impediments to the transformation of elite European systems into systems of mass higher education? And how are the United States and other countries moving toward universal access, lifelong learning, the learning society? These phrases all point in the same direction, toward the breakdown of the boundaries between formal learning in the institutions of postsecondary education and the rest of life, the assimilation of postsecondary education into the ordinary life of the society.

The modern system of higher education in the United States was already in place a century ago; the emergence of modern European systems of higher education is still under way. By 1900, when only 4 percent of Americans of college age were attending college, almost all of the central structural characteristics of American higher education were already evident: the lay board of trustees, the strong president and his administrative staff; the well-defined structure of faculty ranks; in the selective institutions, promotion through academic reputation linked to publication; and faculty readiness to move from institution to institution in pursuit of a career. On the side of the curriculum, the elective system, the modular course, credit accumulation, and transfer based on the transcript of grades were in place by 1900, as were the academic departments covering the known spheres of knowledge—and some not so well known.

Underpinning all was the spirit of competition, institutional diversity, responsiveness to markets and especially to the market for students, and institutional autonomy marked by strong leadership and a diversity of sources of support. The United States had the organizational and structural framework for a system of mass higher education long before it had mass enrollments. Only growth was needed. That happened in plenty, and with surprisingly little strain on a system already adapted to growth and change. Indeed, my view is that until this decade the only major structural change in American higher education over the past century was the invention and spread of the community colleges. These linked easily and casually to four-year institutions through credit transfer.[18] Of course American higher education today differs in many ways from what it was in 1900, but growth and development have not required changes in the basic structure of the system. It is those structural changes that are now taking place, with great difficulty, in Europe and the United Kingdom.

Europe Struggles Toward Mass Higher Education

To what extent have European systems created or introduced some of the chief elements of American mass higher education? These elements may be summarized as size and access beyond 15 percent of the age grade; diversity of the forms of higher education beyond elite universities; diversity of students in respect to social class, age, and ethnicity—including a large proportion of older part-time employed students; a substantial component of vocational-professional education; a high measure of institutional autonomy; modular courses, credit accumulation, and transfer; a strong chief executive and administrative staff; multiple sources of support; a relatively flat academic hierarchy rather than a powerful guild of full professors.

In the past decade, European universities have moved sharply toward mass numbers: in most countries upwards of 30 percent of the traditional college age cohorts are enrolled in some form of higher education. Many countries have a more diversified student population than they did just a decade ago, having seen marked increases in mature and part-time students. Some, like France, have a more diversified system of institutions. On the other hand, the United Kingdom (and Australia) have unified their systems, at least formally reducing the measure of diversity that was previously in place.

Most European nations have tried to give their universities a larger measure of autonomy in curriculum development and the appointment of academic staff, but the limitations are still greater than in most American research universities. They move slowly toward modular courses and the accumulation of course credits and even more slowly toward credit transfer. There are movements in several countries toward the rationalization of academic ranks, but that has been resisted—in some countries successfully. Almost everywhere there is, as in the United States, an increasing use of part-time, casual academic labor, without job security, to deal with declining resources and rapid unpredictable change.[19]

For example, France, like every other European country, is struggling to transform its traditional elite system into one of mass higher education. It is doing better than most countries, having diversified more successfully and moved toward greater institutional autonomy while broadening the resource base. The French speak of a revolution in the culture of the universities, which seems to refer to the changes associated with diversification, autonomy, and a greater involvement of teaching staff in the development of institutional mission and identity. But when one assesses what has been achieved, it is clear that there is still far to go. For example, France suffers overcrowding in many universities to a degree almost unknown in the United States; there is less student-teacher contact; policymakers have not solved the problem of credit transfer between French universities, much less among European Union countries; nor is there easy movement between major fields. Few French universities provide extension courses and continuing education. Moreover, they are only beginning to make the connections between universities and local government, business, and industry that are common in the United States. The traditional marked separation between teaching in the university and research elsewhere remains. France is trying to overcome this last separation by appointing university and grande école teachers to research groups in the National Council for Scientific Research (CNRS), though it seems that this has little effect on students until the few who pursue research enter doctoral programs.[20]

In Germany, a former minister of science and culture in Hesse writes about "governmental failures to support adequately the transformation of the German university into a system of mass higher education by failing to grant sufficient financial support or to contribute reform concepts."[21] Indeed, the resistance to basic reform has prevented Germany from creating a first degree similar to the American B.A. or B.S., developing a mechanism for controlling access to its universities, or charging tuition fees—problems shared with other European countries and all substantial handicaps to developing a coherent system of mass higher education while preserving the elite sector.

Moreover, many academics and administrators in Europe are

aware that mass higher education and institutional autonomy require stronger institutional leadership, but resistance by the academic guilds and governmental bureaucracies is very strong in most countries; rectors (by whatever name) are, with some few exceptions, still elected by the academic community, serve short terms, and have little power to initiate reforms. What reforms have been introduced in the past two decades have come mainly from governmental ministries and serve their interests, especially in shifting responsibility for the increasingly apparent shortcomings of underfunded institutions. The then vice president of the German Conference of University Rectors noted recently: "The latest reforms in the German system of higher education have been introduced primarily for more effective management of scarce resources and with a view to shifting the onus for the functional shortcomings of the overcrowded and underfunded schools from the government onto the institutions of higher education."[22]

For Americans, the diversity of sources of financial support is a crucial issue. In Europe—while there is a great deal of rhetoric about the desirability of wider support for higher education from the private sector, again with many glances in the direction of the United States—it is still the case that central governments provide most of higher education's financial support.[23] In Germany, Evelies Mayer and many others complain about inadequate resources, and, indeed, per capita support for university students declined in almost every European country—in some cases dramatically—during the rapid expansion of enrollments over the past quarter century. But Mayer's assumption, and that of most commentators in Europe, is that the key lies in additional support from the central or regional government. While private industry in Europe has increased its support for university-based research, its contribution is a small fraction of governmental support. Moreover, there are still few private colleges or universities in Europe, and resistance to their creation remains strong.[24] In this important respect, Japan has an advantage over Europe in its large and varied private higher education sector, which enrolls about three-quarters of all students in four-year colleges and universities and 90 percent when one includes the students in two-year colleges. Like Europe, Japan has preeminent state universities wholly funded by central government and, therefore, not highly responsive to the market. But in Japan the private sector defeated government efforts to restrict the growth of higher education in the late

1980s and early 1990s.[25] The private sector in Japan is likely to be even more important in the future than it has been in the recent past. The biggest hindrance to the development of European universities into mass institutions is the continuing refusal by European governments, supported by the majority of academics, to allow universities to charge tuition fees and to retain these funds for their own development and use. "Free tuition"—free only in the sense that the costs of university education are met by taxpayers rather than by the recipients—constitutes a significant entitlement for the mostly middle- and upper-middle-class families whose children go to university, and it is fiercely defended by them and their children. The idea of setting aside a portion of tuition payments for aid to poorer students is not on the table in Europe. Indeed, in many countries the issue cannot even be raised, much less brought to a vote. The resulting underfunding of higher education in most European nations greatly handicaps their capacity to respond creatively to growth, both of knowledge and of enrollments.

Of course, *underfunding* is a comparative concept. In 1993, from the latest data available, the United States spent 2.5 percent of its GNP on higher education, over twice the proportion spent by France (1.1%), Germany (1.0%), or the United Kingdom and Italy (0.9% in both countries). Only Canada at 2.6 percent was higher among the leading industrial nations reported. Canada is exceptional in its very strong commitment to funding higher education from public sources: 2.2 percent of its 2.6 percent total; Japan only commits about 1.0 percent of its GNP to higher education, but over half of that—0.6 percent—comes from private sources. It is the only country among this group similar to the United States in this respect.

The GNP figures are also reported by the Organisation for Economic Cooperation and Development (OECD) by the proportion of support from public and private sources. With respect to the commitment of public resources, the United States at 1.3 percent of GNP is not far from the European countries named, all of which are at 0.9 percent of GNP except for Italy at 0.8 percent. Indeed, if we consider that the 1.3 percent from public sources in the United States includes support for a broad system of mostly public community colleges, whose counterparts (where they exist) elsewhere are not counted as "higher education," we would probably find that public support in the United States is close to that in these other countries for similar kinds of institutions.

The difference lies in the very great discrepancy in the support for higher education from the private sector: student tuition fees, gifts, endowments, and the sale of services of all kinds. In the United States the 1.3 percent of GNP provided by private sources almost matched the public commitment of 1.4 percent, as compared with the 0.2 percent of GNP in France, 0.1 percent in Germany, and a reported "nil" in the United Kingdom.[26] (The reported figures for the United States do not include the substantial tax credits given by federal and state governments for private contributions to higher education, a form of concealed subsidy by government to both public and private institutions and to research in universities and other nonprofit institutions.) These figures from private sources would probably be slightly higher for 1999 in all countries, including the United States, but the discrepancy would remain. Indeed, in the United Kingdom the Dearing Report of 1997 observes that "none of the [European] countries considered were expecting to change significantly the proportion of GDP [gross domestic product] which they devote to higher education."[27]

The advantages the United States has had in coping with the emergence of mass higher education, including the greater financial support by its society, persist as universities on both sides of the Atlantic face the challenges of the new information technologies and their promise of universal access to postsecondary education.

Challenges Posed: Speed of Change as the Enemy of Policy

All the emerging problems call out for thoughtful and sweeping policy responses in higher education. But the very forces generating the new problems hinder the development of broad encompassing policies in response. The rate of change of information technology outruns our capacity to develop sensible policies for its management. All the European countries I have been discussing have had educational policies, some of which have even been successful—like the Land Grant Act of 1862 and the GI Bill after World War II in the United States. But policies for higher education have not until now been undermined by the sudden eruption of new technologies. So, I suggest that the unprecedented speed of technological development in this area is an independent force posing a severe challenge to policymakers.

One indicator of the speed of technological development can be seen in the decline in the costs of computer memory and in the speed with which information can be transmitted across the World Wide Web—the latter known as bandwidth. Both are crucial to the ease and flexibility of IT applications in education as in commercial activity. The tremendous expansion of bandwidth in the past few years is less visible than the fall in the price of personal computers and memory but is at least as important as distance learning becomes more interactive and employs more audio and video elements alongside text.[28]

Equally dramatic in its implications for higher education is the capacity to download single copies of books from the Internet, print them using fast printers, paste and bind them in board covers, and sell them for the same price as those printed in longer runs. The development of this new technology—"books on demand"—raises difficult problems for authors and publishers of books still under copyright but few for books already in the public domain and long out of print—the kind that scholars commonly need and use.[29] Major publishers advertise on-demand titles whose copyrights they own. The Library of Congress and other bodies are putting whole libraries on the Internet, and these will also be available on demand. Commercial bookstores are already promising a book on demand in about 15 minutes at the same price as a traditionally produced book. The Council of Europe claims that the print-on-demand technology is "now capable of producing perfect books at astonishing speeds and with minimum effort."[30] It may soon be easier and cheaper for a university library to print a book and give it to the user than to order, record, shelve, retrieve, and lend as is the current practice.

Libraries have been the heart of the university—laboratories were latecomers. They have been a powerful centripetal force, bringing scholars and students together and keeping them in physical proximity. But storage on the Internet of books, manuscripts, and other scholarly material, including sounds and pictures, is transforming scholarly research and profoundly reducing the importance of the library as the repository of printed scholarly materials. (It reduces the significance of the museum for similar reasons.) A Stanford historian has reported that he spent 10 years in his spare time in the Library of Congress archives locating material for a book on the first meetings of the American Congress. All the documents he needed are now available on the Internet. The kind of research he did will never be done again for studies using materials that are stored on-line. As we know from research on medieval manuscripts, for example, such study can be more accurate and detailed since the manuscript on the Internet allows high magnifications of small illuminations and blurred passages.

Though memory and bandwidth are not literally free for ordinary users, costs are falling so rapidly that they will soon seem free in the way that electricity to light our houses is regarded. As for what to do with this freedom, the applications pour out of university and commercial laboratories, and many will have large consequences for both the public and the private aspects of higher education—for organization, structure, and finance as well as for teaching and learning. The speed of development of software and applications defeats the efforts of scholars to report or analyze it in books; only journalism can seem to keep abreast of the rapidly changing IT world. For example, in fall 1999, the *New York Times* linked several special reports to capture the nature of these developments.[31] While the articles are about the use of the World Wide Web in commercial life, they are relevant to higher education. One important aspect of distance learning is that it is a form of e-commerce, with the same concerns about start-up costs; the nature of the market; the labor force; the quality and attractiveness of the product to its consumers; and its delivery, pricing, and competition.

The very terms of description of this aspect of higher education are offensive to many who entered academic life to escape the ethos of buying and selling that governs so much of modern life. While some tenured professors may escape their effects for a while, these developments will transform the relations of teachers with students, of teachers with teachers, and of students with students. How it will do so is still unclear.

Our capacity to plan rationally is reduced by the uncertainties of technological developments—a separate matter from the speed of development. We cannot accurately predict developments in this field even three years ahead. The new technologies being tested suggest capacities beyond anything we have seen: the rapid delivery of massive amounts of information over ordinary telephone lines and cable installations has already been achieved. Television sets are a cheap and familiar vehicle for Internet communications. Most experts anticipate the convergence of technologies, blurring the lines between different appliances and bringing costs down.

This prediction, however, extrapolates from existing technologies. We may see more fundamental developments in the organization and transfer of information. Sun Microsystems has already announced "a product called Jini that uses Sun's Java programming language to harness the power of millions of computers, from mainframes to palm-sized devices. We now have all the ingredients to build a distributed computing fabric which approaches science fiction."[32] Technological developments carry powerful challenges for higher education—though few have begun to think of their implications.

How quickly or widely will the changing technologies be adopted in different societies? They may require substantial time and effort to master, which could slow their adoption—especially if older technologies fill needs that do not grow rapidly. On the other hand, the new technologies themselves generate "needs" competitively. Moreover, the new technologies may be so much easier and cheaper to use that they transform the population of users and the nature of use.

Apart from the acquisition and adoption of new information technology, there is the question of what individuals and institutions will use them for. For many in affluent societies, how they choose to use their time will determine how they spend their money. But not all choices will be made by individuals deciding how to use their leisure. Many consequential decisions will be made by large corporate bodies: Business and industry may decide to use IT for training and educating their workforce during working hours. Governments may impose regulations on educational institutions that might want to provide continuing education for the labor force. Colleges, universities, and others will compete to provide continuing education and will be making decisions about whether or not to offer credits toward their degrees for courses taken on-line, as well as about ownership of intellectual property displayed on-line.

Information technology is developing fastest in the United States, where openness encourages innovations that challenge elite structures and attitudes. Everywhere, however, the earliest use of IT for lifelong learning is by less prestigious or marginal institutions and by institutions (often the same ones) most strongly oriented to the market for students and other forms of external support. These institutions are likely to be in the private sector, where one exists.

Since lifelong learning by IT threatens traditional structures in such areas as funding and organization, quality assessment, examinations, and the criteria for earning degrees, it threatens the control that European governments exercise over higher education. Will European governments encourage the development of lifelong learning through IT in all their universities and colleges or, as is more likely, try to restrict it to nonelite forms of higher education and to emerging private or semiprivate universities for whose quality and products governments take little responsibility? Or will IT, in its inherent responsiveness to the market, accelerate the partial privatization of state-supported universities, especially in European countries? These uncertainties confound our capacity to see ahead, and that, in turn, affects the capacity to plan as social institutions might do for a development of such enormous importance.

A researcher in this field today has both to look at the emerging scene and also do what I have suggested is impossible: peer into the future to problems and conditions that may obtain in five or ten years' time. Some colleagues and I have been trying to do that in California, attempting first to find out what is going on in our own institutions and their neighbors and then to detect underlying patterns that might provide clues to the development of these technologies in colleges and universities and in the new institutions growing up inside and around the familiar ones.[33] Our early studies suggest two sets of observations: one on the diversification of the new forms of instruction that reflects the enormous diversity of students and subjects, the second bearing on the implications of that diversity for governmental and institutional policy in this area.

First, both for analysis and policy, we must disaggregate the patterns of use of IT very finely along at least four crucial dimensions: the nature of the subject taught; the location of the student—on campus, at home or workplace, or elsewhere; the primary purpose of the instruction—to transmit skills and knowledge or to cultivate mind and character or some combination of these; and the academic talents and motivations of the learner. There may be other important dimensions, but these at least establish the principle of disaggregation.[34]

Second, our policies must reflect the diversity of higher education —no longer an effort to educate a small segment of the population for leading positions in society, but something close to a continuing education of the whole population for life in the twenty-first century. If lifelong learning is to be as varied as its student populations, then policies must be responsive to the nature and goals of the education offered, almost course by course; to the market for knowledge and information among consumers; and to the judgments of the academics who know best who they are teaching and how their students learn.

A central policy issue for research universities is whether and how they will be involved in distance learning through the new technologies. European nations are showing a growing interest in continuing education "not as a luxury but as a personal and national strategy for survival in a highly competitive global economy. Officials also see it as one way to combat Europe's persistently high unemployment rate . . . "[35] The first answer of research universities, which is mostly to pass continuing education on to other agencies, is unlikely to be their last. Pressures will surely lead some European universities more deeply into distance learning. In Norway, a decision has already been made by the universities and colleges—and confirmed by the ministry in May 1999—to the effect that "responsibility for all lifelong learning at a higher-education level will stay with the higher-education institutions."[36]

How these conflicting requirements of function, demand, and pedagogy balance out cannot be the subject of general rules or state policy. On the contrary, policies must encourage experimentation by those who introduce these technologies into higher education, and especially into distance learning. Such policies would give institutions and the people in them the freedom and resources to initiate from below and to experiment in many different directions. But the other side of that coin is that policymakers must accept that experiments may fail in social and educational life as they may in the laboratory.

Policy as Experimentation

The doctrine of "policy as experimentation" is hard for modern governments to accept, gripped as they are by the importance of this area of public life. They are prepared and willing to make large investments in it for the commonweal, but they are inherently unwilling to give resources piecemeal to providers who are "experimenting."

Nevertheless, I believe the expansion of access to lifelong learning through the new technologies, as far ahead as we can see, will take the form of a continuing series of experiments. There are three elements defining experiments in higher education: (1) programs are not standardized, but vary sharply in character, funding, pedagogy, function, and so on; (2) they are transitory, on trial, and not firmly institutionalized; and (3) they are under continual assessment for costs and effectiveness.

The development of IT in higher education as elsewhere is such that we cannot standardize and freeze delivery systems or policies on the basis of what is already successful. Technological developments alone will continually confound efforts to freeze or standardize educational forms. In addition, other factors—for example, variations among academic subjects, in the places and conditions of delivery, and in students' talents and motivations—will make standardization of forms and procedures impossible. This is, in fact, what we have been finding in California where we have tried to draw out the implications for the future.

Another American Advantage: The Idea of University Service

Most observers recognize the existence in the United States of a broad consensus around the notion that everyone should be involved in formal education for as long as possible. This fundamental value underlies the inclusive sentiments and commitments to service and useful instruction that are the defining features of American higher education. It was captured a century and a half ago in Ezra Cornell's statement: "I would found an institution in which any person can find instruction in any study."[37] It found expression also in the Federal Land Grant Act of 1862, which provided federal support for a college in every state "where the leading object shall be, without excluding other scientific or classical studies, to teach such branches of learning as are related to agriculture and the mechanic arts." It was also embodied in the Wisconsin Idea of service by the university to the wider community.[38]

The Wisconsin Idea is of special importance in understanding American attitudes toward lifelong learning and useful studies of all kinds; it is summarized in the University of Wisconsin's motto: "The boundaries of the University are the boundaries of the State." The motto (and it was a commitment as well) incorporated two ideas keyed to service to the community: an elite notion of building more expertise into the affairs of state and "the development of popular nontechnical lectures, which carried the university to the people." This latter pledge led to the development of extension courses and, later, technical courses. Indeed, there was almost immediately "an acceleration of how-to courses which, if they did not show how to make American democracy more democratic, did show many an American who otherwise would have been beyond the effective range of the university how to make himself a more effective farmer or worker."[39] A century later that is a central motivation of the Western Governors University (WGU) and of its many competitors.[40] The WGU is a "virtual" university without a campus or classrooms. All of its courses, developed by the faculty members of the member public universities, are on-line, and delivered electronically to students. In the case of WGU, the university is merely an adaptation of the extension idea to the potentialities of the new information technologies. The crucial difference from the European experience is that in the United States, extension has been *university* extension. Hardly a university in the country, and certainly no great public university, is without an extension division, providing courses "for any person in [nearly] any study."

These perspectives are very like those that introduce a multitude of books and papers on the information revolution. That literature, though often instructive, is produced for the most part by people who are excited by their work in the area and by the potentialities of IT for higher education, both inside and outside traditional institutions. It is imbued with the excitement and fundamental optimism that C. P. Snow identified as the emotional climate of engineers and scientists, in contrast with the pervasive pessimism of humanistic writing in our time.[41]

The Search for Meaning: On the Survival of Elite Research Universities

Like the enthusiasts, I believe that we are in the midst of a revolution in higher and continuing education, although one in its early stages. Along with the enormous positive potentialities of this revolution, it is also clear that the changes may have negative effects on central elements of higher learning and on the traditional institutions and relationships long associated with the pursuit of wisdom as well as on information and knowledge. Most new forms of distance learning thus far are found in elementary language or mathematics courses and in business-related subjects, where they are used to transfer specific skills and knowledge rather than, in historian Gertrude Himmelfarb's words, helping students to appreciate a poem, understand an idea, find significance in a historical event, follow the logic of an argument, inquire into ethical dilemmas, make rational and moral judgments—"all of which require an exercise of mind that calls upon all the human faculties and which no technology, however sophisticated, can satisfy."[42] Research and reflection on the impact of these new technologies must recognize their limitations and disadvantages as well as their undeniable advantages. Among the latter, not least is the potential of the new technologies to enable large parts of our populations to be involved, even if intermittently, in some kind of formal education or organized learning all their lives.

A former president of the Johns Hopkins University, Steven Muller, has speculated on what continuing functions elite universities will have in the future.[43] He believes much library-based scholarship will no longer need to be based inside a university and much undergraduate education also will be carried effectively on the Internet. A question already under discussion, in California as elsewhere, is "how much is much." California public universities, already facing an enormous growth of enrollments in coming decades—and the resulting shortage of student housing, and hopelessly crowded classrooms, libraries, and laboratories—are beginning to discuss whether some fraction of undergraduate studies cannot be completed by students, for full university credit, off campus somewhere—at home or on less expensive satellite campuses. Of course, those alternative venues are not the same, either in cost or in their effects on students. Such courses would be taught on-line by regular academic staff and supported by IT staff. Early speculation mentions anything from 10 to 25 percent of the student's time at the university taken in study at a distance, the latter representing a full year of the traditional four-year course delivered over the Internet. On the other hand, Muller reminds us that laboratory work and training cannot be divorced from direct personal interaction; nor can the students' desire for each other's company be satisfied in virtual classrooms. The advantages of not overcrowding existing university sites or having to build new general-purpose campuses are obvious and compelling. The drawbacks are less visible and uncertain, especially when we project these moves into the next generation of information technologies, including interactive video links or visible virtual classrooms and seminars.

A central and continuing function of the university is carried by the humanist scholar and teacher, concerned not primarily with the transfer of information or knowledge but with the cultivation of critical and independent perspectives and the exploration of meaning. Reflecting on the technological revolution and its implications for humanistic studies, Gertrude Himmelfarb observes, "It takes a discriminating mind, a mind that is already stocked with knowledge and trained in critical discernment, to distinguish between . . . the trivial and the important, the ephemeral and the enduring, the true and the false. It is just this sense of discrimination that the humanities have traditionally cultivated, and that they must now cultivate even more strenuously, if the electronic revolution is to do more good than bad."[44] She warns of the loss of the capacity to read a book, "to study it, to think about it, to reflect upon it." To do that "we should have it in our hands, for that is the only way of letting it into our minds and our hearts."[45]

These are the classic concerns of the humanist scholar in the face of any technologies that come between learner and book or teacher and learner. While we may watch with concern, we need not assume that those values and the relationships that sustain them require that teacher, book, and student must share the same small physical space. The possibilities for elite forms of higher education through distance learning should not be foreclosed. We already see on the Internet advanced scholarly seminars that bring together students and scholars across a continent around an illuminated manuscript on a screen. To deepen those relationships beyond scholarship and research to character-forming may require another leap in the technology that will make prolonged audio and visual interactive connections cheap and easy. It will depend on the motivation and intelligence of teachers and students to make those distant connections a vehicle for the shaping of mind, character, and sensibility, rather than the mere transmission of information and knowledge at present associated with lifelong distance learning.

Conclusion

A knowledgeable European observer of European higher education has suggested that on the whole it is "about 20 or 30 years back" on a continuum that has led the United States toward universal access to higher education. I have taken that as a starting point for inquiry. The same cultural, political, and institutional characteristics that account for the lag of two or three decades in the emergence of mass higher education in Europe also make for a lag in the emergence of universal access. This is not a lag in the technology or its applications, much of which has been invented and developed by Europeans, but rather in the political, legal, economic, and organizational structures that would allow some form of postsecondary education to be made available to the whole society through the use of these new technologies. This lag cannot be found in the European private sector, where competition in markets of all kinds forces business and industry to develop the resources of IT for training and instruction. Indeed, it may well be that universal access to lifelong learning will come to Europe by way of work-based instruction over the web for upgrading the skills and knowledge needed by an educated labor force in a global economy.

The elite-mass-universal access model I set forth in the early 1970s assumed that universal access to higher education would come through increased numbers of students in all countries enrolling and attending—often part-time or at night—nonelite institutions that might eventually and for some provide further links through credit transfer to degree-granting institutions.[46] That has been happening, though still on a modest scale. Information technology now forces a revision of our conception of the conditions needed for universal access: IT allows, and becomes the vehicle for, universal access to higher education of a different order of magnitude, with courses of every kind and description available over the Internet in people's homes and workplaces. That involves profound changes in both institutional structures and attitudes regarding higher education. And it is in these areas that Europe is lagging.

While most European countries are still struggling to complete the structural reforms necessary to institutionalize mass higher education, few university-based academics or administrators have fully appreciated the implications of IT for universal access. Research universities both in the United States and Europe are exploiting the Internet for scientific research and scholarship and, increasingly, for the enrichment of their taught courses and seminars. But IT will have consequences far beyond those already visible in our institutions. Information technology is already corroding boundaries—national, institutional, disciplinary. It is weakening the links of academics to their institutions, faculties, departments, and disciplines. Since so much research can be done outside universities or colleges in the contexts of use, the distinction between pure and applied research is blurred. The library as a central institution of the research university is drastically weakened. Research can be done anywhere, so the distinction between research universities and other kinds of higher education institutions shrinks. Since IT strengthens the market for education, it strengthens students in relation to teachers and blurs the distinction between learning and entertainment.

The new technologies are having a myriad of other consequences —for accountability and assessment, for the ownership of intellectual property and publication, for the use of publication for meritocratic assessment, and thus for the whole machinery of institutional controls put in place in many European countries during their expansion. The most profound effects of IT will be to weaken the distinction between life and learning. As more postsecondary education goes on-line, the character of our familiar universities and colleges, in both Europe and the United States, will inevitably change. The question remains: to what extent can elite forms of higher education survive in the leading colleges and universities on both continents under the pressure of the new technologies, universal access, and changing cultural attitudes. This has been a continuing and disturbing question for the past four decades and remains so as institutions of higher education everywhere move into uncharted waters.[47]

Notes

This essay began as a paper presented to the North American and Western European Colloquium on Challenges Facing Higher Education, sponsored by the William and Flora Hewlett Foundation, Glion sur Montreux, 14–16 May 1998. My thanks to Guy Neave, Oliver Fulton, and Anne Maclachlan for readings of earlier drafts. An earlier version of this paper appears in *Minerva,* 37 (spring 2000), pp. 1–26.

1. M. Trow, "Problems in the Transition from Elite to Mass Higher Education," in *Policies for Higher Education,* from the *General Report on the Conference on Future Structures of Post-Secondary Education* (Paris: Organisation for Economic Cooperation and Development, 1974), 55–101.

2. S. Muller, "The Management of the Modern University," in *University in Transition,* eds. D. Muller-Boling et al. (Gütersloh, Germany: Bertels-

mann Foundation, 1998), 222–30. That view was echoed by Berkeley's chancellor Robert Berdahl at his inauguration in April 1998 and by President Gerhard Casper of Stanford at Berkeley on the same day.

3. K. Edwards, "New Technologies for Teaching and Learning," *CRE Information*, no. 1 (April 1998), 25.

4. E.g., "I have [been] talking about the great success story of higher education in the United States. By contrast, the public K–12 system has been a disaster, a shocking deterioration of a once quite competent enterprise." C. Pings, "The Ongoing Evolution of the American Research University," in Muller-Boling et al., eds., *University in Transition,* 69.

5. This process is explored in M. Gibbons et al., *The New Production of Knowledge: The Dynamics of Science and Research in Contemporary Societies* (London: Sage Publications, 1994).

6. E.g., in 1997 the chancellor of the University of California at Berkeley observed that in his university "industrial funding is moving up the research stream," and described the process in detail. See Chang-Lin Tien, "Research Funding and Its Effect on the Research Agenda," in Muller-Boling et al., eds., *University in Transition,* 45–46.

7. On European academics see O. Fulton, "Unity or Fragmentation, Convergence or Diversity," in *Universities and Their Leadership,* W. Bowen and H. Shapiro, eds., (Princeton: Princeton University Press, 1998). For comparative essays, see B. R. Clark, ed., *The Academic Professions* (Berkeley: University of California Press, 1987), and for the United States, his "Small Worlds, Different Worlds: The Uniqueness and Troubles of American Academic Professions," *Daedalus,* 126 (fall 1997), 21–42, esp. 31–37. A moving account of changes experienced by academics, especially in the humanities departments in American elite research universities over the past half-century, can be found in A. Kernan, *In Plato's Cave* (New Haven: Yale University Press, 1999), esp. 246–75.

8. Clark Kerr is the most notable critic of these trends, on which most commentators agree. See his "Knowledge, Ethics and the New Academic Culture," in *Higher Education Cannot Escape History: Issues for the Twenty-First Century* (Albany: SUNY Press, 1994), 131–56. On the ambivalence of some senior administrators in American research universities towards external research links and consulting, see H. Rosovsky with I.-L. Amer, "A Neglected Topic: Professional Conduct of College and University Teachers," in Bowen and Shapiro, eds., *Universities and Their Leadership,* 123.

9. M. Trow "Problems in the Transition from Elite to Mass Higher Education." While national systems can be broadly described in terms of these development phases, individual institutions may provide education across all these categories, though in different proportions. My paper for the OECD was based on experience of the growth of higher education in the United States, on what I could see of the beginnings of movement beyond elite forms

in the United Kingdom and Western European societies, and on my first experience of Japanese higher education at about that time.

10. See Gibbons et al., *The New Production of Knowledge.*

11. See M. Trow, "American Perspectives on British Higher Education under Thatcher and Major," *Oxford Review of Education* (winter 1998), 111–29; and my "Trust, Markets and Accountability in Higher Education: A Comparative Perspective," *Higher Education Policy,* 9, no. 4 (1996), 309–24.

12. See, e.g., F. Olsen, "'Virtual' Institutions Challenge Accreditors to Devise New Ways of Measuring Quality," *Chronicle of Higher Education,* 6 August 1999 and <http://chronicle.com/free/v45/i48/48a02901.htm>

13. On the origins and development of the American system see M. Trow "Federalism in American Higher Education," in *Higher Learning in America: 1980–2000,* ed. A. Levine (Baltimore: Johns Hopkins University Press, 1993), 39–67.

14. National Association of Scholars, *The Dissolution of General Education: 1914–1993* (Princeton, N.J., 1999) and <http://www.nas.org/study.html>

15. Ibid.

16. Gibbons et al., *The New Production of Knowledge.*

17. See M. Trow, "Class, Race and Higher Education in the United States," in *Democracy in Comparative Perspective,* eds. Larry Diamond and Gary Marks (London: Sage, 1992), 275–93.

18. Others might suggest that the massive growth in federal support for university-based research, starting really during the Second World War, also qualifies as a major structural change, at least in support for the system. But the principle of federal support for research was in place much earlier; here we can debate when quantitative becomes qualitative change. See, e.g., R. Geiger, *To Advance Knowledge: The Growth of American Research Universities, 1900–1940* (New York: Oxford University Press, 1986).

19. On structural and funding problems in European universities, see "The Decline of German Universities," *Science,* 277 (12 July 1996), 172–74 and articles on higher education in Europe in *Science* (2 February 1996), including "European Union." See also "U.S.-Style Universities for Germany?" in *Science* (19 June 1998).

20. See "France: An Elite System Struggles with Mass Education," *Science,* 271 (2 February 1996), 1826–27.

21. E. Mayer, "Whom Do German Universities Now Serve?" in *German Universities Past and Future,* ed. M. G. Ash (Oxford: Berghahn Books, 1997), 192. See also other essays in that volume, many of which stress the continuing power of the Humboldtian ethos to block reforms needed for the transition to mass higher education in Germany.

22. R. Kunzel, "Political Control and Funding," in Ash, ed., *German Universities,* 173. Much the same could be said about the motives behind the interventions by British governments over the past two decades.

23. For important exceptions, and perhaps precursors of the future, see Clark, *Creating Entrepreneurial Universities.*

24. See "U.S.-Style Universities for Germany?"

25. For analysis of Japanese higher education, see I. Amano, "Education in a More Affluent Japan," *Assessment in Education,* 4, 1 (1997), 51–66, and his "Structural Changes in Japan's Higher Education System: From a Planning to a Market Model," *Higher Education,* 34 (1997), 125–39. See also A. Arimoto, "Massification of Higher Education and Academic Reforms in Japan," in *Academic Reforms in the World,* Research Institute for Higher Education, International Seminar Reports no. 10 (Hiroshima: Hiroshima University, July 1997), 21–55; K. Kitamura, "Policy Issue in Japanese Higher Education," *Higher Education* 34 (1997), 141–50; and U. Teichler, "Higher Education in Japan," in *Goals and Purposes of Higher Education in the 21st Century,* A. Burgen, ed. (London: Jessica Kingsley, 1996), 192–209.

26. Organisation for Economic Cooperation and Development, Centre for Educational Research and Innovation, *Education At a Glance: OECD Indicators* (Paris: OECD, 1997). Of course, there is some private support for British universities; e.g., Warwick, Oxford, Cambridge, and the London School of Economics gain substantial support from the sale of services, college endowments, tuition fees from overseas students, etc. But it is unlikely that these amounts add up to a greater percentage of GNP than does income from private sources for German and French universities.

27. National Committee of Inquiry into Higher Education (Dearing Report), 1997, appendix 5, section 10, "The Role and Background to Higher Education in Europe," para. 10.32.

28. See, e.g., S. Schiesel, "Jumping Off the Bandwidth Wagon," *New York Times,* 11 July 1999.

29. See *Freedom to Publish [on demand] Our Cultural Diversity* (Strasbourg: Council of Europe, 1999). See also A. Malcolm, "A Very Short Run: The Arrival of 'Print on Demand'" and "The Future of the Publisher-Author Relationship," *Times Literary Supplement,* 18 June 1999, 14–15.

30. *Freedom to Publish,* 11.

31. "E-Commerce," *New York Times,* 22 September 1999, section D, 1–69.

32. "Science Fiction Power for the PC," *International Herald-Tribune,* 16 July 1998, 1, 10.

33. My colleagues on this project are Dr. Diane Harley of the Center for Studies in Higher Education at University of California, Berkeley, and Dr. Gary Matkin, associate director of the University of California, Berkeley Extension. The first fruits of our work can be found in M. Trow, "The Development of Information Technology in American Higher Education," *Daedalus,* 126 (fall 1997), 293–314, and "Lifelong Learning through the New Information Technologies," *Higher Education Policy,* 12 (1999), 201–17.

34. The bearing of the diversity of higher education on distance learning

deserves separate treatment. A beginning can be found in Trow, "The Development of Information Technology," esp. 294–98. See also B. R. Clark, "Small Worlds, Different Worlds: The Uniquenesses and Troubles of American Academic Professions," *Daedalus*, 126 (fall 1997), 21–42.

35. B. Bollag, "In Europe, Workers and Professionals Head Back to the Classroom," *Chronicle of Higher Education*, 3 September 1999, A87.

36. Ibid.

37. Quoted in R. Hofstadter and W. Smith, eds., *American Higher Education: A Documentary History* (Chicago: University of Chicago Press, 1961), 555.

38. On the involvement of state and land grant universities in distance learning, see The Kellogg Commission on the Future of State and Land-Grant Universities, *Returning to Our Roots: A Learning Society* (September 1999).

39. F. Rudolph, *The American College and University* (New York: Knopf, 1962), 363–65.

40. These themes are developed in my "Lifelong Learning through the New Information Technologies."

41. C. P. Snow, *The Two Cultures: And a Second Look* (Cambridge: Cambridge University Press, 1964).

42. Gertrude Himmelfarb, "Revolution in the Library," *The American Scholar* (spring 1997), 204.

43. Muller, "The Management of the Modern University."

44. Himmelfarb, "Revolution in the Library." The spread of "books on demand" over the web may somewhat reconcile the concerns of humanists with the new technologies.

45. Ibid.

46. Trow, "Problems in the Transition from Elite to Mass Higher Education."

47. For earlier concerns about the impact of mass on elite higher education, see M. Trow, "Elite Higher Education: An Endangered Species?" *Minerva*, 14 (autumn 1976), 355–76.

Chapter Six

Higher Education and Those "Out-of-Control Costs"

D. Bruce Johnstone

To hear most politicians, journalists, businesspeople, and parents talk, the costs of college are out of control. Variations on this theme include allegations that higher education "is the next healthcare industry" or that "these [tuition] increases just can't keep going up" or that the professors and the presidents "just don't get it." This last remark conveys a notion that the (presumably excessive) cost or price increases in colleges and universities are not truly necessary but reveal some combination of greed, selfishness, incompetence, and all-around obtuseness.

A 1997 survey commissioned by the American Council on Education (1998) concluded, "The public worries a great deal about the price of attending college, believes it is too expensive, and thinks the price can be brought down without affecting academic quality." The survey further found that "The public has no idea of why college prices increase . . . [and thinks] that college leaders are indifferent to their concerns about the price of attending college."

Along with the rhetoric about out-of-control costs are references to overpaid and underworked professors, administrative bloat, institutions trying to be all things to all people, presidents and trustees unwilling or unable to manage (e.g., able to add but never to subtract or diminish), and institutions unable to change. Critics have written a veritable shelfful of books criticizing the academy and attacking professors and administrators for waste and profligacy as well as for softness and political correctness. National newsmagazines and television specials have featured (and perhaps helped to create) a widely perceived "crisis in college costs" (Footlick 1998). In 1997 Congress established the National Commission on the Cost of Higher Education (National Commission 1998) and even sent the commissioners back to reconsider their findings when it appeared that the supposedly independent entity might issue a final report that was insufficiently critical of colleges and universities and of the profligacy of which the sponsors of the legislation knew them to be guilty.

A more scholarly literature appeared in the 1990s (Olson 1997), seeking in part to better differentiate between costs (and especially cost *increases*) that are externally imposed, unavoidable, or otherwise justifiable or that enhanced output and cost increases that are discretionary, avoidable, and unrelated to the enhancement of the product or service. Larry Leslie and Gary Rhoades (1995) describe the latter costs as "internally pathological." William Massy (1991, 1996) writes of "the administrative lattice" and the "accretion of unnecessary tasks" to describe talented people working hard to find problems that justify their jobs (and additional jobs) but have little or no clear link to real organizational outputs or products. He also writes of "output creep" to describe the tendency of faculty to produce what they want, as opposed to what the sources of revenue (whether student, parent, government, or other client) want. Patricia Gumport and Brian Pusser (1995) write of the "additive explanation" to account for positions (and costs) whose functions are maintaining and resolving conflicts within the organization rather than directly contributing to organizational product. Robert Zemsky and his colleagues (1999) found evidence to support the contention that higher tuitions at the selective, "name brand" colleges and universities created "margins" for the benefit not of the students (nor presumably of their parents) but of the faculty.

At the same time, faculty and administrators of many colleges and universities feel as though they have been coping with almost perpetual financial challenges, constantly cutting, reallocating, downsizing, outsourcing, and chasing new revenues. More than a few institutions have cut costs so deeply they have lost many of their full-time faculty—and likely much of their former quality. Conventional wisdom notwithstanding, many colleges have also changed profoundly—for example, from a residential Roman Catholic liberal arts college for young women to a secular, coeducational college for part-time, adult students seeking career education in business or the health professions. Entire public systems have lost real resources (mainly full-time faculty and support staff) as well as the ability to keep libraries and equipment up-to-date, even as they have invested in new fields and new technologies. Net tuition revenue for many private colleges has been rising more slowly than their costs—due to unavoidable increases in unrestricted financial aid or tuition discounts, requiring (on top of the steep increases in tuition, or "sticker prices") more and more cuts in personnel and deferral of maintenance. The National Commission on the Cost of Higher Education, far from finding the "smoking gun" of widespread profligacy, reported merely that it was "convinced that academic institutions have done a lot to control costs but they must achieve more in the way of cost containment and productivity improvement" (1998, 15).

Meanwhile, students, supported by their parents, are increasingly clamoring to get into the highest-priced colleges and universities, a sign (for those who believe in markets) of the *worth* of those colleges and universities to both. Finally, in spite of tuition increases, it is still true that any student who is of traditional college age, at least somewhat academically able, and willing to borrow or work part time can attend some college or university regardless of the financial status of that student's family.

Why such a disconnect? How can it be that the American public, along with many scholars and "insiders," seems to believe that the costs of higher education are out of control, or at least terribly excessive, while most (although not all) faculty and many administrators believe the enterprise (or at least their part of it) to be woefully underfunded and efficient to the point of compromising academic values and also believe themselves to be working harder than ever? This chapter examines the costs and prices of higher education and some of the criticisms surrounding American colleges and universities in search of an explanation of this apparent conflict and of some answer to the question of how like a business the American public can expect its universities to be.[1]

The Several Meanings of "College Cost"

The National Commission on the Cost of Higher Education (1998) differentiated among four quite different meanings of the term *col-*

lege costs. The first is what the commission called "production costs." These are the underlying costs of instruction: a function of faculty-student and staff-student ratios, average salaries and benefits (which are partly a function of the ratio of regular full-time to adjunct or other part-time staff), and other operating and capital costs, or at least those attributable to undergraduate instruction. The second—and probably most cited, scrutinized, and criticized—construct of college cost pointed out by the National Commission is tuition, or that portion of production costs passed on to students and parents as the *sticker* or *nominal price.* This is what the press gets most excited about and what is unambiguously and rapidly rising. A third construct of the costs of higher education recognized by the commission is the total package of all parent- and student-borne expenses, including not just tuition but also all other fees and all costs of student living, including lodging, food, transportation, and similar items. Under this construct, the nontuition costs—that is, the costs of student living, books, transportation, and all other reasonable expenses, most or all of which are not under the control of any college or university—vary widely according to whether the student is living at home, in a dormitory, or with others in an apartment and also according to necessary transportation expenses and the standard of living the student has chosen. The real financial impact on students and their families, however, may best be indicated by yet a fourth construction of college costs—the total costs or expenses borne by students and their families *net of financial assistance.*

Production Costs

It may be significant, although curious, that political and popular interest in the allegedly out-of-control costs or prices of higher education focuses solely on *undergraduate* costs, which are thought to drive undergraduate tuition. The costs of graduate and advanced professional education, while a legitimate issue and possibly too high for a number of reasons, may be so inextricably bound together with the costs of research and scholarship as to make them much more difficult to analyze. But it is still a puzzle why journalistic and political attention seems to focus almost exclusively on the costs and prices of undergraduate education, particularly when there is probably more obvious waste elsewhere.

The faculty-student and staff-student ratios together form the construct of cost that drives all of the others (most notably the tuition cost, or price). This is the cost construct that is presumably the most amenable to real control and that ought, therefore, to be the principal object of scrutiny and criticism (if criticism be due). It is also, however, a construct for which we have too little truly useful data at complex universities.[2] The faculty-student ratio is mainly a function of prevailing class size (reflecting in part the richness or leanness of the curriculum) and the average teaching load (reflecting the orientation of the institution either to research and scholarship or to teaching). The staff-student ratio is a function of the richness or leanness of support functions such as academic support (computing, advising, tutoring, and library services); student affairs (psychological and career counseling, recreation, and student activities); and administrative and institutional support functions (admissions, financial aid, institutional relations, and general administration attributable to undergraduate education).

Whatever the assumptions and conventions under which student costs are measured, the real spread, or variance, in per-student costs among institutions is very great. In large part this reflects the expected differences between sectors (e.g., research universities, comprehensive colleges, and two-year colleges), levels of instruction (lower division, upper division, and graduate or advanced professional), and fields or disciplines (especially between laboratory- and equipment-intensive science and engineering fields and most of the humanities and social sciences) (Stringer and Cunningham 1999).

But the more interesting (and more problematic) cost variations are those among supposedly similar institutions—particularly among research universities and liberal arts colleges. These are the variations that gave rise to Howard Bowen's famous observation that, unlike other productive enterprises, higher education lacks any meaningful production function able to tie variations in production costs to prices of inputs and prevailing technologies. Instead, he attributes unit-cost variations, especially among supposedly like institutions, to variations in available revenue (1980). One consequence of these variations is that published data on *average costs* mean very little. Of greater significance to this analysis, however, is the observation that very high unit costs—and thus the very high tuitions that may be their consequence—are more discretionary, presumably more avoidable, and thus all the more open to criticism (Gose and Geraghty 1997).

The fact is, undergraduates in America can be taught at very low cost—especially if the faculty are paid very little, go largely without benefits, carry heavy teaching loads, are generally absolved from expectations of research, institutional governance, and academic or community service, and given minimal support in the way of facilities or professional staff. Or, they can be taught at very high cost—especially if the college has the resources to compete for the best faculty, both with good compensation and with the perquisites of low teaching loads and support for research, and also for a bright and diverse student body, "purchased," in part, with generous financial aid, abundant library and computing facilities, and a rich array of student activities and other support services (Clotfelter 1997). The colleges and universities at the high-cost end of this instructional-cost spread would not admit to costing more to produce the same output, but would claim to be producing a different—and fundamentally more costly—output, or product. Evaluating their output by the learning their students acquire, their developmental advances in character and leadership abilities, and by their acquisition of other values (in part measured by their voluntary philanthropy as alumni), as well as by the great social benefit purchased by very extensive financial assistance, the high-priced colleges and universities would readily admit to being more costly but not necessarily to being any less efficient or productive.

Table 6.1 shows some of the data compiled by Gordon Winston (1998a) that were used by the National Commission on the Cost of Higher Education, which completed its work in 1998. I repeat all of my caveats, particularly that against basing judgments on the available data on average per-student instructional cost by certain gross spending categories.

Time series data on per-student costs, or spending, add another dimension of uncertainty and variability. Table 6.2, from the U.S. De-

Table 6.1
Average Per-Student Spending in 1994–95

Public			Private		
All Public	Public Research	Comprehensive	All Private	Private Research	Liberal Arts
$9,919	$13,448	$9,933	$14,172	$32,014	$15,425

Source: Winston 1998a, 121, table 1.

Table 6.2

Per-Student Educational General Expenditures and Average Annual Rates of Increase by Control and Type, 1977–1995 (constant 1995–96 dollars)

	Public Sector				Private Sector			
	University		4 Year		University		4 Year	
Year	Spending Per Student	Average Annual Increase Previous 5 Years	Educational and General Spending Per Student	Average Annual Increase Previous 5 Years	Educational and General Spending Per Student	Average Annual Increase Previous 5 Years	Educational and General Spending Per Student	Average Annual Increase Previous 5 Years
1995–96	$19,700	1.6%	$13,403	2.2%	$37,200	2.6%	$17,177	2.3%
1990–91	18,237	1.6	12,102	0.3	32,945	3.5	15,417	2.7
1985–86	16,868	1.9	12,283	1.4	27,983	3.3	13,605	2.9
1980–81	15,391	0.4	11,482	1.0	24,040	1.1	11,876	0.7
1976–77	15,112	*	11,020	*	23,395	*	11,533	*

Note: * = no data available.
Source: NCES 1999, Supplemental table 40-2.

partment of Education's National Center for Education Statistics (NCES), using Higher Education General Information Survey (HEGIS) and Institutional Postsecondary Education Data System (IPEDS) data, shows the increase in per-student educational and general expenditures in constant 1995–96 dollars. Although the data are limited, they do not seem to support the notion of out-of-control increases in the costs of production—as long as one accepts that unit costs in a labor-intensive industry like higher education are almost bound to increase somewhat in real terms (i.e., at a rate of increase something in excess of the prevailing rate of inflation).

A more limited time series, but with refinements in the IPEDS data, was used by the National Commission (1998, 6, fig. 2; 166, exhibit 1–3a; and 168, exhibit 1–5) to illustrate the changing proportion of underlying instructional costs that are borne by tuition. The commission reported eight-year (1987–96) increases in "instructional costs" from $7,922 to $12,416 in current dollars in the public sector and from $10,911 to $18,387 in the private sector. Converted to constant 1995–96 dollars (by the Consumer Price Index), this represents for the public sector an eight-year increase of about 12.5 percent, or average real-dollar annual increases of some 1.5 percent. Again, the data are less comprehensive than one might hope for, but again, they do not seem to support a notion of out-of-control increases in instructional costs, particularly in the public sector.

Tuition

It is tuition—or the *annual increases* in posted, or nominal, tuition—that is probably at the root of most allegations of out-of-control costs. Average annual tuition increases for public and private colleges, as compiled annually by the College Board, increased well over 600 percent in the 25-year period from 1974–75 through 1999–2000, with annual tuition increases in the private sector averaging some 15 percent in the last half of the 1980s.

Expressing these increases in constant dollars eliminates the misleading (and inflammatory) effect of general inflation. As shown in table 6.3, the average annual *real* (constant 1999 dollars) tuition increases were still quite considerable. These tuition increases averaged nearly 9 percent annually for the private sector in the last half of the 1980s and almost 6 percent annually in the public sector from the mid-1980s through the mid-1990s. Otherwise in this 25-year period, the average *real* annual increases were mainly in the range of 2 to 3 percent. This is about what one would expect in an economic sector in which unit cost and price increases reflect essentially the economywide average increases in total wages and salaries—without the offsetting savings of productivity advances in other sectors. And if we factor in the very considerable withdrawal of per-student state aid in the public sector, along with the considerable increase in price discounting in the private sector—both of which contributed to the increases in tuition without contributing any net revenue toward operating expenses—the data again do not support the notion of excessive increases in real operating expenditures (with the exception of some private colleges and universities in the latter half of the 1980s).

Tuition, of course, differs from (that is, *is less than*) the underlying instructional costs according to varying levels of nontuition revenue: mainly state tax support in the public sector and endowment earning and current giving in the private sector. It is not the case, however (at least not in the private sector), that the higher the per-student nontuition revenue, the lower the tuition is likely to be—which would be a reasonable expectation under the condition of a fixed production function or unvarying instructional costs, as in an otherwise price-competitive, goods-producing enterprise. Instead, the greater the available nontuition revenue, the *higher* the tuition is apt to be—and of course the *very* much higher the per-student instructional costs are likely to be. Consumers—meaning both stu-

Table 6.3

Average Tuition and Tuition Increases, Public and Private 4-Year Sectors, 1974–1975 to 1999–2000 (constant 1999 dollars)

| Year | Public Sector (4 Year) | | Private Sector (4 year) | |
	Average Tuition	Average Annual Increase Previous Five Years	Average Tuition	Average Annual Increase Previous Five Years
1999–2000	$3,356	2.6%	$15,380	3.8%
1994–1995	2,968	6.7	12,938	2.6
1989–1990	2,217	5.1	11,436	9.0
1984–1985	1,769	2.4	7,882	2.8
1979–1980	1,580	2.8	6,904	0.3
1974–1975	1,386	*	6,793	*

Note: * = no data available.
Source: College Board (1999a, 7, table 5).

dents and parents—can then perceive themselves as getting even more for their already high tuition dollars. And those advocating for the most costly (and pricey) private institutions can point out that tuition, however high in the estimate of some observers and however rapidly increasing, still constitutes only a portion of total under-graduate instructional costs—the other portion being covered by past and present philanthropy.

Thus, the billions of dollars in aggregate endowment and the hundreds of millions in aggregate current giving in the priciest of the private colleges and universities will, for the most part, be used not to cover the underlying essential costs of instruction and diminish the amount that must then be covered by tuition, but rather to cover the costs of measures that provide more expensive (but presumably better) undergraduate education:

—lower student-faculty ratios, lower teaching loads, and better salaries, resulting in the best faculty, who have more time both for their scholarship (and the national prestige that this brings to the institution) and perhaps even for their (relatively few) students;
—an abundance of nonfaculty professional staff (for the support of learning and tutorial centers, recreation, student activities, career counseling, etc.);
—a bigger and better physical plant (e.g., computer labs, gymnasia, theaters, art galleries, student meeting spaces, nicely landscaped grounds);
—the greater academic preparedness as well as greater diversity of the student body that come about through costly financial aid.

In the public sector, of course, a similar defense can also be given: that the tuition paid is only a portion of the actual underlying cost and that the student or family is getting a "bargain" represented by the taxpayer subsidy and measured by the difference between the tuition they are paying and the actual underlying per-student costs of undergraduate instruction. This subsidy is difficult to calculate because it requires certain assumptions about the appropriate portion of costs to be attributed to the education of undergraduates—as opposed to all of the rest of the purposes of public higher education, especially in research and doctoral universities. Nevertheless, as conventionally measured (and granting considerable between-state and even some within-state variation), in-state undergraduate tuition in most state four-year colleges and universities ranges between 25 and 40 percent of full instructional costs. This, however, is a defense only when it is used to convince parents and students that public tuition and its recent increases are appropriate. For politicians, taxpayers, and advocates of the low-cost, low-tuition private sector, observation of the very substantial per-student public subsidy probably only exacerbates the charge that it is the underlying cost of instruction that is excessive.

Total Expenses

Table 6.4 shows some estimated "other-than-tuition expenses" as percentages of the estimated total expenses for a year in college according to the College Board. These may range from 34 percent of total expenses for a year in residence at an average private college to 69 percent for a residential experience at a public college and 62 percent for attendance at a public college while living at home. In fact, since these College Board numbers are from college-reported averages, the actual range is probably much greater. But the point is that dwelling only on tuition seriously underestimates the expense burden that must be met by parents and students, especially in public low-tuition colleges, and even in situations where the low public tuition is combined with living at home.

Putting a range of these student living and other expenses together not with the published average tuition, but with modeled, or reasonable, estimates of high and low tuition in both the public and

Table 6.4

All Other-Than-Tuition Expenses as a Percentage of Estimated Total Expenses, College Board National Averages Estimates

	Private Residential	Public Residential	Public Commuting
Tuition and required fees ($)	15,380	3,356	3,356
All other expenses ($)	8,271	7,553	5,418
Total expenses ($)	23,651	10,909	8,774
"All other expenses" as % of total	34	69	62

Source: College Board (1999a, 6, table 4).

Table 6.5
Total Costs/Expenses Borne by Students and Families, U.S. Colleges
and Universities, 1998–1999 (in dollars)

	Public		Private	
	High Expense	Low Expense	High Expense	Low Expense
Tuition and Required Fees	4,000	1,200	20,000	10,000
Other Educational Expenses	850	700	900	900
Room and Board	5,650	1,800	6,600	5,600
Transportation and Other	1,500	2,000	1,500	1,500
Total	12,000	5,700	29,000	18,000

Source: Estimates by author (Johnstone 1999b, 362, table 13.4 and notes).

the private sectors yields the range of possible total expenses for an undergraduate academic year in the United States in 1998–99. This is shown in table 6.5.

This is the cost—considerably beyond tuition—that most parents have in mind when they give vent to their "college-cost anxiety," and this is the cost that will drive student indebtedness. Much of this cost—such as room, board, transportation, entertainment, and the costs of books and computers—is outside the control of either the institution or the state or federal government. Moreover, most of these costs at public institutions are not costs of college at all but merely the costs of young-adult living and would be incurred in or out of school. Parents and the general public, however, seem to see them as costs of college and want a *solution* to the problem of their magnitude. This then becomes a political problem for governors, state legislators, or the Congress. If the state and federal governments cannot directly force down the underlying instructional costs, if they cannot hold down tuition (indeed, cuts in appropriations by state governments may be largely responsible for public college and university tuition increases), and if they choose not to provide more financial assistance to those who most need it, they can at least *seem* to be responsive to this college-cost anxiety by granting middle-class tax breaks in the form of tax-advantaged savings and tuition prepayment plans.[3]

Net Expenses

The National Commission's information on total and net price of attendance is shown in table 6.6. These data come from the published averages, rather than modeled ranges used for table 6.5, and as such do not show the considerable variation within the sectors or the variation of price discounting by family income, which varies according to the calculated "family financial need" (or its converse, the calculated "expected family contribution"). These calculations, in turn, depend on current income, certain assets, and other family obligations. Total available financial aid (loans and work study as well as grants) has substantially cushioned the increase in total expenses for public and private four-year colleges. Moreover, the greatest percentage increase in college expense net of financial assistance of all kinds has been in the public sector, and especially in community colleges. The least percentage increase in net expense has been (on average) in the four-year private sector.

Table 6.6 also illustrates the concept of *affordability* versus *accessibility*. *Accessibility* refers to the sheer ability of a student to attend college—that is, to come up with the cash, even if only by borrowing. *Affordability* refers to the actual expenses incurred net of the discounting provided by grant aid and the loan repayment subsidies. The portion of financial assistance in the form of loans has increased dramatically, from 41 percent in 1980–81 to 47 percent in 1992–93, to 58 percent in 1998–99 (College Board 1999b). If access only is the exclusive object of financial assistance, then loans may be generally sufficient—and under most circumstances will be more cost-effective (to the taxpayer) than grants.[4] But large student indebtedness, aside from providing no real income redistribution, has other possible or at least alleged downsides. For example, some critics claim that some low income or minority students are likely to be culturally debt averse, while other critics point out that high indebtedness can distort life plans such as marriage or the choice of a socially worthwhile but low-paying career.

Concerns about Tuition

One reason that the public (meaning politicians, journalists, and citizens generally) has not been greatly concerned about the enormous

Table 6.6
Total Costs or Expenses Borne by Student and Family Net of Grants and Total Financial Assistance, 1996

	Average Public 4-year		Average Public 2-year		Average Private 4-year	
	1996 ($)	% change from 1987	1996 ($)	% change from 1987	1996 ($)	% change from 1987
Total Average Expenses Borne by Student and Family	10,759	109	6,761	141	20,003	84
Total Expenses Minus Grant Aid [Affordability]	9,365	114	6,067	159	15,069	81
Total Expenses Minus All Financial Aid [Accessibility]	7,262	95	5,717	169	11,205	64

Source: National Commission 1998, 7.

variation in tuition or total expenses borne by students and parents noted above is because the focus has often been not on the tuition or the total expense itself but only on the annual rate of increase in these numbers. The reason for this seems to be that the annual rate of increase can so easily be compared with another annual rate of cost or expense increase: the annual rate of inflation or the current yearly rise in the Consumer Price Index. The typical headline, usually following the announcement by the College Board of the results of its annual survey of college costs reads, often in bold front-page headlines, "College Costs Again Rise Faster than the Cost of Living!" or "College Cost Increases Exceed Rate of Inflation for the Fourteenth Year in a Row!"

It seems to make little difference to the headline writers—or to the politicians or the rest of higher education cost critics—that the rate of inflation is merely an *average* (weighted) of lots of price increases and that, as in any average, roughly one-half of all the elements that have been averaged must perforce lie above—and another one-half lie below—that calculated average. Nor does it seem to matter that higher education, as a labor-intensive industry, has relatively few opportunities for large scale *substitution* of capital for labor (which is not to be confused with the large scale *addition* of capital to labor that more commonly describes the application of technology to college teaching) and will almost inevitably feature above-average cost-price increases. (This is fundamentally unlike most manufacturing, which can substitute capital for labor, reaping cost-side productivity increases, and holding both cost and price increases below the economywide average.) It would, in fact, be unusual if higher education in general were not in the above average half of the cost/price distribution. But as Footlick (1998) notes in "The Holy Cow! Story: How the News Media Cover College Costs," such explanations are not the stuff of headlines or political speeches.

It is true that some colleges and universities have sometimes managed to hold unit cost increases below the rate of increase of costs and prices in the general economy, evidencing an apparent gain in productivity. The occasion for this is generally either (in the public sector) mandatory cuts forced by the governor or legislature or (in the private sector) falling demand and net tuition revenue. The productivity increase that is reflected in these below average increases in unit costs may have been made possible by a reduction in the number of faculty and staff, by a shift from full-time faculty to part-time, inexpensive, adjunct faculty, or by a reduction in student services. This is a genuine productivity increase only as long as there is no commensurate decline in the output or the quality of the product. This is exceedingly difficult to prove one way or the other. Many educators, however, believe such a diminution of quality to be widespread and thus to have considerably blunted the alleged productivity gains of many of the per-student cost reductions of recent years.

The public's fixation on the rate of increase of *tuitions* rather than the rate of increase in the *underlying costs of instruction* is particularly significant in the public sector. A state can magnify even a modest underlying instructional cost increase by a large withdrawal of public tax revenue requiring an equally large tuition increase that is not at all indicative of what may be happening to the underlying costs of instruction. Data comparing different states and sectors are difficult to compile due to interstate differences in the rates of enrollment increases, faculty compensation, and expenditures earmarked for purposes having little bearing on undergraduate instruction— not to mention the above-mentioned difficulty of comparing changes in quality, or *true outputs*. In the past decade, however, many states have almost certainly decreased the real per-student undergraduate spending, at least as measured by real full-time faculty and professional staff per student, even though the resulting below-average increase in per-student instructional costs has frequently been accompanied by above-average tuition increases as states have shifted the burden of cost from taxpayers to students and their parents.

While the rate of tuition increases gets the headlines, it is the dollar amount of these increases that may generate an enrollment response, particularly in the public sector, where a decline in enrollment may be politically volatile. The question posed is what is the price elasticity of demand for higher education, or what is the anticipated percentage enrollment decline that can be expected from a tuition increase of, say, $100 or $1,000? This question has been the object of both time series and cross-sectional econometric analyses that have consistently shown a small response: in the range of one to two percent for each $100 rise in tuition (Leslie and Brinkman 1989; Kane 1995; McPherson and Schapiro 1998; Heller 1997, 1999). We know little, however, about how this enrollment response may be concentrated in certain college sectors or how it may relate to certain student-family attributes, except that the response seems to be minimal among upper-income and upper-middle-income students, upperclassmen (as opposed to first-time or "about to enroll" freshmen), and among the academically successful and ambitious. Conversely, we can expect there to be a measurable enrollment response to a tuition increase among low-income, academically unsuccessful or ambivalent youth, and among part-time students. The actual nature of this enrollment response, however, can vary from not applying at all or dropping out for a semester of work, to "dropping down" to a lower-cost college near home, or to dropping out altogether never to return.

Out-of-Control Costs: Variations on the Charge

To the extent that higher education costs can legitimately be deemed to be a public policy issue, there seem to be five rather different "charges" that can be aimed at higher education's leadership (broadly defined to include both campus and system CEOs, governing boards, deans and other academic administrators, faculty leaders, and elected officials). The specification or attribution of the charge is important both for understanding cause and for assigning blame—for if there can be no blame, there will likely be no amelioration of the problem.

—*Profligacy or wastefulness.* Charging that colleges and universities are wasteful implies that what they do could be done (in generally the same way or using the same technology) at much lower cost. The charge of profligacy suggests unnecessary or overpaid faculty and staff, unnecessary capital expenditures, insufficient cost controls, and the like.

—*Wrong priorities.* This charge states that while cost increases may (or may not) be justified, or at least explainable, for what colleges and universities are doing, the point is that they are doing too many unimportant or low priority things. The faculty may be busy doing research that is of no interest or foreseeable consequence to anyone, even to other scholars. Or there may be academic programs, however well taught, that have few students or courses taught with little evidence of actual learning or a student affairs staff, also hard-working, but with no enthusiastic participants or evidence of "student development."

—*Timidity, or the reluctance to radically restructure.* Those who make this charge claim that there are altogether new (and ultimately less costly) ways of doing things that may require radical alterations of the production process itself (restructuring) but that would make the process substantially more efficient if the management were only bolder, more visionary, or more forceful in effecting these radical changes.

—*Insensitivity to the student consumer.* While those making this charge may admit that the costs (and especially the cost increases) of higher education may be justified or explainable, they accuse colleges and universities of not making the unusual sacrifices called for by the vulnerability of some of their students (especially those most likely to be dissuaded by tuition increases) and the importance of economic and social justice.

—*Overselling, or overenrolling.* This is the charge that educators have oversold their product, that colleges and universities are admitting and teaching too many "marginal" students—at public expense and with predictably low odds of success.

In Defense of the Academy's Costs and Prices

There are bits of truth in all of these charges. But overall, the charge that higher educational costs are out of control or that tuitions do not reflect value received is overwrought and mainly wrong. Each of the charges listed above can and should be answered—not to everyone's satisfaction, but in defense of the academy, which has taken more criticism on costs than it deserves.

Are We Profligate or Wasteful?

The most general charge is that of profligacy, or wastefulness. The most common defense against this charge is to explain just why higher education is so expensive or why it is so much more difficult for colleges and universities (as opposed to businesses) to economize due to their general "productivity immunity," or absence of ways regularly to substitute capital for labor. A better defense, however, may be simply to dispute the initial observation. As table 6.2 shows, the underlying per-student costs, or their rate of increase, in the tax-supported public sector—where these costs are a legitimate public policy issue—are neither excessive in themselves, nor increasing at excessive rates.

Where most undergraduates are taught—in public community colleges, public comprehensive colleges and universities, and in regional private colleges and universities—salaries have generally lagged behind the general economy, and the ratios of full-time faculty and staff per student in many states have declined (a demonstration of clear cost-side productivity improvement). The cost and pricing structures of the private, well-endowed, pricier colleges and universities are simply not a legitimate public policy issue.

In the public research and doctoral universities, there are undoubtedly pockets of less productive faculty and administrative staff who are working hard at organizational maintenance and at solving very small problems. But this observation yields few specific recommendations for managerial actions that would demonstrably (and usefully) increase productivity and save public resources. In these public research and doctoral campuses, the following points are worth noting:

—Any reversal of the drift of campuses toward the higher-cost end of the per-student cost continuum would almost certainly be bitterly opposed, most of all by governors and legislatures.
—Costs have been lowered substantially already (many would say excessively) through widespread substitution of cheaper part-time and adjunct faculty for full-time faculty.
—Alternative revenues from tuition, fees, research overhead, and aggressive fund raising have already replaced tax support in many public institutions.
—For decades, public universities have been pursuing—and will continue to pursue—standard industry practices such as early retirement, contracting out, decentralized budgeting, electronic transactions and records, on-line and widely shared libraries, and aggressive and innovative marketing.

It is still useful to explain why some things continue to cost as much as they do in higher education. For example, externally imposed regulations or mandates are responsible for many of the supposedly high unit costs. Such outside controls include occupational health and safety regulations, especially affecting research laboratories and academic health centers; paperwork mandates upon offices of admissions and financial aid, where federal regulations are voluminous and ever-changing; and the prohibition against mandatory retirement, which is especially difficult for research universities, where faculty effort must be essentially voluntary and there are few measures (other than retirement) to cure the problem of permanently lapsed productivity. At the same time, while valid, these sorts of restrictions and mandates are probably no more burdensome than those in many other sectors of the economy and are probably an insufficient defense against excessive cost, where otherwise demonstrated.

A similar and more substantial explanation for high costs in some public systems is rigid state finance laws, which exist more to inhibit corruption or outright stealing than to encourage good business practices. For example, as long as state treasurers or comptrollers "sweep" college and university accounts at the end of a fiscal year, returning unspent balances to the state treasury, public institutions will do everything in their power *not* to save, but to spend the money before the end of the year. Institutions even resort to holding excess inventories or making low-priority expenditures, in the perfectly rational and even businesslike effort to avoid signaling that they were overfunded to begin with (Johnstone 1991).

Similarly, public colleges and universities in states with executive line-item budget control may well overspend on some expenditure categories relative to others simply because that is the way the state finance law is written and the budget is passed. The state budget office is not about to delegate to the campuses the "textbook" optimizing authority to shift expenditures among categories until the benefits per marginal dollar are equalized among categories. Finally, some states may well overspend on wages and benefits relative to the local labor market because the governor conducts collective bargaining with the faculty and staff as employees of the state rather than of the public college or university. The institution is then stuck with a compensation agreement to which neither the chief executive officer nor the trustees of the state university were a party. This does not override the observation that these practices can be wasteful and sometimes profligate, but it ought to blunt the notion of higher education's managerial culpability in the waste.

One of the single most common elements of this profligacy charge is insufficient faculty productivity, generally meaning that faculty are teaching insufficient numbers either of students or courses (or both). In response to this charge, I must first note that if it applies at all, it only applies at research and doctoral universities. Faculty at such institutions have low teaching loads for the express purpose of supporting the dominant institutional mission of scholarly productivity. To make time for research, these institutions hold teaching time to (at best) 40 percent of faculty effort or workload—generally about two formal courses per term, plus undergraduate, graduate, and postdoctoral student advising and mentoring. We may have more research and doctoral universities than we need, although governors and state legislators have concurred in, and often initiated, this institutional drift. In any case, however, this is much less a case of inefficient, unproductive, or excessively costly institutions than it is a case of inappropriate missions assigned to some public universities. Finally, it is appropriate once again to observe that most undergraduate students are being taught in community colleges, small regional private colleges, and public comprehensive colleges (sometimes called "universities") where the faculty effort, if anything, is too heavily tilted toward teaching, with insufficient time available for reading and scholarship.

Any amelioration of this problem of insufficient faculty productivity in doctoral and research universities (regardless of its magnitude), would have to follow one or both of two lines. First, some of the lesser research or doctoral public universities would have to be closed or converted into comprehensive colleges, with faculty efforts and workloads altered to bring them into accord with the heavier teaching expectations of the public comprehensive colleges. Even if this could ever be legally, contractually, or politically feasible (highly unlikely), the result would not be a less costly institution, much less a more productive institution, but merely a different institution—and one filled with disgruntled faculty who, having been trained, hired, and initially rewarded as scholars, were now expected to abandon their scholarly work to teach more undergraduates.

Second, the research and doctoral universities could do a better (tougher?) job of holding faculty accountable for the research and scholarly parts of their jobs, imposing heavier teaching obligations on those who, for whatever reason, have become unproductive in their research. There are, however, serious problems with this approach. There is the valid concern that such a policy would, or at least could, stifle academic freedom or be carried out with other, inappropriate, managerial agendas. There is also the likelihood that the volume of good teaching that could be squeezed out of faculty whose research productivity had demonstrably lapsed is almost certainly minimal. Finally, there is the bothersome asymmetry of a policy that purports to increase the amount of teaching demanded from the faculty member whose research is deemed insufficient without a similar determination to increase the research expectations for the faculty member who is an uninspiring or otherwise less than competent teacher.

Actually, the popular assumption that research universities are expensive places to teach undergraduates may be less true than conventionally believed. Research universities have devised ways of holding down the costs of teaching the undergraduate—that is, ways that seemingly enhance productivity—which happen, ironically, to be the very devices that the same critical public frequently castigates them for: large lectures with graduate assistant recitation sections or large-scale reliance on adjunct professors for introductory classes. Any appropriate criticism of underlying unit costs is more validly a criticism of the extent that undergraduate tuitions are cross-subsidizing graduate teaching and the underlying scholarly missions and of the inappropriate recruitment and placement of undergraduate students in research university settings when they would be better served elsewhere. These may be lapses in effective management, but they are not manifestations of unproductive faculty.

A very different defense is appropriate for the so-called high-end providers: those private colleges and universities marked by high costs, high tuitions, substantial institutionally provided financial aid, large applicant pools, and considerable selectivity—for example, the colleges and universities making up the Consortium for the Financing of Higher Education (Clotfelter 1996). This defense is the simple test of the market—that preeminent indication of worth in our economy. Yes, these high-priced (and even more, high-*cost*) colleges and universities have more faculty teaching fewer students with greater support and more physical amenities than seems absolutely necessary to provide an education. For all their implicit per-student subsidy via their large endowments, they may still charge more than some families are willing to pay (although a considerable portion of that cost, as earlier noted, is for room, board, entertainment, and other living costs that most of these students would be enjoying anyway). But the major defense of their high cost is that many students and their families, with plenty of good-quality, lower-cost alternatives, are lining up to make these sacrifices—including the assumption of substantial student debt—because they believe the expense to be worth it. And because there are no public dollars going into this choice (other than the need-based financial aid, most or all of which the students would be entitled to even at an equivalent public college or university alternative), there would seem to be no reason for assuming either the underlying unit costs or the tuitions (pricey though they may be) to be valid public policy issues.

Do We Expend Resources for the Wrong Things?

A different charge from spending wastefully is spending on the wrong things or with the wrong priorities. This can occur in the allocation (or the alleged misallocation) of resources among the legitimately multiple products of the university: scholarship (applied versus basic), teaching (or, more accurately, learning), and service (to the community versus to the discipline or even to private causes). Of course, multiple products are not unique to the university—neither are the other complications such as cross-subsidization, or simultaneous production of these different "products." What is unique—and what invites the constant barrage of charges of wrong priorities—is the absence of a common, undisputed, easy-to-measure, and unambiguous metric such as contribution to profit. A business only has to apply the single metric of profit to each of its products. A university cannot do this—not because it does not want to or know how to but because *it cannot be done*. Of course, it is possible, albeit exceedingly difficult and probably always contestable, to compare the worth or value of advances in historical scholarship, the development of a new method of business accounting, a certain output of baccalaureate graduates, the advancement of basic science that might lead to application, and the learning that may be imparted to graduating some at-risk young adults. But it is only possible with something called academic judgment, not with some clear and unambiguous common denominator like dollars.

The more serious criticism of priorities is not of the priority given one acknowledged product (say, research) over another (such as teaching or learning), however disputed these priorities may be. Rather, it is the criticism of the expenditure of resources and attention for what are not end products at all, but for solutions to non-problems, or for the mere aggrandizement of the organization itself (or worse, of an individual) with no product enhancement. This may be the most valid criticism of college and university management and of excessive costs.

Are We Too Timid to Reallocate Radically?

Underlying the charge of timidity is the notion that universities have been managed too much for the benefit and comfort of the faculty and administration—unlike businesses that are, at least in theory, managed for the stockholders and that (if they are truly successful) do not hesitate to lay off long-time workers, close a factory, move across the Mexican border, or drop or add entire product lines in order to enhance revenue and lower costs.

The criticism of timidity also has some validity. Many (by no means all) college presidents, provosts, and deans are sensitive to, and solicitous of, their faculty in ways that have no counterpart in business or even most other public agencies. This sensitivity—correlated with the genuinely influential role of the faculty—is not typical of all colleges and universities. Rather, there is a continuum of authority sharing. At one end are authoritarian institutions, where faculty senates are nonexistent or at least nonfunctional (although there are frequently strong faculty unions) and where the president controls all decision and directs all organizational (including faculty) behavior. At the other end are the schools that are run collegially, where faculty have very great influence, and even authority, not only over the curriculum and matters of faculty membership (i.e., appointments and promotions), but even over the definition and direction of faculty work itself. Proximity to the authoritarian end of this continuum correlates quite directly with low per-student instructional cost. The lower the cost of production (which implies a lean staff, generally low pay, and extensive reliance on part-time and adjunct faculty), the more authority tends to be held by the president and management—and in general the lower the prestige of the faculty and the selectivity of the undergraduate student body. Conversely, the greater the deference to the faculty, the higher the per-student costs tend to be—and also the greater the faculty and institutional prestige and the selectivity of the student body.

However—and this point is critical—administrative deference to the faculty does not cause the higher costs (and tuitions). Rather, it is the abundance of revenue—from endowments, current giving, research overhead, and a strong student market position—that affords the institution the luxury of strong collegial faculty governance and the ability to be deliberative about (or reject altogether) radical change. Conversely, it tends to be the college that is underendowed, reliant on part-time faculty, unable to be selective in admissions, and dependent upon an ever-changing market niche that generally cannot afford the additional time and occasional wrong decisions associated with shared decision making. In this construction, what a trustee, politician, or businessperson may see as administrative timidity is more a purposeful choice of the governing style of the most prestigious and successful colleges and universities. It is clearly not a governing style conducive to abruptly changing the institutional mission or to forcing a change in the productive behavior of the faculty. But most colleges and universities do not need abrupt alterations in mission. Nor can top faculty be attracted to places where presidents, deans, and trustees are trying to direct professional behavior—especially under the rubric of making them more productive.

This is not to say that many administrators (especially deans and department chairs) of prestigious colleges and universities could not be a great deal more effective as managers, at least in part by becoming more decisive and forceful. Nor is it to claim that some colleges and universities have not suffered, both financially and academically, from presidents who became captive to, rather than leaders of, their faculty. But as a general rule, colleges and universities are managed with just as much forcefulness, decisiveness, and even authority as is demanded by the nature of the institution; its faculty; and most of all, its mission.

This defense may beg the question about the alleged need for radical change. For example, the charge of timidity sometimes alleges that most universities are far "behind the wave" of instructional technologies, refusing to recognize that the lecture and even the "seated course" may be mainly obsolete and that much instruction can take place via the Internet, through e-mail, or over fiber-optic lines. Consultants, pundits, and journalists making such charges tend to be enamored with the University of Phoenix and other institutions promising to deliver instruction via instructional television, the Internet, or other technologically aided, essentially self-paced, means. In an earlier published prediction about "patterns of finance" in the future, I wrote:

However, most traditional-age undergraduate students engage in higher education for purposes other than, or at least in addition to, learning: for the prestige of being admitted to a selective institution, for the fun of college life, and for the social learning that comes of interacting with fellow students, professors, and other adult professionals. Such students will achieve few if any of these life goals from the Internet or from other forms of self-paced learning.

By this reasoning, radical new patterns of higher education finance predicated on conceivable "out of the box" possibilities presented by the new learning technologies are likely to have a major cost-reducing impact more on firm-specific and continuing professional education, or on personal or recreational forms of postsecondary education, but not on mainstream undergraduate education nor on elite graduate higher education, except when such education is enriched—and made more expensive—as additional resources are brought to it. (Johnstone 1998, 252)

A final note of defense against the charge of timidity: even if the above comments prove to be wrong, and higher education gets overtaken by new providers unimpeded by existing organizational forms and uninhibited by the established norms and values of the academy, this will not prove that the current leadership is or was wrong in not attempting to radically restructure the colleges and universities of today. The institutions in such an unlikely scenario will almost certainly have to be entirely new ones or institutions forced into radical change not by visionary or exceptionally courageous leadership but simply by financial catastrophe.

Are We Insensitive to the Financial Difficulties of Students?

Clearly, higher education, at least as we know it, is a costly enterprise, both in and of itself (i.e., the production cost) and in its price, or tuition. Just as clearly, it is possible for most institutions of higher education to provide instruction (ignoring, for a moment, scholarship and other outputs that are legitimate and important products of many institutions) at less cost per student, and also, if necessary, to price this instructional product at an even lower net tuition. It is at least intuitively likely that there are some, perhaps many, students who could profit from higher education (and from whose higher education society would also profit) who are dissuaded from college in part because of its expense (tuition less aid), even if other factors, such as poor academic preparation and low interest, also contribute to their failure to pursue a higher education. We also know that these "dissuaded" students are disproportionately from low-income, African American, Latino, and Native American families and are older or perhaps even high school dropouts. And finally, we know that without at least some higher education, the chances that this group will enjoy middle-class opportunities are very greatly diminished.

The critical question in this line of inquiry is whether this disproportionality is so great and so unjust that its diminution—that is, an increase in college participation among these hitherto underserved populations—must supercede other criteria for the allocation of revenue within higher education, including such conventional criteria as the quality of faculty scholarship and the preferences of conventional entering students. The "waste" of higher educational resources under this construct is an extreme case of misplaced priorities, in which some would claim that most expenditures (at least in publicly supported higher education) can be considered wasteful until the grossly unequal participation rates have been more nearly equalized—to the extent this can be remedied through the reallocation of public resources. The remedy would feature very substantial increases in financial aid. These could be paid for, if necessary, by substantial cuts elsewhere in the institution. In this case the intent would not be to appease budget cutters or to meet some ephemeral standard of efficiency or productivity but to attain a new priority: the more nearly equal participation by socioeconomic class, to the extent this can be secured with financial aid. Or, the necessary and substantial increases in need-based financial assistance could be realized from very high tuition increases to upper-middle and upper socioeconomic classes, and the introduction of a policy of "high tuition–high aid."

However, high tuition–high aid has serious practical and political liabilities (Johnstone 1999a). For example, governors and legislators may like the part about high tuition but be less positive about high aid. Also, we know relatively little about the enrollment behavior of the "marginal" student—that is, the student for whom the decision to go to college, where to go, and whether to persist is truly an open decision, particularly susceptible to variations in tuition and financial aid. Clearly, the need for a very major increase in need-based financial assistance (or even a rollback in some tuitions) is not what most of the conventional critics have in mind when they speak and write of waste and out-of-control costs in higher education. And just as clearly, the brightest and most highly motivated students—especially if they are from affluent families—are going to continue to attend the most selective colleges; and greater equality will assuredly not be served if only the public colleges foreswear all other traditional funding priorities in order to pour maximum resources into additional financial aid for the poor and the ambivalent. A tentative answer to the "insensitivity" charge, then, is that the issue, however profoundly important, is probably not one that can be solved by shifts in higher education's spending priorities.

Are We Overselling Our Product?

"Overselling" as a construct of excessive cost, or waste, signals a number of practices, all suggesting to the critics not so much excessive spending per student but excessive numbers of students. For example, some U.S. colleges and universities accept students for university, or baccalaureate, studies (including those accepted into two-year "transfer" programs), who would be deemed academically unacceptable for what could be called "university studies" almost anywhere else in the world. They are accepted for baccalaureate study in the United States in spite of the fact that they have not yet mastered the learning expected of the graduate of an academic secondary school. Part of the alleged "waste," therefore, is the considerable need for remediation in U.S. colleges and universities. Critics of this practice see it as paying for the same education twice.

Another part of alleged waste (again, true mainly of the nonselective college) is the high drop out, or noncompletion, rate.[5] The British use the term *wastage* for *dropping out,* implying that obtaining less than higher education's first degree is a waste of time and money—for the student as well as the taxpayer. And even for those who ultimately graduate, the prolongation of the time-to-degree—frequently accompanied by an excessive number of *credits*-*to-the-degree*—is considered by some critics to be a waste of time and resources.

Furthermore (or so it is alleged), some of these marginal students are encouraged to take—again, at taxpayer expense—more higher education than is likely to benefit either them or the larger society. Thus, students for whom a two-year degree may be a "stretch," albeit an appropriate one, are told that they ought to seek a bachelor's degree; those who finish (if barely) the bachelor's degree are told that they ought to pursue a master's. And so it goes until American universities are producing, at public expense, far more Ph.D. degrees than is appropriate either for the students, the disciplines, or the taxpayer paying the bill. And although this overselling may occur under the noble banners of *opportunity* or *equality,* the real interest of the academy is said to be in its own jobs and in the revenue students bring with them in the form of public funds or tuition.

Portions of this broad charge of waste are simply exaggeration. For example, some public systems are denying entry into a senior college to any student in need of remedial work in any core subject. Trustees or governors advocating such a policy may be quite content for these underprepared students to be given remedial instruction, still largely at taxpayer expense, at a community college or in the local school system. But the true production cost of remedial instruction—a function mainly of student-teacher ratios and average faculty or teacher compensation—is not necessarily any higher at a senior college or university than at a community college or a high school. In fact, at the level of a senior college or university, the remediation will almost certainly be done with part-time adjunct faculty or graduate students or, in any event, non-tenure-track staff, whereas at the high school or community college, it may well be performed by regular teachers at much higher rates of compensation.

Furthermore, it is not clear that a community college or night school setting is more conducive to learning than a baccalaureate college or university for students deemed to be marginal or underprepared. Part of the reason that this admittedly marginal student might be underprepared is that he or she was totally unmotivated (or worse) by the social and instructional ambience of the high school. If so, it is likely that a night school will have much the same "feel." Clearly more research is necessary on which institutional settings are more conducive to learning for different kinds of marginal or underprepared students. But if this student is to be given a second chance (and the case in favor of this seems overwhelming—but is not the topic of this chapter), this second chance could be provided equally or more cost-effectively by the right program in a senior college or a university than in some less collegiate or university-like setting.

But in the end, the charge that higher education is being wastefully oversold—in effect, overenrolled—can only be answered by placing a value on the very high level of accessibility and the second chance offered uniquely by American higher education. And we seem to have settled that issue. Particularly as long as college preparedness in America is so overwhelmingly affected by the socioeconomic setting of the family, the school, and the neighborhood, American values will demand the second (and third) chance that our extraordinarily accessible colleges, both public and private, provide. Virtually open access to, and second and third chances to succeed at, higher education are indeed costly. But these features may also be among the most cost-effective ways of fixing at least some of the problems of a society in which higher education is increasingly important to economic and social opportunity and traditional preparation for college continues to be so overwhelmingly correlated with socioeconomic class, race, and ethnicity.

Conclusion

All higher education is costly, and its unit costs can be expected to continue to increase like those of any other very labor-intensive service—that is, at rates somewhat in excess of the rate of increase in the costs of living. Higher education's costs can increase at much greater rates if revenues increase commensurately. Likewise, higher education can find economies and cut unit costs when revenue falls short. There is, however, little evidence of out-of-control cost increases, especially in the public sector, where cost-effectiveness is a more legitimate public issue.

Naturally, colleges and universities must be especially vigilant about costs (and, admittedly, more so than many have been in the past) because of several features of the enterprise: its labor intensity; its legitimately multiple yet hard-to-measure products; and the essentially professional nature of its principal producers (the faculty), who have control over their own time and considerable, but highly inefficient, involvement in all decision making. The relatively new public pressure for attention to productivity and cost-effectiveness is a good thing. However, there is abundant evidence that much or most (but not all) of higher education is both well managed and lean, particularly given what it is being asked by society to accomplish. A little more thoughtful defensiveness on the part of college and university leadership would be welcomed.

Notes

1. I write with some biases. Although I have studied, written about, and taught graduate courses on the economics and finance of higher education for more than 20 years, my most vivid lessons in the finance of higher education have come from 9 years as president of the largest comprehensive colleges of the State University of New York system and another 6 years as chancellor of that system, which consists of 29 state-operated institutions, 30 community colleges, and the "contract colleges" of the private universities of Cornell and Alfred. In almost every one of those 15 years (and frequently more than once in a single fiscal year), I and my administrative team have had to cut faculty, staff, and operating expenses (on more than one occasion extending to the removal of tenured faculty), totaling approximately 20 percent of the full-time faculty and staff of the state-operated system (Johnstone 1992).

2. We have so little useful data on the underlying production costs of college not because we lack either institutional or aggregate cost data, but because the production costs of undergraduate instruction are deeply embedded within the costs of graduate and advanced professional education, research, and community service. Furthermore, production costs include indirect administrative and support costs—not to mention the much more complicated cost of capital and debt service—that must be allocated according to some simplifying, but not always edifying, assumptions. Depending on the assumptions and accounting conventions used, the costs attributable to undergraduate instruction can be made to seem higher or lower (Jones 1999). The National Association of College and University Business Officers has an ambitious project to develop a uniform methodology for the reporting of costs, prices, and subsidies. The [University of] Delaware Study of Instructional Costs and Productivity is compiling research university unit cost data (see Middaugh 1998, 1999).

3. That these middle-class tax breaks probably do little to alter the actual savings behavior of parents and more importantly may do little or nothing to alter the enrollment behavior of students has been pointed out by critics of these plans (among whom I count myself). Our greatest concern is not that prepaid tuition or college savings plans are bad or even that they are largely ineffective but that governors and legislators are being allowed to "walk away" believing that they have solved a problem, while nothing has been done either for the genuinely poor (who are effectively excluded from these middle-class plans) or to affect the underlying costs of instruction (Hauptman and Rice 1997; Roth 1999).

4. The cost-effectiveness of student loans is an exceedingly complex mat-

ter to determine. In the first place, a student loan is actually a mixture of a student- or parent-borne expense (the present discounted value of the amount actually repaid) and an effective grant, represented by the present value of the stream of public subsidies, including the in-school interest subsidy, any interest subsidy at the repayment stage, and the implicit subsidy of the guarantee, which allows a far lower rate of interest than would be possible for unsecured student borrowing generally. Depending on the interest rate, the actual value of money (i.e., the appropriate discount rate), the in-school grace period, losses through default, and the true administrative and servicing costs, student loans can be a great deal less expensive to the taxpayer than an equivalent amount of outright grants, only minimally less expensive, or any point in between.

5. Other countries (e.g., Italy) also have prolonged times-to-degree and high rates of noncompletion. However, the culprit in these countries is almost certainly the form of instruction, or the virtual absence of attention to pedagogy or learning, rather than to the number of entering students or their lack of preparedness.

References

American Council on Education (ACE). 1998. *Research on public perceptions of college costs and student aid.* Washington, D.C.: ACE.

Anxiety over tuition: A controversy in context. 1997. *Chronicle of Higher Education Special Report,* 30 May, A10–19.

Bowen, H. R. 1980. *The costs of higher education: How much do colleges and universities spend per student, and how much should they spend?* San Francisco: Jossey-Bass.

———. 1981. Cost differences: The amazing disparity among institutions of higher education in education costs per student. *Change* January–February: 21–27.

Brinkman, P. T. 1989. Instructional costs per student credit hour: Differences by level of instruction. *Journal of Education Finance* 15 (summer 1989): 34–52.

Clotfelter, C. 1996. *Buying the best: Cost escalation in elite higher education.* Princeton: Princeton University Press.

College Board. 1999a. *Trends in college pricing.* Washington, D.C.: College Board.

———. 1999b. *Trends in student aid.* Washington, D.C.: College Board.

Davis, J. 1997. *College affordability: A closer look at the crisis.* Washington, D.C.: Sally Mae Education Institute.

Footlick, J. K. 1998. The holy cow! story: How the news media cover college costs. *Presidency* 1, no. 1 (spring 1998): 29–33.

Fossey, R. 1998. Condemning students to debt: Is the college loan program out of control? *Phi Delta Kappan* 80 (December): 319–21.

Gose, B., and M. Geraghty. 1997. Comparisons of tuition rates raise tough policy questions. *Chronicle of Higher Education,* 30 May: A15.

Gumport, P. J., and B. Pusser. 1995. A case of bureaucratic accretion: Context and consequences. *Journal of Higher Education,* 66, no. 5: 493–520.

Hartle, T. W. 1998. Clueless about college costs. *Presidency* 1, no. 1 (spring): 20–26.

Hauptman, A. M., and L. Rice. 1997. Coordinating financial aid with tuition tax benefits. *Brookings: Common and uncommon sense from the Brookings Institution,* no. 28 (December).

Heller, D. E. 1997. Student price response in higher education: An update to Leslie and Brinkman. *Journal of Higher Education,* 68, no. 6: 624–59.

———. 1999. The effects of tuition and state financial aid on public college enrollment. *Review of Higher Education* 23, no.1: 65–89.

Ikenberry, S. O., and T. W. Hartle. 1998. *Too little knowledge is a dangerous thing: What the public thinks and knows about paying for college.* Washington, D.C.: American Council on Education.

Institute for Higher Education Policy. 1999. *The tuition puzzle: Putting the pieces together.* Report prepared for the New Millennium Project on Higher Education Costs, Pricing, and Productivity. Washington, D.C.: Institute for Higher Education Policy.

Johnstone, D. B. 1991. Productivity and cost containment: The challenge of public sector budgeting. *Policy Perspectives* 3, no. 2 (February): 22B–23B.

———. 1992. *Working Papers in a Time of Fiscal Crisis.* Albany: State University of New York, Office of the Chancellor.

———. 1993. *Learning productivity: A new imperative for American higher education.* Albany: State University of New York, Office of the Chancellor.

———. 1998. Patterns of finance: Revolution, evolution, or more of the same? *Review of Higher Education* 21, no. 3: 245–55.

———. 1999a. Financing higher education: Who should pay? In *American higher education in the twenty-first century: Social, political, and economic challenges,* edited by P. G. Altbach, R. O. Berdahl, and P. J. Gumport. Baltimore: Johns Hopkins University Press.

———. 1999b. *The high tuition–high aid model of public higher education finance: The case against.* Albany: National Association of System Heads, Office of the SUNY Chancellor.

Jones, D. 1999. *An alternative look at the cost question.* Boulder, Colo.: National Center for Higher Education Management Systems.

Kane, T. 1995. *Rising public college tuition and college entry: How well do public subsidies promote access to college?* Cambridge, Mass.: National Bureau of Economic Research.

Leslie, L. L., and P. Brinkman. 1989. *The economic value of higher educa-tion.* New York: Macmillan.

Leslie, L. L., and G. G. Rhoades. 1995. Rising administrative costs: Seeking explanations. *Journal of Higher Education* 66, no 2: 187–212.

Massy, W. K. 1991. Improving academic productivity: The next frontier. *Capital Ideas* 6, no. 2.

———. 1996. *Resource allocation in higher education.* Ann Arbor: University of Michigan Press.

Massy, W. F., and A. K. Wilger. 1995. Improving productivity: What faculty think about it—and its effect on quality. *Change,* July–August: 10–20.

McPherson, M., and M. Schapiro. 1998. *The student aid game.* Princeton: Princeton University Press.

Middaugh, M. F. 1998. How much do faculty really teach? *Planning for Higher Education* 27, no. 2 (winter): 1–11.

———. 1999. Instructional productivity of systems. In *The multicampus sys-tem: Perspectives on practice and prospects,* edited by Gerald Gaither. Sterling, Va.: Stylus.

National Center for Education Statistics. 1997. *Digest of education statistics.* Washington, D.C.: U.S. Government Printing Office.

———. 1999. *The condition of education 1999.* Washington, D.C.: U.S. Gov-ernment Printing Office. <http://nces.ed.gov>

National Commission on the Cost of Higher Education. 1998. *Straight talk about college costs and prices.* Phoenix: American Council on Education and Oryx Press.

Olson, J. E. 1997. The cost-effectiveness of American higher education: The United States can afford its colleges and universities. In *Higher educa-tion: Handbook on theory and research,* vol. 7, edited by John C. Smart. New York: Agatha Press.

Roth, A. 1999. State-sponsored, tax-advantaged college savings plans: A study of their impact on contemporary understanding of the public-ver-sus-private responsibility to pay for higher education issue. Ph.D. diss., University at Buffalo, Buffalo, New York.

Stringer, W. L., and A. F. Cunningham. 1999. *Cost, price and public policy: Peering into the higher education black box.* Indianapolis: USA Group Foundation.

Twigg, C. 1999. Improving learning and reducing costs: Redesigning large-enrollment courses. Troy, N.Y.: Rensselaer Polytechnic Institute, Center for Academic Transformation.

U.S. Congressional Budget Office. 1991. *Student aid and the cost of postsec-ondary education.* Washington, D.C.: Government Printing Office.

U.S. General Accounting Office. 1998. *Higher education: Tuition increases and colleges' efforts to contain costs.* GAO/HEHS-98–227. Washington, D.C.: Government Printing Office.

Winston, G. C. 1998a. College costs: Subsidies, intuition, and policy. In *Straight talk about college costs and prices,* edited by the National Commission on the Cost of Higher Education. Phoenix: American Council on Education and Oryx Press, 117–27.

————. 1998b. *A guide to measuring college costs.* Discussion Paper no. 46, *Williams project on the economics of higher education.* Williams College, January.

————. 1999. Subsidies, hierarchy, and peers: The awkward economics of higher education. *Journal of Economic Perspectives* 13, no. 1 (winter): 13–36.

Zemsky, R. et al. 1999. *Market, price, and margin: Determining the cost of an undergraduate education.* Philadelphia: Institute for Research on Higher Education, University of Pennsylvania.

Part Two ～

Within the Academy

Chapter Seven ～

The Liberal Arts
and the Role of Elite
Higher Education

Nannerl O. Keohane

This is not the first period in history when large-scale technological and social change has transformed higher education. The campus as we know it is the multilayered result of many such changes over the decades—in governance, curriculum, and student access. Yet through all these transformations, some version of the traditional liberal arts preparation for the baccalaureate degree has survived. Today some observers fear, and others hope, that liberal education has finally become obsolete.

We live in what pundits call a "knowledge society," in which mastery of certain kinds of information is essential to success. As a result, nontraditional knowledge purveyors are springing into action everywhere—corporations training workers, for-profit "universities," new high-tech companies marketing degrees. In every part of our lives, sophisticated technologies offer exotic new ways of conveying information, and theoretically provide almost unlimited access to it.

In such a world, what is the place of a traditional liberal arts education? At least for the moment, we are helped by evidence that higher education brings quite tangible benefits in earnings over time (Clotfelter 1999). The first step in the process is the baccalaureate degree. Prestigious institutions that confer this degree in the humanities and sciences are highly competitive. Students may seek these degrees more for their networking benefits or the power of the "brand name" than for the kind of education offered. But consumer preferences rooted in such factors tend to have a long life.

Thus young people who want to hold power, make money, or make a difference in the world still flock to such colleges and universities. Another way to describe the aspirations of these students is to say that they wish (or their parents wish them) to become, or remain, members of the "elite." An ambivalence in the meaning of this word works to the benefit of selective colleges and universities. We describe these institutions as elite because they choose their students carefully from a much larger pool of applicants and offer an expensive education by the most distinguished faculty members they can attract. Because their graduates, even if not born to wealth and privilege, are disproportionately represented in privileged and powerful positions in society, these institutions are also associated with the concept of the elite in a socioeconomic sense.

This conjunction poses some tricky issues in our society: "elitism" is often regarded as inherently undemocratic, perpetuating historical inequities. But the benefits of spending four years in these highly specialized settings at a formative time in life, with talented peers and magnificent resources for learning, are quite significant. Our job is to make sure that these institutions are truly open to bright students of all socioeconomic backgrounds and that we provide them with the very best liberal arts education we can devise for the world they will go on to lead.

How Do We Defend the Liberal Arts Today?

Familiar defenses of liberal education offer a beautiful ideal, playing on the multiple meanings and linguistic roots of the key word *liberal*. This form of education was first designed in classical times for free persons, rather than slaves or metics. It also frees the mind, offering personal liberation from ignorance and constraint. In a recent essay, William Cronon traces the meaning of *liberal arts* beyond the root Latin *liber*, providing affinities with Old English *leodan*, 'to grow,' and *leod*, 'people,' as well as the Greek *eleutheros* and Sanskrit *rodhati*, 'one climbs,' 'one grows.' As Cronon summarizes this ideal, "Liberal education is built on these values: It aspires to nurture the growth of human talent in the service of human freedom" (Cronon 1999).

These aspirations of a liberal arts education overlap with some of the goals of contemporary culture. Self-development is an attractive concept for many people. But neither peace of mind nor social success is guaranteed by the baccalaureate degree. Many paths promoted on TV, or in the kinds of seven-step handbooks available in airport bookshops, promise a much more direct way of reaching such goals. It is hard to explain to our contemporaries, raised in a society of sound bites and instant gratification, how the oblique routes taken by the liberal arts through arcane and apparently useless forms of knowledge lead to many different worthwhile destinations (Graber 1995).

Justifications of the liberal arts usually focus on skills or competencies, the basic habits of mind and spirit instilled by such an education. The ability to read, write, and converse with supple ease and interest; a familiarity with human history and diverse cultures; some understanding of the scientific method; and appreciation of art, quantitative reasoning, critical thinking—these are the markers we use in describing what we aim to do.

All these claims, I believe, are sound; but how do we accomplish these goals? The next few pages spell out some key assumptions that lie behind justifications of liberal education and its distinctive character.

The Value of Discipline

A liberal education achieves its goals first by training the mind in a disciplined way, as one trains the body in physical fitness to improve health and prolong life. Learning Greek verbs is an especially dry example of such exercise, like performing a certain number of push-ups every day. The liberal concept of a discipline is broader and more expansive, more akin to a life regimen.

Undergraduate students are typically exposed to a wide range of subjects in their early college years. This gives them some conception of the foundations and forms of knowledge available to them. Then we require them to choose an area of concentration, a major subject, believing that the organized pursuit of knowledge brings special benefits. This approach differs from that of the dilettante by positing intriguing relationships among the different parts of a particular form of human understanding and demonstrating confidence that pursuing these relationships with sustained persistence bears its own fruit.

For the student who does not intend to pursue the major subject in greater depth through graduate education, this discipline becomes an end in itself. It turns out not to matter a great deal, from the point of view of intellectual growth and later benefits, which discipline is chosen. The acquisition of the habit of mental discipline includes learning how to pursue different parts of a complex subject, to impose the right kinds of questions on unfamiliar material in order to find the key to understanding. This is a large part of what we mean when we say that liberal education teaches people how to learn rather than to master a technical skill that may someday become obsolete.

Some of the same benefits in mental acuity can, of course, be gained by mastering a technical skill. In the case of liberal education, however, the mental discipline itself is the basic point, rather than the content of what is learned. If undergraduates choose to concentrate in an interdisciplinary program, or design their own majors, they cannot simply be a potpourri of whatever happens to interest the student at the time. We insist that there be a clearly structured path through the material that brings the same benefits of mental discipline as traditional majors. Programs that fail to honor this requirement have become something else—a Chatauqua, or an intellectual cruise ship menu, but not a liberal education.

The Delights of Exploration

A second tactic employed in liberal education is wide-ranging intellectual exploration. This open-ended quality might seem to be the opposite of the requirement for mental discipline; but experience has shown that these two facets fit together with exceptional facility and reinforce each other.

One of the mechanisms for encouraging exploration is the distribution requirement. Undergraduates in most institutions must become minimally familiar with several different types of knowledge. Fascinated (or discomfited) by the large number of courses offered for a baccalaureate degree, students are guided not only by the requirement that they choose a major subject, but also that they obtain some familiarity with each of the basic areas of knowledge. This encourages suppleness of mind and lays the groundwork for future exploration of different aspects of the world.

Furthermore, some of the most formative moments in a liberal education occur outside the classroom. A campus (especially a residential campus) provides multiple encounters with other students and faculty members in extracurricular activities, sports, and volunteer service. Bringing together seekers of knowledge across the generations, the campus is a uniquely powerful setting for such structured yet serendipitous exploration—a "free and ordered space," in Bart Giamatti's felicitous phrase (1988).

This kind of exploration is especially useful in educating citizens (Barber 1992). Members of large, complex modern communities who understand something about science, technology, culture, human nature, and politics will be better prepared to make well-informed decisions about what kinds of policies, or political leaders, deserve support. They will be more cautious about accepting bold claims that turn out to be false, less subject to manipulation by those claiming superior knowledge.

Equally important, a taste for intellectual exploration and the acquisition of skills that enable one to indulge that taste are important keys to personal satisfaction. The person who is encouraged to be curious and knows how to satisfy curiosity is a more interesting friend or colleague and more comfortably at home in solitude. Mental resources that enrich leisure time, direct travel plans, and widen one's personal horizons, are of great value throughout life.

One of the best descriptions of this benefit of a liberal education comes in Montaigne's *Essays*. Montaigne's favorite place to write was the tower library on his estate with a view of the vineyards and grain fields, a ceiling carved with some of his favorite quotations, and lines of books around the shelves. He hit upon a lovely image to describe the connection between his omnivorous reading, reflection, and writing and the place where he did these things with such pleasure: the image of the "back room of the mind." He thought of his own mind as a kind of tower library to which he could retreat even when he was far from home, a place filled with quotations from wise people, experimental thoughts, jokes, and anecdotes, where he could keep company with himself (Montaigne 1958, 39).

Montaigne suggested that we all have such back rooms in our minds and that the most valuable and attractive people have rich and fascinating intellectual furniture rather than a void between their ears. I often tell students that a liberal education furnishes that space and ask them to notice how the most interesting people, the people they really like spending time with, have well-furnished mental back rooms.

The Ideal of a Common Language

One of the traditional justifications for a liberal education has been that the leaders of a society should have some common reference points. Shared familiarity with certain works of art, literature, and music to which allusions could be made provided a kind of elegant shorthand within which arguments and claims could be couched without having to spell out the layers of meaning and implication in every new idea. Acquisition of such a common language was the primary form of upward mobility for members of the lower classes in many stratified societies. By learning the symbols used by the elite, the young person could emulate them and thus, by assimilation, join them.

At a time when knowledge has burgeoned so greatly that various curricula provide quite different approaches to the common goal of a liberal education, it is hard to assume that graduates will all have read even a small number of generally acknowledged classics. Nonetheless, some kind of familiarity with the major cultural accomplishments of the Western world (and increasingly of other cultures as well) and the basic frameworks of the natural sciences and mathematics still provide a rudimentary common language for leaders these days.

This ideal has yielded some interesting permutations in the increasingly pluralistic society of the United States, where people of many different backgrounds, cultures, languages, and beliefs aspire to leadership. Many faculty members today stress multicultural understanding while retaining the ideal of a shared, structured curriculum. Their goal is a curriculum that does justice to the core of the liberal arts developed in the West and also to the contributions of other cultures to human understanding and enrichment.

When such a complex combination is successful, students from many backgrounds can recognize themselves in the curriculum. As a result, they are more motivated to participate in this educational experience. Future leaders learn some valuable lessons about the cultural expectations and accomplishments of the diverse people with whom they will work. This creates considerable pressure on curricular choice and internal coherence; it also provides the stimulus for some very interesting juxtapositions of knowledge. Fortunately, the faculties of many institutions have designed rigorous yet flexible curricular structures that incorporate nontraditional as well as classical kinds of knowledge.

A common language derived from a similar education, even in such an attenuated form, is a valuable asset in an increasingly global world. Corporate, nonprofit, and governmental leaders increasingly have no choice but to engage in multinational cooperative endeavors. They readily appreciate the value of some common reference points. Congruent goals—in business or elsewhere—smooth the way, but things are made much easier where the informal context of conversations includes some shared signposts of experience and understanding.

Thus, paradoxically, this third feature of a liberal education has become even more important in a period of growing international contacts and rapid social and technological change. Common reference points make it easier to work past the inevitable misunderstandings that arise from differing cultural expectations, the nuances of different languages, and the implications of different historical experiences.

The Value of Values

One further practice in the traditional liberal arts education that has been regarded with some suspicion over the past few decades is reemerging as a significant asset: training students to think carefully about values in human life. This goal is rooted in the conviction that both the individual and society are better off if people are trained to consider critically the consequences of their behavior for themselves and others.

In the past, a liberal education was openly and specifically value-oriented, proposing to make students more virtuous human beings. Such claims can seem quaintly irrelevant or even dangerous today. We are acutely aware of the pitfalls of narrow sectarianism, the contradictory teachings of different ethical and religious systems, and the huge divergence in human cultural practices. Faced with the consciousness of such diversity, the most prudent course may seem to be to avoid any claims about teaching ethics or building character in the classroom.

Thoughtful observers, however, are concerned about several features of modern society that stem from a breakdown of ethical awareness. The erosion of the standards of civility that ease human interaction, the rising tolerance for cruelty and violence, the increasing incidence of cheating and fraud: these are all disturbing aspects of our world today. To reverse such tendencies, there is renewed emphasis on character-building or civics education in primary and secondary schools, and a well-defined movement toward teaching ethics in professional-school curricula. Given the ancient connection between a liberal education and developing character, it seems especially shortsighted to ignore the place of education in ethics during the undergraduate years. Thus, many campuses are developing education in ethics as part of the liberal arts experience (Shapiro 1999).

In its modern guise, teaching ethics does not mean imposing particular creeds or theological systems. Instead, students are taught to think clearly about ethical dilemmas just as they learn to reason more carefully in other areas. Students draw upon texts and historical models as well as extracurricular experiences that stimulate and focus such thinking and apply these lessons in their own lives. They are encouraged to think about what they value and admire in others and aspire to become themselves. The goal is to help students of many different religious and moral beliefs live a more ethically informed and sensitive life.

An excellent example of such moral education is the Kenan Ethics Program at Duke University. This program provides support for developing courses in ethics across the curriculum, beginning with the first-year writing program. It also gives students many opportunities to connect their formal learning with morally relevant experiences such as community service. The dual goals of the Kenan Program are to ensure that students engaged in community activities will be more likely to pause and reflect on the implications of what they are doing and that those who are pondering moral issues in the classroom will be more likely to seek ways to put their learning into practice.

There are interesting links between this form of education and the roots and character of the liberal arts. Moral education stems from the same core axioms as liberal, moral, and social philosophy: the value of the examined life, the basic equality of members of the human species, and the ideals of individual freedom and self-control. Yet the impulse to provide ethical education derives also from themes closely identified with conservatism in our culture: respect for tradition, the concept of honor, and awareness of the fragile complexity of institutions and of the impulses toward destructive cruelty that can mar even the most beautiful human moral and religious systems.

What Kind of an Elite?

The four themes sketched out above do not cover the entire range of accomplishments of a liberal education; they do, I think, provide a good sense of the basic assumptions that lie behind this form of education and some idea of the keys to its success.

What about the audience for whom this kind of education has traditionally been intended—the children (most often, in the past, the young men) of the privileged classes, preparing to take their places in the leadership of a society, as clerics, warriors, barons, professors, artists, senators, doctors, lawyers, corporate CEOs? How do we square this aspect of a liberal education with our contemporary beliefs in equality and advancement by personal merit rather than the accidents of birth?

One familiar way of dealing with this quandary is to explore the two different facets of the word *elite* I alluded to earlier. In one sense, *elite* refers to those who are privileged by class or caste. In many societies, these privileged persons are expected and given the opportunity to govern, guide, or manage others. Another meaning of *elite* embraces what Thomas Jefferson called the "aristocracy of talent," the naturally gifted of whatever social background who have the personal qualities to excel in their professions and lead other people. These are the students elite institutions have attempted to enroll in recent decades.

American society, like most societies these days, has mingled these two concepts in an uncertain brew. By precept (and sometimes fortunately in practice as well), we provide higher education for all who can benefit from it, without regard for family background or privileged access to resources. Yet a young person from a privileged background is clearly more likely to enroll in a school that offers a liberal education. Others may have formal access to such an education, but the access may be (or seem to be) more difficult. There are many reasons for this: the cost of the education; earnings foregone while getting it; lack of information about available scholarship and admissions opportunities; the absence of appreciation of and, thus, support for this kind of education in the family or social group; and uncertainty about what such an education involves and whether the student will fit in.

This gap between our goals and our situation raises several troubling questions about elitism in our society. We need to face these questions directly and honestly if we are to understand, articulate, and carry forward our educational mission. Our colleges and universities, supported by our federal and state governments, have for many decades attempted to bridge the gap between precept and practice (McPherson and Schapiro 1998). This was done by providing generous financial aid for talented students of all backgrounds and attempting to share information about these opportunities widely. There are signs that this commitment may be crumbling, both on campus and in government, as financial aid practices, attitudes toward affirmative action, and tax policies are changing. Given the consumerist mentality of parents and students and the benefits that accrue to an institution from recruiting talented students, financial competition among schools for the "best" students has sharpened markedly. A sense of entitlement appears to be growing up among some talented students from well-to-do families: they feel that they should be given "merit" aid to demonstrate that the college or university really values them and wants them to attend. In such a climate, the pressure to use financial aid funds to attract students from more affluent backgrounds has become significant.

Except in a handful of the very wealthiest schools, this brings about a reallocation of scarce funds from disadvantaged students to those with more conventionally attractive admissions credentials. In both federal and state government, pressures from vocal middle-class families worried about the price of education and shifts in ideology that undermine the principle of government support for an education accessible to all, have had a similar effect. The largest single form of federally supported financial aid is no longer allocated to those most in need, but rather, through recent changes in tax laws, to those who vote most consistently—the middle and upper-middle class.

If these factors are not addressed, we will see the reversal of a direction that has lasted for more than a century: the opening of selective colleges and universities to more and more gifted and ambitious students of varied backgrounds. The result will be the recreation of enclaves of the privileged, offering the benefits of a liberal education, while those from less privileged socioeconomic classes obtain their education in less desirable circumstances and with fewer opportunities. This should cause concern to anyone who worries about the increasing tendency toward a winner-take-all society in which those who have inexorably get more and those who don't fall further behind (Frank and Cook 1995). More fundamentally, this trend should worry everyone who is committed to the ideal of a liberal education for all talented young people prepared to embark upon such a course and to educate one another in doing so.

Who Benefits from a Liberal Education?

Commitment to equality of access for talented students does not mean that everybody ought to be given a liberal arts education. This raises another issue that needs to be faced directly in defenses of this kind: who should get such an education?

Statements about the worth of a liberal education make clear that this experience is valuable in fundamental ways. These have to do with the kind of person one becomes, the richness and satisfaction of life, and the ability to contribute meaningfully to one's community. Of my four key assumptions, only one—the third—has anything to do with a specific group or class of leaders. All the others touch on aspects of a full human life that are relevant for everyone, not just those who will occupy positions of power or special responsibility. If we can make the case for the fundamental value of a liberal education in personal growth and fulfillment, how can we justify only a small percentage of students having the benefit of this experience?

The only way to justify this situation in our democratic society is to admit that the kind of intellectual talent that enables students to benefit from a liberal arts education, like all other forms of talent, is not evenly distributed across any population. A liberal education works best—in fact, it truly *only* works—for students who have qualities of mental acuity, curiosity, and intellectual stamina that prepare them for such a demanding regime. For those who possess this particular form of talent, a liberal education is, for the reasons I've sketched out, a wonderful preparation for life. For those who do not, other kinds of education, personal experience, and community involvement can lay the groundwork for a satisfying life. Our task as a society should not be to try to route everyone through the same kind of education. Instead, we should think creatively about different educations and life experiences that lead to fulfillment for people with varied talents and capacities so that each individual can have a shot at living life to the fullest. This means recognizing that a liberal education is one way, but not the only way, to prepare people for a rewarding life.

Intellectual quickness, in the form of the ability to understand complex issues and find solutions, is an essential attribute of leadership in several areas of human life. Thus it should not be surprising that there is a positive correlation between those who benefit from a liberal education and those who tend to wind up in positions of leadership. Our most pressing task is to make sure that all those in our democratic society who possess this quickness, and the aspiration for leadership, are given the best education possible. Family circumstance alone should not determine who gets such opportunities. There are many entrenched barriers to the realization of this goal, including very unequal preparations in primary and secondary school and unequal forms of family and community support and encouragement. But such barriers should not deter us from doing our best to identify talented young people early in their lives and give them the tools and encouragement they need to prepare for a liberal education.

It is important also to be clear that these generalizations hold for people of *all* backgrounds, including members of racial minorities. *The Shape of the River* (Bok and Bowen 1998) provides compelling evidence that, measured by their long-term success in life and ability to provide significant leadership for their communities, students from minority backgrounds, including both those from disadvantaged and more privileged families, benefit greatly from study in selective colleges and universities. We must make sure that we are truly educating leaders for all kinds of professions and all parts of our increasingly pluralistic society.

How Well Do We Live Up to Our Claims?

Some contemporary critiques of colleges and universities recognize the value of what we claim to do but fault us for falling down on the job in any one of a number of ways. These critiques take several forms. I have addressed, at least in passing, a couple of them above: that we have diluted the traditional liberal arts curriculum beyond recognition by pandering to new groups and forms of knowledge or that we have deformed our admissions standards in order to offer a liberal arts education to people with nontraditional preparations and of many different backgrounds. Although we have not addressed these issues with complete success, I am confident that we are on the right track.

Another concern of the gloomsters comes closer to hitting its target, in my view: that we do not often enough provide our students with the exhilarating educational experience promised by our ideals and our promotional brochures. To live up to what we promise requires close attention to the educational needs of all our students— their diverse backgrounds, personal experiences, degrees of preparation and readiness. It also requires that we put undergraduate teaching high on the priority list for support in institutions that, increasingly, have multiple purposes and opportunities.

Selective liberal arts colleges today, as a group, do an especially good job of emphasizing teaching while not neglecting the importance of faculty research (Astin 1999). Research universities provide a stellar alternative model. They offer students access to a broader range of courses and interdisciplinary programs and to potential involvement in truly cutting-edge research in many more fields than smaller institutions can provide—even smaller institutions of very high quality. However, because of the range of other activities and responsibilities in these larger institutions—professional education, graduate training, large medical complexes, distance learning, agricultural or technical research, government consulting—it is easy for the devotion to baccalaureate education to be diminished or submerged. Indeed, even liberal arts colleges are not immune to such cross-pressures.

Sustaining our ability to offer an excellent liberal arts education while fulfilling all our multiple missions requires an imaginative, multifaceted strategy and the institutional will to pursue such a strategy (Rhodes 1994). We must think in new ways about the activity of teaching, the interconnections between teaching and research, the value of information technology, the role of graduate students, and our expectations of both partners in the close student-faculty engagement we call a liberal arts education.

What Matters to the Faculty?

According to our critics, the key to our problem lies here: most professors at a modern research university teach infrequently and ineffectively, spending their time in esoteric research of dubious social value to impress their professional peers and carve out an easy sinecure for life. What really motivates faculty members? Most young professionals who choose to become faculty members in a school of arts and sciences assume that they will teach undergraduates, and many look forward eagerly to doing so. They have recent experience of great teachers with passion and charisma, teachers who inspired their own vocation. They also recall dull or distant teachers and are convinced that they would never inflict such poor teaching on their own students.

Over time, this fresh eagerness is dissipated by the realities of professional life. Faculty members at a research university are expected to engage in many different types of work—teaching undergraduates, supervising graduate students, research, service to the discipline, consulting, service to the university—as well as juggle family and personal responsibilities. In stark contrast to the stereotype of the "lazy professor," many, perhaps most, faculty members work intensively, for long hours. Overwork is only part of the problem. Teachers are also subject to "burnout" over time, unless they can refresh their skills and reignite their excitement in the classroom. As more undergraduates come to college deficient in basic skills, teaching introductory material can be especially onerous. It is easy to become jaded with entering the mind of the uninitiated in order to bring yet another generation up to speed in the rudiments of the discipline.

For all these reasons, hours spent teaching tend to become fewer, rather than more, as faculty members develop other professional skills and find it rewarding to exercise them. My generalization holds not only for indifferent teachers but even for professors with well-developed skills who enjoy their students. The linguistic conventions that refer to teaching *loads* and research *opportunities;* to the effectiveness of promising a very light course load when wooing a faculty superstar to another university; and the appeal of time released from teaching as a reward for service on campus—all these factors demonstrate this consistent preference.

Yet most scholars continue to prefer the university campus with its multigenerational set of scholars to the rarified atmosphere of a research institute, except for the occasional sabbatical. The urge to share one's knowledge with others, to lead others along the path of discovery in one's discipline, continues to be one of the major motivations for the life of scholarship for mature as well as younger professors. So why is research, especially, preferred to teaching as an intellectual pursuit?

Part of the answer lies in the incentive structure for faculty members. Research universities—and increasingly, other types of institutions—rely heavily on research productivity in making decisions about which faculty members to employ on a long-term basis. It is easier for administrators to obtain "objective" estimates of successful research than successful teaching, at least by the metrics we conventionally employ. Asking other professionals to judge their peers' research provides the most clear-cut way of deciding which professors are likely to continue to be productive, highly regarded members of the faculty.

Successful research is the best single indicator of that elusive trait we call "quality of mind," the intellectual sharpness and vigor that we want to ensure in our faculties. If professional peers find work provocative and relevant, this is our best indication that faculty members will teach their students material that is fresh, challenging, and well-grounded, rather than reading from yellowing lecture notes designed to play well to an undergraduate audience. Research success also transfers easily from one institution to another and thus makes a faculty member potentially more marketable. This has obvious implications for salary and status differentials.

Our conventional assessment structures thus provide powerful incentives for ambitious faculty members to concentrate on research. But it would be wrong to assume that such incentives are the only factor. The joys of pure research are great, and the fruits of successful intellectual endeavors are profoundly rewarding both personally and to one's students and colleagues. For many faculty members, nothing is more exhilarating than a discovery that works out as the researcher passionately believed it would. In many more cases than the public usually recognizes, research results are also important to society as a whole. Even apparent candidates for the infamous Golden Fleece Award can be unexpectedly fruitful in helping us to understand ourselves and the world. The structure of ancient, "dead," languages can form the basis of our most sophisticated computer languages today.

However, teaching can also be a deeply rewarding activity. A brilliantly successful lecture or seminar can be as exhilarating as any other experience in life. Indeed, unless a faculty member is one of a handful of truly outstanding scholars in his or her field, teaching is often more likely to be rewarding than research, since path-breaking research findings are less likely to be part of one's daily fare. Because our systems for professional assessment and establishing salary and other forms of institutional support as well as our professional status systems are so intricately bound up with research success, however, it is difficult for a professor who cares deeply about teaching to sustain this passion in the face of multiple institutional messages that research is more valued. If research universities are to be successful in sustaining a strong liberal arts education as part of their mission, they will have to change this. Teaching must be deeply valued, and our incentive and reward structures must reflect this evaluation.

Rethinking the Incentive Structure

All faculty members at elite research universities and liberal arts colleges should be expected to demonstrate their ability to do research and to remain current in their fields. But every faculty member should not be judged simply by the standards of the most productive researchers, as though research were the only thing that mattered in the university. Faculty members and administrators need to work together to find more reliable ways to measure excellence in teaching and then provide significant rewards to professionals who teach well. Both institutional recognition and generous salary increases should be realistic goals for fine teachers, not only for scholars with strong name recognition on other campuses.

One of the most notable features on campus these days is the changing composition of the professoriate. Fewer scholars are hired for conventional tenure-track posts; more are employed in part-time or full-time contract work, with an emphasis on teaching. Research expectations for such faculty members are much less than for tenure-track professors, and it is important that they feel valued by their institutions and be motivated to teach well. This is another reason for making sure that we reward fine teaching and demonstrate that we esteem those who excel in this craft. The issue is one of reallocating limited institutional resources. It would be unrealistic to expect that salary competition and demand for the faculty members most productive in their research will dramatically diminish, but we can bend our efforts toward cutting back on other institutional expenditures to free up money to support good teaching.

A professor invited to join the faculty of arts and sciences in an institution that aspires to offer a fine liberal arts education should expect to engage in undergraduate teaching. The alternative—a two-tiered faculty with one part concentrating solely on research and graduate education and the other on undergraduate teaching—may have been successful in certain institutions in the past. But the costs in morale can be significant, with damaging results for the enterprise of undergraduate education. The graduate faculty risk losing the intellectual energy and zest that comes from involvement with bright undergraduates, as well.

In any case, a significant portion of the budget of the arts and sciences division of any modern college or university is provided by tuition-paying parents of undergraduates or by state funding provided specifically to make such an education possible. This makes it imperative for us to involve some of the energies of virtually all faculty members in the endeavor of providing high-quality teaching as one of the obligations of their employment. To do so successfully, we need to find ways to sustain the love of teaching in young faculty members even as they encounter significant incentives to engage in other activities.

Rethinking the Teacher's Craft

Teaching and research are, ideally, deeply symbiotic. Helping students understand the process of discovery and engaging them in some form of independent inquiry should be one of the basic goals of a liberal arts education. At the same time, sharing knowledge and learning from the questions and insights of students can jolt a teacher's stagnant preconceptions and suggest whole new ways of looking at the world. This, at least, is the ideal. In reality, of course, neither teaching nor research is always exhilarating. Both pursuits involve repetitive work that is not inherently rewarding. Few teachers look forward to grading, but then neither do we enjoy writing yet another peer review of a badly written research paper for potential publication. Like every profession, scholarship involves both routine work and intellectual excitement. It is important to find ways to keep the routine to a minimum and introduce new sources of intellectual excitement.

Preeminent among these sources should be the new instructional technologies. It is true that cyberspace can never match the unique advantages of the physical place where students live and learn together, with multiple opportunities for education both inside and outside the classroom. And the personal interaction between teacher and student will always remain central to the particular qualities of liberal learning. But the amplification of new, exciting ways of conveying and sharing knowledge can be one of the most important ways of preserving the excitement of teaching for faculty members and of involving students deeply in their own education. Rather than seeing such technologies as a threat to the liberal arts, we should take full advantage of their radical possibilities.

Well-designed computer programs are effective substitutes for routine drills in language instruction and can provide introductory materials in a variety of disciplines. At the other end of the spectrum of learning, computer assistance in doing independent study can facilitate student and faculty research. Mid- or upper-level courses can be enlivened with clever exercises and simulations, increasingly available in every discipline. In certain fields, programs for grading quizzes on basic material are available and will surely become even more sophisticated. Communication among students and between students and faculty members is enhanced by the use of electronic mail, chat rooms, syllabi and question sets posted on the web, and numerous other electronic aids. With appropriate incentives and support, faculty members can find exciting new ways of conceptualizing material to be shared in class.

These ways of rethinking the teacher's craft promise also to make better use of faculty time with students. The lecture format works well for faculty members who are gifted in presentation and skilled at involving even large classes in substantive classroom discussion. For many faculty members, however, there are better ways to spend teaching time. As more material is shared through innovative computer programs and less in the conventional lecture format, more time is available for seminars, discussion sections, one-on-one research projects, small group tutorials, and other forms of close interaction that clearly bring benefits to student learning.

Supporting faculty members who want to think freshly about familiar material through team teaching with a colleague from another discipline; rotating courses so that no faculty member is permanently "stuck" with an undesirable assignment; encouraging faculty members who are talented teachers to provide guidance to colleagues in settings where such guidance is not directly tied to the assessment process—all these and many other ways of helping teachers rethink their craft should be developed on every campus, and the best practices should be shared with colleagues elsewhere.

Faculty members should also think in fresh ways about the role of graduate teaching assistants. Too often, TAs are assigned the routine tasks of teaching, those associated with the mundane drudgery of the craft. As a result, they have a hard time getting excited about teaching or learning much about its splendid opportunities. To compound the problem, parents and students regard them as a deficiency in the program of the university. Employing TAs is seen as inserting an intermediate layer between the student and the "real" professor.

In fact, with the right opportunities and support, many graduate teaching assistants are outstanding teachers, with the high degree of excitement and fresh commitment that comes with the first opportunity to engage in their professional craft. Many have an insouciant ability to communicate ideas directly and effectively to undergraduates. Giving TAs the chance to participate in designing their courses and reconceptualize the material and to discuss their experiences with the professor and other graduate students not only trains TAs to teach but also contributes significantly to the richness of the undergraduate experience. By the time they have almost completed their dissertations, many graduate students can do a fine job of teaching a course on their own, especially with appropriate guidance and support from faculty members in their field. Conceived and carried forward in this way, the use of graduate teaching assistants can be a real plus for the university curriculum, a venture in intergenerational scholarly discovery, rather than a deficit.

Finally, it is important for faculty members—and, indeed, for universities and colleges more generally—to clarify the institution's expectations of undergraduate students. One of the primary sources of teacher burnout is student apathy. If students come to our campuses for an undergraduate degree assuming that the admissions process is the ultimate test, that they can float through four years with a "punched ticket," working only on things that immediately appeal to them, the implicit bargain we call liberal education is not possible. We need to be clear from the start about institutional expectations for their contribution to this partnership.

Candidates for a degree in the liberal arts should be aware that they have been chosen for their intellectual promise and apparent aptitude for the demands of this particular form of learning. Students, and their parents, should understand that a high degree of intellectual engagement and a willingness to live through periods of intellectual austerity, difficulty, and challenge are essential to a successful education and its promise for greater personal and professional reward in later life. If students are not willing or able to operate within these constraints, they should be encouraged to find some other form of preparation for the future.

Conclusion

In a speech to the graduating class of Duke University in 1931, President William Preston Few said, "As I look back over the life of man, I think I can trace a long historic conflict that has been waged through all civilization between beauty and fullness of life without a moral meaning, on the one hand, and austerity and barrenness along with religious intensity, on the other." Few went on to speculate on the unresolved conflict in the human spirit, "[which] has produced that strange ebb and flow so conspicuous in all human history. It has always been difficult for human society to preserve the gains made generation after generation, and any high and enduring civilization still awaits the synthetic power . . . to combine a full and beautiful living with moral energy and enthusiasm for the causes of humanity" (1931).

Few's description of this historic struggle reminds us that it has never been easy for societies to combine material success, aesthetic achievement, and technological progress with a true belief in the dignity and value of every person and a moral commitment that all should share in the benefits of a good life. Failure to achieve this synthesis has, as Few notes, contributed to the decline of many civilizations over time.

One of the main purposes of a liberal arts education today should be to prepare tomorrow's leaders to tackle this challenge. Of course a liberal arts education provides no guarantee that leaders will avoid

Few's dilemma; some of history's most vivid examples of failures to achieve his ideal had a classical education. Nonetheless, building a "high and enduring civilization" that effectively melds both these impulses is an aspiration worth instilling in our students. And, today as in the past, a strong liberal arts education provides our best hope that leaders might understand both the power and the difficulty of this goal and dedicate themselves to achieving it.

References

Astin, A. W. 1999. How the liberal arts college affects students. *Daedalus* 128, no. 1 (winter): 77–100.

Barber, B. 1992. *An aristocracy of everyone: The politics of education and the future of America.* New York: Ballantine.

Bok, D., and W. G. Bowen. 1998. *The shape of the river: Long-term consequences of considering race in college and university admissions.* Princeton: Princeton University Press.

Clotfelter, C. 1999. The familiar but curious economics of higher education: Introduction to a symposium. *Journal of Economic Perspectives* 13, no. 1 (winter): 3–12.

Cronon, W. 1999. Only connect. *Liberal Education* 85 (winter): 6–12.

Few, W. P. 1931. Duke University architecture discussed by President W. P. Few. *Duke University Alumni Register* 17, no. 6 (June): 195–97.

Frank, R. H., and P. J. Cook. 1995. *The winner-take-all society.* New York: Free Press.

Giamatti, B. 1988. *A free and ordered space: The real world of the university.* New York: W. W. Norton.

Graber, R. B. 1995. *Valuing useless knowledge: An anthropological inquiry into the meaning of liberal education.* Kirksville, Mo.: Thomas Jefferson University Press.

McPherson, M. S., and M. O. Schapiro. 1998. *The student aid game: Meeting need and rewarding talent in American higher education.* Princeton: Princeton University Press.

Montaigne, M. de. 1958. *Complete essays,* translated by D. Frame. Book 1, essay 39. Stanford, Calif.: Stanford University Press.

Rhodes, F. H. T. 1994. The place of teaching in the research university. In *The research university in a time of discontent,* edited by J. R. Cole, E. G. Barber, and S. R. Graubard. Baltimore: Johns Hopkins University Press.

Shapiro, H. T. 1999. Liberal education, moral education. *Princeton Alumni Weekly,* January 27.

Chapter Eight 〜

The Technological Revolution

Reflections on the Proper Role of Technology in Higher Education

Jack M. Wilson

There is little disagreement with the view that universities need to change in response to the revolution in information technology. There is consensus agreement that the world has changed dramatically and that our students must be prepared to survive and thrive differently in the new environment. But how? Exactly how should universities change? What are the immutable values of the university? How will universities be able to afford the changes? How will the faculty, students, facilities, and curriculum change? On these questions, there is little agreement.

The lack of agreement does not preclude a plethora of opinions. At one extreme, faculty organizations are expressing their concerns about the effects of change on the academy. At the other, venture capitalists are dumping hundreds of millions, perhaps billions, of dollars into new educational ventures that purport to be the wave of the future. Bricks and mortar are viewed as passé, while everyone embraces "virtual education." The lack of agreement about just what constitutes virtual education is no barrier to the rapid formation of virtual universities in every state and region.

The incompatible time scale of change for technology and for human beings simply makes the problem more intractable. The other issue that has attracted a lot of energy in higher education is diversity. While diversity involves finally coming to grips with issues that have been with us for centuries, technology involves trying to cope with factors that change faster than anyone can possibly accommodate. Technology will undergo a 100 percent change roughly every two years. People, individually or collectively, change very slowly.

The rapid pace of change depends upon the pace at which computing, communication, and content develop. Three laws underlie the changes. Moore's Law tells us that the power of computing doubles every 18 months. The bandwidth law tells us that communication bandwidth (unit communication capacity) doubles about every 12 months. Metcalf's Law tells us that the value of a network increases by the square of the number connected. These three laws combine to change the world in dramatic ways on a time scale so much faster than the usual university responses that the effects, not surprisingly, are disconcerting to everyone.

On a much slower time scale, we are discovering much more about how human beings learn. The cognitive sciences and other educational research are yielding results that have serious implications for how we organize our learning communities. These principles are now being adapted into new learning environments.

The Future of the University

There is no one simple solution for how universities will change, but there are emerging patterns and some practices that appear to be both consistent with our community's values and with the changing world. It may be that one effect of the overall change will be to differentiate universities further as we serve a more diverse and rapidly changing world.

Focus, Differentiation, Mass Customization, and Globalization

In the early part of the twentieth century American universities differed significantly by mission. Institutions would focus on teacher education (normal schools), liberal arts, land-grant universities, selective brand-name universities, engineering schools, regional institutions, and so on. During the second half of the century there was convergence of mission as schools became comprehensive research universities. This was at least partially the result of Vannevar Bush's vision of the role of research in the university. The normal schools became universities; the liberal arts colleges began hiring and promoting faculty based upon their research; and the engineering schools became technological universities. The differences have surely not been eliminated, but the direction was confluent.

In the 1980s and 1990s institutions began to run up against some of the limits of this convergence. The cost of higher education was actually advancing faster than the cost of health care. Parents began to look hard at their higher education expenditures. Legislators turned their attention to the cost of higher education. Perhaps the cost of having every institution be all things to all people would be just too high. In at least a few cases, institutions began to consider how to differentiate themselves from one another.

Babson College is one outstanding example of focus and differentiation. The college decided that it would focus on entrepreneurship and use that focus to drive itself to national preeminence. Today it is recognized as a world leader in entrepreneurship education. The Thunderbird School of International Business is another example. It is hard to believe that a world leader in international business education could develop at an abandoned air base in Arizona, but it did. Focus and differentiation made the difference. The California Institute of Technology is a prestigious example of differentiation. Caltech decided to remain small and to keep its focus on a very small high-quality undergraduate program in science and engineering and world-class research and graduate programs in a few science areas. The 1999 *U.S. News and World Report* ranking of colleges and universities catapulted Caltech into the number one position. Once again, this was a victory for focus and differentiation.

At the other end of the higher education pecking order, the University of Phoenix has become the fastest-growing university and one of the largest by focusing on providing convenient, commodity-level education in high-demand areas and making access easy and schedules flexible. In this, Britain's Open University paved the way decades earlier.

It is much too early to declare the arrival of the era of differentiation, but there seems to be an indication of a trend. This trend appears to include a movement toward mass customization. Until recently, mass customization was an oxymoron. Today it is a central tenet of the information economy. Dell Computer has grown to be the world's largest supplier of personal computers by building every computer to order. The young upstart has eclipsed companies that clung to the old model of mass production, channel distribution, and large, specialized inventories. Amazon.com elbowed its way into the clubby book business with a brash business model that tied them far more directly and personally with every customer. Amazon.com customers often receive book recommendations based upon their past reading, buying, and browsing patterns. The new economy industries know their customers and treat each one individually. Each business experience is customized to the customer, but it is done on a mass-production scale.

Mass customization in higher education would mean that education would become much more responsive to the individual student's needs rather than addressing general needs and assuming that every student would fit into general programs. Mass customization is often confused with being "student centered." Although the student-centered approach to education can indeed be a part of mass customization, it is a very different concept. A student-centered learning environment, which is part of many (if not most) undergraduate innovations, refers to transferring the focus of the activity from the instructor to the student. Rather than having teachers work hard while students listen, the student-centered environment expects the students to work hard while the faculty member listens.

The confusion about a student-centered environment and the market forces of mass customization have caused some to fear a shift to a "the customer is always right" approach to higher education. "Is a student-centered university providing a better product for its customers?" wonders Frank Furedi in the *Times Higher Education Supplement.* "No it is not. The marketization of higher education is forcing universities to be driven by concerns that have little pedagogic value," he concludes (1999).

What Furedi fears is an education system that panders to the wishes of its students. A student-centered environment, however, does not do this. It is designed to provide for the needs of its students, not simply to gratify their desires. A student-centered environment requires more of a student, not less. My own university, Rensselaer, has developed studio courses, which replace the traditional separate lecture, recitation, and laboratory with an integrated combination that scales back lecturing while increasing the hands-on activity of the students. Some have suggested that Rensselaer is requiring more of the students in our studio courses than we required of students in the past. That is probably accurate.

Mass customization might also mean that education is delivered in multiple formats and uses multiple explanatory examples that meet the needs of a diverse student population. Traditional lectures require that the instructor stereotype the student to some extent. There is not enough time to bring forward examples that appeal to everyone's interest and draw on everyone's experiences. In a science lecture, the lecturer has to pick a few examples from the many possible options to illustrate each concept. The instructor does this based upon his or her knowledge of student interests, learning styles, experiences, mathematical abilities, and so on. In a technology-based environment, one need not restrict the number of examples or make often-unwarranted assumptions about the characteristics of the students.

This approach could include the development of degree programs that draw on "best of breed" programs from several institutions. The National Technological University, for example, combines courses from several institutions to create new degree programs, and this could be the harbinger of a future trend. It has already appeared in a more restricted form as schools collaborate to meet the needs of students. At General Motors, engineering employees can pick from programs that combine courses from (for example) Stanford, Rensselaer, and Purdue. The final degree may come from any of these institutions.

As the previous example shows, higher education is being freed from the geographic restrictions of the past. This globalization of education runs counter to the trend toward differentiation. Differentiation in many areas of higher education may no longer occur regionally. While students were once compelled to accept programs from a local institution, today they may have a choice of programs provided by universities that are far away. For example, the two largest providers of on-the-job master's level engineering education to General Motors' engineers are Rensselaer and Purdue. Many of General Motors' employees are in or near Michigan, but the two state universities have a much smaller presence. At Rensselaer's Hartford, Connecticut, campus, Rensselaer departments find themselves in competition with programs from Stanford, Carnegie Mellon, the Massachusetts Institute of Technology (MIT), and others. Often these programs are even provided by and billed through the

Rensselaer Hartford campus. In industry, this has been dubbed *coopetition.*

Globalization has also led to the formation of global brand names in higher education. Recently, MIT concluded a cooperation agreement with Cambridge University that created a multinational brand in technological university education and research. The British government agreed to provide $109 million and to raise $26 million from private sources to create the new center, based in Britain (MIT and U. of Cambridge 1999; MIT, Cambridge team up 1999). Prior to that, MIT had concluded a large agreement to provide Singapore with higher education services (Singapore hires MIT 1997), and received a $25 million gift from Microsoft for the distance-learning portion of the relationship (Microsoft will give MIT 1999).

The entry of the top-ranked universities into the distance-learning market has been astounding to some of the more traditional observers. Distance learning has often been viewed as the province of correspondence schools or "diploma mills," and not the business of the top Carnegie Research I universities. With MIT now entering the arena, Stanford long established as a distance-learning leader, and countless other schools vying for the market, distance learning has gone mainstream. New York University has gone so far as to spin off their distance-learning program as a for-profit venture called NYU On-line. Their plan is to augment the $1.5 million investment from NYU with capital raised from private venture-capital sources (NYU starts for-profit 1998).

The Wharton School of Business at the University of Pennsylvania, Johns Hopkins University, and Teachers College at Columbia University took a different tack. Rather than creating new private ventures, they teamed up with Caliber, a joint venture of MCI and Sylvan Learning Systems, to offer their programs at a distance. The programs involved are all top ranked, and although they did not evolve in the way their proponents expected them to, they clearly show that high-quality distance learning is well established.

In their rush to enter the distance-learning market, universities have not always been careful to take into account the lessons learned from the centuries of higher education. Many distance programs are driven by technology and not pedagogy. Technology is a powerful force that must be reckoned with, but centuries of history and the recent research coming out of the cognitive sciences on how human beings learn will have much to say about where this technology will take us.

The Relentless Forces of Computing, Cognition, and Communications

Advances in computing, communications, and cognition are both driving and enabling the rapid change in higher education. We have become the victims of our own success. The research of our faculty and students has created a relentless flood of new possibilities and new demands. The advances in computing and communications have been rapid, spectacular, and quickly applied by society. Understanding the learning process has taken much longer and is much more slowly adapted by society. I use the term *cognition* to describe the research on learning and particularly the applied research that has shown the importance of engagement, interaction, collaboration, and specific instructional strategies.

Ever since the invention of the microprocessor, the performance of computers has been doubling every 18 months. This is directly related to the number of components that can be fit on a chip and is thus linked to the minimum size of each component. Advances in basic physics and engineering have kept this rate of improvement accurate for over five decades. The basic physics is in place to keep this going for another few doubling periods at least. At the same time, the cost of equivalent computing power halves every 18 months. These related factors create a challenge for universities to meet.

Communications technologies are developing even faster. The bandwidth density in fiber is doubling every two years, but that is only half the story. Fiber is being laid and wireless systems are being deployed so quickly that bandwidth is doubling in less than a year. These two doubling laws tell us that we will see more change in technology in the next two years than we have in the last few decades.

The convergence of computing and communications has led to the development of massive networks. Metcalf's Law tells us that the value (economic and otherwise) of a network scales as n^2 where n is the number of persons connected. This helps to explain the enormous values that Wall Street assigns those companies that appear to have locked the most customers into their networks. Companies like America On-line (AOL), Amazon.com, and eBay have established networks of users that are so much larger than their competitors' networks that the value comparison is overwhelming. The proposed recent merger of AOL and Time Warner graphically demonstrates the value assigned by Metcalf's Law. In the resulting company AOL will own 55 percent of the merged company to Time Warner's 45 percent. This is in spite of the fact that Time Warner has four times the revenues of AOL and has its roots in one of our oldest and largest publishing empires. The market clearly assigns greater values to AOL's network than it does to Time Warner's revenues.

These three laws tell us that what is hard today is easy tomorrow. They also contribute to the relentless nature of these technologies—relentless, because they will indeed change everything whether we want them to or not, whether we engage or not, and whether we like the result or not. We have no choice in this matter. We *will* change. The issue is: *how* will we change?

In the early part of the twentieth century, the automobile was the relentless technology. It built the greatest industry of the middle part of the century, and it irreversibly changed the way we live our lives. It changed the way we work, live, and go courting. It led to the rise of the suburbs, the creation of shopping malls, the decline of the inner cities, the collapse of mass transit, and the spread of smog. We did not consciously choose these things. For the most part, they just happened. One would like to think that if we had been more proactive about the process, the world would be a better place today.

Trends in Higher Education

Suddenly, even Wall Street thinks that education is an opportunity. It has been suggested that over $1.7 billion has been invested in new ventures in an effort to tap an education market estimated at over $600 billion annually (Marchese 1998).

There are those who think that higher education as we know it will be displaced by other alternatives. Stephen Talbott argues that this will indeed happen and that it is the universities' own fault (Talbott 1999). While Talbott seems disturbed (even angry) about these prospects, Lewis Perelman is positively welcoming. He remarks, "I've analyzed and forecasted trends that, I am increasingly confident, will lead eventually to the collapse of the academic system in a way and for reasons that are basically the same as those that led to the collapse of the Soviet system" (1993). Perelman does not think that there is any hope at all for reform in higher education and thinks that reform is a complete waste of time. In his words, "I have no interest in reform; and, when asked, I discourage others from wasting time and money on it. Education reform over a period of decades has proven to be either unnecessary, futile, irrelevant, or even downright harmful" (1997).

Some take a matter-of-fact approach that may neglect some of the subtleties of the changes while recognizing their inevitability. De-wayne Matthews, from his post as director of student exchanges and state relations at the Western Interstate Commission for Higher Education (WICHE), assumes that "programs can be structured around asynchronous learning" (1998). As we will see, this certainly requires a much more calibrated approach. One needs to ask: which programs? for what audience? under what circumstances? An asynchronous program for a motivated adult learner in a discretionary program may be the ideal solution. An asynchronous program to teach calculus to young adults with the expectation that over 90 percent of them will be able to use calculus in the next course is a much more difficult proposition. WICHE was a prime mover in the Western Governors University (WGU), and the WGU programs reflect his matter-of-fact approach. It may be that some issues accepted at face value require a deeper analysis.

Others in higher education are in denial. They hide behind platitudes of "immutable values" and "centuries of stability." A university administrator responded to one of my talks by asserting that the current structure of higher education was the "stable product of long evolution." I pointed out that the dinosaur was one of the most stable products of long evolution, but that evolution does not create "stable products." It will be important to understand the core values and practices and to see how they play out in this changed environment.

Responses of the University

Some faculty members view change with quite a bit of trepidation. I have been asked more than once, "If you can put my course on a website, then why would you need me any more?" I always answer, "If you can be replaced by a website, then you should be replaced by a website." The question reveals both a lack of self-confidence and a severe misconception about the nature of the educational interaction.

If professors are viewed as purveyors of information, then they surely can be replaced by high-quality websites and CD-ROMs. A writer in *Prism* asked, "If a student can zoom the best professors into his or her living room, then what is to happen to the rest of the country's professors?" I've heard this misconception expressed in many forms. It again assumes that the role of the professor is only that of presenter of information. That is much too narrow a view of what a professor does. If the first worry were true, then professors would have been replaced long ago, first by books, then by audio tapes, and then by video tapes. If the second were true, then we would surely have been replaced by live televised courses.

Technology for the Learners' Sake

Each of these technologies (book, audio tapes, video tapes, and television) has had a time of hype followed by disillusionment (at least on the part of the proponents). They all have their place, but they all failed to replace the professor—because they cannot do what a *good* professor does. A good professor interacts with the students, stimulates them to think, prods them into new insights, motivates them through personal interaction, and provides a role model for intellectual inquiry.

Visiting an outstanding website can be an illuminating and exciting experience from which one can even learn. Watching a superstar give a lecture can lead to the same results. Neither of these can replace the experience of two or more minds making their way through a complex concept together. Whether students interact with students or with their professors, working on a problem or concept collaboratively is a special learning experience. The best professors have always generated these kinds of interactions in their classes. This is not a new issue, but it is often ignored when technology-enhanced learning or distance learning is discussed.

This does not mean that technology cannot be used to allow and even enhance such interactions. It means instead that using technology to automate lecturing does not a professor make. Technology can be used to allow more meaningful kinds of interactions at a distance. Technology can allow simulations and group activities that stimulate these kinds of interactions. Unfortunately, technology can also have the effect of damping down these kinds of interactions. It all comes down to the design of the learning experience. Technology by itself neither guarantees nor inhibits quality. The design and the delivery of the educational experience are the critical factors.

Well-designed technology-enhanced classrooms incorporate communication, (written, electronic, peer discussion, face-to-face, and electronic face-to-face). as part of the educational experience. Well-designed courses focus on the quality of the educational experience. Focusing on the total educational experience means that one looks beyond what happens in the classroom to all the other parts of the educational experience as well: to the admissions process, residence facilities, student support systems, testing procedures, career counseling facilities, and the like.

Technology for Technology's Sake

Another misconception about the proper role of technology is summed up by the popular mantra "no technology for technology's sake." That is an appealing but misleading piece of advice. Because technology has become part and parcel of every profession, it is important for the students to focus on the technology. Ability to use technology in creative, even astounding, ways depends upon a deep knowledge of both the potential and limitations of technology. It presupposes a deep understanding of the technologies themselves.

The need appears even greater when one realizes that the rate of change of technology will continue to restructure most professions over the coming years. Graduates need to have an ability to use technology, to evaluate technology in the context of their professions, and to learn and adapt new, presently unknown technologies to their work. It is often noted that, to the uninitiated, any new technology is essentially indistinguishable from magic. Perhaps it is this effect that causes the often seen bipolar reactions to technology of either uncritical acceptance or visceral rejection. These are both inappropriate responses that need to be replaced by critical evaluation. Technology needs to be included both for its own sake and to enhance the learning experience. Both are valid goals, and both should be assessed in any innovation.

Residential Education

The effect of technology on residential education is of serious concern to many (Farrington 1999). Will the University of Phoenix (or one of its many competitors) put the local colleges and universities out of business? There is no easy answer to this question. The differentiation of mission that is likely to occur suggests that there will be many different kinds of institutions vying for students' attention.

In light of our understanding of how people learn and the value of student-student and student-professor interactions in the educational process, we would expect that the residential university would continue to have a place in the spectrum of higher education. When it comes to the education of young adults prior to their entry into the workforce, residential higher education has much to recommend it. Technology will improve both the quality of residential undergraduate education and its chance for survival.

Technology can break down the barriers of distance and allow cross-cultural collaboration in spite of geographic isolation. Many of the traditional liberal arts colleges are found in rural or small town settings. In an earlier era, the cloistered environments were thought to be conducive to focusing on learning and allowing opportunity for reflection. The other side of that coin is the risk of provincialism, lack of diversity, and the inaccessibility of urban and global experiences. These smaller undergraduate colleges also find it difficult to offer the student the broad range of courses and experiences that are available at the large research universities. Technology can help demolish those obstacles.

Technology is allowing institutions to share courses, research experiences, and cross-cultural experiences without regard to distance. One such example at Rensselaer had students at Hong Kong's City University and at Rensselaer sharing a weekly graduate class in Survival Skills for Astrophysicists. A large portion of the class was devoted to student presentations. Using video-conferencing and live Internet-based data collaboration, these students saw each other present their work and could view the materials in real time at high resolution. The professor could poll the class periodically for feedback with an Internet question-and-answer tool that immediately displayed student responses. The hardest part of class organization was picking a time suitable for both groups. We finally settled on breakfast for the Rensselaer students and dinner for the Hong Kong students.

Even the smallest liberal arts college in the central United States can now link itself with nearly any major institution in the world. The dramatic advances in bandwidth described earlier mean that this kind of collaboration will get better, cheaper, and more widespread.

Technology and Pedagogical Innovation

Research in the cognitive sciences has reinforced and extended what has long been known. Students learn more from doing than from watching. Students learn better when engaged in group activities instead of solo activities. Students learn as much from one another as from the professor. Students learn more when more is expected of them. Students have a diversity of learning styles, interests, and experiences. None of these insights has anything to do with technology. Most have been known in one form or another for decades. Technology has made possible pedagogical innovations that address these precepts, innovations that were not driven by technology but that are indeed enabled by technology.

Steve Ehrmann of the American Association for Higher Education looked at the application of Arthur Chickering's "Seven Principles for Good Practice" to technology-enhanced learning (Chickering and Ehrmann 1999). These principles come from an understanding of how human beings learn and not from any technological imperative, yet Ehrmann shows how these principles guide good practice in technology-enhanced learning. The seven principles are: (1) good practice encourages contacts between students and faculty, (2) good practice develops reciprocity and cooperation among students, (3) good practice uses active learning techniques, (4) good practice gives prompt feedback, (5) good practice emphasizes time on task, (6) good practice communicates high expectations, and (7) good practice respects diverse talents and ways of learning.

Peter Denning expands upon the themes of interactivity and the faculty member as part of a social process in "Teaching as a Social Process." He concludes, "In spite of the stress, the good news for students and teachers is that learning is more than information transfer, that automation can affect at most the information-transfer part of learning, and that the teacher is indispensable" (1999). I would disagree with his conclusion that technology can only affect information transfer, but I support fully his conclusion that the teacher is indispensable.

The best curricular innovations use technology to facilitate the kinds of interactions described in the seven principles. There are many bright spots—current teaching methods and curricula that others can use as inspiration and encouragement. Creative faculty members have invented many ways to apply technology to the creation of outstanding learning environments that satisfy different local conditions and target various goals. Most draw upon a common research base in learning and the generally accepted principles outlined above.

A working group at the National Research Council identified a number of promising innovations in science and mathematics at various colleges and universities. A partial list illustrates the diversity in approach and the common bonds of interaction, engagement, collaboration, and peer teaching:

—lecture-based models: active learning systems (Ohio State, Oregon State)
—Mathematics Emporium (Virginia Tech)
—peer instruction/concept tests (Harvard)
—interactive demonstrations (Oregon)
—workshop physics, math, and other courses (Dickinson)
—studio courses (Rensselaer)
—Physics by Inquiry (Washington)
—lab models: Tools for Scientific Thinking (Tufts-Dickinson)
—RealTime Physics (Dickinson-Oregon)
—recitation models: cooperative problem-solving (Minnesota)
—tutorials in introductory physics (Washington)
—mathematical tutorials (Maryland)
—distributed education models: Sloan Asynchronous Learning Network
—live on-line learning, such as LearnLinc and other web-based approaches
—increased involvement in undergraduate research

It may be instructive to compare a few of these innovations to highlight the various approaches to reform. Some of these models did not seek to challenge the primacy of the lecture or the lecturer. Those examples focused on reforming the lecture, engaging the student, and incorporating collaborative learning. The interactive lecture demonstrations at Oregon and Ohio State do that through a protocol that has students make predictions and discuss lecture demonstrations before and then after performing the demonstration. The demonstrations are often selected because they stimulate known misconceptions, force the student to take a stand, define that stand, and then confront the student with the actual result, which is often at variance with the predicted outcome. The creation of this cognitive conflict and the animated discussions that are generated lead to enhanced student learning.

At Harvard, Eric Mazur has invented a system of peer learning in lectures that asks questions about concepts, lets the students make predictions, asks them to discuss those predictions with peers, and then resolves the concept through discussion, demonstration, or derivation.

The initiators of other projects, such as Tools for Scientific Thinking, decided that the best way to reform a science course was through the laboratory. The physics programs of the universities of Minnesota, Washington, and Maryland targeted the recitation. For some, the separation of lecture, recitation, and laboratory found in many science and mathematics courses was unnecessary and unhelpful. They envisioned a course in which students would work in groups at tables where they could set up experiments, discuss, collaborate, or listen as appropriate. There would be minilectures but no long monologues. Students would move back and forth between listening, discussion, and hands-on activities according to educational need and not according to an inflexible schedule. Rensselaer applied these concepts in the context of a large research university, creating the studio courses (Wilson 1997a and 1994), while Dickinson College did a similar thing in the small liberal arts college with the creation of the workshop-course series (Laws 1991). Each of these models has garnered its share of national attention, and each has been replicated many times around the world.

There were those who felt they needed to break the bonds of both space and time. These were the anytime/anyplace advocates who developed web-based asynchronous courses that would allow the students to work on their own schedules and in their own locations. These courses were easy to build and held out the prospect of an inexpensive way to deliver higher education to the masses. They could also address the problem of education for the older learner, whose work or family obligations made site-based education inaccessible.

Unfortunately, technology-based learning, and particularly web-based learning, is often viewed as the solution to a variety of problems. Some institutions view it as an alternative to growth. In California, where higher education is going to have to educate 30 percent more students in the next 10 years, anytime/anyplace web-based education is seen as the way to avoid the substantial investments in bricks and mortar that would be required (and are probably impossible to obtain) to educate the additional students in site-based programs. This growth, dubbed "tidal wave II" by advocates, remains a controversial political issue. The California state university system expects to grow by 42 percent and to have an additional 12,000 to 15,000 new students each year, which is the equivalent of an entire new campus. In the western part of the United States, growth is the primary problem identified. The Western Governors University was formed with high hopes of addressing the needs of these rapidly growing western states, although California's decision to go it alone—with the formation of the California Virtual University—inhibited the reach of the program. Each of these cases has encountered substantial difficulties in implementation. Other institutions view asynchronous education as an opportunity to provide access where none existed before. In Maine, educators viewed it as a way to bring unavailable programs to learners. Some view technology as a way to control costs, while others fret that technology is driving an escalation of cost in higher education.

The Sloan Foundation's Asynchronous Learning program supported the creation of prototypes and provided a forum for the large number of institutions that were racing to embrace asynchronous, web-based learning. In short, anytime/anyplace asynchronous education is seen as the prescription for a variety of problems facing higher education. Although this approach will undoubtedly play a role in addressing these problems, the solutions are not nearly as easy as many first thought.

Despite the obvious advantages of increased access and reduced cost, asynchronous learning programs have to surmount a number of obstacles that could have been foreseen based upon earlier research in asynchronous environments using other media. While technology changes rapidly, relentlessly, and dramatically, people change infinitesimally slowly. Asynchronous courses have always been most effective for the highly motivated learner or for non-mission-critical educational experiences. It has been much more difficult to use asynchronous courses to address the less-motivated learner and to ensure high success rates. For example, asynchronous learning has been successful in providing the education needed to prepare engineers for certification in Microsoft, Cisco, Novell, Java, and other technologies. It is also terrific for leisure-time education in things like photography or home medicine. It is usually not known how many persons start but do not successfully complete these programs, because they are rarely tracked. The only thing that is important is that enough individuals come out the other end of the pipeline to meet market needs.

There are many courses that are mission-critical and do not have the benefit of highly motivated students. The introductory college-level calculus course is a good example. At selective institutions, we expect retention and success rates that approach 90 percent. Complete reliance on asynchronous education has not yet proved practical for this level of retention. An example of a mission-critical course in industry might be the maintenance courses for airline mechanics. This is not at all discretionary, and one needs to approach 100 percent success. In those many cases where anytime/anyplace courses have not proven themselves, there are many alternatives that modify the proposition to be either anytime or anyplace or even a combination of anytime/anyplace with anyplace.

Distance-learning courses that use satellite or video-conferencing technologies are excellent examples of anyplace education. Most of the early work in technology-based distance learning focused on these kinds of anyplace education. Students could be gathered together at downlink sites or video-conferencing rooms to participate in learning that broke the bounds of space but required that students participate at the same time. Educators quickly recognized that this kind of distance education built upon the lecture method in its least interactive forms. In a desire to ensure interactivity, educators added the ability to call in or fax in to the professor. Later some students were given keypads to participate by answering multiple-choice questions from time to time. Video-conferencing allowed the instructor to see the students and introduced an element of personal interaction—as long as the number of interacting students was kept small enough. The level of interactivity in these kinds of courses depended critically upon the skill of the instructor in using the technology in an interactive manner. In the worst case, the instructor would resort to uninterrupted lectures with very little interactivity. In many ways, these kinds of courses just pushed the back wall of the lecture hall out a few thousand miles.

The Virginia Tech Mathematics Emporium is a clever instance of anytime education. The Mathematics Emporium was set up in a vacant shopping center near the Virginia Tech campus. In that sense, it is place-bound but not time-bound. Students can walk in at a time convenient to them rather than at a set time. The Emporium uses quite a bit of information technology and is operated by faculty, staff, and teaching assistants on a rotating basis. If the student really wants a lecture, they are available on video tape. Not surprisingly, that is not a popular option. Rutgers University has used a similar approach to teaching physics, with remarkably similar experiences. They set up the walk-in physics facility in an old World War II–era Quonset hut on campus.

A number of organizations have deployed hybrid systems that have a portion of the course delivered asynchronously and a portion synchronously. The particular proportions can be adjusted to be appropriate for the content, the audience, and the instructor's preferences. At Rensselaer, we often refer to this as the "80-20 model," because 80 percent asynchronous and 20 percent synchronous is often our starting point in the design (Lister et al. 1999). The 20 percent synchronous instruction can be done by web-based audio, video, and collaborative data sharing with live on-line tools like the LearnLinc system used at Rensselaer and Lucent Technologies. The actual percentage can be set small enough to be efficient and flexible and provide for student access but large enough to increase the success rate for students enrolled. The figure 20 percent is not a magic number but is adjusted based upon the audience and material. These hybrid approaches that use both synchronous and asynchronous learning techniques are often referred to as interactive distributed learning (IDL) systems (Wilson 1996).

A web-based IDL approach to teaching need not involve only a single distinguished professor. Rather, the web can be a networking tool, representing a collaborative approach. Teleconferences using video, audio, and the World Wide Web offer great potential for conducting courses simultaneously at multiple sites. These models do not mean that one expert broadcasts to many students. Instead, the network connects faculty and students in peer interactions. Division of participants into experts (faculty) and novices (students) is much too coarse a sieve. IDL courses may involve individuals of varying expertise and diverse backgrounds. In a traditional course, for example, there may be senior faculty who are world-class experts in their subjects, other faculty whose expertise is outside of the subject area, graduate students who are bright but inexperienced, undergraduate student assistants who have only rudimentary knowledge of the subject but lots of enthusiasm, and the actual students who are enrolled in the course. Each of these participants has a significant role in the interactions in the course. It is particularly important to consider the level of student-to-student interaction. In a graduate course offered simultaneously to residential students and to students in the workplace, there is an entire range of expertise. On any specific topic, the most knowledgeable person may well be a student in the workplace.

Guides for Technology in Higher Education

Decades of experience working with universities that are applying technology has led me to formulate a set of rules of thumb, which I irreverently dubbed the "Ten Commandments for technology in higher education" in a presentation to the National Science Foundation (Wilson 1999). Here they are (slightly adapted):

1. Restructure around the learner. Neither overemphasize nor underemphasize technology.

2. Build upon research results that inform design; don't try to reinvent the wheel.

3. Remember that technology has an intrinsic educational value beyond helping students learn better.

4. Do systematic redesign and not incremental add-ons. There is always a tendency just to add on a few computer experiences to everything else. By definition this costs more, creates more work for faculty, and adds to the students' burden. An innovative approach changes exercises rather than adding poorly integrated ones.

5. Benchmark your plans and build upon examples of systematic redesign. Do not automate the lecture. Find the best examples and build upon them.

6. Count on Moore's Law ("what is hard today is easy tomorrow"). For example, computer processing power and bandwidth have consistently improved.

7. Cost is an important aspect of quality. There is no lasting quality if there has been no attention to cost. There are more than enough examples of expensive high-quality solutions. We need more examples of inexpensive high-quality solutions.

8. Avoid pilots that linger. Design for a large scale and for pilot projects only as a prelude to scaling up. It is easy to design innovative educational experiences that work for small groups. It is harder to address the needs of the 1,000 students taking calculus I at the large research university.

9. Develop a balance between synchronous and asynchronous distributed learning.

10. There is no longer any way to do good scholarship without technology, and there is no longer any way to teach good scholarship without technology.

Libraries and Other Resources

As more and more universities move toward any of the models that bend the rules of space and time, it will be a challenge to provide the resources and support that have been expected in residential higher education. The library has always assumed a central role in higher education. Accrediting teams and evaluation teams are fond of counting volumes and measuring "holdings" as some kind of metric for quality. Technology changes that equation rather significantly. It provides both opportunities for access and challenges. The World Wide Web has made many resources available as easily as sitting at your terminal, pointing, and clicking.

The rise of distributed learning has raised the issue of how universities can provide library access to students who may be thousands of miles from campus (Luther 1998). Brian Hawkins puts the library into the larger context when he considers how universities should respond to the challenges of distributed learning in an article in *EDUCOM Review* (1999). The digital library promises to provide access to almost everything more easily than a Washington, D.C., resident can visit the Library of Congress. In spite of major efforts to achieve this, the promise remains largely unfulfilled.

Changing What We Teach As Well As How We Teach

As universities deploy new learning environments to meet students' and society's needs, it will not be a one-size-fits-all approach. Universities will analyze their historic roles, their current missions, their prospective audiences, and a plethora of other variables and choose the approach that most closely meets these needs.

For example, in 1997 Rensselaer formed the new Faculty of Information Technology with 125 faculty members drawn from almost every discipline. From the beginning, the intent was to offer a bachelor of science degree, a master of science degree, and a doctorate in Information Technology (IT). Research of the new faculty would focus on the cross-disciplinary applications of IT. After examining the educational issues that we have been discussing, the Faculty of IT concluded that the BSIT should focus on a residential program that would be built around IT-intensive, interactive studio courses. The Ph.D. was seen to be a smaller, much more theoretically focused, residential program.

The MSIT was seen as much different. Five factors seemed to be of key importance: (1) there is a severe shortage of IT professionals, (2) the shortage leads to very high salaries for new BS graduates, (3) the shortage makes it difficult for anyone to leave employment to return to school, (4) the shortage leads to massive cross-training of others in related fields into IT, and (5) the rapid change of technology mandates a continuous updating even for those with excellent credentials in IT.

For these reasons, we felt that the MSIT program should be designed around the paradigm of IDL (interactive distributed learning), which was discussed earlier. We expect to deliver the education to the workplaces and the homes of employed persons. This will allow the further education of IT professionals in the workplace. It will enable the cross-training of people in related fields into IT. It will help IT professionals to update their skills as the technology advances. It would not require that an individual leave employment to undertake graduate work. This need for continuous education (Wilson 1997b) is a characteristic of many of today's professions and professionals.

As universities respond to these relentless technologies, they will do so according to their own values, their own histories, their own audiences, and their own missions. The example above is only one specific instance of how a university responds to these circumstances.

Support for the Changes

Universities coping with the relentless nature of change have had a variety of support sources. Nearly every disciplinary organization maintains standing committees that address these issues. The National Research Council has considered the issues of digital libraries, and its Committee on Information Technology has prepared a report on their effects on higher education in science, mathematics, engineering, and technology education.

Several national organizations are organized to help with the diffusion and dissemination of the innovations in higher education. Among these are the following:

—The EduCause National Learning Infrastructure Initiative (NLII), which has initiated a number of partnerships between institutions that band together around specific approaches to innovation (Twigg 1994; National Learning n.d.).
—Pew Center for Academic Transformation, which is funded at over $8 million to help institutions reform their undergraduate programs to enhance quality, increase access, and constrain cost (Pew Grants 1999; Pew Program n.d.). The first two are noncontroversial goals, but the last has raised eyebrows.
—AAHE Teaching Learning Technology Roundtables (TLTR), which have taken a very traditional approach to a very nontraditional issue. The TLTR programs stimulate the formation of stakeholder groups at institutions undergoing change. These roundtables give voice to both the aspirations and the fears of the faculty, staff, and students. The TLTR list-serve is one of the most active sources of information about innovations at universities (Gilbert 1996; Teaching Learning n.d.).
—The Instructional Management System group. With hundreds of universities and commercial vendors preparing materials for uses in newly designed courses, the need for standards became clear. Groups under the auspices of the NLII began meeting to discuss both the standards and the process for developing those standards that could simplify interoperability and ease the adoption of new materials. Eventually, a decision was made to spin the group off into a new organization (Instructional Management n.d.).

Conclusion

There is no doubt that higher education faces challenges that are unprecedented in this or the previous century. The rapid and relentless advances in computing and communications technologies have stimulated and enabled creative new ways for institutions to address the educational needs of the learners. The disparity between the rapid dramatic technological changes and the consistency of human interactions has made this a slower and more difficult transition than many expected.

There are now many examples of educational innovations that both accommodate the rapid change of technology and are based upon an understanding of how human beings interact and learn. These new environments are changing and will continue to change higher education in many ways. While the second half of the twentieth century was marked by the convergence of university characteristics, the first half of the twenty-first century may see increased emphasis on differentiation, globalization, mass customization, and focus.

Traditional universities will find it difficult to respond to these changing circumstances. There will be increased pressure from nontraditional higher education providers. Proprietary universities, virtual universities, and corporate universities will continue to grow. Nevertheless, higher education enters the next millennium as strong as it has ever been. The relentless pressure of communications, computing, and cognition is driving change. Some changes are completely foreseeable; others are not. Universities can chose either to lead the changes or follow behind. By rapidly adapting the technological advances of computing and communications and applying research in learning in a context where their core values remain unchanged, universities will survive the "Internet tsunami" and even thrive through the century. There has never been a more exciting time to work in a university.

References

Chickering, A. W., and S. C. Ehrmann. 1999. Implementing the seven principles: Technology as lever. *AAHE Bulletin.* <http://www.aahe.org/technology/ehrmann.htm>

Denning, P. J. 1999. Teaching as a social process. *EDUCOM Review* (May–June). <http://www.educause.edu/ir/library/html/erm9932.html>

Farrington, G. C. 1999. The new technologies and the future of residential undergraduate education. *EDUCOM Review* (July–August). <http://www.educause.edu/ir/library/html/erm9949.html>

Furedi, F. 1999. *Times Higher Education Supplement,* 22 October.

Gilbert, S. W. 1996. Making the most of a slow revolution. *Change* 28, no. 2 (March–April)10–23.

Hawkins, B. L. 1999. Distributed learning and institutional restructuring.

EDUCOM Review (July–August). <http://www.educause.edu/ir/library /html/erm9943.html>

Instructional management system. N.d. <http://www.imsproject.org/>

Laws, P. 1991. Calculus-based physics without lectures. *Physics Today* 44, no. 12 (December): 24–31.

Lister, B. C., M. M. Danchak, K. A. Scalzo, W. C. Jennings, and J. M. Wilson. 1999. The Rensselaer 80/20 model for interactive distance learning. *EduCause '99* (October). <http://www.pde.rpi.edu/presentations/index .html>

Luther, J. 1998. Distance learning and the digital library. *EDUCOM Review* (July–August). <http://www.educause.edu/ir/library/html/erm9842 .html>

Marchese, T. 1998. Not-so-distant competitors: How new providers are re-making the postsecondary marketplace. *AAHE Bulletin* (May). <http ://www.aahe.org/bulletin/bull_1may98.htm>

Matthews, D. 1998. Transforming higher education: Implications for state higher education finance policy. *EDUCOM Review* (September–October). <http://www.educause.edu/ir/library/html/erm9854.html>

Microsoft will give MIT $25-million for educational-technology research. 1999. *Chronicle of Higher Education,* 15 October.

MIT and U. of Cambridge announce $135-million joint venture. 1999. *Chronicle of Higher Education,* 19 November.

MIT, Cambridge team up. 1999. *CNET News.com,* 5 November

National learning infrastructure initiative. N.d.<http://www.educause.edu /nlii/>

NYU starts for-profit unit to sell on-line classes. 1998. *Chronicle of Higher Education,* 16 October.

Perelman, L. 1993. *School's out: Hyperlearning, the new technology, and the end of education.* New York: Avon Books.

———. 1997. *Technos Quarterly* 6, no. 3 (fall).

Pew grants to focus on classroom technology. 1999. *Chronicle of Higher Education,* 2 July.

Pew program at the Center for Academic Transformation. N.d. <http://center .rpi.edu>

Singapore hires MIT to audit its engineering schools. 1997. *Chronicle of Higher Education,* 23 May.

Talbott, S. 1999. Who's killing higher education? Corporations and students: The unusual suspects. *EDUCOM Review* (March–April). <http://www .educause.edu/ir/library/html/erm99024.html>

Teaching, learning, and technology roundtables. N.d. <http://www.tltgroup .org/>

Twigg, C. A. 1994. The need for a national learning infrastructure. *EDUCOM Review* 29: 4–6.

Wilson, J. M. 1994. The CUPLE physics studio. *Physics Teacher* 32 (December): 518.

———. 1996. The virtual university. *Proceedings of the International Conference of the American Society for Engineering Education.* Washington, D.C. (June).

———. 1997a. *Re-engineering undergraduate education in the learning revolution.* Boston, Mass.: Anker.

———. 1997b. Distance learning for continuous education. *EDUCOM Review* 32, no. 2 (March–April): 12–16. <http://www.educause.edu/pub/er/review/reviewArticles/32212.html>

———. 1999. Creating new learning environments for higher education. In Workshop on Improving Undergraduate Education in the Mathematical and Physical Sciences through the Use of Technology. *Preliminary Report. National Science Foundation* (20–22 July). <http://www.wcer.wisc.edu/teched99/>

Chapter Nine

Academic Change and Presidential Leadership

Richard M. Freeland

Point: American universities are conservative institutions, resistant to change, preoccupied with internal issues, and largely unresponsive to evolving societal needs. *Counterpoint:* American universities are agencies of social progress, promoting new thinking and technical innovation, encouraging experimentation, and deeply involved with nonacademic problems of all kinds, including the well-being of their surrounding communities.

Point: the university presidency is an enfeebled position, much diminished from an heroic past, buffeted by conflicting interest groups, hamstrung by governance constraints, and fundamentally unable to provide the leadership needed for academia to respond to changing needs. *Counterpoint:* the presidency may have lost its mythic authority, but presidential leadership remains an essential prerequisite for any successful program of planned change in academic institutions.

Point: stripped of real power, the presidency has lost its appeal except for those who crave the appearance above the reality of power and love to work long hours for little reward while sacrificing any semblance of normal life. *Counterpoint:* the presidency continues to provide opportunities to make a significant impact upon one's own institution as well as to influence events outside the university while also offering rich possibilities for professional satisfaction—and even joy.

Contradictory statements like these about the adaptability of universities and about the strength of the contemporary university presidency abound in the vast literature on higher education, and thoughtful voices have advanced each of the positions cited above. The reality is that truth can be found in every one of these statements and that each is valid for some institutions and some presidencies some of the time.

But it is not enough to nod in all directions on urgent questions. Doubts about the responsiveness of academic institutions to changing needs and about the ability of presidents to lead efforts of planned change are frontal challenges to academia's social effectiveness. We need to know what we think about these matters, and—to the extent that we agree with the negative proposition in each of these cases—we need to do what we can to strengthen the performance of our universities.[1]

This chapter represents a personal coming to terms with these issues. My thoughts are informed by two kinds of experience. First, for nearly 30 years I have held administrative positions in higher education, including the deanships of two university-based colleges; the academic vice-chancellorship of a large public system; and, most recently, the presidency of a major private university. Second, in 1992 I completed a study of change among American universities during the 51-year period from 1930 through 1980, based on a close analysis of eight universities in Massachusetts.[2] These engagements with academic life have heightened my appreciation of the negative side of each of the arguments to which I have referred and caused me to be highly attentive to critics and reformers. In the end, however, I have found the positive proposition more compelling than the negative in each case.

This chapter affirms three propositions. First, American universities have an impressive record of adapting to changing circumstances and needs over long periods of time. Second, university presidents have consistently played indispensable roles in the change process. And third, the presidency continues to be a deeply rewarding position for those who are interested in administrative work, love higher education, care about institutions, and believe that universities make a critically important contribution to the well-being of our nation.

Do Universities Change with the Times?

Among academia's many critics, no theme is repeated more frequently nor with a greater undercurrent of moral indignation than the charge that colleges and universities are unresponsive to social needs and excessively resistant to change. I first became familiar with this pattern of commentary as a graduate student in the 1960s, when higher education was under assault from students who wanted their campuses to be more socially engaged, communities who wanted them to be more permeable, and governmental leaders who wanted them more involved in social and economic problem-solving. In those days, traditionalist faculty and stubborn administrators who tried to focus on the core missions of education and research readily became symbols of an industry preoccupied with its own concerns to the exclusion of pressing public business. Legions of reformers—in government, in the foundations, in community organizations, in the media, and in academia itself—sought ways to make the university more receptive to their concerns.

The institutional disarray that occurred in many colleges and universities in the late 1960s and early 1970s as the pressures for reform played themselves out produced, in subsequent years, some cooling of ardor for the socially engaged campus and a renewed appreciation for the special and enduring qualities of academic institutions. Despite this change of atmosphere, the charge that universities are unresponsive to changing social needs is no less a staple of the critical literature today than it was 30 years ago. In many ways, the persistence of this complaint is remarkable. If one reviews the record of American higher education since World War II, it would be hard not to conclude that colleges and universities have been impressively adaptable and highly attentive to the most urgent public issues of the day.

During the war years of the 1940s, academia created special training programs for military officers and technicians, designed accelerated courses of study to get manpower into the field quickly, and spawned a new generation of interdisciplinary research centers that produced technological innovations essential to the war effort. With the return of peace, the nation's campuses became major contributors to reconversion, first by expanding to accommodate veterans seeking admission under the GI Bill, then by creating a continuing research capability that provided much of the scientific and technological basis for national defense and economic progress during the Cold War.

Still later, during the egalitarian era of the 1960s, universities grew rapidly to meet increased demand for admission to college, participated actively in the effort to extend access to minority youth, and took on increasing responsibility for social progress in urban America. In the 1970s and 1980s, as public attention shifted toward issues of economic revitalization, universities were once again in the middle of the change process, creating new partnerships with industry while generating many of the technical innovations and entrepreneurial organizations that produced the nation's current economic vibrancy.

When one surveys the contemporary academic scene, the pattern of academic involvement with societal issues continues to be apparent. Is there a crisis in the K–12 system? Higher education is replete with efforts to reform teacher education, partner with elementary and secondary schools, and identify effective schooling policies. Is there a call for new initiatives to exploit the economic and medical potential of the life sciences? Universities are spawning research programs and designing new curricula. Is there a need for renewed attention to the despair of inner-city communities? Universities are responding to governmental calls for partnerships with urban communities. Is it vital that young Americans master the challenges of changing technology? Universities are racing to retool themselves and provide the requisite facilities and programs. The record varies, of course, from institution to institution, but the broad pattern of engagement with urgent social challenges seems very clear.

Despite this history, participants in higher education can readily see why outsiders so often perceive our institutions as rigid and disconnected. For one thing, academics do have a responsibility to focus on educational and intellectual issues of lasting significance, and this can lead us to resist pressures to work directly on social problems that can more appropriately be addressed by other kinds of institutions. Indeed, cycles of change in academia are intentionally slower than in business or politics, at least with respect to activities that involve long-term institutional commitments, which tend also to be the zones of academic life that get the most public attention. A new undergraduate major will not produce graduates for three or four years after it is initiated and will frequently require funding of tenured faculty positions and specialized facilities. A change in degree requirements has long-term implications for departmental budgets. Changes in these areas need to be carefully considered. In addition, public perceptions of higher education are often dominated by the actions of a limited number of highly visible, elite institutions, and these campuses are often the slowest to change. Far less media attention gets focused on the hundreds of community colleges, four-year public colleges, and urban universities for whom responding to social needs is central to their missions.

Perhaps most important, even the most casual observer of academia is familiar with the painfully slow, highly participatory deliberative processes through which institutional decisions are made. The perception that our governance arrangements often provide a means by which entrenched interests can resist change has much validity, and corporate executives who participate in higher education as trustees and members of public governing boards are routinely horrified by the Byzantine workings of this system. Even a passionate advocate for higher education can sympathize with the fabled CEO of Monsanto, who characterized managing a university as his worst nightmare.

Indeed, my own perceptions as a young administrator in the 1970s had much in common with our critics on this point. As an assistant to a reforming chancellor at a new urban campus of a major state system, I was keenly attuned to the urgencies of the 1960s regarding social conditions in cities. It was hard for me to understand the resistance of faculties to developing programs that disadvantaged young people so clearly needed or to adopting flexible admissions policies to give students from nontraditional backgrounds a better chance or to embracing alternative forms of study so that working people, or those who could not get to campus, could have access to higher education. These concerns led me, some years later, to undertake a systematic research project on the problem of institutional change. Trained as a historian, I studied long-term patterns of development at a diverse set of universities to see how adaptable they had been and what forces had tended to promote or to impede change. I focused on eight universities in Massachusetts, on the theory that I could understand the process of adaptation better if I looked at a disparate set of institutions operating in a common external environment. I studied these schools from the 1930s through 1980, following each from a time of severe financial constraint, through the crises of World War II, to the postwar expansion, the uncertainties of the 1950s, the baby-boom years of the 1960s, and into the downturns and reversals of the 1970s.

What I found surprised me. All eight universities underwent dramatic changes over this span of years. Harvard finally broke the mold of its WASPy, New England heritage to emerge as the leading modern research university of the world. The Massachusetts Institute of Technology evolved from a mostly undergraduate engineering school into a great center of research and advanced education in basic science. Tufts outgrew its past as a locally oriented Ivy League wannabe to become a highly competitive and selective New England college. Brandeis was born and quickly established itself as one of the leading universities of the country. Boston University, Boston College, and Northeastern moved beyond their roots as urban, commuting institutions to become, in different ways and to varying degrees, regional and national universities. The small, unimpressive state college in Amherst mushroomed into a major public university and became the flagship of a three-campus system with burgeoning centers in Boston and Worcester. It was impossible to review this history without being impressed by the resilience, adaptability, and creativity of these institutions and their leaders.

Even more important, I was forced beyond the reformist biases with which I began my research to conclude that changes at these several institutions had produced, in the aggregate, an impressive range of societal benefits not only for Massachusetts but also for the region and the nation. At the end of the period they offered far more opportunities for study across a wider array of fields to a greater diversity of students than they had at the beginning. These institutions had greatly multiplied their overall scholarly productivity and had played major roles in the ascendance of American scholarship to international leadership in field after field. Their collective impact on the regional economy was equally unarguable: spin-offs from their research laboratories powered the economic rejuvenation of a region that was struggling and stagnant at the beginning of the period, while their programs attracted talent to the area and their budgets became major sources of jobs and purchasing power. They strengthened Massachusetts and New England in countless social dimensions as well, most dramatically in the area of healthcare, where they fueled Boston's emergence as one of the world's major centers of medical research and clinical care.

Does this impressive record of adaptation and social contribution mean that higher education's critics are just plain wrong? Not entirely. The histories that I studied contained numerous examples of just the kind of petty, self-serving, cantankerous behavior that often leads to the labeling of higher education as resistant to change. In addition, universities in Massachusetts were much more responsive to some challenges than to others. In particular, campuses were more receptive to changes that contributed to their institutional standing—for example, raising admissions standards or enhancing scholarly work—than to those that served important social purposes but added little institutional glory.

The moral I found in my study is not that universities are virtuous and are unfairly criticized. The moral is that despite the validity of many criticisms about the character and organization of higher education, despite the often infuriating nature of our decision processes, academic institutions have, over time, found ways to adapt to evolving societal needs, and these adaptations, broadly considered, have produced extensive social benefits.

The key to understanding the patterns of change I have described lies in a deeper analysis of the workings of our system of higher education than is typically offered by our critics and detractors. The charge that administrators and faculty who ought to be concerned with the public good are too often preoccupied with narrow institutional interests contains much truth (though I was also deeply impressed with the statesmanship and social commitment of numerous leaders at the institutions I studied). In the end, however, neither the intentions of academic leaders nor their social values are as significant in determining broad directions of institutional development as the critical literature suggests. The story of academic change at the institutions I studied was not fundamentally about good and bad leaders—though leadership mattered greatly, as I argue below—but about the impact of an array of driving forces on large, complex social institutions.

Scholars of organizational change have advanced alternative theories about the forces that drive universities. One tradition has argued that academic institutions are moved by the play of ideas—debates about institutional mission, curricular content, and pedagogical theory. A second school of thought has focused on internal power relationships, seeing change as the outcome of struggles among key institutional constituencies. Still another theme in the literature stresses competition among campuses as the most powerful determinant of change. My own studies have convinced me that each of these approaches has merit and that long-term patterns of institutional change reflect complex interactions among ideas, power struggles, and competitive pressures in particular campus settings.

The historical record among universities in Massachusetts makes it plain, however, that over an extended period the competition for resources and prestige has been the deepest and most pervasive force determining trajectories of institutional evolution. The theoretical implication is quite clear: if one wishes to understand why a university is pursuing a particular pattern of change, one needs to look first to the competitive contexts in which that institution seeks students, faculty, and dollars, then to the context in which it competes for recognition and status. Those who criticize academia for refusing to change are missing the forest for the trees. Any fair examination of the historical record will show that they do change. Change occurs not primarily because of the moral qualities of individual leaders, important as these are, but because universities, like businesses, function in a highly competitive environment in which they must adapt or die.

The most challenging conclusion from my study was this: processes of interinstitutional competition—powered as they often are by the interests of campuses or of dominant campus constituencies— nonetheless, in the aggregate and over the long run, produce adaptations that serve the interests of society. Growth and change in higher education mirrors growth and change in the broader economy. Competition and self-interest may not always display the most appealing qualities of academics or corporate leaders, but they nonetheless drive institutional systems that are impressively adaptable and serve our nation remarkably well.

Are College Presidents Really Important?

Just as observers differ about the responsiveness of universities to changing societal needs so, too, do they disagree about the importance of presidents in the change process. The traditional view, of course, is the stuff of legend. Even moderately well-informed students of academic history know tales of the great nineteenth- and early-twentieth-century presidents who built the first modern universities and became leading public figures in the process: Eliot of Harvard, Gilman of Hopkins, Angel of Michigan, Butler of Columbia, Harper of Chicago, to name only a few. Viewed through the prism of these histories, the university was and is the lengthened shadow of its leader, and it is not possible to imagine the greatness of the institution without the greatness of the president.

Most would agree that the modern university is far more complex, and far less susceptible to presidential authority, than its turn-of-the-century counterpart. Today's universities are much larger; the intellectual territory they cover is much vaster; the constituencies they serve are more varied; their financing is more complex; and their interactions with other institutions, especially governments at both the state and federal levels, are more extensive than was the case for even the most highly developed universities a hundred years ago. Despite these changes, the belief that presidential leadership is the key to campus progress continues to hold sway among important commentators. One of the leading proponents of this notion is James Fisher, who has argued that "our future rests on the bold, decisive leadership of college and university presidents nationwide" (Association of Governing Boards 1984, 11–14). In recent years, Fisher has produced a series of volumes on the presidency of colleges and universities, finding numerous examples of success stories and extracting from them maxims to guide those who seek to run their institutions more effectively (Fisher 1984, 1991; Fisher, Tack, and Wheeler 1988).

The conviction that presidents are essential to institutional progress has spawned another familiar theme in the literature on higher education: the characterization of the presidency as an enfeebled position, so weakened by the demands of academic governance, so hemmed in by contending forces, so daunted by the complexity of fragmented campus communities, that incumbents are challenged merely to survive, let alone to lead. The Association of Governing Boards' Commission on the Academic Presidency put this conclusion succinctly in its 1996 report: "the greatest danger we see in this new era of growing doubt and demands is that colleges and universities are neither as nimble nor as adaptable as the times require. Why? Because the academic presidency has become weak" (11). The commission's call for a revitalized presidency echoes numerous recent assessments.

Among scholars of higher education, the finding of a diminished presidency does not necessarily lead to worry that universities are in trouble or cannot adapt. On the contrary, the most fashionable analysis among social scientists is that the importance of the presidency is vastly overrated as a factor in institutional progress and that change occurs as a result of far more complex intrainstitutional dynamics than suggested by champions of the presidential perspective.

The classic statement of this thesis was produced by Michael Cohen and James March in their 1974 study of academic leadership. Cohen and March acknowledge the symbolic role of the president and even the importance of a president's ability to articulate a vision capable of energizing a campus community, but they expressed deep skepticism about the substantive impact of presidential activity on the actual work of the university. Perhaps the most thoughtful contemporary proponent of this perspective is Robert Birnbaum, who asserts that colleges are "cybernetic" (or self-regulating) systems that "evolve not by one omniscient and rational agent but by the spontaneous corrective action of the college's parts." In Birnbaum's view the president has important functions to fulfill but is unlikely to significantly influence the institution's long-term pattern of development (1988, 21).

My own research, as well as my direct observations, provides some support for both the presidential and the cybernetic perspectives. Indeed, the argument advanced in the preceding section—that the direction of institutional change is largely determined by a university's competitive position—suggests that structural factors are of decisive importance in shaping the developmental trajectories of universities. Among the campuses I studied, it was apparent that each acquired, over time, areas of competitive advantage and vulnerability; broad patterns of development tended inexorably, with or without presidential intent, toward outcomes that maximized institutional resources and prestige. This fact explains one of the most striking aspects of the campus histories I reviewed—the continuity of change trajectories across long periods of time and successive presidencies.

Two twentieth-century Harvard presidents, Lawrence Lowell in the 1910s and 1920s and Nathan Pusey in the 1950s and 1960s harbored decidedly mixed feelings about the shift in their institution's emphasis toward research and graduate work that had been championed by their predecessors, Charles Eliot and James Conant, and away from undergraduate education. Both Lowell and Pusey advanced policies that ran counter to this trend. Yet Harvard evolved steadily toward its current identity as a modern research university. The forces compelling the nation's oldest university to accept a future that opportunity offered and preeminence required were simply too strong to be more than mildly impeded by the interventions of contrarian presidents.

At the other end of the status spectrum, the founders of the Boston campus of the University of Massachusetts sought to create a kind of elite, public-sector New England college focused on undergraduate liberal education in the arts and sciences with few, if any, professional programs and minimum attention to urban issues or to advanced graduate work. If ever a leadership vision was doomed by a campus's structural position it was here. In time, UMass-Boston became what its situation demanded that it be: a diversified urban campus with a mix of undergraduate programs in professional fields and the arts and sciences, active interactions with the urban community, and, of course, ambitions at the doctoral level. Ultimately UMB found chancellors who would affirm—and provide leadership toward—this destiny.

So the structure of a university's position is important and imposes significant constraints on administrative discretion. But structure isn't everything. Institutions do need to make decisions about where and in whom to invest and how to evolve. These things do not occur automatically, and it is possible to make mistakes. Some institutions flourish and others languish. Some move along a well-defined course of development, while others drift in a confusion of competing priorities.

Boston University in the 1950s and 1960s was a textbook case of institutional drift. While the president focused on creating a proper physical campus for the once-dispersed university community, academic directions were never clearly articulated, and by the end of the period the university was headed for serious financial trouble. It was only when the trustees appointed a strong-willed, clear-thinking president, John Silber, that BU found its bearings and began to make significant progress toward viability as a diversified, second-level, regional, and increasingly national, university. A similar change occurred at Boston College under a very different kind of president. In 1970, BC was in deep financial trouble under a president who had been seriously disoriented by the turmoil of the student protest movement. The institution's impressive rise in both material fortunes and academic recognition over the next 20 years cannot be separated from the steady, understated, collegial leadership of the new president, Father J. Donald Monan, SJ.

I looked hard among the institutions I studied to find instances where universities made significant progress on a unified pattern of development across an extended period of time in the absence of strong presidential leadership—or a strong leadership team centered around a president. I couldn't find any. This is not to say that a well-established academic community—a Harvard or an MIT—could not add strength under a weak president, especially during a period of financial prosperity; both institutions have demonstrated the contrary. Nor would I argue that a midrange institution could not survive and even achieve some successes with mediocre leadership; my studies contained examples of this phenomenon as well. But put the question more sharply: Can an institution sustain a coherent pattern of institutional repositioning in which mission is reconceived, competitive strategies are altered, constituencies are modified, and financial arrangements are recast—in short, can it execute a basic adaptation to changed circumstances—in the absence of effective presidential leadership? I would argue that such a result is very unlikely. My studies of eight universities over a 51-year period yielded no examples.

The reason that presidents remain important is not hard to grasp. The forces that bear on academic institutions are complex. External pressures—competing campuses, changing student markets, the academic professions, donors and legislators, public policies, neighboring communities, economic conditions, intellectual and technical change—present the institution with a myriad of opportunities or threats that must be seized, ignored, or countered. Internal pressures from the various departments and disciplines, both academic and administrative; students; faculty leaders; trustees; and budgets also present a daunting set of choices. If one accepts, as I do, that institutional change requires an integrated strategy in which some possibilities are pursued and others neglected, in which decisions must be made as to where to invest energy and resources, then it is difficult to imagine how the chaos of forces that beset a modern university can be tamed into a consistent pattern of change in the absence of a guiding consciousness. That consciousness cannot be a committee (and often not a leadership team either), and it certainly cannot be an impersonal social dynamic. Some decisions need to be made by a leader with a workable vision of where the university is going as well as the skill to organize institutional resources in pursuit of that vision.

Both my studies and my observations have led me to the conclusion that there is no substitute for an effective university president. This is not because we need heroes to save us from confusion. It is because there is an essential leadership function implicit in any complex social system, universities included, that can be performed only by an individual, and that function involves much more than the symbolic and rhetorical performances that even cynics concede a president must provide.

Those who worry that an academic culture that withholds legitimacy from presidential leadership will weaken higher education and compromise our social functions are right. No sensible person would want to return to the days of authoritarian presidents who could ride roughshod over faculties or impose their wills without consultation or debate. The principle of shared governance is a measure of progress in academia, not decline. But we need to recognize that presidents have a valuable, even indispensable, role to play, and that the best interests of higher education and of the society it serves require that we foster institutional cultures and shape decision processes that appropriately support those attempting in good faith to fulfill that need.

The Satisfactions of the Job

It is a short step from depicting the presidency as an exceptionally difficult job to seeing it also as an undesirable one. Those who yearn for bygone days and lament the absence of larger-than-life presidents, tend to argue that the diminished presidency of today simply cannot attract the kind of talent that aspired to academic leadership a century ago.

It is, of course, impossible to compare the ability of today's presidents with those of an earlier era, but my suspicion is that the perceived differences have more to do with the changed character of the university—indeed with changes in contemporary culture regarding authority—than with the actual capacities of academic leaders. Whatever qualities today's presidents may possess, however, there can be little doubt that the historic picture of the heroic president has been replaced in popular imagery by a conception of the college or university president as careworn, harassed, and constrained— more likely to be the mediator or campus politician so memorably described by Clark Kerr (1963, 29–41) than a commanding educational leader.

It may be unbecoming for a sitting president to comment on the satisfactions of the job. It may also be unwise. And yet I am inclined to write on this subject because I find the opportunities offered by the presidency so profoundly engaging and feel so strongly the importance of encouraging capable young academics that I see administrative work as both valuable and rewarding. So with apologies and qualifications appropriate to the fact that in my case the jury is still out, let me devote the last part of this essay to a personal reflection on my experience as a university president.

From the perspective outlined earlier in this essay, the importance of institutional adaptation in higher education, I have been extremely fortunate in the campus I have the opportunity to lead. Northeastern University, at the time of my appointment, had recently embarked upon a course of fundamental repositioning, and it has been my charge from the trustees to realize the potential of a radically altered vision of the university. I have thus been asked to lead precisely the kind of change process about which I have written, and I have been invited to do so at a university that I had studied as a scholar and for which I had developed a deep respect long before the idea of becoming its president was anything more than a remote fantasy.

Here is a brief summary of Northeastern's situation. Founded in 1898 to provide education for young Boston men from working-class backgrounds, the university evolved over its first 90 years as a classic urban campus. It focused on practical programs in fields such as engineering and business, mostly at the undergraduate level. It adopted a pattern of cooperative education so that students could earn income to pay tuition. To reduce costs, it built no dormitories, operated with minimal facilities, and offered little campus life beyond its classes, many of which were held in rented rooms in nearby city buildings.

In a state where public higher education remained notoriously underdeveloped well into the 1960s, Northeastern served the need for low-cost, accessible education met in other states by large public universities—and it flourished in the process. By the mid-1960s the university had gone co-ed and built a skeletal campus with a few dorms; its enrollment had ballooned to 45,000 (mostly commuting) students; and it had eight undergraduate colleges, fledgling graduate programs and research centers, deep ties to Boston's neighborhoods and area businesses, a huge evening program for adult learners, and satellite campuses at several sites around metropolitan Boston. In 1967 President Asa Knowles proudly proclaimed NU to be the largest private university in the country. Five years later the Carnegie Commission on Higher Education identified it as one of the nation's model urban universities.

As the conditions of higher education locally and nationally evolved in the late 1970s and 1980s, Northeastern continued to do what it historically had done. It expanded further. It added some programs and improved the campus. Essentially, it maintained the mission and competitive strategy that had worked so well during its first 75 years. Unfortunately, structural changes in Northeastern's environment—especially the growth of public higher education in Massachusetts combined with the declining numbers of high school graduates—were steadily eroding the viability of those traditional patterns. By the late 1980s, the institution was forced to admit almost all applicants in order to maintain the scale on which its financial health depended.

The roof collapsed in 1990 when the university failed to meet its freshman enrollment goals by a wide margin, a harsh jolt of reality that struck a second time with equal force the following year. For a tuition-dependent institution like Northeastern, a modest enrollment shortfall presents a serious problem. The reduced enrollment numbers of 1990 and 1991 pushed the university to the edge of bankruptcy.

The enrollment crisis prompted Northeastern's leadership to reassess the university's position within the highly competitive arena of Massachusetts higher education. That rethinking led to the recognition that the school's historic role as the low-cost provider of accessible education for the local community had been taken over by the public sector, which could offer a credible alternative at a much lower price, and that to compete effectively in the future Northeastern would need to raise its academic standards significantly and attract students more by the value and reputation of its educational programs than by their cost and accessibility.

Impelled by this vision and led by an extraordinarily effective president, Jack Curry, the university embarked on a program of systematic downsizing combined with ambitious efforts to increase admissions selectivity and enhance the campus while improving the quality of academic programs. By the mid-1990s—the time of my appointment—Northeastern had achieved financial stability at significantly lowered levels of enrollment and costs and had taken the first critical steps in building heightened academic standards and improved reputation. In just five years the university had jettisoned patterns and policies developed across the previous nine decades and set off on an entirely new course as a "smaller and better" Northeastern. Those who doubt the capacity of universities to adapt to changed circumstances need to take a close look at the remarkable achievements of Northeastern in the early 1990s.

Following my appointment in 1996, my charge from the board has been to help Northeastern realize the "better" part of the "smaller-better" formula that has guided the institution since the early 1990s. To carry out this charge, it has been necessary to engage the campus community in an extended dialogue about what kind of "better" university we want to be. The process has required intensive efforts by many people. We have examined each of our colleges to find niches in which we can excel. We have reviewed graduate education and research activities to identify areas of advantage. We have invested in new facilities to increase our residential capacity. We have rethought cooperative education less as a means for students to earn income to pay educational costs and more as a powerful form of learning that can appeal to outstanding students on a national and even international basis. We have wrestled with the challenge of honoring important Northeastern traditions—such as our accessibility to students from modest backgrounds and our links to the urban community—while also repositioning ourselves at a higher level of academic recognition. We have had to reconsider many aspects of our organization to provide much more effective student support than was possible (or expected) when we were offering a low-cost education to huge numbers of undergraduates.

We are, of course, only in the early stages of this transformation, and we are a long way from achieving our goals. But progress so far is encouraging, and we are looking to the future with confidence that we are on the right track. Some future historian will need to assess the merits of our efforts. My challenge here is to reflect on the rewards of the presidency as I have experienced them.

I should confess at the start that I love being president of Northeastern. There have been tensions and difficulties, of course, and the amount of work to be done has more than justified the image of the presidency as highly demanding. But these challenges were to be expected and have not detracted from the many satisfactions of my job. The personal interactions have been especially rewarding. The presidency has given me the chance to work with a talented and dedicated institutional community, including many members who have been ready to participate energetically in the change process. It has allowed me to interact with trustees, many of them alumni, who care deeply about the well-being of the university and to meet with other alumni who are eager for news of their alma mater and ready to provide support. My responsibilities have also brought me into contact with an intriguing range of accomplished people beyond the Northeastern community, including political and business leaders, honorary-degree recipients and campus visitors, and reporters for the major media.

The fact of having presidential authority has also been rewarding. I have found it enormously satisfying, after many years as a middle-level administrator, to be able to make decisions and to act—to build a new residence hall, to create an endowed professorship, to change scholarship policy, or to direct resources toward any one of dozens of other worthy projects. There has also been the fun of working across a wonderfully broad range of issues—intellectual, political, financial, aesthetic, and social. For anyone with the instincts of a generalist, the university presidency is a rare opportunity indeed.

Best of all has been the satisfaction of working with students who are excited by the experience we are providing them and often remarkably appreciative of our efforts to enhance that experience. Few professional moments can exceed in pure deliciousness a commencement ceremony in which the president gets to stand before the graduating seniors and their parents and to hear their thunderous cheers and to know that one has done something good for all those young lives. John Gardner has summarized my feelings about the Northeastern presidency perfectly: "what could be more satisfying," Gardner once wrote, "than to be engaged in work in which every capacity or talent one may have is needed, every lesson one may have learned is used, every value one cares about is furthered?" (1968, 32). For all its pressures and problems, the university presidency offers just such an opportunity.

The satisfactions I have mentioned so far are almost certainly available at many universities, and I commend them to those who are considering administrative work. From my perspective, however, none of these experiences goes to the heart of the presidential opportunity. At the center of my experience has been the awareness that the fortunes of an immensely valuable social institution, one lovingly nurtured over a century by many gifted and dedicated people, one that does work that is vitally important to me personally, has been entrusted in some degree to my care and that I am having the opportunity to help that institution find a new way to survive, to flourish, and to make a social contribution during the next period of its existence. The thing I would most want to believe, at the time I step down from this position, is that the university has negotiated the transition on which we have embarked and has arrived securely at a new position in the constellation of American colleges and universities.

The opportunity to lead this change process has provided the greatest satisfactions of my presidency. The challenge has been, in the first instance, intellectual. I have needed to understand this institutional community—its history, its sense of purpose, its values, its capabilities—and to find in these materials ways of characterizing who we are, what we care about, and where we need to get to that both engage the enthusiasm of key constituencies and work as a competitive strategy in our current circumstances.

The intellectual challenge has been engaged, of course, in a social context. My thought processes have not occurred in an office with a closed door. They have proceeded through countless conversations with members of the Northeastern community, through the work of several committees that we have created to reflect on one or another aspect of our situation, and through extended discussions within a leadership group of senior administrators and faculty members. In the end, though, it has been my job to identify in the ideas that have emerged at least the broad outlines of a direction for the university and to find a way of expressing that direction in words. Nothing so far has given me greater satisfaction than the positive responses I have received to our formulation of an "aspiration" for Northeastern that summarizes our character and purpose and gives us a foundation on which to build.

What began as an intellectual challenge quickly became an organizational and political one. The broad themes of our aspiration needed to be translated into an operational plan. Fortunately, we reached the point where this planning activity was required at the same time that we were due for a decennial reaccreditation visit, and we were able to use the extensive process of institutional review associated with reaccreditation to craft goals and strategies that would advance the purposes we had identified. Under the leadership of a very effective provost, the campus community was able, over a period of two years, to turn our aspiration into an action and assessment plan that tells us, in specific and measurable terms, how we need to change a broad range of institutional activities.

We are currently in the third stage of the change process. Neither a broad sense of direction nor a detailed plan of action has real value unless a group of institutional leaders puts energy into bringing about these changes and unless the dozens of university departments, both academic and administrative, are prepared to make the adjustments of focus and increases in effort necessary to accomplish these purposes. So, Northeastern's leadership team is currently engaged in aligning the efforts of units across the university behind our aspiration and our plan. The senior vice presidents, each of whom is responsible for a broad sector of institutional life, are working with the departments reporting to them to formulate unit plans that reinterpret their work in these terms and set standards of accomplishment necessary to achieve our goals.

While all of this planning activity has kept part of our attention focused on long-range goals, we have been taking concrete steps in the directions we have identified. We have understood that such planning is a continuing, organic process, that it would be foolish to postpone action until we have completed detailed plans in all areas, and that there is a healthy interaction between thinking about the future and taking practical steps in the present. So we have invested a great deal of effort in improving our performance in areas ranging from admissions recruitment to student support to faculty hiring to sponsored research to physical facilities to public relations. Positive results from these initiatives, as registered by increases in the number and quality of applications, improved retention rates, outstanding appointments, and external recognition have been rewarding and have encouraged all of us to keep investing in the change process. We have also committed ourselves to a capital campaign, knowing that we cannot become the better university we have envisioned unless we become less dependent on tuition for financing than we historically have been. The enthusiasm of key supporters and donors—many of them longtime members of our governing boards and alumni with deep institutional roots—for our vision of a new Northeastern and for the progress we are making in getting there has been extremely rewarding.

The challenges of actually accomplishing the goals we have articulated and of acquiring the resources we need are, of course, far more daunting than those we have faced so far. Yet I approach the work that lies ahead with the same excited sense of opportunity that I have experienced in the first stages of the change process. Large, complex institutions like Northeastern are the vehicles modern society has created to do its most important work. As Jean Monnet has said, "institutions are more important than individuals, but only individual men and women can transform and enrich the things which institutions transmit to successor generations" (Lewis 1988). My colleagues and I have been given the chance to transform an important institution that has great personal significance for each of us. What opportunity could be richer?

Conclusion

I have written this chapter for a volume intended, unashamedly, to celebrate American higher education. I was pleased to participate in this project because I believe so deeply in the value of academic work and regard many of the criticisms directed at higher education as shallow. The point-counterpoint construction I used at the beginning of this chapter, however, works both ways. There is a counterpoint for each point I advanced here, and there is much truth in the arguments against positions I have espoused. I would not want to be understood as an apologist for the status quo. There are many ways higher education could serve society better. We could find more varied ways to strengthen the competitive positions of our institutions while also serving a range of societal needs. It is discouraging to see so many colleges and universities seeking to improve their positions by pursuing more-or-less interchangeable versions of institutional models associated with a handful of elite campuses. It is equally disheartening to realize that we have done much less than we should have done to shift the focus of our universities away from the preoccupation with research that has dominated academia since the 1960s and back toward undergraduate education and to see how little progress we have made in reintroducing coherence into undergraduate curricula that have grown ever more chaotic over the last 30 years. There is unfinished work at the graduate level as well, especially the challenge of better preparing doctoral students for their most important responsibility—undergraduate teaching. We could be doing much more in the external arena as well, especially in strengthening our public schools. The list goes on.

So we need critics. We also need other institutions—government agencies, foundations, and corporations—to push us to do things that we would not do without their interventions. We need advocacy groups to prod us in such areas of social change as diversity and the environment. The forces of the academic marketplace may produce many important adaptations, but the market is an imperfect mechanism for assuring that higher education makes its maximum contribution to society. For this same reason we need leaders who see both the beauty and potential of academic institutions as well as their proclivity for self-serving behavior. The challenge to such leaders is the same in every era: to find ways to make academic communities reach their highest potentials while also flourishing in the intensely competitive arena in which they must exist. It is my hope that this essay encourages a few of my colleagues to seek the challenges of the presidency in order to find their own solutions to this continuing dilemma.

Notes

1. We cannot assume, of course, that everyone agrees that the "points" cited are negative propositions, while the "counterpoints" are positives. For example, many conservatives accuse higher education of being excessively responsive to social pressures and, indeed, given to chasing after the latest fad rather than attending to traditional values and core academic concerns.

2. All references in this chapter to universities in Massachusetts are taken from Freeland (1992).

References

Association of Governing Boards of Universities and Colleges. 1984. *Presidents will lead—If we let them. Report of the Commission on the Academic Presidency*. Washington, D.C.: Association of Governing Boards of Universities and Colleges.

———. 1996. *Renewing the academic presidency: Stronger leadership for tougher times. Report of the Commission on the Academic Presidency*. Washington, D.C.: Association of Governing Boards of Universities and Colleges.

Birnbaum, R. 1988. *How colleges work*. San Francisco: Jossey-Bass.

Cohen, M. D., and J. G. March. 1974. *Leadership and ambiguity: The American college president*. New York: McGraw-Hill.

Fisher, J. L. 1984. *Power of the presidency.* New York: Macmillan.

———. 1991. *The board and the president.* New York: Macmillan.

Fisher, J. L., M. W. Tack, and K. J. Wheeler. 1988. *The effective college president.* New York: Macmillan.

Freeland, R. M. 1992. *Academia's golden age.* New York: Oxford University Press.

Gardner, J. W. 1968. *No easy victories.* New York: Harper & Row.

Kerr, C. 1963. *The uses of the university.* Cambridge: Harvard University Press.

Lewis, F. 1988. *The New York Times,* 13 November.

Chapter Ten 〜

Graduate Education and Research

Jules B. LaPidus

From time to time in the history of higher education, certain countries have become the focal points for advanced study and scholarship, attracting students and scholars from all over the world to pursue their intellectual interests and often to obtain advanced degrees. Starting in the 1950s, the United States became such a place, particularly in the sciences, engineering, and other disciplines closely associated with the development of American business and industry. There were several reasons for this. One was the significant investment in graduate education and research made by the federal government. Successes in science and technology during World War II led Vannevar Bush to publish his famous paper, "Science: The Endless Frontier," which urged the government to make this investment in the national interest. Congress responded by appropriating money for the establishment and funding of a host of agencies, including the National Science Foundation and programs to support university research associated with graduate programs.

The increased demand for college education, some of which was related to the GI Bill and the opportunities it created for veterans to go to college, led to an expansion in higher education that created a demand for faculty. By the late 1950s, going to graduate school was not just a matter of pursuing scholarly interests, it was also a good career decision. In addition to a burgeoning academic job market, industries showed increasing interest in hiring Ph.D.s. This development was related to rapid advances in technology, much of which grew out of the scientific and technological advances that came out of World War II. Sputnik and the space program, which led to new concepts in microelectronics and computing, and the development of biotechnology in the 1970s and 1980s created entire new industries with a high demand for scientists and engineers at the Ph.D. level.

In all of these activities, the United States led the world not only in new discoveries and concepts, but also in the conversion of these ideas into practical realities. In addition, the United States had developed an unrivaled capability in graduate education and research, particularly in the sciences and engineering. The combination of these factors—new discoveries, increased investment by both the private sector and government, intense interest in careers in science and technology (particularly among young people), and opportunities to pursue those careers—created an atmosphere of excitement and enthusiasm for graduate study and research in science and technology that was paralleled in the other doctoral fields by the prospects of an expanding academic job market. At the same time, the increasing number of people with baccalaureate degrees sparked a revolution in master's-degree education, converting what had been seen by many as, at best, a way station in the Ph.D. process into a sought-after and increasingly necessary professional credential.

During the last 50 years of the twentieth century, American graduate education continued to grow both in numbers and in prestige. By the end of the century, the American approach to graduate education was serving as a model for much of the world. Doctoral production had risen to well over 40,000 each year, and the number of master's degrees approached 400,000 annually. But while the numbers are impressive, they do not reflect the many changes that took place in every aspect of graduate education during this half century. In particular, the changing relationship between graduate education and careers and the advent of distance technology, mediated through the Internet, are causing a shift in the way graduate education is perceived by students, the education and business communities, and the public at large.

In the course of this chapter I intend to provide sufficient background to give some sense of the enterprise, and also to comment on the major changes—demographic, programmatic, procedural, technological, conceptual, and cultural—that are defining the next phase in the development of graduate education in the United States.

A Brief History

Although graduate education in America began in the late nineteenth century, the changes in this sector of higher education after World War II, particularly between the late 1950s and the early 1970s, really define what it had become by the beginning of the 1990s. Clearly, the major characteristic of American graduate education was growth—in the number of students seeking admission, in the number of institutions offering graduate degrees, and in the number of students obtaining master's and doctoral degrees. Between 1960 and 1976, the number of doctoral degrees awarded tripled to about 32,000 a year, and the number of master's degrees increased from about 80,500 to more than 300,000 annually. During this same time period, the number of institutions awarding doctoral degrees increased from 208 to 307, and the number awarding master's degrees from 621 to 979.

Part of the development of graduate education during that time was the conversion of normal schools into regional state universities. Most of these institutions continued to concentrate on programs in education, developing master's and certificate programs to meet the postbaccalaureate needs of their primary constituents. Some of them eventually developed doctoral programs, for the most part in education and related fields. In addition, the rapid development of community colleges created a demand for faculty, giving rise to the Doctor of Arts degree, intended specifically for those who wanted teaching positions in these institutions. This was essentially a non-research, course work–oriented program focused on the teaching of a discipline at the level of the first two years of college. Although this degree is still offered in some places today, it was not particularly successful in fulfilling its objectives, and most institutions that had started these programs dropped them by the early 1980s.

This period of expansion was followed by a decade of relative stability (GUIRR 1989). Enrollments in doctoral institutions leveled off, and the number of doctoral degrees held fairly constant at between 32,000 and 34,000 per year. Master's degrees continued to increase annually until 1976, when they peaked at about 317,000. The apparent stability in numbers was misleading. Steady numbers of Ph.D.s masked a pronounced demographic change, characterized by a large decline in the number of American men and an increase in the number of women and foreign students receiving the degree.

Prior to 1950 most graduate students were white males in their mid- to late 20s. There were very few American minority students or foreign students and relatively few women. That situation began to change in the 1970s, dramatically for American women and for foreign students in the United States on temporary visas, and slowly for American minorities. By the mid-1990s the typical American graduate student was most likely to be a woman in her 30s, married, with dependents, and getting graduate education on a part-time basis (Syverson 1996).

The period from 1978 to 1988 was one of diversification, particularly in the number and kinds of institutions involved in academic research. Competition for research support, faculty, and students increased in response to greater availability of research funds. The source of these funds also became more diverse, with industry and some states investing more heavily in applied research—usually related to economic development. In addition, universities interested in expanding their research capabilities (or being pressured to do so by state legislatures) invested more of their own resources in this kind of activity. The result was a decentralizing of the academic research establishment from a relatively small number of established research universities to a much larger group of institutions aspiring to become active and competitive in research. In a way, this was echoed in Great Britain by the conversion of the polytechnics into universities.

This diversification of the academic research enterprise was not accompanied by a rise in student enrollment, which tended to remain relatively stable. But toward the end of the decade, specifically in 1986, the numbers of both doctoral and master's degrees awarded began to increase, in many cases fueled by a dramatic increase in the number of foreign degree candidates. As a fraction of total degrees awarded, those awarded to foreign students more than doubled for both degrees. This combination of factors led to a situation described in the GUIRR report:

If it was not clear earlier, it became so by the end of the 1979–1988 decade: The historic relationship between university research and graduate education was under stress from virtual steady-states in university enrollments and over-all production of new doctoral researchers, on the one hand, and mounting pressure to expand basic research activities, with or without instructional components, on the other. With the overall ratio of students to faculty remaining constant over the past decade, expansion occurred in part by creating extra-departmental research centers and institutes and hiring non-teaching researchers to operate them. While graduate education in the United States continues to include significant research components, what appears to have changed is the extent to which expanding academic research programs include instructional components. (1989, 1–9)

This change was not as extreme as it might have seemed. In a way, it was an expansion of the experiment-station model familiar in fields like agriculture and engineering in land-grant universities. These units had always employed a mix of faculty and nonfaculty research personnel as well as graduate student research assistants. Much of what they did was contract research unrelated to graduate programs and often inappropriate for dissertation research. But the changes went much further than that. Universities were actively seeking to expand their research support from private sources, primarily industry. Particularly in the rapidly developing biotechnology and computer industries, the interface between universities and private industry was growing more permeable as faculty members became involved as principals in new companies. Faculty had to attempt to keep their commercial interests separate from their role as advisers of graduate students. This issue continues to be important as universities develop new kinds of relationships with a wide variety of for-profit organizations.

Changes in Field of Study Preferences

Many of the changes that occurred at the doctoral level through 1988 have been commented on by William Bowen and Neil Rudenstine (1992). In general, degree production in the sciences and engineering had increased. This was particularly striking in the biological sciences. Degree awards in the social sciences had remained fairly level and had declined in the humanities. At the master's level, the most striking change during the past 30 years has been the growth of practice-oriented master's degrees; they now constitute roughly 85 percent of all such degrees awarded (Conrad, Haworth, and Millar 1993). By the mid-1990s, the number of master's degree awards in education had declined and the number of business degrees had grown, so that each represented approximately 25 percent of the degrees. The number of master's degrees awarded in engineering had remained about the same, but the number of social science degrees had declined and those in the health professions had increased.

At both degree levels, the changes in field preferences were the result of a number of factors. Among these were the availability of support for research and students; student interest in certain fields; job opportunities; and the broader political, economic, social, scientific, and technological changes that affected the way people lived, learned, and worked. Clearly, there has been a shift to the life sciences and health professions. Much of this is related to exciting and important new discoveries that stimulated public as well as student interest in these fields in the 1980s and 1990s just as the space program and the advent of computers stimulated interest in engineering and physics in the 1960s and 1970s. In particular, the reconceptualization of the biological sciences and the opportunities inherent in molecular biology and genetics led to redesign of graduate programs and closer ties with business and industry. At the master's level, the MBA grew dramatically, reflecting not just a growing interest in careers in business but a tendency in the corporate sector to require this kind of advanced degree for people seeking managerial positions.

Multidisciplinary, Interdisciplinary, and Area Studies Programs

Another change in the nature of graduate study that began in the 1970s has to do with the way research was actually carried out in several fields. It became common practice for students in some fields (e.g., physics and biochemistry) to work together in groups, with each student having responsibility for certain parts of a project. This was an industrial model and raised serious questions about the independent nature of doctoral work, but the practice has become widespread and universities have adapted to it (Council of Graduate Schools 1991). In a parallel development, individuals in different fields with a common research interest began to work together across disciplinary boundaries. This was usually referred to as multidisciplinary research.

To move from multidisciplinary teams working together on research problems to interdisciplinary research required a more fundamental change. For the most part, the increased interest in interdisciplinary studies was motivated by scholarly interest in areas of study that simply were not amenable to unidisciplinary or even multidisciplinary approaches. The rapid expansion in knowledge in almost every field illustrated the artificiality of disciplinary boundaries and the constraints they often imposed in understanding problems and finding approaches to their solution. Some individuals became immersed in fields other than their own to the point where they could think creatively using knowledge of both (or several) fields. This, coupled with the aforementioned shifting of student, faculty, and public interest (the latter often reflected in funding priorities), gave rise to research groups in areas such as cognitive science; neuroscience; environmental science; atmospheric science; material science; bioengineering; and later, in fields such as bioinformatics. In many cases, these research groups provided the foundation for the development of interdisciplinary graduate programs, which developed their own paradigms and processes.

In addition, there was an expansion in the concept of area studies. At one time this term had been used primarily to describe programs focused on a particular geographic area. Programs like Latin American studies or East Asian studies brought together people from a variety of disciplines, primarily in the social sciences and humanities, to bring their expertise to bear on issues affecting a country or world area. Starting in the 1970s, largely in response to social and political pressures, this concept expanded to include gender and ethnic studies, giving rise to women's studies, Black studies, and a variety of other programs.

Information Technology, The Postcomputer University, and the Post-Internet University

Beginning in the 1960s and 1970s when computers began to pervade the way universities did their business and faculty and students studied and did their research, it quickly became apparent that a sea change was occurring. At first it was mainly a matter of doing things faster. The slide rule and the Friden calculator were relegated to the academic attic, replaced by hand-held electronic calculators that provided incredible power at lower cost. Word processors became available and changed the dynamics and style of dissertation writing. But doing calculations and revising manuscripts were not new activities; computers merely made it possible to do these things faster.

By the early 1980s a different kind of change was beginning to occur. *The Oxford English Dictionary* had become available in electronic form, which made it an infinitely more useful resource, since it could be sorted and searched in ways that were impossible in hard copy. That icon of academic scholarship—the library card catalogue —gave way, with much hand-wringing and dire predictions about the end of scholarship, to on-line catalogues that could be accessed from home computers. It became possible to do incredibly complex mathematical calculations in minutes rather than years, thus making certain kinds of research practical for the first time. It was now possible to manipulate variables and run simulations and, with rapidly developing sophistication in computer graphics, to convert numbers into manipulable and moving visual images. This affected everything from the study of molecular interactions to choreography. At the same time, many scholars, particularly in areas like classics, art history, economics, and literature were incorporating the use of computers into their studies, and in the arts computers were being viewed not just as tools, but also as integral parts of the way creative artists thought about their fields. The postcomputer university had a dramatic effect on the way work was done, and it affected every field of scholarship and creative activity. With all of that, however, there was relatively little effect on the way people interacted with each other. For that to change, we needed the Internet.

Michael Schrage, speaking at a recent meeting, suggested that "The digital technologies restructuring enterprise and academe are far less about the creation and management of new information than the creation and management of new relationships" (1998). Each passing day seems to corroborate that insight, particularly as we try to comprehend the role of the Internet in graduate education and research. From the perspective of doctoral education, the use of the Internet as a readily accessible source of data and information appears to be very useful. A number of universities are requiring that all doctoral candidates submit their dissertations in digital form, and these are immediately made available on the World Wide Web (Networked Digital Library of Theses and Dissertations <www.ndltd.org>). An enormous amount of textual and statistical information is readily available on the web, and for students and faculty in all disciplines, the web is rapidly becoming a primary source of reference material. Research universities have viewed the availability of a superb library as an absolute requirement for mounting world-class doctoral programs. The development of digital libraries is broadening access to this kind of resource and creating new opportunities for scholarly research. It will also force scholars to deal with intellectual property issues as well as nagging questions about the quality of information available on the World Wide Web. In some ways this situation exemplifies the issues of technology and education: incredible opportunities fraught with pitfalls for the unwary. Peter Lyman has pointed out that, "On the Web there are writers but no authors or authorities, everything is published, and its value is determined by readers" (2000).

One of the most interesting developments is the "collaboratories," whereby investigators in different locations can work together, perform experiments by remote control, analyze data, and discuss results—all in real time. The head of the Space, Physics and Aeronomy Research Collaboratory based at the University of Michigan recently observed that while "controlling instruments from afar was one of the original goals . . . it gradually became clear . . . that researchers value the collaboratory more for giving them a venue for discussion and debate." The collaboratories eventually phased out the technically difficult remote control aspects and concentrated on "being able to talk about what they're seeing rather than being able to twist or turn some dials on an instrument" (Kiernan 1999).

These examples represent new ways of interacting that can facilitate the work of faculty and graduate students. They also raise to a higher level of intensity questions of intellectual property rights, access to data, and in a very different sense the development of consortial graduate programs involving students, faculty, and facilities from a number of different institutions. Particularly in the case of real-time collaborative research, it is easy to visualize consortial graduate programs organized around specialized facilities or resources. One of the concepts that has influenced institutional decisions about the initiation of graduate programs has been the question of "critical mass," by which is meant gathering together in one place a sufficient number of people to make a graduate program intellectually viable. Access to the Internet makes that concept meaningless with respect to place.

In addition to the effect of the Internet on research, there are obvious implications for all aspects of education. At the level of the master's degree and postbaccalaureate certificate programs, there has been intense interest in the use of technology as a way of providing education to large numbers of students. Although this idea is not new (closed-circuit and interactive audio-video systems, video and audio cassettes, and similar techniques have been in use for some time), the implications of the World Wide Web as an educational resource are dominating almost all discussions of higher education. The rush to the Internet as the solution to every educational question is both exciting and alarming. There is no question that the availability of courses and other educational material on-line provides great convenience for students who have the discipline to study and learn on their own and in their own time. Whether these techniques will replace classroom teaching is more problematic. In those virtual universities that make extensive use of on-line courses (e.g., Walden or the Open University), tutorial sessions and other meetings with instructors take place at regular intervals and are deemed essential to the learning experience.

The relationships between asynchronous education and education in real time, between live interactions and virtual ones, between the teaching prerogatives of the faculty and the learning prerogatives of the students, and between the development of educational content and the systems used to provide that content to students are among the most critical issues facing higher education today. Much of the discussion of these vexing topics has been focused on convenience and cost-effectiveness, for both student and education provider. The conversation is now beginning to shift to consider the educational questions. M. Edmundson has suggested that "on-line education's greatest contribution to the academy won't be its efficiency or its accessibility" but that "It will force us to decide whether we are going to continue our current evolution into mere conveyors of knowledge, or become seekers after something akin to wisdom" (1999). That issue is still unresolved.

These developments in the nature of graduate programs underscore an important fact of American graduate education: rather than being isolated from the real world, as some of its critics believe, it has been responsive to intellectual and scientific developments as well as to changes in technology and in student and public interest without relinquishing responsibility for maintaining high standards of scholarship. In this context, perhaps the most striking changes that have occurred in graduate education are related to the way people view the acquisition of advanced education as part of their lives. At the doctoral level, this has focused mainly on how graduate education prepares people for jobs and careers related to their education as scholars. At the postbaccalaureate level, the concern has been primarily about how people who have left the university and are in the work force continue to get the kind of education they need in order to remain employable and advance in their careers. The rest of this chapter will be devoted to exploring these topics in some detail.

Graduate Education in the 1990s

This brief recapitulation of the history of graduate education in the United States in the post–World War II period serves to set the stage for graduate education in the next century. Clearly, however, not knowing what demographic, social, economic, and technological changes will take place during this period prevents us from knowing what stories will be played out on that stage. Some predict the end of universities as we know them. Others predict that degrees will become obsolete and will be replaced by different kinds of certification. The only thing we can be sure of is that the future will not simply be the past writ large. Particularly in graduate education and research, areas that by definition are operating at the edges of what we know and how we think, future developments will be radically different from what we have seen in the past.

American graduate education as it now exists is an enormous enterprise, in terms of students (1.8 million), annual degree production (43,000 doctoral degrees and 400,000 master's degrees), institutions offering graduate education (1,800) and areas of specialization (1,000). It is characterized by a lack of any national coordinating entity, giving rise to a complex group of public and private institutions, each with a great deal of autonomy. It serves the postbaccalaureate educational needs of an increasingly diverse population and maintains an amazingly high level of quality over such a heterogeneous system. In order to explore these and other themes in graduate education, however, it is necessary to treat doctoral and master's education separately, as well as to consider two other important but nondegree programs: certificate programs and postdoctoral programs.

Doctoral Education

As the 1990s began, doctoral education was a booming enterprise. As mentioned previously, doctoral degree production had been increasing each year since 1986, and by 1997 had reached 42,705, its highest annual level ever. A number of large-scale scientific projects were under way, including the human genome project and the development of the superconducting supercollider. The power of computers was increasing at a tremendous rate, making previously undreamed of computing power available in every laboratory and library, home and office. Large databases were being developed in the humanities and social sciences, and access to scholarly material was improving dramatically in all fields. American doctoral education, particularly in the sciences and engineering, was widely regarded as premier in the world (Haworth and Smart 1996; LaPidus, Syverson, and Welch 1995).

Above all, American doctoral education and the American research university were considered to be amazingly successful at producing world-class research and world-class researchers on a scale hitherto unknown. It was this combination of capacity and excellent programs that continued to attract students and scholars from all over the world to study in the United States. For the same reasons, and because so many business and education leaders in other countries had received some or all of their graduate education in the United States, American doctoral education became the model for the development of research doctoral programs in countries whose expanding economies required the concomitant expansion of their graduate programs. As Stuart Blume points out: "The attractiveness of the North American model has derived from the fact that it has seemed able to ensure effective and efficient training of researchers on a much greater scale than has been usual in European universities" (1995, 23).

But there were problems. Educators had long been concerned that the development of graduate education could be detrimental to undergraduate education, since increasing pressures to obtain research funds and to be productive in research tended to draw the faculty away from involvement in undergraduate teaching. This was the topic of much comment in the education and popular press and the subject of many campus task forces and symposia. The issue was usually couched in terms of values and the reward system of universities. Leaders in the higher education community were unambiguous in their commitment not just to maintaining an appropriate balance between graduate research and undergraduate teaching, but also to demonstrating that research and teaching were complementary activities.

At the same time, however, the various rankings and ratings of universities, based almost entirely on the research reputations of their faculties and their ability to generate external funds for the support of research, tended to have a dampening effect on efforts to devote more faculty time to teaching. Unfortunately, the academic community as well as the general public persist in viewing higher education as a hierarchy based on research reputations rather than as a rich and diverse system based on serving the needs of different kinds of students. Universities continue to grapple with this issue and to try to move it beyond the simplistic dichotomy of teaching versus research to the more relevant concern about the enhancement of learning in an atmosphere characterized by scholarly inquiry.

The Doctoral Job Market

By the mid-1990s another factor appeared. Several studies in the late 1980s projected shortages of scientists and engineers as well as expanding academic opportunities in most fields (Bowen and Schuster 1986; Bowen and Sosa 1989; Atkinson 1990). The promise of an expanding academic job market, however, evaporated under the desiccating influence of major cutbacks in funding, particularly by state governments, and a series of events, such as the end of the Cold War, that had direct effects on the funding of universities. The terms *downsizing* or *rightsizing* came into prominence with respect to both universities and industrial organizations, and academic as well as industrial hiring of Ph.D.s declined. While the availability of academic jobs in the humanities had been relatively low for at least 20 years, it suddenly appeared that there was a shortage of jobs, academic or otherwise, for Ph.D.s in the sciences and engineering. By 1992, new Ph.D.s in physics, mathematics, chemistry, and engineering were reporting some difficulty in getting their first jobs. Tenure-track positions in research universities became scarce in all fields, and universities increased their use of part-time faculty. This was particularly unsettling to young scholars who had entered graduate school in the mid- to late 1980s and who now felt they had been misled.

The relationship between doctoral education and the job market is far from simple, and a great deal of misinformation and mythology surrounds the issue. In the popular and even the academic press the impression seems to be that most Ph.D.s are prepared by their graduate education for tenure-track positions in research universities and that failing to obtain such positions means their education has been wasted and they are failures. This impression is false on almost all counts. First of all, most doctoral programs try to prepare students to function as independent investigators, rather than to fill any specific job. This has been a problem, since relatively few students find jobs where doing independent research is all that is required. Second, there is a great deal of variation by field. In many of the sciences and in engineering, most Ph.D.s have sought industrial employment, and that number has been slowly and steadily increasing over the past 25 years. In the humanities, most Ph.D.s have been interested in academic jobs, and most have found them. But the issue is more subtle than just finding jobs. While it is true that the overwhelming majority of students in the humanities envision tenure-track positions in research universities as the ideal career path, most humanities Ph.D.s have never obtained these positions and have instead found their way to other types of faculty positions in universities or colleges. A minority have chosen nonacademic careers.

Articles that appeared in the press during the mid-1990s concerning this issue have been characterized by a bitterness and sense of disillusionment on the part of students, faculty, administrators, and other commentators that was unusual and disturbing to everyone connected with graduate education. I have written a more detailed description of this period (LaPidus 1997a; 1999). Universities began to pay increasing attention to student career goals and to the quality of the graduate experience—prompted in part by the vagaries of the job market and by discontent with the ambience of doctoral programs. Whether inspired by a student suicide, a concern about the paucity of tenure-track academic positions, a feeling that graduate students were being exploited, or general unhappiness about relationships between students and advisers, the education press and the programs of professional meetings reflected widespread concern. In addition, many people believed that doctoral education was too narrow, too focused on the dissertation, too concerned with learning more and more about less and less.

The considerable literature that developed about Ph.D.s and the job market was dominated by several themes: that universities had overproduced Ph.D.s by not letting the job market influence the size of their doctoral programs; that faculty members were misleading students into going to graduate school in order to maintain a source of cheap labor for undergraduate teaching and to help with faculty research projects; and that students, having survived the rigors of graduate school and obtained the Ph.D., were entitled to jobs doing independent research, preferably as tenure-track faculty in research universities (LaPidus 1997b).

There are two very different issues being considered here. One has to do with whether the United States is producing too many Ph.D.s. The other concerns the nature of doctoral education. With respect to the first, opinion is sharply divided. Although unemployment for Ph.D.s continues to be very low (2 to 3%), the fact that some Ph.D.s are having difficulties getting the jobs they want has led to criticism of graduate programs for admitting too many doctoral students. While it is true that the research and teaching obligations of a department are factors in determining the size of their doctoral programs, they are only part of the story. The availability of resources such as space, equipment, libraries, computing capability, and financial support for students also are important considerations. But the most difficult aspect of dealing with the size of doctoral programs may be related to the notion of providing educational opportunities to meet student demand regardless of the current or prospective states of certain career options.

There are those who believe that universities should take active steps to reduce the size of their doctoral programs. Because of the highly decentralized nature of graduate education, this kind of approach cannot be mandated nationally but is a matter for individual institutions and, in the case of public universities, state government to consider. The motivation is usually related to a combination of job-market concerns, availability of resources, and the desire to improve the quality of students admitted and to provide them with a better graduate experience. There are also attempts to provide better data about the availability of jobs for Ph.D.s. This is fraught with problems because of the difficulty in predicting or projecting what will happen to job opportunities during the time it takes to get a Ph.D. It is somewhat ironic that now, when many universities in the United States are considering decreasing doctoral production, most other countries are going in the opposite direction, although there are signs that this is beginning to change in some places (United Kingdom, Japan, France).

The second question involves the nature of doctoral education and how it related to jobs and careers. Probably the best statement to have appeared on this point was by John Armstrong: "The training of new Ph.D.'s is too narrow, too campus-centered, and too long. Furthermore, many new Ph.D.'s have much too narrow a set of personal and career expectations. Most do not know what it is they know that is of most value. They think that what they know is how to solve certain highly technical and specialized problems. Of course, what they really know is how to formulate questions and partially answer them, starting from powerful and fundamental points of view" (1994, 21). There is great interest in broadening the graduate education of doctoral students to better prepare them for a variety of jobs and careers.

New Approaches to Change in Doctoral Education

The past few years have seen a spate of studies that use words like *reinvent, reengineer, rethink,* and *reform* when discussing doctoral education (COSEPUP 1995; Patel 1995; Tobias, Chubin, and Aylesworth 1995; National Research Council 1998). For the most part, these studies have defined the purpose of doctoral education as transcending preparation for any one career and have recognized the need to take into account, in the design of doctoral programs, the need to prepare students to use their skills in a variety of ways (LaPidus 1997c). The remedies prescribed fall into several broad categories, and one way or another, many universities are investigating them.

Doctoral education is not job training, and people with the ability to function as independent problem-solvers can use that skill in ways tangential or even peripheral to their formal education. This reality is often difficult to understand, since there is a tendency among students and those who support graduate education to view as successful only those whose job descriptions match the field of specialization on their transcripts. A major activity in many graduate schools is the development of programs to provide better guidance to doctoral and postdoctoral students about career options and possibilities, particularly outside of the academy (LaPidus 1995).

One approach involves modifying the doctoral curriculum to provide students with a broader range of knowledge than that encompassed by their dissertation specialties. This usually is done by adding courses or other educational experiences to prepare students for a wide variety of jobs and careers. Some universities have designed minors and certificate programs in areas ancillary to the major field. In addition, they have developed courses and workshops on so-called transferable skills such as project planning, report writing, communication skills, and time management. These developments have been particularly striking in countries where doctoral study was often limited to one student, one research problem, and one faculty member. American doctoral programs, on the other hand, have long been characterized by a combination of courses, seminars, and dissertation research. There were indications, however, that this curriculum was becoming too focused on topics closely related to the dissertation research topic.

Another approach has been to develop special programs that resemble internships. Preparing Future Faculty is a program that has involved hundreds of doctoral students who have had the opportunity to spend time with faculty and students in a variety of institutional settings. A number of institutions have developed programs consisting of partnerships with business, industry, and government that allow students to get real-life experience in different kinds of career settings.

There are several programs designed to provide better information about the kinds of jobs and careers available to Ph.D.s. Departments in many institutions are inviting former students to return and give seminars on their experiences. Graduate students avidly seek this kind of information, which has unfortunately often been lacking in their programs. One of the reasons for this is that many advisers of doctoral students have spent their entire careers in research universities and may have little or no knowledge of other settings for the pursuit of scholarly work. This makes it difficult for them to serve as effective advisers about career options. The problem is more acute in the humanities than in the sciences. Most academic scientists have some contact with colleagues in nonuniversity laboratories and thus know something about alternate careers. This is not the case for humanists, many of whom cannot imagine satisfying and fulfilling scholarly lives outside the academy. One approach to solving this problem has been to provide students with guided experiences that introduce them to different kinds of careers. The Woodrow Wilson Foundation, in its project on Alternatives to Academic Careers for Humanists, has developed three programmatic initiatives: awards to departments that encourage graduate students to gain nonacademic experience as part of their graduate education; awards to students who use their academic training in non-academic internships in business or industry; and support of post-doctoral programs in areas outside of the university.

Just how graduate students have been faring is shown by a recent study that surveyed 6,000 Ph.D.s who had obtained their degrees in six disciplines (English, biochemistry, electrical engineering, political science, mathematics, and computer science) at 60 U.S. universities from 1983 to 1985 (Nerad and Cerny 1999). The major purpose of the study was to find out what had happened to these people and how they related their careers to their graduate education. In the report cited here, which concentrates on Ph.D.s in English, the findings in many cases not only run counter to general impressions, but are also often counterintuitive. By 1995, 53 percent of the English Ph.D.s held tenure-track positions, but only 9 percent of these were in top-ranked research universities. A total of 73 percent held some kind of academic appointment, and 16 percent were in business, government, or the nonprofit sector. Of the 814 individuals who responded, only 5 were involuntarily unemployed and seeking work.

Respondents were asked a number of questions about their programs and, most pertinent here, what they would do differently and what they thought graduate programs should do differently. The great majority, regardless of which employment sector they were in, indicated satisfaction with their current jobs and said they would still get a Ph.D. in English if they had the opportunity to do it over again. Their comments about changes they would like to see in doctoral programs were very revealing in that they were all generic rather than discipline directed. They thought programs should be smaller, that students should have more assistance in learning how to teach, and that there should be improved career services and more emphasis on interdisciplinary studies.

The kinds of approaches described here and the results of the Nerad-Cerny study represent a philosophical or cultural change. They involve a shift away from what some perceive as an overemphasis on the research interests of the faculty toward a broader view of the educational aspects of the program. Sufficient concern has been expressed by graduate students, faculty, and administrators that change appears to be taking place. Much of this change centers on the responsibilities of the adviser and the relationship of that role to the role of mentor. Graduate schools have approached this issue gingerly because of well-established attitudes of faculty autonomy. Times have changed, however, and schools are much more receptive to generic approaches aimed at improving faculty-student relationships than they were several years ago. That in itself represents a change in culture. An example is the suggestion in an article that appeared in *Science* a few years ago: "It is not enough for faculty members to give good lectures and engage in world-class research. As educators, faculty members must also be concerned about providing a welcoming and supportive environment for their colleagues and their students. Constructive attitudes, a caring approach, open communication channels between faculty and students, and good will can go a long way toward enhancing successful outcomes for students and young faculty members" (Dresselhaus, Franz, and Clark 1994, 1393).

There is a growing understanding that a supportive environment in graduate school is not incompatible with high academic standards. Many if not most faculty have always known this, but those who have not have caused considerable problems for graduate students. Bad or indifferent advising is not characteristic of any school or discipline; it varies with individuals, and graduate schools are beginning to address this problem in very direct ways. The most obvious sign of this is the great interest in mentoring and in improving the lives of graduate students.

The 1990s have been a watershed in the American concept of doctoral education. The driving force in doctoral education continues to be the knowledge needs of the discipline. It is still based firmly in the Humboldtian model of faculty and students seeking that knowledge together, modified by the American adaptation of combining dissertation research with a fairly extensive course work program. What is different is the idea that the programs are no longer being considered solely as research apprenticeships driven by the interests of the faculty, but also as educational experiences related to the learning and career objectives of the students.

The Future of Doctoral Education

As we begin a new millennium, doctoral education in America faces several problems. This enterprise has been enormously successful in producing high-quality research and research scholars. Some of these scholars become faculty members at the wide range of colleges and universities that characterize American higher education. Others find positions in industry, business, government, and professional practice. People continue to be attracted to advanced studies out of interest and the desire to devote their professional lives to seeking and disseminating knowledge. Americans have considered supporting this activity, whereby bright and talented people can realize their intellectual potential and contribute to our knowledge of the world, a wise investment of public and personal funds. That investment is called into question when the recipients of this education cannot find, or believe they cannot find, opportunities to use it productively.

American graduate education is going through a sorting-out process. Educators, elected officials, and interested members of the public are reexamining many basic assumptions in the light of the way the system has evolved and the values that students, faculty, and the public at large hold about higher education. Most doctoral recipients find good and productive careers in a variety of areas. What is so striking and disturbing is the fact that so many of them have been socialized through their experience at research universities to believe that only tenure-track positions in research universities are worthwhile academic careers.

Universities have continued to view the Ph.D. as the appropriate credential for college and university teaching. The cliché of the Ph.D. as "union card" is firmly established in the public understanding. In looking at the complex higher education system that has developed in America, many are apt to ask, "Why do you need a Ph.D. to teach in a community college or, for that matter, in anything but a research university?" The answer was best expressed several years ago by a colleague who was president of a community college. In talking about the old argument about the balance between teaching and research, he observed that the issue was not teaching or research but rather scholarly teaching or nonscholarly teaching, and that there was no excuse for nonscholarly teaching. That is why I continue to believe that doctoral education is an appropriate preparation for a variety of careers. This is certainly borne out by the experience of former students, as reported by Nerad and Cerny.

Doctoral education is an American success story. People undertake the arduous path to the Ph.D. and beyond because they want to explore their intellectual and scientific interests and need to develop the skills to do so. Certainly they want jobs that allow them to pursue those interests and get paid for doing so. For the overwhelming majority, this is what happens. Good public policy demands that we invest in providing educational and career opportunities for those with the ability, drive, and passion to pursue them. This truly is a golden age for scholarship and research. That is why so many young people want to continue their studies. We close that door at our peril.

Master's and Other Postbaccalaureate Education

Postbaccalaureate education is comprised of a number of different kinds of programs characterized most broadly by their focus on a discipline, field of study, or professional activity. Many people use the term to refer to nondegree academic experiences, such as certificate programs or individual courses, seminars, and workshops intended for individuals with baccalaureate degrees. It is never used to refer to doctoral education. In practice, the master's degree has dominated this area of higher education—in number of students, number of programs, and general design and philosophy.

Today, roughly 85 percent of all master's degrees are practice-oriented, with only 15 percent being traditional arts and sciences degrees. Most master's programs are freestanding, that is they are not intended as part of the preparation for another degree and, increasingly, are not based on any specific undergraduate major. The majority of students in these master's programs are part-time students who view the master's degree as an important and perhaps essential credential to obtain in order to advance in their careers. Thus, a very large market exists for job- and career-oriented postbaccalaureate education available at times and places that are convenient for people who work full time.

As this need and desire for continuous education has expanded, graduate certificate programs have become so popular that they now constitute perhaps the most rapidly growing segment in postbaccalaureate education. Certificate programs are not a new idea. They usually represent a relatively short-term concentrated educational experience that is highly focused on a particular topic or perhaps a technique. The award of a certificate rather than a degree recognizes successful completion. Certificate programs are totally unregulated and may be offered by universities, professional societies, or any other entity that chooses to do so. As might be expected, these programs are highly attractive to both employers and employees (Hamblin 1998; Patterson 1999; Irby 1999).

The future relationship between certificates and master's degrees is a subject being widely discussed in the graduate community. Some feel that rather than get a master's degree, students will develop portfolios representing their educational experiences, most of which will be recognized by certificates (Langenberg 1997). Others believe that certificates will become modules that can be used as parts of master's programs. In either case, a major issue will be how to evaluate all these diverse educational credentials.

Dramatic changes in the nature of work, the makeup of the workforce, and the form and shape of the education system that is evolving to accommodate these developments are challenging many long-established assumptions about the relationship between education and work. These issues can only be described briefly here, but they are being exhaustively discussed throughout the higher education and business communities.

Access to Postbaccalaureate Education

In terms of access to master's education, Donald Spencer predicted in 1986 that distance education, especially by technological means, would probably accelerate and that "widespread adaptation of these delivery systems at the Master's level will depend largely on the cost effectiveness of those technologies, as well as on the level of student satisfaction" (3). His analysis of master's education has been right on the mark and serves as a solid foundation for understanding current trends, not just in master's programs, but also in certificate programs and, to some extent, in doctoral education. The higher education establishment has embraced the idea of distance education enthusiastically, and we are in a period of very rapid development, particularly with respect to the use of instructional technology.

Postbaccalaureate education has been a leader in developing ways to meet the educational needs of working students. Thirty years ago that meant either offering classes on campus at night or on weekends or having faculty members travel to an off-campus site, often a high school or community center, to meet a class of local residents in the evening. These arrangements continue today, augmented by a variety of systems and methods for delivering education to people. These include real-time, two-way video (often on in-state networks); satellite downlink (including some national and international providers such as National Technological University); surface mail; video tapes; audio tapes; the World Wide Web; other computer usage; telephone conferencing; short-time, summer, or weekend residencies; e-mail; and fax. These technologies can be used in the workplace; in regional centers operated by academic and/or industrial organizations, either alone or as consortiums; in education centers developed for this purpose by private companies (e.g., Sylvan Learning Centers); or directly in people's homes.

This plethora of education delivery systems offers working students the opportunity to get courses and programs on a schedule that meets their needs, thus opening up educational opportunities for the growing number of students who would find it difficult or impossible to attend regularly scheduled classes at a university.

The Changing Nature of the Education "System"

The huge market for postbaccalaureate education is attracting many new kinds of education providers. A booming distance education market has emerged, and its players range from Western Governors University to the University of Phoenix, from Sylvan Learning Centers to the Michigan Virtual Automotive College, from the Open University to over 1,000 corporate universities (Marchese 1998). The number of academic institutions, corporations, Internet entities, and other organizations that now comprise the world of higher education is growing explosively with no regard for state, national, international, or traditional academic boundaries.

For-profit educational companies that will work with universities to develop courses and programs for delivery in a variety of formats and sell them to a variety of users are bringing about some of the most interesting changes. New York University and National Technological University have spun off for-profit corporations to develop educational materials (courses, certificate programs, and graduate programs) and sell them to companies or universities. Several companies are providing a number of services to universities, including converting courses to an electronic format, training faculty to teach on-line, and maintaining servers. This often allows institutions to quickly become players in the distance education market. Aside from the obvious financial aspects, nagging questions about who is determining the agenda, reminiscent of the questions raised in the early

1980s about university-industry research relationships, are surfacing again.

Currently there are some 1,400 corporate universities in the United States (many of which operate globally because of the multinational aspects of their businesses). They are as different from each other as universities are and are primarily concerned with providing the education needed by a company's employees in order to ensure that the company can compete successfully. All companies are interested in having knowledgeable employees—provided that knowledge is used to advance the company's strategic objectives. Many develop relationships with universities through which courses and other educational experiences can be provided to employees. For many corporations, however, the issue is not so much contracting for external educational services as it is capturing their own corporate culture and knowledge base and transmitting it within the company.

Alliances, consortia, and partnerships are being formed at a great rate, and many are proving to be extremely complicated. Some, like the California Virtual University, close before they ever accept students. Western Governors University, a virtual university comprising educational offerings from 17 different states, projected thousands of student enrollments and has been very disappointed in the exceedingly low interest shown by the public. Along with Florida State University and the California State University System, Western Governors University formed or tried to form alliances with the Open University of Great Britain to try to utilize that school's experience in providing postbaccalaureate education through distance learning techniques to large numbers of students. For a variety of reasons, these approaches have not been successful. Clearly, we are in a period of great activity and change in higher education. Many new things are being attempted. Some will succeed, others will fail. The important thing is for us to learn by these experiences so that the educational enterprise becomes better able to provide high-quality education suited to student needs.

The nature of the postbaccalaureate education enterprise is beginning to mirror the increasingly fragmented way students are approaching postbaccalaureate learning: in smaller segments, at different times and places, in different formats, and from different providers. The separation of the responsibility for the intellectual quality of course content from the equally demanding but primarily technical responsibility for delivering that content in an effective

manner raises a host of questions about the nature of postbaccalaureate education and the relationship between students and faculty.
Prime among them is how universities define their educational priorities in a post-Internet world.

Conclusion

Graduate education is once again undergoing dramatic and deep-
seated change. Part of that change is being prompted by technological
developments that are altering forever the ways in which we utilize
information and communicate with each other and that will affect
teaching and learning (including research) at all levels. Part is responsive to an economic and social milieu that is making basic alterations in the way people live and in how, when, and where they work
and further their education. Finally, part is a market-driven response
to the continuing educational needs of an ever-growing postbaccalaureate workforce. In this atmosphere, the traditional driving forces in
graduate programs (i.e., the knowledge needs of the disciplines and
the practice needs of the professions) have been joined by a third important force: the educational and career needs of the students.

Graduate education in America, always characterized by its combination of formal course work and research, is becoming even more
programmatic. Much of this is a response to student, employer, and
public demands for clearer links between education and careers. At
the doctoral and postdoctoral levels, a major issue is how to retain
the intensity and depth of the research experience while embedding
it in a context of career options for the participants. In addition, the
opportunities provided through technology for the development of
collaborative research activities are turning the "invisible colleges"
of the disciplines into virtual universities. This is already leading to
new structures and concepts of graduate programs. At the master's
and certificate level, the system that appears to be developing is one
of different kinds of educational providers catering to consumer educational needs in a variety of ways. Patrick Callan and Joni Finney
(1998) have pointed out that this system exists primarily in the eyes
of the beholders, and they have used the term *system of users* to refer to this kind of educational melange.

I believe that universities will continue to be significantly involved
in whatever new education systems develop. The particular nature

and extent of that involvement will vary by institution, especially given the extraordinary range of institutional type and mission to be found in higher education. But the role of the traditional university as the primary provider of graduate education and thus as the definer of what is an acceptable level and standard for this kind of education may be changing, particularly at the postbaccalaureate level. Universities may become partners in loosely defined educational coalitions whose structures, objectives, methods, and motives change to reflect current needs and user demands.

Historically, universities have provided a unique setting and a particular context for higher education, one that may well define their role in an uncertain future. At their core, they have been more about education than training, more about knowledge than information, and, ultimately, more about scholarship than research. In each case, the difference is between considering the acquisition of specialized learning as an end in itself or as the beginning of a process that leads to a higher level of understanding. As graduate and postbaccalaureate education become more involved with the short-term career objectives of students and as the rapid development of the Internet leads us from e-mail to e-commerce to e-education, there is a tendency to be concerned with short-term answers rather than with long-term questions. If this happens in graduate programs, universities will have turned from the education of scholars to the training of technicians, and society will be the ultimate loser.

References

Armstrong, J. A. 1994. Rethinking the Ph.D. *Issues in Science and Technology* 10, no. 4 (summer): 19–22.

Atkinson, R. 1990. Supply and demand for scientists and engineers: A national crisis in the making. *Science* 248 (27 April): 425–32.

Blume, S. 1995. Problems and prospects of research training in the 1990's. In *Research training present and future*. Paris: Organisation for Economic Co-operation and Development.

Bowen, H., and J. Schuster. 1986. *American professors: A national resource imperiled.* New York: Oxford University Press.

Bowen, W. G., and J. A. Sosa. 1989. *Prospects for faculty in the arts and sciences.* Princeton: Princeton University Press.

Bowen, W. G., and N. L. Rudenstine. 1992. *In pursuit of the Ph.D.* Princeton: Princeton University Press.

Callan, P. M., and J. E. Finney. 1998. *The changing contours of higher education: The policy implications of an emerging system.* Paper presented at the Postbaccalaureate Futures Colloquium, Aspen, Colo., 1 November.

Committee on Science, Engineering, and Public Policy (COSEPUP) of the National Academy of Sciences, the National Academy of Engineering, and the Institute of Medicine. 1995. *Reshaping the graduate education of scientists and engineers.* Washington, D.C.: National Academy Press.

Conrad, C. F., J. G. Haworth, and S. Millar. 1993. *A silent success: Master's education in the United States.* Baltimore: Johns Hopkins University Press.

Council of Graduate Schools. 1991. *The role and nature of the doctoral dissertation.* Washington, D.C.: Council of Graduate Schools.

Dresselhaus, M. S., J. R. Franz, and B. C. Clark. 1994. Interventions to increase the participation of women in physics. *Science* 263 (11 March): 1392–93.

Edmundson, M. 1999. Crashing the academy. *New York Times Magazine,* 4 April, 9.

The Government-University-Industry Research Roundtable (GUIRR). 1989. *Science and technology in the academic enterprise: Status, trends, and issues.* Washington, D.C.: National Academy Press.

Hamblin, J. A., ed. 1998. *Certificates: A survey of their status and a review of successful programs in the United States and Canada.* Washington, D.C.: Council of Graduate Schools.

Haworth, J. G., and J. C. Smart, eds. 1996. Doctoral programs in American higher education. In *Higher education: Handbook of theory and research.* Vol. 11. New York: Agathon Press.

Irby, A. J. 1999. Postbaccalaureate certificates. *Change* (March–April): 36–41.

Kiernan, V. 1999. Internet-based "collaboratories" help scientists work together. *Chronicle of Higher Education,* 12 March, A22–23.

Langenberg, D. N. 1997. Diplomas and degrees are obsolescent. *Chronicle of Higher Education,* 12 September, A64.

LaPidus, J. B. 1995. Doctoral education and student career needs. In *Student services for the changing graduate student population,* edited by A. S. Pruitt-Logan and P. Isaac. San Francisco: Jossey-Bass.

———. 1997a. Issues and themes in postgraduate education in the United States. In *Beyond the first degree,* edited by R. G. Burgess. Buckingham, England: Society for Research into Higher Education and Open University Press.

———. 1997b. Why pursuing a Ph.D. is a risky business. *Chronicle of Higher Education,* 14 November, A60.

———. 1997c. Doctoral education: Preparing for the future. *CGS Communicator* 30, no. 10 (November).

————. 1999. Scholarship and the future of graduate education in science and engineering. In *Science careers, gender equity, and the changing economy.* Cambridge, Mass.: Radcliffe Public Policy Institute and the Commission on Professionals in Science and Technology.

LaPidus, J. B., P. Syverson, and S. Welch. 1995. Postgraduate research training in the United States. In *Research training present and future.* Paris: Organisation for Economic Co-operation and Development, 159–94.

Lyman, P. 2000. Risk, tribe and lore: Envisioning digital libraries for post-baccalaureate learning. In *Postbaccalaureate futures,* edited by K. Kohl and J. B. LaPidus. Washington, D.C.: Oryx Press.

Marchese, T. 1998. Not-so distant competitors. *AAHE Bulletin* 50, no. 9 (May).

National Research Council. 1998. *Trends in the early careers of life scientists.* Washington, D.C.: National Academy Press.

Nerad, M., and J. Cerny. 1999. From rumors to facts: Career outcomes of English Ph.D.s. *CGS Communicator* 32, no. 6 (August): 7.

Patel, C. K. N. 1995. Reinventing the research university. In *Proceedings of a Symposium held at UCLA on June 22–23, 1994,* edited by C. K. N. Patel. Los Angeles: Regents of the University of California.

Patterson, W. 1999. Certificate programs raise important issues. *CGS Communicator* 32, no. 9 (October): 3.

Schrage, M. 1998. *Tangled web(s): The rise of the absent-networked professor and the "translucent" college.* Paper presented at the Postbaccalaureate Futures Colloquium, Aspen, Colo., 1 November.

Spencer, D. S. 1986. The masters degree in transition. *CGS Communicator* 19 (January): 3.

Syverson, P. 1996. The new American graduate student. *CGS Communicator* 29 (October): 8.

Tobias, S., D. E. Chubin, and K. Aylesworth. 1995. *Rethinking science as a career: Perceptions and realities in the physical sciences.* Tucson, Ariz.: Research Corporation.

Chapter Eleven

College Students Today

Why We Can't Leave Serendipity to Chance

George D. Kuh

One of the few topics about which pundits, policy wonks, higher education scholars, and blue-ribbon panels agree is the subpar quality of undergraduate education. Many observers place the blame on students, calling this current cohort whiny, self-centered, politically apathetic, career-obsessed, and materialistic (Hayworth 1997; Sacks 1996).

But students alone are not responsible for all the alleged shortcomings in collegiate quality. Colleges and universities are said to be inefficient and focused on the wrong things; many admit poorly prepared students primarily to generate revenues (Carlin 1999; Finn and Manno 1996). The curriculum is typically fragmented and incoherent, devaluing substance by awarding academic credit for such courses as Introduction to Tennis and dating and cultural diversity seminars. Faculty persist in lecturing to classrooms of disengaged students. Three-quarters of all campuses offer remedial courses, and about 30 percent of all students take one or more (Hansen 1999). An unacceptably high fraction of college graduates are barely literate according to some (Wingspread Group 1993). Particularly susceptible to such criticisms are the large, organizationally complex, research-intensive universities from which, allegedly, the typical student graduates "without knowing how to think logically, write clearly, or speak coherently" (Boyer Commission 1998, 6).

Those who hold these views either overlook or discount important contextual factors and indicia about the undergraduate experience that point to a different conclusion. For example, a majority of the college students enrolled in the 1990s were involved in altruistic social activities in high school or college and are no more cynical about contemporary society than any other age cohort (Astin 1997; Hayworth 1997). Incidents of institutional negligence surely exist with regard to undergraduate education, but most colleges and universities are responding to legitimate complaints. For example, some large universities such as Indiana University and the University of Iowa have increased instructional capacity by modifying faculty assignments and adding sections of high-demand courses to increase course availability. Also, both public and private institutions are offering "guarantee" programs, whereby students who follow a mutually agreed upon plan of study will be able to register for all required courses within a four-year period; students who do stick to their plan of study but do not get the classes they need can take these classes later at no additional cost. Critics are silent about these and other efforts to enhance collegiate quality, efforts such as classroom-based learning communities, freshman interest groups, service learning programs, and a host of other initiatives to improve teaching, learning, and student support services.

Undergraduate education is a large, diffuse enterprise spread across several thousand institutional settings. Thus, it is impossible to accurately describe the college student experience in a single chapter or even a book-length manuscript. That said, most of what I will say in this chapter applies more or less to the majority of colleges and universities using primarily synchronous instruction (as contrasted with asynchronous and virtual learning environments) in their undergraduate programs.

Higher Learning in the United States: As Good As It Gets

The key quality question is whether undergraduate education is adequately preparing students to be self-sufficient, economically productive, and civically responsible after college (Shapiro 1997). In this section I discuss four factors that are frequently overlooked when making judgments about collegiate quality. They are (a) the inexorable evolution of American higher education toward universal access, (b) a romanticized view of the undergraduate experience of previous generations, (c) the considerable differences between student and faculty viewpoints, and (d) the absence of comparative data about the performance of students and institutions over time.

Changing Expectations: Higher Education Is for Everyone

Perhaps the best indicator of collegiate quality is the century-long continual increase in demand. Between 1900 and 1950, the U.S. population increased about 100 percent while college enrollments jumped 1,000 percent, doubling every 15 years or so. Even so, by 1940 only 1.5 million students were participating in higher education, less than 10 percent of the eligible traditional-age population. Up to this point, colleges and universities were perceived to be (and generally behaved like) elitist institutions, discriminating against the poor, African Americans, and women (Bonner 1986). Indeed, the prevailing view from colonial times through the first half of the twentieth century was that higher education was intended only for educational and societal leaders. The Servicemen's Readjustment Act of 1944 along with other factors changed forever who could go to college and what college was for. Enrollments doubled during both the 1950s and 1960s. Between 1975 and 1990 enrollment growth slowed some—to about 23 percent—but it has increased slightly since (Hansen 1999). By 1997 over 14 million students were enrolled in colleges and universities including more than 12 million undergraduates. Almost two-thirds of all students who graduated from high school during the 1997–98 school year were attending some type of postsecondary institution six months later. This 1997–98 cohort was 41 percent, or 535,000 students, larger than the 1973 cohort (Mortenson 1999, 5). Record undergraduate enrollments are expected through the first decade of the twenty-first century, with the number of new high school graduates predicted to increase about 10 percent between now and 2009.

Thus, during the last half century, higher education evolved from an elitist system to one of universal access. One result is that the public is much more aware of what happens on college campuses. Another is that people today have high, perhaps unreasonable, expectations about what higher education can and should do for individuals and society. The individual benefits of higher education are frequently calibrated in pecuniary terms—that is, just how much more money do college graduates make compared to other groups? This is one topic where the public perception is consistent with the data. For example, according to the U.S. Census Bureau in 1998 the average income of families where the head of household has a high school diploma is $48,434 compared with $85,423 for the average family where the head of household holds a bachelor's degree. And generally speaking the more education one has, the more one earns. On average a master's degree means about $16,000 more a year or $101,670; doctoral degree holders made $123,796. No wonder that most people (about four-fifths) think that high school graduates should go to college if they are able (Immerwahr and Harvey 1995). In fact, more people want their children to attend college than ever before, correctly perceiving that they need higher education not only to move into or remain in the middle socioeconomic class but also to obtain the skills and competencies required to thrive in a rapidly changing world. If collegiate quality were a legitimate concern, it is unlikely that hundreds of thousands of families would annually spend a significant portion of their income on college costs and employers would uniformly prefer candidates with college degrees.

A wider, deeper, more colorful pool. Another factor that does not receive enough attention when estimating collegiate quality is the expanded range of human diversity now represented on college campuses. Once the province of the young, colleges are enrolling an increasing number of older students. The proportion of college students 25 years of age or older is now about 45 percent, up from 28 percent in 1970 (Hansen 1999). More than three-quarters (77%) of the 3.5 million new students who attended college in the 1970s were women (Mortenson 1998). Today, so many more women than men enroll that policymakers and educators are discussing how to increase the number of men who matriculate. The complexion of college classrooms is much more colorful today, particularly in regions of the country populated by large and growing numbers of people who belong to historically underrepresented groups. The increase in the college-going rate of African American college students is fairly dramatic; in 1983 only about 38 percent of African Americans went on to some form of postsecondary education in the year immediately following high school graduation; in 1998 this figure was 61 percent compared with 67 percent of Caucasians (Mortenson 1999). Hispanics, however, remained underrepresented in 1998 with only about 47 percent of Hispanic high school graduates going on to college.

Today's students are also different in less visible ways from earlier cohorts. The proportion of children living in single-parent families grew about 2.5 times between 1960 and 1986 (Hansen 1999). About 26 percent of freshman in 1997 were from divorced families, three times more than in 1972. In the past 15 years suicide attempts by college students increased by about 23 percent and eating disorders by 58 percent (Gallagher 1995). More students today have been hospitalized for psychiatric reasons and have serious psychological problems requiring psychoactive medication. In short, more students than ever before are coming to college psychologically damaged (Levine and Cureton 1998).

Another difference from previous generations is that many students today are unrealistic about what it takes to do well in college. Though they studied less in high school compared with previous cohorts, record numbers got Bs or better in their high school courses (Sax et al. 1997). High school teachers are awarding more A grades than ever, almost 32 percent in 1997, compared with 12.5 percent in 1969. At the same time more than two-fifths (43 percent) of college freshmen say they need to improve their reading and study skills; about the same percentage expect to earn at least a B average.

Many more students today have learning styles that differ from those of previous cohorts and from those of their teachers. Perhaps as many as two-thirds of the students on a given campus prefer field-dependent approaches to learning, which means they perform best when working in small groups on activities that have applications to concrete, real-world issues and situations. In contrast, most college instructors are field-independent learners, preferring strategies such as observing, listening, abstract analysis, and individual reflection (Schroeder 1993). These learning-style differences make working with college students more challenging because most faculty and staff members were not themselves exposed to active and collaborative learning strategies while they were college students nor were they subsequently trained to use these approaches.

Another noteworthy difference between undergraduates today and those of earlier eras is the role of employment while attending college. Four-fifths of all students work while going to school. Of this group, about a third describe themselves as full-time employees who attend college. The rest are primarily college students who work ostensibly to help meet college expenses (King 1998), although many also use their earnings to purchase items not necessarily related to success in college, such as CD players, televisions, and car insurance. While most faculty members realize that some students must work in order to pay for college expenses, a nontrivial fraction also perceive employment to be an unfortunate and frequently unnecessary distraction that dilutes the amount of time and energy students can devote to their studies.

Bigger is neither better nor worse. One of the effects of the exponential growth in student enrollments was a reversal in the proportions of students attending private and public schools Whereas prior to 1950 the majority enrolled in private colleges, today more than three-quarters attend public institutions. As a result, the average size of public colleges and universities increased. About 60 percent of all students now attend universities with 10,000 or more undergraduates. These changes coupled with the changing characteristics of students could have had deleterious effects on student satisfaction. But there is little evidence that this has occurred. For example, about 80 to 85 percent of all students report being generally satisfied with their college experience (Kuh and Hu 1999), a figure that has not changed much over the past two decades. About three-quarters say that if they had it to do over again they would choose the same institution. These percentages vary slightly (3–5%) by sector. As one might expect, students at smaller, more selective independent schools are somewhat more satisfied.

Though student satisfaction with the overall college experience is generally high, satisfaction with specific aspects of college can vary considerably. The area in which students tend to be the least satisfied is academic advising, though it is not always clear which advising issues concern them. What students want from their advisers probably changes over time as their major field interests evolve and they get more experience with the college environment and learn more about themselves and their career options and opportunities. Upper-division students want more of a mentor-guide relationship, expecting their adviser to help them understand why and how what they are doing fits their life goals, questions that usually do not have easy answers.

Employers also seem to be relatively satisfied with the graduates they employ. Of course, college graduates could perform better in such areas of practical competence as time management, decision making, and working effectively with people from different backgrounds. But on balance employers are generally satisfied with the quality of preparation their employees received, especially in their major fields (Gardner 1997).

Collegiate Quality in Earlier Eras: Not as Good as We Remember

Another factor affecting judgments about collegiate quality is the rosier-than-justified recollections of the performance of previous student cohorts. Suggestions that today's students are inferior or less serious about their studies compared with their predecessors often are overstated or contradicted by the historical evidence (Kuh 1999a). The first point to keep in mind is that students of every generation want pretty much the same things from college: preparation for a good job, some knowledge about a wide variety of topics relevant to their lives and the world in which they will live after college, and a modicum of self-discovery in the form of a broader understanding of themselves. For example, in the post–Civil War decades most students aspired to mercantile and industrial positions. The Morrill acts of 1862 and 1890, which gave states government land to use for higher education, stimulated the introduction and expansion of applied programs of study that helped boost enrollments; most students and their families saw such preparation as more relevant and attractive than the classical approach that emphasized the study of philosophy and ancient languages. "Learning for earning" was important to WW II veterans because many had spouses and children to support. Students in the 1950s were called "the silent generation" (Brubacher and Rudy 1997, 349) and "unabashedly self-centered" (Jacob 1957, 1) because they were interested primarily in advancing their own careers, not expanding their minds or examining their social and political beliefs. Then as now, of course, substantial variation existed in student attitudes and performance between as well as within institutions.

The second point is that today's students *seem* so different from those of earlier eras because the cohort to whom they are almost always compared is from the 1960s (Kuh 1999a). Using this period as the benchmark is unrealistic because it was, for better or worse, a historical aberration in terms of certain societal attitudes and behavior. Among the things for which the decade of the 1960s is best remembered is student activism primarily focused on national political and social issues. This was not, however, the only period when students expressed their concerns to an extent that disrupted college activities. Students in the 1700s and 1800s frequently rioted, often about their food and living conditions. During the opening decades of the 1800s students became frustrated with the monotonous classical curriculum and the piety and discipline heaped on them by their teachers. In protest (which in hindsight seems like a much-needed educational revolution) students on many campuses formed debating clubs and literary societies to add some intellectual zest to the dull academic routines of college life (Rudolph 1990). Later, in the 1930s, students at more than a few institutions participated in annual spring student strikes to call attention to the rise of fascism abroad and on occasion to campus-specific issues (Horowitz 1987).

But the 1960s overshadow all earlier periods of student protest. Indeed, this decade saw "the most portentous upheaval in the whole history of American student life" (Brubacher and Rudy 1997, 349) because of a unique confluence of social, political, and economic factors. The baby boom caused a spike in the number of college students. The civil rights movement and the Vietnam War energized students to publicly witness their political, social, and intellectual views. Reducing the age of majority from 21 to 18 realigned the nature of institutions' relations with their students from in loco parentis to that of educational provider and client. The result was that colleges had more of a consumer contract with their students than the traditional paternalistic relationship. Moreover, student activists often coupled larger social and political issues with demands for changes in what they considered to be irrelevant institutional structures and requirements. Faculty members occasionally agreed with and rallied support for student grievances.

Despite all of this, however, as in previous periods of student activism most students were only spectators to the protests, though media coverage sometimes made it seem as if large fractions of students were involved. More important, the reasons this generation went to college did not differ appreciably from those of their counterparts of earlier eras. For example, about the same proportions of students in the late 1960s and the late 1990s attended college to get a better job (74%) and to gain a general education (60%) and thought it was important to influence the political structure (16%), raise a family (71–73%), and be recognized as an authority in their field (63–66%) (Astin et al. 1997). Among the more counterintuitive differences between the two cohorts is that almost a third of the students in the late 1990s said they want to become community leaders, compared with only 15 percent in 1970.

So it seems that, with the exception of a couple of frequently cited attitudinal items (making a lot of money, developing a meaningful philosophy of life), college students today generally want from college what previous generations wanted: an experience that changes them for the better and prepares them for life after college, preferably without seriously challenging their core values and beliefs. The evidence suggests that for most students college attendance is associated with these desirable effects, though their teachers usually are not satisfied with the degree to which students take advantage of the learning opportunities colleges provide (Astin 1993; Pace 1990; Pascarella and Terenzini 1991). Indeed, it seems that faculty members of every era have been underwhelmed with the performance of their students, a phenomenon due in large part to fundamental personality differences that will be discussed in the next section.

Students Are from Earth, Faculty Members Are from Another Planet

The disparity between students' and faculty members' views of certain aspects of the undergraduate experience can be enormous. Nationally, almost twice as many faculty (79%) as students (42%) say it is important during college to develop a meaningful philosophy of life (Sax et al. 1996; Sax et al. 1997). At my university, 80 percent of first-year students in fall 1997 indicated that career preparation was a very important goal for attending college, but only 20 percent of my faculty colleagues agreed. Less than a quarter of faculty (24%) nationally think students are well prepared academically (Sax et al. 1996). Again, at my university two-thirds of the entering fall 1997 students thought they were well prepared for college-level work contrasted with only 6 percent of the faculty. For better or for worse, at almost three-quarters of all colleges and universities faculty complaints about students have increased (Levine and Cureton 1998).

These competing views about what college is for and perceptions of questionable student ability, spurious motivations, and lackluster performance reflect fairly sharp differences between the vast majority of people who go to college and the tiny fraction who aspire to and ultimately become faculty members. Nationally, less than one-half of one percent of college freshmen want to be college teachers (Astin et al. 1997). Even if this fraction rises somewhat during the college years in the most selective institutions, the proportion of students giving serious thought to an academic career rarely approaches 5 percent of the student body. All this is to say that those aiming at an academic career differed from their peers in every college-going cohort in their reasons for attending college, the emphasis they placed on intellectual matters, their learning styles, and their vocational interests. These differences in personality and aspirations contribute to inevitable tensions and misunderstandings about priorities and the expectations and standards faculty members have for student performance. Most important, in the eyes of their faculty, undergraduates as a group have always fallen well short of taking full advantage of the learning resources and opportunities college offers. Because the frame of reference used by faculty members of every era to evaluate their students has been people like themselves, it is no surprise that faculty members tend to be somewhat disappointed in the performance of most college-student cohorts.

Lack of Empirical Performance Indicators

Everyone has an opinion about collegiate quality and student performance. Though much good research on college students is available, few comparative data exist to compare the performance of undergraduate cohorts at different points in time. For this reason it is almost impossible to make definitive statements about the relative quality of the student experience across decades. That said, there is some evidence suggesting that similar proportions of students from the 1960s, 1970s, 1980s, and 1990s made substantial gains during college in such areas as critical thinking, self-directed learning, social development, general education, and preparation for further study (Kuh 1999b). In four other areas (writing, vocational preparation, teamwork skills, facility with computers) the percentages of students in the 1990s reporting substantial gains were greater than in earlier decades. However, declining proportions of students reported comparable progress in personal development, awareness of different philosophies and cultures, understanding of science, appreciation of literature, and understanding of the arts.

Critics point to the fact that graduation rates have remained essentially flat over the past 50 years as evidence of both subpar collegiate quality and the recalcitrance of faculty members and administrators to devoting time and resources to improve learning conditions. However, it could be argued that because record numbers of more diverse students are enrolling, institutional productivity has actually increased as recent college-going cohorts are completing baccalaureate degrees at about same rate (40% within 4 years, 46–48% within 5 years, 53–55% within 6 years) when compared with more homogeneous cohorts that moved through a somewhat more selective system in earlier eras.

Given that access to higher education has become nearly universal, stability in key indicia is not disappointing but an indicator of strong performance. It is also important to keep in mind that historically higher education was not designed to induce profound changes in college students or society. The colonial colleges were founded to, among other things, preserve and transmit religious and cultural traditions to subsequent generations. According to the missions of many colonial colleges the only groups to be "changed" were indigenous peoples, which usually meant converting American Indians to Christianity. There is no reason to expect, nor do the data show, that college is a transformative experience for the vast majority of students. For example, less than 7 percent of students even at selective colleges experienced significant personality change as a result of attending college (Clark et al. 1972). In part, this may be due to the dualistic, transitional stages of intellectual development that characterize most traditional-age students (Baxter Magolda 1992; Perry 1970) and that dampen prospects for transformational personality change even under developmentally powerful learning conditions. At the same time, the quantitative data describing college students probably underestimate the demonstrable impact of college attendance. For example, the university experience lifts many first-generation college students to higher socioeconomic levels. This can affect every dimension of their lives after college, including family relations, where and how they live, with whom they interact on a daily basis, and their social and political views. Many such students manage the transition successfully if not smoothly. Others have more difficulty shedding one social identity for another (London 1996).

American colleges and universities are educating more people than ever before from a much larger, deeper, and more diverse pool of undergraduates. Both the proportion and number of people with a postsecondary education are at unprecedented levels, far exceeding those of any other country. On balance, this is an impressive record of accomplishment in the context of dramatic contextual and demographic shifts.

Improving the Undergraduate Experience

Among the more important functions of undergraduate education is to expose students to new ideas and experiences that challenge familiar ways of thinking and behaving and prepare them to be productive, civically responsible members of society. Against this yardstick, undergraduate education in the United States is an undisputed success story. At the same time, the world for which today's college students are preparing is vastly different from that of earlier generations. The rapid pace of change demands that students be able to meet head-on and respond intelligently to unprecedented challenges.

Until recently, college was thought to be a rite of passage from ignorance to knowledge (Ogilvy 1994). Obtaining a baccalaureate degree implied being substantively prepared for one's life work. Today, however, the functional relationship between a college degree and postcollege employment is more ambiguous than at any time in the past century. Few majors lead directly to traditional careers; there are, in fact, few traditional careers left. The nature, structure, and activities of today's workforce are very different from that for which college graduates have been traditionally prepared. Knowledge workers now compose about a third of the workforce, reflecting the changing character of the workplace—including where work is performed (Kull 1999). Sixty percent of all employees are working in unsupervised, self-managed teams in nontraditional settings or telecommuting (Boyett and Snyder 1998). In the next decade perhaps as many as half of all workers will be temporary, contract, or part-time employees. For this reason, employers today are less interested in how much college graduates know and more concerned about whether they can obtain and apply new information in productive, creative ways and can anticipate and address the emerging needs of their organizations (Education Commission of the States 1995; Rutherford 1998).

The shift in the relative importance of acquired knowledge contrasted with the ability to find and use relevant, high-quality information is a direct result of the "waves of transformation" (Rowley, Lujan, and Dolence 1998, 91) washing over virtually every sector of the economy, flooding workplaces, schools, and homes with amounts of information unimagined just a decade ago. To flourish in the workplace of the future, people must be able to communicate effectively, understand their organization's strategic goals and values, manage and discern patterns in massive flows of information, work well with others in a world in which economic and social problems are increasingly abstract and complex, and master perpetual learning technologies such as desktop computers and the World Wide Web. Therefore, it is essential that undergraduates acquire, at a higher level than ever before, the skills for discovering, synthesizing, and applying new information, identifying and evaluating alternative approaches to problem-solving, and working collaboratively with people from different backgrounds. They must also exhibit workplace competencies such as the ability to identify key tasks without supervision, plan and manage complicated and sometimes competing tasks, and respond to unanticipated problems (Rutherford 1998). These skills, competencies, and attitudes are often equated with lifelong learning, spawning such terms as continuous learning and perpetual learning (Norris 1996; O'Donnell 1996; Ogilvy 1994).

The task of higher education has never been more complex and challenging. Most colleges and universities are not organized to help their students develop these kinds of competencies. Indeed, no higher education system anywhere in the world is set up to do so.

Channeling Student Effort: Enhancing Student Learning

In order for students to acquire the skills and competencies they need, institutions must intentionally arrange their resources to engage students more fully in the kinds of experiences that produce the greatest gains in these areas. How students spend their time is the single most important variable in this equation, more important than their background characteristics or where they go to college (Astin 1993; Pascarella and Terenzini 1991). Thus, knowing what students do while in college is essential to estimating collegiate quality and focusing institutional resources on improving undergraduate education.

Full-time traditional-age students study between 8 and 12 hours a week (Kuh et al. 1997); however, they watch television an average of 20 hours per week (Sax et al. 1997). Assuming that students should study two hours for every hour in class, or 30 hours per week, this means an academic effort shortfall of at least 10 hours per week. White students and students of color do not differ appreciably with regard to the amount of academic effort they put forth. However, the patterns of effort differ somewhat, as minority students devote more effort to course learning and less effort to social activities. However, they differ only in trivial ways with regard to the outcomes they report when study results control for variables such as academic background, major, and socioeconomic status (DeSousa and Kuh 1996; Kuh and Hu 1999; Watson and Kuh 1996). None of these measurements, however, take into account omnipresent learning technologies including Internet access to the World Wide Web. Even so, an overall average of about 10 hours a week spent preparing for class is—for better or worse—comparable to the amount of time spent studying by students at Harvard about 100 years ago (Rudolph 1990).

A more constructive approach to understanding college student performance and college quality is to examine the patterns of activities in which students engage and what these patterns yield in terms of desired outcomes of college. Toward this end my colleagues and I examined data from 51,155 students at 128 colleges and universities who completed the College Student Experiences Questionnaire between 1990 and 1997 (Kuh, Hu, and Vesper 2000). Using a combination of analytical techniques (factor analysis, cluster analysis, MANOVA) we found 10 distinctive groups of students based on their patterns of college activities (studying, interacting with faculty and peers, reading, writing, and so forth) and their self-reported progress in important areas of educational and personal development. The 10 groups are disengaged, grind, recreator, socializer, collegiate, scientist, conventional, individualist, artist, and intellectual. Briefly describing 5 of these groups will be sufficient to make the pertinent points.

The disengaged group made up about 18 percent of the total (9,327). They were distinguished by having both the lowest overall scores on "sum of effort" (sum of responses to all college activities items) and "total gain" (sum of responses to all 23 gains items). The grind group comprised about 15 percent of the total (7,668) and had the highest academic-effort score but the second lowest overall sum-of-effort score and second-lowest total-gain score; that is, they studied a lot but did very little else and reported making very little progress in desired outcomes (only the disengaged had a lower total-gain score). The recreator group comprised about 10 percent of all students (5,248). They were well above average in the amount of time they spent in sports and exercise but fell in the lowest third on most outcome measures. The individualist group (3,780, or 7 percent of the total) reported an above-average amount of substantive peer interaction and involvement in cultural and performing-arts activities but relatively little contact with faculty members; even so, they had the second highest total-gain score. Finally, the intellectual group (2,745, or 5%) had both the highest sum-of-effort score and the highest total-gain score. In other words, they actively engaged in a variety of educationally purposeful activities while in college and made the most progress on the wide variety of desired outcomes.

These data show that students developed skills and competencies consistent with the activities to which they devoted effort, a finding consistent with other research (Astin 1993; Pace 1990; Pascarella and Terenzini 1991). For example, the two groups with the lowest overall amount of reported gains were the disengaged and the grinds. The disengaged group also had the lowest overall-effort score; that is, they did very little in any category of activity—course learning, reading and writing, interacting with faculty members and peers, and so forth. The grinds focused almost all of their effort on course-related activities including reading and writing but devoted very little effort to other activities such as peer or faculty interaction or cocurricular activities. Apparently, placing too much emphasis on a single activity—such as the socializer (social interaction with peers), recreator (sports and recreation), artist (cultural and performing-arts activities), and grind (academics)—produces at best only average (and more frequently below-average) gains.

Most disturbing are the large numbers of disengaged students who did very little of anything while in college and the recreators whose effort devoted to sports and leisure activities was out of balance in light of the gains they reported. The disengaged and recreators were about equally distributed across all but the most selective colleges and, taken together, comprised more than one-quarter of all undergraduates. Adding together the disengaged, recreator, and grind groups, it appears that more than two-fifths of undergraduates were not engaged in a reasonable balance of educationally purposeful activities.

We Can No Longer Leave Serendipity to Chance

It has always been difficult to get students to do all the things that matter most to being successful during and after college. This is particularly true for students who go on to college immediately following high school because of the psychosocial developmental issues that are common to this age group. That is, the majority of 18-to-22-year-old undergraduates are fixated on and consumed by managing social relations and developing personal identity, especially in the first year or two of college. But there is some evidence to suggest that it may be even more difficult today than previously to get students to engage in the kinds of activities that the research shows matter most to their learning and personal development.

Forty years ago students were fairly homogenous in background and age. Most went off to the university immediately after high school. They took a full load of classes, lived on campus, and ate meals together. If they held jobs, it was probably only for a few hours a week on campus. Colleges were smaller and core curricula were more common, which resulted in larger numbers of students having similar intellectual experiences at least in the first (and probably the most important) year of college. Social life was focused on campus-based events and activities, putting students in frequent contact with same-age peers who were studying similar ideas and concepts and experiencing many of the same psychosocial challenges. They saw their teachers at least several times a week in the classroom and also occasionally at the library, local grocery store, campus cafeteria, athletic field, and so forth. Such interactions swiftly socialized them to the way things were supposed to be done. Events and activities such as course registration, weekly convocations, and athletic contests were, in essence, "natural" ritualistic exercises that compelled conforming behavior. Granted, participating in such activities was not typically a profound learning experience; and some groups of students, most often women and minorities, frequently found it more difficult to identify with and participate as full members of the campus community in certain of these activities. On the whole, though, relatively little institutional effort was directed toward helping students figure out what was required to succeed and how to do it. What was then constructed to be a fairly homogenous student culture was generally left to its own devices to perform this important socialization function.

Today, more than 40 percent of students attend college part time. The vast majority live off campus. Even at large universities that are described as residential, students are essentially commuters after the first year, living off campus in apartments and condominiums. This lifestyle choice limits the amount of time they spend on campus and, therefore, their exposure to many learning and personal development opportunities, such as taking advantage of cultural and performing-arts events. The classroom is the one point of contact with the institution that all students have in common. But for various reasons, anything resembling a coherent intellectual experience is but a distant memory at all but a handful of small colleges. The curriculum is specialized and fragmented, largely due to unplanned expansions and contractions. The increased number of different courses is, in large part, a function of the knowledge explosion and resulting specializations within disciplines. Students prefer the convenience of registering for classes on-line or by telephone to talking face-to-face with an adviser. An increasing number of classroom instructors are part time, and many don't know enough about the institution and its programs to accurately advise their students. To bring coherence to the academic program, students must construct it themselves.

This is to say that the majority of undergraduates today do not enjoy and benefit from the kinds of routine and often intense interactions with peers and faculty members that not only help them figure out how their institutions work but also foster intellectual and social development. They do not acquire the tacit knowledge needed to perform at a high level in various learning venues on and off campus. While a majority of Americans are participating in higher education, student access to the institutional resources needed to succeed academically and socially is often severely limited, depending on one's background. Students from the lower-income brackets, for example, remain at the highest risk of dropping out. A shrinking fraction of students are involved in leadership positions in clubs and organizations and other cocurricular activities that helped previous generations of undergraduates make meaning of their college experiences inside and outside the classroom and also contributed to valued outcomes of college, such as learning how to work with people from different backgrounds, becoming aware of different philosophies and cultures and ways of life, and applying what they are learning to different circumstances.

To take advantage of the resources for learning that colleges provide, students must understand and learn how to do what is expected of them academically and socially. To insure that this happens, colleges and universities can no longer afford to leave serendipity to chance and assume that students will learn on their own what the research shows they must know and do to succeed in college. This realization is prompting wise people at all types of institutions to ask such questions as: What are the assumptions about teaching, learning, and students that are congenial to the tasks at hand, and which ones are counterproductive? What is the best way of organizing the curriculum and students' out-of-class experiences to more fully engage students in learning? How can we break down the barriers that seem to separate academic and student affairs in order to increase the complementarity of students' in-class and out-of-class activities? What forms of assessment will yield the data needed to guide and evaluate the efficacy of institutional improvement efforts? The inescapable implication is that we must be more intentional about using good practices in undergraduate education to arrange socialization and learning experiences that induce students to take advantage of the multitude of learning opportunities college offers and bring coherence and meaning to their studies.

These observations coupled with the information presented earlier about how today's students differ from earlier cohorts suggest that helping today's undergraduates successfully navigate the undergraduate experience cannot be accomplished through minor adjustments or tinkering. "Re-thinking all functions from the perspective of student learning means treating *all* contacts with students as potential learning opportunities—including faculty encounters out of class, student activities, residence life experiences, and the campus social environment" (Ewell 1997, 14).

Countering Counterproductive Thinking

A few widely held shibboleths discourage thoughtful, productive discourse about the nature of students and institutional cultures and block colleges from fashioning the kinds of responses that these challenges require. One of the more problematic is that student learning is primarily a function of the formal curriculum. This belief is at odds with the literature on student development accumulated over the past five decades that shows that students' out-of-class experiences are as important to student learning and success after college as classroom activities. In large part this is because students spend far more time outside the classroom in the company of peers, coworkers, and family members than in a lecture hall, laboratory, or studio. Interactions with peers mediate many important higher-order skills including thinking analytically and logically, seeing relationships between ideas, and understanding one's own abilities and interests. In addition, the most profound learning often comes through concrete experience when the deeper meaning of knowledge is revealed and internalized. Such experiences foster both intellectual and social development and affect the way people think and behave. This is why students frequently report that study abroad, service learning, internships, and cooperative work arrangements are among their most memorable learning experiences (Kuh 1993, 1995) and employers routinely favor applicants with such experiences (Gardner 1997).

Another shibboleth is that learning is fundamentally a solitary intellectual activity. Most learning is a product of social activity, not isolated individual endeavor. It often best occurs in settings where learners are known by name and respected as individuals, feel comfortable, interact with people from backgrounds different from their own, take intellectual risks, assume responsibility for their learning and social welfare, and participate in community affairs. Unfortunately, most colleges and universities are organized and function as if students' social lives and their academic lives are independent. In Jane Tompkins' view, "There's too much emphasis on matters related exclusively to the head and not enough attention given to nurturing and attitudes and faculties that make of knowledge something useful and good" (1996, 206). Many faculty members ignore what students do outside the classroom or how students' personal lives affect their learning. Most student-affairs professionals have little firsthand information about (and too often little interest in) what happens inside the classroom and how students' academic experiences affect their lives outside the classroom.

Practical Strategies for Engaging Students

One characteristic of engaging learning environments is that they have clear, coherent goals and are managed with policies and practices that are consistent with the institution's espoused values (Chickering and Reisser 1993; Flint and Associates 1999; Kuh et al. 1991).

Various forms of learning communities and service-learning programs are designed with these principles in mind.

Learning communities typically are made up of small numbers of students who are co-enrolled in two or more courses. Some are exclusively classroom based and others have a residential component. The organizing principle is to create "communities of learners," whereby the social fabric connects students to one another. Thus, the tacit knowledge and ethic of belonging that was taken for granted several decades ago is produced by intentionally bringing together groups of students focused on academic tasks in the one venue they have in common: the classroom. Participation in these programs does not always produce immediate improvements in grades, persistence rates, or outcomes. In part, this may be because the students for whom certain types of learning communities are designed have academic profiles that are not as strong as those of the typical student. The University of Missouri-Columbia and Indiana University, Bloomington, offer residential freshman interest groups (FIGs), clusters of about 20 students co-enrolled in the same two to three courses and who live in close proximity in campus housing. The academic backgrounds (college entrance examination scores, high school class rank) of FIG participants at both schools were slightly below that of their non-FIG peers in the early years of implementing these programs. Even so, FIG students tended to persist at essentially the same rates as their somewhat better-prepared counterparts and reported similar levels of satisfaction with their college experience. In addition, they were more likely to return to live on campus in subsequent years, suggesting that participating in a FIG may have had an indirect positive effect because students who live on campus benefit more from college than their peers who do not.

Service learning also has direct ties to the academic program. It is usually a course or major-field requirement, and the experience is supervised by a faculty member, often with the assistance of a professional staff member who coordinates the service-learning program. Service learning puts students in real world situations (typically off-campus) where they encounter numerous opportunities to apply what they are learning in the classroom and vice versa. In fact, the impact of a service-learning experience on such abilities as problem-solving and critical thinking is heightened when service and academic study are tightly linked and augmented with periodic, structured reflection (Eyler 1999). A host of other positive outcomes also appears to be associated with service learning, including openness to and appreciation of diversity and higher levels of moral development. Both learning communities and service learning programs reflect good practices in undergraduate education in that they are carefully designed efforts to connect students' academic and social experiences using the vehicle of participation in activities that are consistent with an institution's educational mission.

Quality Assurance through Feedback, Assessment, and Action

Finally, colleges and universities need to monitor and evaluate their efforts to encourage students to take greater advantage of the learning resources provided. Identifying the patterns of student engagement is, as suggested earlier, an essential first step toward developing policies and practices and targeting resources to channel student behavior toward educationally purposeful activities. It is necessary to determine for whom a learning improvement intervention is intended and to collect data over time to assess the relative impact of participation (net of student background characteristics). Data should be analyzed at various levels (including such variables as year in school and major field as well as individual student, program, and institutional levels) to ensure that certain groups of students are not being screened away from certain types of resources and that students are benefiting from programs. Comparative indicia are needed to allow individual institutions, affinity groups (sector, special mission), and state systems to benchmark student and institutional performance against their peers in order to estimate collegiate quality. An initiative that promises to yield such data is the National Survey of Student Engagement, a multiple-year study supported by the Pew Charitable Trusts that will collect information about the use of good practices in undergraduate education from several hundred thousand undergraduate students at about 1,000 four-year colleges and universities.

In addition to collecting good information, institutions must use it productively. Failure to act is in large part a function of institutional will. A case in point is the male social fraternity system that many colleges and universities continue to host despite evidence showing that on balance much of the behavior of those groups is antithetical to academic values and that the intellectual and personal development of the members of many of these groups is blunted compared with other students, especially in the first year of college (Pascarella, Flowers, and Whitt 1999). Fraternities are powerful socialization vehicles. The combination of campus-specific information and national research underscores the need for institutional interventions. Examples of such initiatives include those recently undertaken at the University of Maryland-College Park to revitalize its Greek system and at Colgate University and DePauw University, where groups are prohibited from adding new members until they are sophomores— that is, after they have managed a successful academic and social transition to university life independent of the powerful conforming fraternity culture. The dynamics of addressing this and related student-culture challenges (including similar behaviors and consequences associated with male athletic teams) are complicated and demand cooperation from a diverse set of constituents ranging from alumni, governing board members, legal counsel, and student-life professionals and strong leadership and support from senior campus administrators. Often the president must be involved to persuade the various stakeholders to take actions consistent with the university's espoused values, sound educational theory and practice, and institutional assessment data.

Conclusion

College students today are more diverse in every way than their counterparts of just two or three decades ago. The differences that present the greatest challenges to faculty and professional staff members are inadequate preparation for college-level work and challenging precollege personal and family experiences that may have adversely affected students' social and psychological well-being. Despite these differences, students today generally want pretty much the same thing from their college experience as previous generations. They want to acquire the skills and competencies that will allow them to prosper economically and live self-sufficient lives after college. They also want to learn things about themselves, others, and the larger world that will improve the quality of their thinking. On balance, this seems to happen for most students to a degree comparable to earlier undergraduate cohorts.

Despite the complex contextual and environmental factors mentioned in this chapter, collegiate quality across all sectors appears to be as good as, and perhaps better than, in any previous era. That is, in the absence of incontrovertible evidence comparing the quality of undergraduate student learning and personal development across decades, it seems reasonable to conclude that learning productivity in U.S. colleges and universities is not as poor as most critics assert or as good as apologists claim. Most important, institutions of higher education are doing what the majority of people want and expect them to do in terms of undergraduate education: giving record numbers of students an opportunity to develop their potential and prepare themselves for life after college.

That said, the dramatic changes in the demographic characteristics of college students and the escalating pace of change in the external environment make the role of higher education both more important and more challenging than at any previous period. For this reason, the baccalaureate experience at American colleges and universities can and must be improved. Some of the challenges are relatively new, such as how best to use emerging forms of technology to produce desired collegiate outcomes and to cultivate in students at a higher level than ever before the discernment skills needed to critically evaluate the quality and utility of information available electronically from an increasing number of providers. Other challenges are long-standing, such as arranging college transition experiences and shaping student cultures so that they appropriately socialize students to academic values and encourage them to use the university's vast intellectual and cultural resources. Perhaps the most important challenge is more consistently infusing in educational practice what the theory and research show to be promising approaches to teaching and learning. Indeed, more is known today than ever before about the pedagogical tactics and strategies that actively engage students in learning activities and yield the greatest gains in educational and personal growth. Closing the gap between theory and practice in undergraduate education is essential to ensuring the well-being of individuals and the future of our society.

References

Astin, A. W. 1993. *What matters in college: Four critical years revisited.* San Francisco: Jossey-Bass.

———. 1997. The changing American college student: Thirty year trends, 1966–1996. *Review of Higher Education* 21, no. 2: 115–35.

Astin, A. W., S. A. Parrott, W. S. Korn, and L. J. Sax. 1997. *The American freshman: Thirty-year trends, 1966–1996.* Los Angeles: University of California, Los Angeles, Higher Education Research Institute.

Baxter Magolda, M. B. 1992. *Knowing and reasoning in college: Gender-related patterns in students' intellectual development.* San Francisco: Jossey-Bass.

Bonner, T. N. 1986. The unintended revolution in America's colleges since 1940. *Change* 18, no. 5: 44–51.

Boyer Commission on Educating Undergraduates in the Research University. 1998. *Reinventing undergraduate education: A blueprint for America's research universities.* Stony Brook, N.Y.: Carnegie Foundation for the Advancement of Teaching.

Boyett, J. H., and D. P. Snyder. 1998. Twenty-first century workplace trends. *On the Horizon* 6, no. 1: 1, 4–9.

Brubacher, J. S., and W. Rudy. 1997. *Higher education in transition: A history of American colleges and universities.* 4th ed. New Brunswick, N.J.: Transaction.

Carlin, J. F. 1999. Restoring sanity to an academic world gone mad. *Chronicle of Higher Education,* 5 November: A76.

Chickering, A. W., and L. Reisser. 1993. *Education and identity.* 2d ed. San Francisco: Jossey-Bass.

Clark, B., P. Heist, M. McConnell, M. Trow, and G. Yonge. 1972. *Students and colleges: Interaction and change.* Berkeley: University of California, Center for Research and Development in Higher Education.

DeSousa, D. J., and G. D. Kuh. 1996. Does institutional racial composition make a difference in what Black students gain from college? *Journal of College Student Development* 37: 257–67.

Dolence, M. G., and D. M. Norris. 1995. *Transforming higher education: A vision for learning in the 21st century.* Ann Arbor, Mich.: Society for College and University Planning.

Education Commission of the States. 1995. *Making quality count in undergraduate education.* Denver, Colo.: Education Commission of the States.

Ewell, P. T. 1997. Organizing for learning: A point of entry. Discussion paper presented at the 1997 AAHE Summer Academy, Snowbird, Utah.

Eyler, J. 1999. The civic outcomes of service-learning: What do we know? *Peer Review* 2, no. 1: 11–13.

Finn, C. E., Jr., and B. V. Manno. 1996. Behind the curtain. *Wilson Quarterly* (winter): 44–53.

Flint, T. A., and Associates, eds. 1999. *Best practices in adult learning: A CAEL / APQC benchmarking study.* New York: Forbes.

Gallagher, R. P. 1995. *National survey of counseling center directors, 1995.* Alexandria, Va.: International Association of Counseling Services.

Gardner, P. D. 1997. Are college seniors prepared to work? In *The senior year experience: Facilitating integration, reflection, closure, and transition,* edited by J. Gardner, G. Van der Veer, and Associates. San Francisco: Jossey-Bass.

Hansen, E. J. 1999. Essential demographics of today's college students. *AAHE Bulletin* 51, no. 3: 3–5.

Hayworth, J. G. 1997. The misrepresentation of Generation X. *About Campus* 2, no. 4: 10–15.

Horowitz, H. L. 1987. *Campus life: Undergraduate cultures from the end of the eighteenth century to the present.* New York: Knopf.

Immerwahr, J., and J. Harvey. 1995. What the public thinks of colleges. *Chronicle of Higher Education,* 12 May: B1–2.

Jacob, P. 1957. *Changing values in college.* New York: Harper.

King, J. E. 1998. Too many students are holding jobs for too many hours. *Chronicle of Higher Education,* 1 May: A72.

Kuh, G. D. 1993. In their own words: What students learn outside the classroom. *American Educational Research Journal* 30: 277–304.

———. 1995. The other curriculum: Out-of-class experiences associated with student learning and personal development. *Journal of Higher Education* 66: 123–55.

———. 1999a. Student bashing: An unseemly academic tradition. *About Campus* 4, no. 3: 2–4.

———. 1999b. How are we doing? Tracking the quality of the undergraduate experience, 1960s to the present. *Review of Higher Education* 23, no. 2: 99–119.

Kuh, G. D., and S. Hu. 1999. Unraveling the complexity of the increase in college grades from the mid-1980s to the mid-1990s. *Educational Evaluation and Policy Analysis* 21: 1–24.

Kuh, G. D., S. Hu, and N. Vesper. 2000. "They shall be known by what they do": An activities-based typology of college students. *Journal of College Student Development* 41:228–44.

Kuh, G. D., J. S. Schuh, E. J. Whitt, and Associates. 1991. *Involving colleges: Successful approaches to fostering student learning and personal development outside the classroom.* San Francisco: Jossey-Bass.

Kuh, G. D., N. Vesper, M. R. Connolly, and C. R. Pace. 1997. *College Student Experiences Questionnaire: Revised norms for the third edition.* Bloomington: Indiana University Center for Postsecondary Research and Planning.

Kull, M. D. 1999. Knowledge markets: A primer. *On the Horizon* 7, no. 4: 12–13.

Levine, A., and J. S. Cureton. 1998. Collegiate life: An obituary. *Change* 30, no. 3: 12–17, 51.

London, H. B. 1996. How college effects first-generation students. *About Campus* 1, no. 5: 9–13.

Mortenson, T. G. 1998. Men behaving badly. . . . Where are the guys? *Postsecondary Education Opportunity* 76: 1–8.

———. 1999. College continuation rates for 1998 high school graduates. *Postsecondary Education Opportunity* 84: 1–8.

Norris, D. M. 1996. Perpetual learning as a revolutionary creation. *On the Horizon* 4, no. 6: 1, 3–6.

O'Donnell, J. J. 1996. The digital challenge. *Wilson Quarterly* (winter): 48–49.

Ogilvy, J. 1994. The information revolution. *On the Horizon* 2, no. 4: 1–2, 4.

Pace, C. R. 1990. *The undergraduates: A report of their activities and college experiences in the 1980s.* Los Angeles: Center for the Study of Evaluation, UCLA Graduate School of Education.

Pascarella, E. T., L. Flowers, and E. J. Whitt. 1999. Cognitive effects of Greek affiliation in college: Additional evidence. Paper presented at the annual meeting of the Association for the Study of Higher Education (November), San Antonio.

Pascarella, E. T., and P. T. Terenzini. 1991. *How college affects students: Findings and insights from twenty years of research.* San Francisco: Jossey-Bass.

Perry, W. G., Jr. 1970. *Forms of intellectual and ethical development in the college years: A scheme.* New York: Holt, Rinehart & Winston.

Rowley, D. J., H. D. Lujan, and M. G. Dolence. 1998. *Strategic choices for the academy: How demand for lifelong learning will re-create higher education.* San Francisco: Jossey-Bass.

Rudolph, F. 1990. *The American college and university: A history.* Athens: University of Georgia Press.

Rutherford, P. 1998. Competency-based training: The link between education and workplace excellence. *On the Horizon* 6, no. 6: 7–8.

Sacks, P. 1996. *Generation X goes to college: An eye-opening account of teaching in postmodern America.* Chicago: Open Court.

Sax, L. J., A. W. Astin, M. Arredondo, W. S. Korn. 1996. *The American college teacher: National norms for the 1995–96 HERI faculty survey.* Los Angeles: University of California, Los Angeles, Higher Education Research Institute.

Sax, L. J., A. W. Astin, W. S. Korn, and K. M. Mahoney. 1997. *The American college freshman.* Los Angeles: University of California, Los Angeles, Higher Education Research Institute.

Schroeder, C. C. 1993. New students: New learning styles. *Change* 25, no. 4 (September–October): 21–26.

Shapiro, H. T. 1997. Cognition, character, and culture in undergraduate education: Rhetoric and reality. In *The American university: National treasure or endangered species?* edited by R. G. Ehrenberg. Ithaca, N.Y.: Cornell University Press.

Tompkins, J. 1996. *A life in school: What the teacher learned.* Reading, Mass.: Addison-Wesley.

Watson, L. W., and G. D. Kuh. 1996. The influence of dominant race environments on students' involvement, perceptions, and educational gains: A look at historically black and predominantly white liberal arts institutions. *Journal of College Student Development* 37: 415–24.

Wingspread Group on Higher Education. 1993. *An American imperative: Higher expectations for higher education.* Racine, Wisc.: Johnson Foundation.

Chapter Twelve ⌇

Governance
The Remarkable Ambiguity

George Keller

Governance: the word itself is ambiguous. It implies administration of the affairs of an organization, as in *a well-governed hospital.* It also implies tight control, as in *a valve that governs the steam intake,* or major influence, as in *an expert coach often governs the outcome of a game.* It connotes management, as in *the governance of a state's higher education system.* (The word derives from the Latin verb *gubernare,* to steer.) Most frequently today, however, the word has a political implication, suggesting some sort of sovereignty that derives in part from the constituents, who have considerable influence.

For colleges and universities, especially in the United States, governance usually refers to the part that the teaching scholars play in the administration, control, standards, and long-term management of the institutions at which they work. Here, too, there is considerable ambiguity. Colleges and universities have been present in Western society since the twelfth century (Baldwin 1971; Haskins 1923; Rashdall 1936). But how they should be governed is still in dispute. These social institutions have officers called presidents, chancellors, trustees, or even (in Europe) rectors magnificus, but the prerogatives, parameters of authority, and responsibilities of those leaders are to this day uncertain and ambiguous. The reasons are many.

For one thing, the ownership and sponsorship of colleges and universities vary. Some are arms of the national state, some are branches of the local state or county government. Some are limbs of a religious denomination. Some institutions are private nonprofit corporations whose trustees are their legal owners, and some are profit-making businesses with stockholders. For another thing, the range and heterogeneity of colleges and universities are vast. The Salvation Army College for Officers in California has 60 students and offers one degree, while Ohio State University and the University of Texas at Austin have nearly 50,000 students each and provide numerous programs and degrees.

Great Britain's Oxford University resembles a holding company for several historic colleges. The DeVry Institutes, which teach business and technology but supply no collegiate frills, are part of a for-profit growth company that adds a new college or two every year. Some U.S. institutions are historically mainly for African American or American Indian students; some religiously controlled institutions are like Loma Linda University, which is chiefly for Seventh-Day Adventists. There are colleges of art, music, law, and naval architecture and colleges devoted to dental hygiene, Bible studies, agriculture, and international business. In the United States there are around 1,500 accredited two-year colleges and 2,200 four-year colleges and universities.

Scholars and students of U.S. higher education often like to use the country's large universities as an archetype for their analyses of campus governance. But the better-known, larger, doctoral-degree-granting universities constitute no more than 200 of America's 3,700 institutions of higher education. To a large extent, most of the best-known universities serve one of the several functions of colleges and universities: the discovery of new knowledge. Many of these universities are research factories, with half or more of their teaching done by graduate students and by adjunct and part-time instructors. These noted universities primarily serve the nation by providing new findings, new ideas, fresh approaches.

Because the U.S. economy increasingly needs new findings to stay competitive and because the media are addicted to the new, the faculty at these institutions are more and more what Henry Rosovsky, a former Harvard dean, calls "stars." The top scholars are frequently well-known intellectual entrepreneurs, sometimes earning more than $400,000 a year from several sources (Finkelstein, Seal, and Schuster 1998, 80–83; Crainer and Dearlove 1999, ch. 5), which has "given many of them immunity from institutional control" (Rosovsky 1998, 125). Moreover, the best-known universities often have in their midst excellent professional schools that tend to operate nearly autonomously from the central university. These powerful and frequently quite rich schools of law, business, or medicine greatly reduce the possibilities of smooth universitywide governance and presidential management (Muller 1994). The 200 or so large research universities best exemplify the dour characterization of American campus governance and management as "a prototypic organized anarchy" (Cohen and March 1974, 3).

In their preoccupation with unearthing or creating new knowledge, the better-known research universities are addressing only one of the functions of the nation's colleges and universities. A separate set of 350 to 400 institutions serves another need of society: educating young persons so that they become aware of civilization's intellectual, artistic, literary, political, and religious heritage. These colleges, from Williams, Swarthmore, and Davidson to Reed, Grinnell, and Occidental, and including several fine religiously affiliated colleges, usually have a minority of professors who conduct research and write articles and books with prodigious scholarship. But the institutions and their faculties are more dedicated to dissemination than to discovery, to developing intellectual and aesthetic acuity than to methodology and metaphysics. They are often bastions of exceptional teaching.

Such colleges of the liberal arts tend to be small in size, with 2,500 students or fewer, usually contain no professional schools, and exhibit something close to the rhetorical ideation of *a community of scholars*. At these campuses the professors and the president and his or her staff often share the governance and priority-shaping rather amicably. The result is somewhat akin to the administration of a large Congregational Church or a small-town hospital.

By far the largest number of American colleges and universities serve the function of preparing the nation's workforce. These are the land-grant universities with schools of agriculture and specialized colleges of nursing, business, education, engineering, and social work. Also included are public and private institutions with major programs in computer science, graphic art, medical technology, creative writing, accounting, and fashion design. In this category too are religious seminaries; graduate schools for psychological counseling; and higher education programs to help train better deans of students, campus finance officials, and college analysts and officers. The governance at these state colleges and underendowed private colleges and universities tends to be more contentious, fragmented, and politically and financially driven—with deans, vice presidents, and trustees or regents often playing a more forceful role. The presence of faculty unions at some institutions in this third group often complicates the governance procedures and skews governance issues somewhat.

Then there is a fourth layer of accredited colleges and universities, which educates one-third of all U.S. undergraduates—primarily in basic literacy, quantitative calculations, technical job training, and adult education (Grubb 1999). These are principally the public two-year community colleges, but the layer includes many small, underfinanced private colleges, too. The governance of these colleges usually leans toward a more hierarchical and centrally directed form, with faculty concurrence and approval rather than full collaboration being sought. Here, too, faculty and other staff are often unionized and there are numerous part-time faculty, so shared governance is difficult.

Thus, America's colleges and universities display at least four different modes of campus governance, depending on the societal function of the institution. And each of these modes has a variety of different styles and manners for running institutions and for deciding on priorities for expenditures and academic emphasis. Also, of course, each institution's governance pattern will shift a little depending on the personality, skill, and ambitions of its president and the composition of its board of trustees or regents. Election of a new state governor, changes in the state higher education commission (Gaither 1999), new legislation, or recent rulings of the courts may alter the governance activities at state colleges and universities. An example is the federal government's Title IX, and the courts' interpretations of the act, both of which have altered how universities recruit for and organize their athletic programs and facilities. Governance increasingly comes from outside as well as inside (Berdahl 1989).

Fashions in Governance

As if the matter of governance in American higher education were not protean enough, the historical circumstances and fashions in campus governance change from time to time. In early-nineteenth-century America, the small colleges were governed mainly by their outside trustees, who were largely nonacademic lay persons (Metzger 1989). Then in midcentury, strong presidents scrambled to build enrollments and gather financial support, and they governed commandingly over the faculty, many of whom were callow tutors. As the colleges and universities slowly filled with more mature and scholarly faculty in the last third of the nineteenth and early decades of the twentieth centuries, and as large universities began to appear, American professors began to emulate their European counterparts and assert themselves as partners with the trustees, presidents, and deans in governing their institutions and deciding on priorities for the future (Cowley 1980). The American Association of University Professors, the AAUP, was founded in 1915 to argue for faculty rights and greater freedom from trustee and presidential prohibitions and dismissals. Over the next century the quasi-profession of academic scholars expanded greatly, became more diverse and important, and pressed hard for "shared governance," where the faculty would codirect the colleges and universities at which they worked (Metzger 1987; Mortimer and McConnell 1978).

By the 1960s, faculty power in campus governance had reached its zenith, especially at most research universities and many of the liberal arts colleges and state institutions. Historian of American academics and academic governance Walter Metzger observed that by 1966, "The AAUP joined with the American Council on Education and the Association of Governing Boards to formulate a statement on shared authority that gave professors some voice in every sphere of governance and a predominant say in matters of professional concern" (Metzger 1987, 196).

Shared governance is still the often-invoked ideal for many four-year-college professors and campus executives. What it means is that the management of a college or university should be collaborative, with some areas requiring joint decision making and other areas primarily the responsibility of either the faculty or the administrators and trustees. Thus, with significant matters such as long-range planning, general allocation of financial resources, and the location and design of new campus buildings, a shared endeavor by the faculty, administrators, and trustees should be the norm. But the AAUP-ACE-AGB "Statement on Government of Colleges and Universities" (American Association of University Professors 1966) states that faculty members should have "primary responsibility" for determining educational matters such as the curriculum, requirements for all degrees, methods of instruction, research, the content of courses, the selection and promotion of colleagues, and "those aspects of student life which relate to the educational process." The president has the primary responsibility for administering all board-of-trustee policies and campus operations, selecting the deans and other academic officers, and speaking for the institution. He or she also has "a special obligation to innovate and initiate" and "at times, with or without support, infuse new life into a department." The trustees, who are legally the final authority, are primarily responsible for the overall fiscal health and the fundamental mission and educational policies of the institution.

The joint statement of 1966 recognizes that it is a set of guidelines not a blueprint and that campus governance will vary according to the type, size, and sponsorship of the college or university. In effect, it urges maximum consultation and courtesy among the constituent groups and avoids laying out very clear boundaries of authority. So, naturally, there are ambiguities. For example, which aspects of student life relate to the educational process? Admissions? Residence halls? Athletics? Also, faculty decisions about the curriculum and courses are more than merely educational matters; they affect the financial condition and the attractiveness of the college to potential students. Likewise, administrative budget making can affect the educational capabilities of the faculty. A noteworthy omission in the 1966 joint statement is the absence of suggested protocols for dealing with financial matters or difficulties.

The 1960s and early 1970s were the high point of American campus *governance*—as contrasted with administration, management, and leadership, which are the other three of the four necessities for running a college or university. At numerous large universities and activist colleges radical students wanted a voice in governance, as did some junior staff members attracted to the "power to the people" rhetoric of the time. Dozens of institutions replaced their faculty senates with more broadly representative college or university senates. Direct democracy briefly became the vogue, even though universities are intellectual corporations and not primarily political entities. In his Godkin lectures at Harvard in 1963 Clark Kerr noted, "There is a 'kind of lawlessness' in any large university with separate sources of initiative and power . . . There are several 'nations' of students, of faculty, of alumni, of trustees, of public groups. Each has its territory, its jurisdiction, its form of government . . . [the president] is mostly a mediator. The first task of a mediator is peace" (1963, 36). It was a piercing overstatement, but it caught the sense of stalemate on many campuses; the preoccupation with power and broad political representation of the 1960s and 1970s; and the crippling of forward action, new campus initiatives, and institutional focus. Too much governance on campus can contribute to a lack of collaborative planning for the future and sound financial and academic management (Benjamin et al. 1993).

Inevitably, a reassessment and restructuring of college governance took place, especially as changing demographics, reduced financial support, new technology, and novel patterns of admissions and attendance in higher education became more apparent. Also, at its 1972 convention, the AAUP decided to pursue collective bargaining and establish more faculty unions, causing the AAUP to lose some membership and national influence. By the late 1970s, several scholars of higher education such as T. R. McConnell and Kenneth Mortimer noted a mounting dissatisfaction with the 1966 AAUP statement and its call for shared authority. McConnell and Mortimer saw "three flaws" in the concept. First, "it does not describe actual governance patterns in a majority of institutions," especially community colleges, historically black colleges, underfinanced private colleges and universities, and religiously affiliated institutions. Second, it ignores the rise since the mid-1960s of faculty unions and collective bargaining, which introduced adversarial rather than collaborative decision-making practices. And third, the AAUP statement neglects to factor in the growing intrusion of "external forces":

> In our view, "academic" issues, such as faculty status, and "fiscal" issues, such as the reassignment of vacant positions due to retirement, termination, or the phasing out of existing programs, are inescapably interdependent; and more emphasis should therefore be placed on the principle of joint endeavor . . . We think it is unrealistic for the faculty to argue that such considerations [as the balance of schools of thought in a discipline or affirmative action standards] are irrelevant and . . . require little, if any, administrative participation. It is equally unrealistic for the administration to argue that fiscal matters related to academic affairs are adequately decided without faculty participation. In sum, we argue that those concerned with college and university governance should eschew the search for separate areas of authority and look for ways to enhance joint involvement. (Mortimer and McConnell 1978, 271–72)

Soon after, more institutions felt the need to engage in strategic planning and decision making and in better financial management as the costs of higher education began to rise faster than the Consumer Price Index (Keller 1983). Sharper administration, shrewd, farsighted and competitive management, and stronger leadership became as vital as democratic governance. By the late 1980s, Jack Schuster could write that "the faculty appears to be retreating from a strong commitment to governance" (1989, 95). Faculty senate meetings sometimes could not muster a quorum. In the same text, I wrote, "Something new is emerging, the exact outlines of which are still unclear. But what is clear is that the 'unique dualism' (Corson 1960, 43) that has characterized university administration in the post–World War II period is crumbling, and new forms of academic management are being tried" (Keller 1989, 133).

A Structural Fault in Academe

Underneath all these difficulties of governing and managing colleges and universities is something more fundamental: a structural fault in the organization, privileges, and leadership of scholarly institutions and the behavior of their professors. The flaw is the product of centuries of university evolution and is thus time-honored and extremely hard to correct. No one has analyzed the flaw better than the late James S. Coleman, who at one point called the governance of contemporary colleges and universities a "medieval anachronism" (1973).

In the late medieval years, when universities were embryonic, they were organized into small communities, like the craft guilds of their time. The masters organized and scheduled their own lectures, performed outside jobs, and collected their own fees. There was no central administration; instead, a discipline for the *universitas* was collectively imposed. Usually the masters, like monks, could not marry and had to uphold scholastic standards and profess a given faith, as was the case at Cambridge and Oxford universities until the late nineteenth century. The income of the early scholars was small and somewhat unpredictable, but the masters were a close, self-controlled community and familiar with their students. (Recall that Thomas Jefferson designed the University of Virginia so that the masters each lived with students in a house.) Their time was free, but as Coleman notes, "university rules invaded their whole lives."

As universities in later centuries became larger and more secular and began to receive monies from political and other sources rather than solely from students, the scholar-teachers and their sponsors gradually scaled back the medieval controls over the members' lives. The professors married, became diverse religiously, and felt free to teach what they wished. They ceased being a close, self-regulating community. But they remained advocates of the campus as a community and fought against the imposition of central administrative controls and the pull to become merely skilled workers in the evolving modern, purposeful corporations. To this day professors are not regarded as employees, though everyone else at a college is so regarded. Most American professors continue to see themselves as independent semiprofessionals, free to lecture or consult off-campus, conduct research instead of teach, and own a business on the side. They see their time as their own, not belonging daily to the college or university at which they work.

Yet the modern college or university is a major institution in today's more intellectually grounded and information-rich civilization. Some large universities have an annual operating budget of more than $1 billion, and resemble a holding company or conglomerate. They cannot avoid being well-managed and behaving more like a corporate actor in most cases. Smaller colleges, especially, are pressed to select a market niche to serve in order to remain viable and to be more strategic and focused in their initiatives.

Professors have been glad to become salaried workers and to receive secretarial help and their own offices, telephones, and computers like corporate executives. But they usually have been unwilling to exchange control of their own time for their increasingly considerable salaries. In fact, they spend more time on their own scholarship, consulting, writing, or doing research for the federal or local government, a foundation, a profit-making corporation, or a government agency (Slaughter and Leslie 1997). There has been a concomitant erosion of higher education's central activity of teaching in both course load and quality of instruction (Cuban 1999). But the professors continue to talk about the community of scholars, and they demand a full partnership in the governance of the institutions to which they are attached, even as their allegiance to their home college or university and to fellow scholars on campus becomes more tenuous.

And then there are the AAUP and other union organizers arguing for more pay, lifetime tenure, and the privileges of valuable full-time employees at a corporation—at the same time they are battling for the freedom of independent professors to teach when, what, and however they wish and to earn as much as they can from outside assignments or enterprises.

James S. Coleman described the structural fault in academic organizational life this way:

> The faculty members have the rights of members of a community— control over their own activities and their time—without the normative constraints and demands that such a community provides. They have the rights of employees of a purposive corporation—the security of a salary and the other perquisites of such employees—without the obligation to give up control over their time for use toward a corporate goal.
>
> The effect of this structural fault is to create a status with special privileges, a status with the autonomy of a community member, the security of a corporate employee, and the obligations of neither. (1973, 397)

To govern a leading academic institution today is to deal heavily with gifted, avant-garde intellectual entrepreneurs who cling to medieval notions of community control over their own activities while wanting to help run a multimillion-dollar organization that has become a central institution in modern society. It is a formidable task. To try to overcome the structural fault and to assist in contemporary campus governance and management there appear to be new efforts on three fronts.

The first is an attempt by several academic provosts and presidents to prod faculty members into restoring some of the discipline, values, and self-regulation of their community life if they wish to help govern (Cahn 1986; Kennedy 1997). Donald Kennedy, biologist and former president at Stanford, for example, observes that faculty often stress the importance of academic freedom and faculty rights and privileges but "little is said about duty." "Little is to be found in the academic literature about the nature of faculty responsibilities. It is part of the tradition of freedom, perhaps, that in higher education there are no job descriptions, no annual performance evaluations. But one result is that expectations of the professorate are murky, and public understanding murkier still" (1997, 2–3). In Kennedy's opinion, "The missing information amounts to a lesion in accountability, which I think has much to do with the rising chorus of national discontent with higher education" (vii). He therefore calls for a "shift in loyalty," with greater attention by the faculty to the needs of the institution and its students and with a renewed sense of obligation and self-regulation.

A second effort is to invent a novel form of governance and management through standing strategic priorities and budget committees and other joint faculty-administration bodies instead of the we-they dual governance of the past half century (Keller 1983, 1989; Schuster et al. 1994). The third is to virtually set aside faculty governance and manage the institutions like market-savvy corporations with faculty employed as nontenured teachers in a salaried, businesslike way and assigned to work at times that the students prefer. This is happening primarily in the fast-growing for-profit sector, at companies such as the DeVry Institutes, the University of Phoenix, and ITT Education Services.

Despite the Difficulties

Clearly, the governance of American colleges and universities is varied, often fractious, and fundamentally impaired. It causes many lay trustees to roll their eyes and some outside business leaders, parents, and politicos to seethe and occasionally bluster about academe's elephantine movements, unusual privileges, and inability to make decisions and innovate smoothly.

And yet, the remarkable fact is that American higher education has somehow managed to carry on quite successfully, so well that many regard America's colleges and universities as among the world's best and the most strategically layered to fulfill society's needs for highly educated and skilled talent in numerous arenas. Moreover, a surprising number of colleges and universities have transformed themselves into substantially different and superior institutions during the past three decades. Among universities, Boston College, Boston University, Carnegie Mellon, Duke, Furman, Georgetown, Hampden-Sydney, the University of Miami, New York University, Notre Dame, Stanford, and Xavier University of Louisiana are only a dozen of the larger institutions that have reengineered their organizations to become more estimable. Such colleges as Babson, Colgate, Connecticut, Elon (North Carolina), Grinnell, Macalester, Occidental (California), St. Mary's (Maryland), Spelman, Stevens Institute of Technology (New Jersey), Trinity (Texas), and Webster (Missouri) constitute only a portion of the numerous smaller institutions that have changed their clienteles, programs, and reputations.

Hugh Davis Graham and Nancy Diamond identify a group of ambitious universities that have elbowed their way into the ranks of America's important research universities (1997); and many liberal arts colleges from Roanoke College in Virginia to Whitman College in Washington state have been renovating themselves to join the ranks of the country's outstanding such colleges. Wheaton College in suburban Chicago has remade itself from a decent Bible college into an institution that Edward Fiske in his *Guide to Colleges* calls, "arguably the finest Evangelical college in the country." Berklee College of Music in Boston has become a worldwide center for the training in and study of jazz, folk, and rock music; and the University of California-San Diego has emerged as a premier enclave for higher education in the sciences.

The frequent allegation that American higher education has not changed while the country's economy, religion, culture, and technology have been transformed is only partly correct. It is true that much of the basic structure of higher education is similar to that of a century ago, but much new wine has been poured into the dusty bottles. And an entirely new kind of wine—technologically enhanced education that can be delivered over great distances—is now being added at a headlong rate.

How have many of the nation's colleges and universities been able to move so nimbly when their governance procedures are so sclerotic and unsettled? Again, the reasons are many. One could point to new mandates by some legislatures or pressures from boards of trustees, to the actions of aspiring and alert faculty members and deans at numerous campuses, or to presidential leaders—from the imperious John Silber at Boston University, strategic Richard Cyert at Carnegie Mellon, and prescient James Duderstadt at the University of Michigan to the spirited Jane O' Brien at Hollins College and warmly insistent John Slaughter at Occidental College.

W. H. Cowley, one-time president of Hamilton College in New York and the first David Jacks Professor of Higher Education at Stanford, found through his research that presidential leadership was very often decisive for an institution's climb to eminence.

Name a great American college or university, and you will find in its history a commanding leader or leaders who held its presidency . . .

> Our American social system, as well as its political system, thrives or falters depending on the quality of its leadership. Colleges and universities, focal institutions in the life of the nation, need especially strong leaders. By this I do not mean that presidents should autocratically make policy themselves. Instead, they should see that policy gets made—and made wisely—by faculty and trustees, and that it gets carried out. (Cowley 1980, 70)

Certainly strong presidential leadership has made the difference at institutions as varied as Maricopa Community College in Arizona and Michigan State University. And today it is the primary factor in the rise in stature at numerous colleges and universities. For instance, at the Mississippi University for Women, President Clyda Rent has battled to save the college, which has educated persons such as writer Eudora Welty and the first woman appointed to the Mississippi Supreme Court, from being closed by the state. She herself planted flowers and bushes because when she took office the appearance of the campus had been neglected for decades. She has increased the endowment, state appropriations, and enrollment; rallied the dispirited faculty; and restored the college, the first public college for women in the United States, to educational eminence. In another instance, at the University of Maryland, Baltimore County, a post–World War II creation, President Freeman Hrabowski has brought the relatively new medium-sized university to the edge of scholarly distinction; fought for several new buildings, including a superb library; and established with the help of foundation dollars one of America's finest programs for talented African American undergraduate scientists and mathematicians.

But these and other visionary, energetic presidents are careful to involve their faculty and trustees in the determination of initiatives and priorities. As higher education scholar Paul Dressel writes: "Determination of priorities is meaningless unless there is wide involvement of faculty, clientele, board, and influential fund sources. Thus the administrative responsibility for determination of priorities must be a shared one, and it must, in great part, be related to the governance pattern" (1981, 85).

Today, faculty committees are actually more numerous at most institutions than ever before, and some professors very much want the faculty to have more power in deciding major matters. But when hard decisions need to be made or bold new ventures approved, most faculty have little stomach for such distressing tasks. Again Paul Dressel, "Now that institutions are facing the necessity of some reduction in activities . . . faculty members are not much inclined to take a major role" (1981, 81).

To understand governance it is necessary to distinguish between authority, influence, and power. The legal authority of universities is vested in the board of trustees and in its selected chief executive officer, the president. The faculty, however, have considerable power, ranging from enormous influence at the research universities to a fair amount at many community colleges and small, poor private colleges. Power, the ability to shape and force policies and practices, is distributed at most academic institutions among an array of parties: students; alumni; radical, ideological, or militant groups; famous or noisy professors; rich donors; strong trustees or regents; deans; state leaders (for public institutions); the media; the courts; religious leaders; and others. Sometimes, a tiny band of firebrands can temporarily become so powerful that they override all the traditional forms of governance, as happened at Cornell University in 1969 when angry, gun-toting students calling themselves the Afro-American Society seized power on campus (Downs 1999) and overrode both presidential authority and faculty influence.

In most cases, though, where a college or university has made considerable changes or increased its quality, as at Rutgers and Princeton universities in New Jersey, there has been a delicate interplay between presidential leadership, faculty initiatives and guidance, and trustee and alumni support. An example is the transformation of Elon College in North Carolina from a destitute, small, religiously affiliated college with mostly local students to a most attractive and innovative college (the third-largest private institution in the state) with students from many other states. President J. Fred Young sparked the move, but Elon's dedicated faculty brought in outside speakers; went on retreats; attended national workshops on such subjects as critical thinking and writing across the curriculum; organized teaching workshops; and, with the help of a genial, insistent provost, devised a remarkable new curriculum. Elon's trustees kept pressing the president and supported him with financial contributions. President Young also received major help from several unusually able persons on his staff, even a maintenance director to whom the students annually present thank-you letters and posters (Keller 1997a).

The Virtues of Ambiguity

It may be that the very lack of clarity about how all colleges and universities should be governed has been a huge contributor to many institutions' ability to be agile and especially responsive to new conditions. An ironclad and historically developed scheme of strictly correct governance procedures would probably have stymied campus changes. After all, the idea of shared governance, akin to the U.S. government's separation of political powers, is a conservative device to prevent rash, ill-considered acts. Like the battles between the U.S. Congress and the executive branch, the campus checks can sometimes be paralyzing. Today's colleges and universities, however, live in a time of unusually rapid shifts. They cannot afford to be blocked from exploring new organizational forms, academic programs, delivery systems, faculty arrangements, and financial schemes.

Currently, presidents and deans generally consult their faculties on important policy or personnel issues; and many campus executives create special committees and task forces, on which professors are usually in the majority, to study and advise them on prickly problems or proposed initiatives. Faculty members usually maintain a dominant role in the appointment of new colleagues and the promotion and tenure of teaching scholars. Therefore, a kind of mutual deference between faculty and administrators exists, especially at the four-year institutions.

But in a time of changing demographics, worsening student preparation for college-level study, a digital communication revolution, escalating costs of undergraduate education, and continuing and expanding higher education for adults, the management of change—and stronger leadership for such change—has become as important as participatory governance and efficient administration of weekly campus operations (Keller 1997b). So the ragged protocols of dual governance are usually still observed, like displays of good manners; but stronger, more active leadership is being called for in academe (Eaton 1995; Chait, Holland, and Taylor 1996; *Stronger leadership* 1996), and new external factors are compelling colleges and universities to modernize their operations. The management of change in academe has been pushed to center stage, much as governance captured center stage from 1960 to 1980.

Faculty influence in governance has also suffered from one of the most fundamental shifts in U.S. higher education in decades: the increasing sway of the marketplace and higher education's consumers over professorial dominion (Riesman 1980; Kuttner 1997; Yergin and Stanislaw 1998). Traditionally university professors have decided, for the most part, what students need to learn. Now the faculties are increasingly being urged to provide instruction in subjects preferred by the paying students, the graduates' employers, and some state officials. We are moving from a teacher-led higher education to what is euphemistically called a "learner-centered" higher education (Barr and Tagg 1995). This shift—like the pressure for better institutional planning, decision making, financial management, and strategic change—tends to pull professors toward a professional serving role and away from a commanding governing role where they design what the students should learn and how and when they can learn it.

In the face of this upheaval, faculty governance has both yielded and stiffened. That is, a number of professors, recognizing that they may have been a bit narcissistic and inattentive to new educational needs, have sometimes allowed others to guide them into offering novel subjects and employing new methods of instruction. Other scholars, however, have insisted that a college is more than a service station and that they, like doctors, know better than their younger attendees the requisites and most valuable components of intellect for the more democratic, international, and scientific society of the future. At numerous faculty department and faculty senate meetings, especially those at the research universities and liberal arts colleges, fervid arguments can be heard from many learned scholars for continuing the faculty's prerogatives of controlling the curriculum, the ingredients for receiving a degree, and the directions of institutional change. Faculty governance lives, even if its influence has been diminished slightly and its practice assumes a greater variety of forms each year.

Most remarkable of all is that despite the famous conservatism of faculty governance bodies, their reluctance to accept changes at their institutions, and their fierce allegiance to some medieval privileges, many colleges and universities have changed, and continue to adjust to new conditions and new discoveries. Yes, some irritated faculties from time to time pass votes of no-confidence in their president, and some presidents and boards of trustees or regents institute changes over stubborn faculty objections. But, all in all, a tactful, fragile doctrine of mutual deference is currently in force at many institutions, rough hewn though its edges are.

Miraculously, the balancing act somehow works in most cases. And just possibly, the ambiguous combination of faculty governance that protects centuries-old academic privileges and practices and modern presidential and lay trustee governance that nudges the institution toward necessary accommodations to novel conditions and fiscal realities is a surprisingly good one. It seems to provide a nice equilibrium between the two indispensables of academic life: tradition and innovation.

References

American Association of University Professors. 1966. Statement on government of colleges and universities. *AAUP Bulletin* 52, no. 4: 375–79.

Baldwin, J. 1971. *The scholastic culture of the Middle Ages, 1000–1300.* Lexington, Mass.: D. C. Heath.

Barr, R., and J. Tagg. 1995. From teaching to learning: A new paradigm for undergraduate education. *Change* 27 (November–December): 12–25.

Benjamin, R. et al. 1993. *The redesign of governance in higher education.* Santa Monica, Calif.: RAND.

Berdahl, R. 1989. Shared governance and external constraints. In *Governing tomorrow's campus,* edited by J. Schuster and L. Miller. New York: American Council on Education/Macmillan.

Cahn, S. 1986. *Saints and scamps: Ethics in academia.* Totowa, N.J.: Rowman & Littlefield.

Chait, R., T. Holland, and B. Taylor. 1996. *Improving the performance of governing boards.* Phoenix: American Council on Education/Oryx Press.

Cohen, M., and J. March. 1974. *Leadership and ambiguity: The American college president.* New York: McGraw-Hill.

Coleman, J. S. 1973. The university and society's new demands upon it. In *Content and context,* edited by C. Kaysen. New York: McGraw-Hill.

Corson, J. 1960. *Governance of colleges and universities.* New York: McGraw-Hill.

Cowley, W. H. 1980. *Presidents, professors, and trustees: The evolution of American academic government.* San Francisco: Jossey-Bass.

Crainer, S., and D. Dearlove. 1999. *Gravy training: Inside the business schools.* San Francisco: Jossey-Bass.

Cuban, L. 1999. *How scholars trumped teachers.* New York: Teachers College Press.

Downs, D. 1999. *Cornell '69: Liberalism and the crisis of the American university.* Ithaca, N.Y.: Cornell University Press.

Dressel, P. 1981. *Administrative leadership.* San Francisco: Jossey-Bass.

Eaton, J. 1995. Where have all the higher education leaders gone? *Council [for Aid to Education] Comments* 2 (April): 1–2.

Finkelstein, M., R. Seal, and J. Schuster. 1998. *The new academic generation: A profession in transformation.* Baltimore: Johns Hopkins University Press.

Gaither, G., ed. 1999. *The multicampus system: Perspectives on practice and prospects.* Sterling, Va.: Stylus Publishing.

Graham, H. D., and N. Diamond. 1997. *The rise of American research universities: Elites and challengers in the postwar era.* Baltimore: Johns Hopkins University Press.

Grubb, W. N. 1999. *Honored but invisible: An inside look at teaching in community colleges.* New York: Routledge.

Haskins, C. H. 1923. *The rise of universities.* New York: Henry Holt.

Keller, G. 1983. *Academic strategy: The management revolution in American higher education.* Baltimore: Johns Hopkins University Press.

———. 1989. Shotgun marriage: The growing connection between academic management and faculty governance. In *Governing tomorrow's campus,* edited by Jack Schuster and Lynn Miller, 133–40. New York: American Council on Education/Macmillan.

———. 1997a. The college that transformed itself. *Planning for Higher Education* 25 (spring): 1–12.

———. 1997b. Examining what works in strategic planning. In *Planning and management for a changing environment,* edited by Marvin Peterson, David Dill, and Lisa Mets, 158–70. San Francisco: Jossey-Bass.

Kennedy, D. 1997. *Academic duty.* Cambridge: Harvard University Press.

Kerr, C. 1963. *The uses of the university.* Cambridge: Harvard University Press.

Kuttner, R. 1997. *Everything for sale: The virtues and limits of markets.* New York: Alfred Knopf.

Metzger, W. 1987. The academic profession in the United States. In *The academic profession: National, disciplinary, and institutional settings,* edited by B. Clark. Berkeley: University of California Press.

———. 1989. Academic governance: An evolutionary perspective. In *Governing tomorrow's campus,* edited by J. Schuster and L. Miller. New York: American Council on Education/Macmillan.

Mortimer, K., and T. R. McConnell. 1978. *Sharing authority effectively.* San Francisco: Jossey-Bass.

Muller, S. 1994. Presidential leadership. In *The research university in a time of discontent,* edited by J. Cole, E. Barber, and S. Graubard, 115–30. Baltimore: Johns Hopkins University Press.

Rashdall, H. 1936. *The universities of Europe in the Middle Ages.* 3 vols. 2d ed. Edited by F. M. Powicke and A. B. Emden. New York: Oxford University Press.

Riesman, D. 1980. *On higher education: The academic enterprise in an era of rising student consumerism.* San Francisco: Jossey-Bass.

Rosovsky, H., with I.-L. Ameer. 1998. A neglected topic: professional conduct of college and university teachers. In *Universities and their leadership,* edited by W. Bowen and H. Shapiro. Princeton: Princeton University Press.

Schuster, J. 1989. Governance and the changing faculty condition. In *Governing tomorrow's campus,* edited by J. Schuster and L. Miller. New York: American Council on Education/Macmillan.

Schuster, J., D. Smith, K. Corak, and M. Yamada. 1994. *Strategic governance: How to make big decisions better.* Phoenix: American Council on Education/Oryx Press.

Slaughter, S., and L. L. Leslie. 1997. *Academic capitalism: Politics, policies, and the entrepreneurial university.* Baltimore: Johns Hopkins University Press.

Stronger leadership for tougher times. 1996. Report of the Commission on the Presidency. Washington, D.C.: Association of Governing Boards.

Yergin, D., and J. Stanislaw. 1998. *The commanding heights.* New York: Simon & Schuster.

Chapter Thirteen

Understanding the American Academic Profession

Martin J. Finkelstein

How far the American academic profession has fallen over the past quarter century! From its once pristine high estate of the 1950s and 1960s, it has descended (plummeted) to barely a notch above *lawyers* in the minds of government policy leaders, the press, and the general public. Especially over the past decade, it has become the subject of popular exposés, such as Charles Sykes's *Profscam* (1988) and Martin Anderson's *Impostors in the Temple* (1992). In most popular discussions of higher education these days, especially when the subject turns to spiraling college costs or the neglected state of undergraduate education, professors are at once identified as the major source of the problem and the major obstacle to reform.

How can we account for this precipitous fall from grace? What are the precise terms of the indictment of the American professoriate? How well do the indictments hold up to systematic examination of the evidence and knowledgeable analysis? In what ways are they on target or wide of the mark? And what accounts for these public perceptions—however accurate or inaccurate they may be?

It is useful to remember that as late as the mid-1960s, the American academic profession was drawing favorable ratings at the very top in polls of public confidence in occupational groups, right alongside judges and physicians (Bowman 1938; Ladd and Lipset 1975). Over the ensuing 20 years, American higher education experienced unparalleled growth—significant increases in the community col-

lege sector, the expansion of a large public system of higher education, and the concomitant expansion in the ranks of the professoriate. Two associated developments are relevant here: The first is the
extraordinary growth in demand for college faculty through the early
1970s. This industrywide seller's market fueled a golden age of compensation growth, liberal awarding of early tenure, and extension of
"professional" conditions of employment to faculty at all reaches of
the higher education system (at former public teachers colleges,
small church-related liberal arts colleges, as well as two-year community colleges). The second development is the enormous growth in
college participation rates—not only by the traditional 18-to-22-
year-old age cohort but by adults of all ages—resulting in exploding
demands on the public purse and vastly expanding the group of
stakeholders in the enterprise.

The growth of the professoriate and its privileges amid increasing
public funding and scrutiny would, in and of itself, certainly provide
the conditions for a less starry-eyed and more discriminating assessment of American professors. But that condition is not by itself
quite sufficient to account for the fall from grace. The basic premise
of this chapter is that the confluence of increasing public awareness
and scrutiny and a widening misunderstanding of—or public confusion about—the purposes of higher education generally and of the
research university in particular has contributed to a growing chasm
between the citizens of the academy and the citizens of the public
polity. Moreover, we as educators have done a very poor job indeed of
bridging that chasm and bringing to the body politic a thorough understanding of the role of the American academic profession—and its
astonishing success from a cross-national perspective.

The Emerging Indictment

A cursory review of the "muckraking" literature on the American professoriate identifies at least four major aspects of the public indictment of the faculty:

—*Scurrilous motives.* Professors, it is alleged, are less interested in
  serving the public than in serving themselves. They focus on pursuing their own research (95% of it insignificant) at the expense
  of their "real job," educating students. They are actively engaged

in a "flight from teaching," animated by a "relentless drive for advancement" (Sykes 1988) and demonstrate a "lack of loyalty to students and institution" (Smith 1990).

—*A poorly developed work ethic.* Professors, it is alleged, are perpetually seeking to "minimize classroom contact hours" (the "flight from teaching" mentioned above) so they can "do their own thing." Granted professional autonomy, they have whittled away their classroom responsibilities to the point that many teach less than six hours per week, and some do not teach at all.

—*Complacency.* The tenure system promotes laziness and indifference and protects incompetence ("deadwood") and irresponsibility (not meeting obligations).

—*Lack of accountability.* Tenure protects professorial autonomy, resulting in the faculty's being free to do as they will without being held accountable for their actions (e.g., not meeting their classes, etc.).

What's Wrong with This Picture?

How tenable are these four indictments? How is it that these charges —each of which contains a grain of truth—have been distorted in their interpretation into a fundamentally flawed picture that illuminates less than it personalizes and blames? At the root of these indictments, I would argue, is a fundamental lack of understanding of the traditional academic role—faculty as practitioners of a discipline *and* as institutional employees—and of the role of research universities. At their root as well is an unfamiliarity with the realities of what faculty do and a lack of appreciation of extant accountabilities (to their field, to their institution). Finally, these indictments reveal a misunderstanding of the institution of faculty tenure—what it is and what it is not.

The Role of Academics at Research Universities

At least part of the public misunderstanding of what research universities are is "historical." That is, research universities in the United States developed in a certain peculiar fashion (vis-à-vis other national systems). In continental Europe, universities were organized from the beginning around graduate professional education (in medicine, theology, and law) and only incidentally developed "arts colleges" to prepare students for entry to the university (Pfnister 1984). Moreover, these professionally oriented universities were seats of training and learning but were only infrequently the home of national research enterprises. In France and Germany, the two leading continental systems, research institutes were typically founded outside the university as separate single-purpose entities (Wolfle 1972).

Universities developed very differently in nineteenth-century America. In the United States, the foundation for what became the research university was the residential undergraduate college, imported from England by the Puritans and modeled after Cambridge and Oxford (Morison 1956). It was upon the foundation of this indigenous, undergraduate English college that Harvard, Columbia, and other leading American universities (often reluctantly) superimposed "graduate schools" in the late nineteenth century. Indeed, the only U.S. institutions to transplant the German university model directly—Johns Hopkins and Clark, which were founded as exclusively graduate institutions and centers of doctoral training and research—failed early and miserably until they added undergraduate divisions allowing them to be viewed as "real" colleges in the American style.

Thus, a basic tension between undergraduate education and research-graduate education was structurally built into the American system from the very beginning. Typically, at the turn of the twentieth century, it was graduate education that found itself with the "short end of the stick." Thus, for example, as late as 1900, President Charles W. Eliot at Harvard was appointing faculty primarily based on their character as gentlemen who would be a good influence on undergraduates rather than upon their scholarly prowess (he was even a bit suspicious of those sallow scholars who spent too much time in the library or laboratory) (Veysey 1965). It was not until after World War II, and especially after Sputnik, that graduate education and research displaced the primacy of the collegiate model (Kerr 1998); and it was the massive infusion of federal research funds by the Department of Defense and other agencies that shifted the balance—not the faculty. As Clark Kerr argues, once federal research funds became the largest single source of revenue for research universities, it was administrative leaders as much as faculty who put their imprimatur on the transformation.

This brief history is important for two reasons. First, it clarifies the emergence of research universities as key instruments of the national interest spurred primarily by government in the decades following World War II. And it clarifies as well their central purpose as the nation's research and development laboratories—a role that is distinctively American and at least as critical as their role in undergraduate education. Second, it prepares us to understand what emerged in the United States as the dual organization of the academic profession: responsibility to the discipline as well as to the employing institution. Concurrent with the development of the research universities in the late nineteenth and early twentieth centuries was the development of the disciplinary associations and professional societies. The purposes of these associations was to advance their disciplines at least in part by articulating and maintaining standards of research and ensuring the quality of graduate training required for entry to the discipline.

Once embarked on an academic career, the new Ph.D. has two focuses for his or her attention. First stands the invisible organization of all universities' departments in his or her discipline across the United States. New Ph.D.s must seek professional recognition from colleagues in these other national departments because the promotion and reward systems at their employing institutions are, in fact, based on reputation and accomplishment in the discipline (Alpert 1985). It is upon this external professional evaluation that most universities make their personnel decisions. Not coincidentally, it is upon the review of these professional peers that all federal research funds are awarded. What this means, of course, is that the faculty member's job, not merely from his or her own perspective but from the perspective of the employing institution, is to advance the institution's reputation in the discipline—preferably while winning huge federal grants and contracts.

The second focus of the new Ph.D.'s attention is on teaching. Universities require that faculty members' teaching be evaluated by their students and that faculty contribute service to both the institution and the broader community. But these purely institutional responsibilities must be seen in the context of the larger picture: the mission of the public research university, shaped in large part by government. That mission is reflected in the financing of research universities. On average, the typical public research university receives less than half of its annual revenue from tuition and state subsidies (this is the portion supporting undergraduate education); the remaining 50-plus percent comes from research grants, contracts, corporate support, and so on (this is the portion that supports the research and development mission) (Slaughter and Leslie 1997).

The faculty role at these institutions is organized to respond to these institutional realities, and it does so quite admirably. The point here is that the system has been organized to channel faculty energies into the "real" mission of public research universities—only a small part of which is undergraduate education. That mission, shaped by government in the post–World War II period, continues to arouse an ambivalent public reaction rooted in the historical supremacy of undergraduate education in the popular mind.

Interpreting the institutional behavior of a professional group in terms of an individual motive such as selfishness, as critics have, probably makes good copy but falls completely wide of the mark. There are, to be sure, more or less self-serving individuals in the U.S. professoriate (as there are in the law and the medical professions), but the role of the professor at the public research university requires that they aggressively pursue their own research in order to advance the institutional mission. It may be that we have too many public research universities (the subject of a recent debate in Texas [Selingo 2000]), or it may be that professors trained in research universities are seeking to turn their small colleges into research universities. But these are different matters, issues of institutional leadership and resistance to "mission creep." It is not professors as individuals who are the problem.

Understanding the Realities of Faculty Work

If the priorities of faculty work appear, in fact, to be mission-critical and shaped by appropriate organizational (system) incentives rather than the result of a quest for personal self-aggrandizement, what about the view that faculty simply don't work hard enough and are subject to no accountability? Over the past three decades, the United States, in contradistinction to nearly all other nations, has developed a rich repository of data about its college teachers. My colleague Jack Schuster and I are in the process of organizing the findings of some 16 national surveys of the American academic profession conducted between 1969 and 1999, as well as basic federal data sources on university employees and academic scientists. There is a plethora of data related to these questions that remains largely unmined. In what follows, I bring some of these data to bear on the questions of faculty workload and faculty privilege.

Overall workload. Academic work has intrinsically fuzzy boundaries. While we all agree that meeting a class several times weekly, serving on a committee, grading student papers, counseling students, or writing an article that is published by a respected journal in one's discipline is work, what about reading a book in one's discipline? What about reading a book about the changing needs of college students? What about speaking to a community group? What about thinking about a class? What about interacting with department colleagues on professional issues in the discipline? What about doing off-campus consulting in one's field? Where does academic work begin and end—especially in the Internet age?

While these definitional issues will always remain, there are some data that provide national or statewide estimates of faculty work. A convergent portrait of an approximately 50-hour workweek has remained constant over the last quarter century (Yuker 1984; Russell 1992; Finkelstein, Seal, and Schuster 1998; Meyer 1998). It is frequently higher in research universities (closer to 60 hours) than in community colleges and varies somewhat by field and family or household responsibility. Recent evidence from the Campus Computing Survey (Green 1999), the 1999 Faculty Survey of the Higher Education Research Institute at the University of California, Los Angeles (Saxe 1999), and from several new studies (Finkelstein, Frances, Jewett, and Scholz 2000) suggest, moreover, that the infusion of information technology into the academic program over the past few years has probably increased that estimate by as much as 5 to 10 percent. This is because electronic mail now allows students 24-hour-a-day, 7-day-a-week access to their teachers, and faculty are spending considerable time in learning the new technologies and in revising their course materials to integrate newly available resources from the Internet. The available evidence suggests that most of this increased workload has gone uncompensated (Frances 1999; Maitland, Hendricksen, and Dubeck 2000) and has emerged as the single greatest stressor in faculty work life (Saxe 1999).

The pervasiveness of teaching. Faculty not only work long hours; they spend a lot of that time, one way or another, on their teaching. Table 13.1 details the percentage of their time that faculty spend in teaching and research across the spectrum of institutional types. Two points are striking. First, is the significant amount of their time faculty devote to teaching rather than research. Overall, faculty spend two-fifths to two-thirds of their time on teaching and about one-seventh to one-third of their time on research. Second is the rather significant variation in teaching effort, depending on institutional type. And this is a crucial contingency. What it demonstrates is that the allocation of faculty effort follows institutional mission fairly closely: more involvement in research at those institutions whose mission it is to advance knowledge and more in teaching at those institutions with primarily teaching missions.

Moreover, there is evidence that faculty have maintained, or even expanded, their interest in and concern for the teaching of undergraduates. The data in table 13.2 tell what will be for many a very encouraging story: American faculty report their own interest in un-

Table 13.1

Mean Percentage Time in Teaching and Research for Full-time Faculty, 1984–1997

Variable	CFAT 1984	NSOPF 1988	NSOPF 1993	CFAT 1997
All FT faculty	(4,331)	(515,220)	(509,602)	(4,244)
Mean % time teaching	65.7	57.1	53.6	63.1
Mean % time research	15.0	17.2	20.1	18.8
Research universities	(1,057)	(143,700)	(141,594)	(1,170)
Mean % time teaching	50.6	43.4	37.1	34.8
Mean % time research	28.6	30.2	37.1	34.8
Doctorate-granting universities	(544)	(81,230)	(76,207)	(353)
Mean % time teaching	60.6	46.2	45.7	54.9
Mean % time research	19.1	23.9	26.5	25.8
Comprehensive universities	(1,365)	(134,030)	(131,419)	(1,020)
Mean % time teaching	67.4	63.9	59.6	63.5
Mean % time research	11.8	11.8	14.4	17.6
Liberal arts colleges	(342)	(38,430)	(39,221)	(386)
Mean % time teaching	73.1	66.9	62.8	68.4
Mean % time research	8.2	10.4	11.8	13.7
2-yr Community colleges	(1,024)	(96,150)	(103,529)	(1,314)
Mean % time teaching	80.0	73.4	71.2	77.3
Mean % time research	4.6	4.0	4.9	5.2

Key: CFAT —Faculty Survey, The Carnegie Foundation for the Advancement of Teaching. NSOPF—National Study of Postsecondary Faculty, National Center for Education Statistics, U.S. Department of Education.

Table 13.2

Faculty Interest in the Education of Undergraduates 1969–1999

	CFAT 1969	HERI 1990	HERI 1993	HERI 1996	CFAT 1997	HERI 1999
Total N	345,912	29,771	35,478	33,968	4,450	33,785
All full-time faculty	62.0	76.4	80.0	81.5	82.1	82.1
(N)	(337,815)				(4,305)	
Research universities	52.9				72.7	
(N)	(163,052)					
Doctorate-granting institutions					76.5	
Comprehensive universities	68.5	74.1	77.7	80.0	83.8	81.1
(N)	(130,929)					
Liberal arts colleges					92.6	
2-yr institutions	76.1	84.6	88.0	86.3	87.0	83.8
(N)	(43,834)					
Other institutions					NA	

The figures in this table present the percentage of faculty who "strongly" or "somewhat" agree with the statement, "Faculty at my institution are interested in the education of undergraduates."

Institutional stratification for the CFAT69 survey is universities, four-year colleges, and junior colleges. Data for this survey are thus integrated into the following three types of institutions: research universities, comprehensive universities, and two-year institutions, respectively. Institutional stratification for the HERI survey is all institutions, comprehensive universities, and two-year institutions respectively.

Key: CFAT—Faculty Survey, Carnegie Foundation for the Advancement of Teaching. HERI—Higher Education Research Institute.

Source: Saxe 1999.

dergraduate education (in contradistinction to research and graduate education) to be on the rise. In 1997, fully four out of five faculty agreed "very much" or "somewhat" that faculty interest in undergraduate education is rising compared to about three out of five in 1969. Consistent with the reported rise in faculty interest is a decline in the percentage of faculty reporting that the quality of undergraduate education is declining.

This strong growth of interest in undergraduate education, while generally pervasive, does, of course, vary across the higher education spectrum. The data show that while the greatest interest has been and remains at the historically freestanding liberal arts colleges, the research universities—often the most criticized—have not escaped the broader peaking of interest.

The increasing pressure to publish. The data above suggest at least two tentative conclusions: faculty allocate more effort to teaching and less to research than is commonly assumed; and where there is variation in teaching and research effort, rational institutional incentives, based on variation in mission, are largely responsible. The data in table 13.3 reinforce those conclusions. They suggest first that faculty perceive considerable external pressure to publish because "it is difficult for a person to achieve tenure if he or she does not publish" and they perceive further that the pressure has increased over the past five years—not only in research universities, where it was already very high, but even more so at the doctoral and master's institutions. Indeed, at research and doctoral universities, about one-third of the faculty agree with the statement "I frequently feel under pressure to do more research than I actually would like to do." What emerges here then is a picture of professionals juggling a variety of sometimes incompatible responsibilities in response to institutional incentives that are intended to promote mission-related behavior.

Research orientation versus teaching orientation. If, on the one hand, faculty report increasing external pressure to do more research and publication, the available evidence suggests limited opportunity for faculty to act upon such pressures. Since 1969, the Carnegie surveys have asked faculty to describe their "orientation" to teaching versus research on a continuum from primarily teaching to primarily research. Those data are displayed in table 13.4. What these data show are a very modest increase (5%) between 1969 and 1997 in the proportion of faculty who report themselves "leaning or heavily oriented to research" from about 25 to 30 percent and virtually no change in the proportion of faculty who report themselves "leaning or heavily oriented to teaching"—about 40 percent. While these orientations appear to reflect the pattern of our findings on the distribution of actual faculty effort—they do suggest, in terms of absolute magnitude that there remains a differential of about 10 percent between faculty research orientation and actual research time and effort. That is, faculty remain proportionately more oriented to research than the demands of their jobs allow.

While, most generally, this means that a certain tension is built into the faculty reward system requiring a delicate balancing act between teaching and research, there are, at the same time, real institutionally structured parameters within which that balancing act must be

Table 13.3

Faculty Peceptions of the Salience of Research and Publication at Their Institutions (Total Full-Time Faculty = 4,450)

Responses	All Faculty	Research Universities	Doctoral Universities	Master's Universities and Colleges	Baccalaureate Colleges	Associate of Arts Colleges
(Item 32g): Teaching effectiveness should be the primary criterion for promotion of faculty.						
Agree/somewhat agree	55.3	20.1	36.5	58.7	69.6	84.1
(N)	(4,393)	(1,200)	(364)	(1,054)	(405)	(1,372)
Agree	27.2	6.6	14.0	24.5	34.3	48.7
Somewhat agree	28.1	13.5	22.5	34.2	35.3	35.4
(Item 40b): In my department it is difficult for a person to achieve tenure if he or she does not publish.						
Agree/somewhat agree	54.9	95.1	89.1	66.3	47.5	1.7
(N)	(4,339)	(1,206)	(364)	(1,054)	(398)	(1,317)
Agree	42.7	85.6	74.5	42.1	26.6	—
Somewhat agree	12.2	9.5	14.6	24.2	20.9	1.7
(Item 40d): I frequently feel under pressure to do more research than I actually would like to do.						
Agree/somewhat agree	19.3	30.5	33.3	23.6	18.3	2.2
(N)	(4,336)	(1,204)	(363)	(1,052)	(399)	(1,318)
Agree	7.5	12.9	15.4	8.9	5.5	—
Somewhat agree	11.8	17.6	17.9	14.7	12.8	2.2
(Item 48b) Thinking about your own situation, do the following faculty activities count more or less today for purposes of faculty advancement than they did five years ago? "Research and/or other creative work"						
Count more	28.6	32.6	43.5	41.3	37.8	7.1
(N)	(4,289)	(1,201)	(363)	(1,053)	(400)	(1,273)
Count less	9.3	10.3	9.4	10.8	8.3	7.4
Count about the same	43.6	50.0	36.6	33.2	38.5	49.6

Item 32g is a 5-point scale item (strongly agree, somewhat agree, neutral, somewhat disagree, strongly disagree). Numbers 40b and 40d are 6-point scale items (strongly agree, somewhat agree, neutral, somewhat disagree, strongly disagree, not applicable). Number 48b is a 4-point scale item (count more today than five years ago, count less today than five years ago, count about the same as five years ago, don't know).

Source: 1997 Survey of Faculty, Carnegie Foundation for the Advancement of Teaching.

Table 13.4
Actual and Preferred Distribution of Effort

	Actual					
	Teaching	Research	Service	Professional Growth	Administration	Consulting
All faculty	53.8	20.1	5.7	4.7	12.8	2.6
New faculty	51.3	22.5	5.8	4.9	13.2	2.2
Senior faculty	55.1	18.9	5.6	4.7	12.6	2.9

	Preferred					
	Teaching	Research	Service	Professional Growth	Administration	Consulting
All faculty	48.6	26.6	5.4	8.0	7.9	3.3
New faculty	45.5	29.5	5.3	8.3	8.2	2.8
Senior faculty	50.1	25.1	5.4	7.8	7.8	3.5

Percents represent percentage of total time (100%). Details may not add to total because of rounding.
Source: Finkelstein, Seal, and Schuster (1998), 66.

performed. Faculty cannot simply do what they want to advance their own personal agendas—that is, act out their own research-teaching orientation. External organizational incentives, which vary across the higher education spectrum according to institutional mission, provide a critical set of boundaries within which the faculty must operate.

In sum, the evidence suggests that faculty work long hours; and they work on the activities of teaching and research in proportions that are congruent with the missions of their employing institutions.

Reconfiguration of the faculty workforce. Perhaps no single trend has more powerfully affected faculty workload than the reconfiguration of the faculty workforce that has been under way for at least the past decade. The data in figure 13.1 chronicle the dramatic increase in the use of part-time faculty (Sloan Foundation 1998); and Finkelstein, Seal, and Schuster (1998) have chronicled the dramatic increase in non-tenure-eligible, full-time faculty appointments. Indeed, the latest IPEDS data suggest that the majority of new full-time hires since 1995 have been nonregular, term appointments. While these changing appointment practices have been most notable in the community colleges and liberal arts colleges, the research universities have not been immune—especially in fields such as English, foreign languages, mathematics, and others.

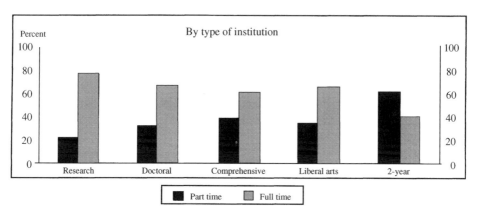

Figure 13.1
Percentage of Postsecondary Instructional Faculty and Staff, by Employment Status, Fall 1992
Source: U.S. Department of Education, National Center for Education Statistics, National Study of Postsecondary Faculty, 1993.

How does the move to a contingent workforce affect faculty work-load? The available evidence suggests that, much like technology, contingent appointments drive increases in faculty workload. It may be obvious how the appointment of increasing numbers of part-time faculty whose responsibilities begin and end with the course they are being paid to teach leaves more of the burden of curriculum development, student advising, governance, and department management to a shrinking number of core permanent staff. Less obvious is how the appointment of term or temporary full-time faculty affects department workload. When we compare the activities of "regular" versus temporary full-time faculty as reported on the U.S. Department of Education 1993 National Faculty Study (table 13.5), we find that full-time term appointees whose principal activity is teaching tend to teach more than regular faculty and to spend much less time in research, administration-governance, and student contact. These different activity patterns are discernible across all types of four-year institutions and across most academic fields—although the regular faculty versus term faculty activity differential is particularly striking in the humanities (English and foreign languages) and the natural sciences.

These data suggest that a two-tiered system of academic appointment has taken hold at four-year colleges and universities (including research universities) that distributes teaching about evenly but distributes most other work activities onto a smaller number of core, permanent faculty. And as non-tenure-eligible, full-time appointments become the norm among new hires, this increasing concentration of all nonteaching work in a shrinking core continues to accelerate.

The Myth of the Well-Paid Professor

In the popular mind, American professors not only work little while pursuing their own advancement but also manage this self-serving feat while drawing attractive compensation.[1] This is the myth of the well-paid professor, and myth it is! Figure 13.2 charts the growth in faculty compensation between 1970 and 1995, with separate lines for current versus constant dollars. The story is unambiguous: while average salaries calculated in current dollars have nearly quadrupled in the past quarter century, average salaries in constant dollars have barely recaptured their 1970 levels, following two decades of gradual

Table 13.5

Work Activities among Faculty Whose Principal Activity Is Teaching

	Regular		Term	
	% Male (N = 168,028)	% Female (N = 65,239)	% Male (N = 18,112)	% Female (N = 21,590)
All Faculty				
Teaching (mean %)	58.5	63.5	60.8	72.1
Research (mean %)	19.9	14.7	10.4	8.1
% with no publications during career	10.3	11.9	28.9	29.1
0 hours informal contact with students	10.9	9.6	20.9	13.5
Did not engage in funded research	62.9	69.1	74.3	75.4
Research universities	(N = 50,996)	(N = 13,375)	(N = 4,176)	(N = 6,706)
Teaching (mean %)	50.0	52.0	55.0	67.4
Research (mean %)	28.2	23.8	13.3	10.6
% with no publications during career	7.6	7.7	29.1	29.7
0 hours informal contact with students	14.1	11.3	26.7	13.6
Did not engage in funded research	48.8	52.5	70.9	64.7
Other Four-Year Institutions 14,884)	(N = 117,062)	(N = 51,864)	(N = 13,936)	(N =
Teaching (mean %)	62.2	66.5	62.5	74.2
Research (mean %)	16.3	12.3	9.5	6.9
% with no publications during career	11.5	13.0	28.9	28.8
0 hours informal contact with students	9.5	9.1	19.2	13.5
Did not engage in funded research	70.3	74.3	75.9	81.9

Source: National Study of Postsecondary Faculty, 1993, U.S. Department of Education.

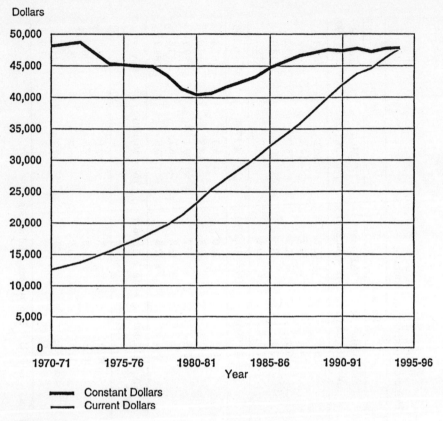

Figure 13.2
Faculty Salary Trends: Average Salary of Full-time Instructional Faculty on
9-month Contracts in Institutions of Higher Education, 1970–71 to 1994–95
Source: U.S. Department of Education, NCES, Digest of Education Statistics: 1996
(NCES 96-133), 242-43, table 229, based on data from the Integrated Postsecondary
Education Data System (IPEDS) "Salaries, Tenure, and Fringe Benefits of Full-time
Instructional Faculty" surveys.

erosion. The static picture is reaffirmed by at least one additional da-
tum. When one compares trends in average faculty salaries (adjusted
for inflation) to trends in average salaries (also adjusted for inflation)
of other professionals—in health, law, and engineering—one finds a
relatively constant faculty salary disadvantage on the order of one-
third over the past 20 years (see table 13.6).

While these data appear to suggest that the worst may be over,
that the losses of the 1970s and 1980s have been regained, and that

Table 13.6

Academic Salaries Compared with Those of Other Professionals,
Adjusted for Inflation, 1979–1997

Year	Average Adjusted All Rank Faculty Salary[a] ($)	Average Adjusted Professional Salary[b] ($)	Faculty Salary Disadvantage (%)
1979–80	47,547	61,114	29.0
1980–85	46,240	62,849	36.0
1985–90	52,515	65,599	33.0
1991	53,578	71,716	33.9
1992	53,936	71,095	31.8
1993	53,430	70,821	32.6
1994	53,685	70,505	31.3
1995	54,206	70,301	29.7
1996	54,408	70,732	30.0
1997	54,293	69,421	27.9

Notes: Salaries adjusted for inflation using the Consumer Price Index for All Urban Consumers, 1998=100 base.

[a]Based on AAUP salary survey.

[b]Professionals include health professionals, lawyers, computer and mathematics professionals, natural scientists, and engineers who have at least a master's degree and whose earnings were reported in the *Current Population Survey.*

the American faculty has recaptured their economic position of 1970, figures 13.3 and 13.4 suggest differently. When we examine trends in entry-level salaries of new assistant professors, we find that as a proportion of median family income, entry-level salaries have actually declined during this past quarter century. Moreover, when we compare salaries in the public versus the private sector, we find an entirely new and disturbing trend. While compensation in the public sector outpaced faculty compensation in the private sector until about 1980, thereafter we see a reversal in which average compensation in the private sector surpasses that in the public sector, and the gap is widening. This suggests that the financial condition of the public sector of higher education, which accounts for two-thirds of the academic profession and of the student body has been weakened during the 1990s. That does not augur well for the majority of the profession.

The above analysis, of course, focuses on full-time faculty only. While full-timers are the usual objects of popular "muckraking," it

1970-71 to 1997-98

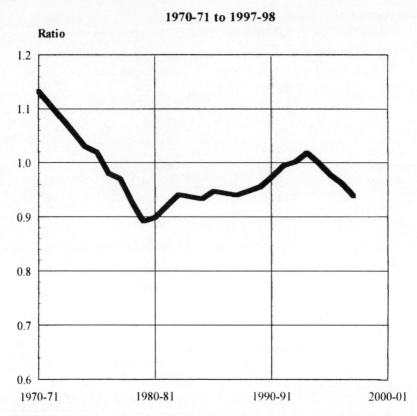

Figure 13.3
Ratio of the Average Salary of Assistant Professors to the Median Family Income

Note: The ratio is calculated using current dollar series for both the average assistant professor's salary and the median family income. The salary data starting with the academic year 1970–71 is compared with the median family income starting with the calendar year 1970. The plot spans gaps in the salary data for the years 1971–72, 1973–74, 1983–84, 1986–87, and 1988–89.

Source: The ratio is calculated using data downloaded September 20, 2000, from the U.S. Department of Education, National Center for Education Statistics, *Digest of Education Statistics: 1999* website (tables 240 and 37), <http://www.nces.ed.govpubs 2000/digest99>

should be understood that the part-time professoriate in America may now outnumber the full-time professoriate; and the compensation of part-timers is even more problematic. The available data suggest that they are paid predominantly on a course-by-course basis and at a rate that is a fraction of the per-course pay of full-timers.

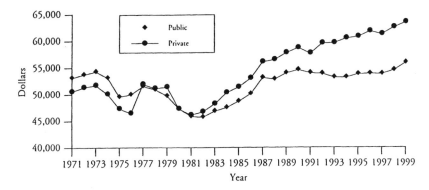

Figure 13.4
Inflation-Adjusted Average Salaries at Public and Private-Independent Institutions, All Ranks, 1970–71 to 1998–99
Source: American Association of University Professors, "Annual Survey of Faculty Salaries," 1999.

Moreover, most, even those who may teach what amounts to a full-time load, receive no benefits—not only for healthcare but also basic disability and Social Security (Gappa and Leslie 1993).

Understanding Tenure

There is no more vilified institution or practice within American higher education than the tenure system. As I suggested above, the critics are concerned about two issues in particular: first, that tenure promotes laziness and complacency, undermining the quest for excellence in higher education; and second, that tenure protects "deadwood" and incompetence.

In addressing these concerns, it is important to understand what academic tenure is and what it isn't, and how it developed in the United States. In the British system, tenure at Oxford and Cambridge conferred "fellowship" or membership in the university corporation. This fellowship constituted a legal property interest. In the continental universities, tenure was simply the designation for the employment status of a particular group of civil servants who were part of the permanent workforce in a department of national government, the universities (Metzger 1973; Cowley 1980). Tenure as we know it was a late arrival to the American system, becoming a formal part of American practice in the "1940 Statement of Principles on Academic Freedom and Tenure" of the American Association of University Professors (1961). Put another way, tenure has been the modal practice for academic appointments in American higher education for about 60 out of 360 years (the last one-sixth of our history). Prior to its arrival, the general practice that evolved in the nineteenth century, in marked contrast to that in Europe, was one of offering annual appointments to faculty (especially at the major public universities). Such annual appointments might lead, at the discretion of the institution, to "indefinite" appointments (i.e., appointments with no specified term). As Walter Metzger (1973) demonstrates in his painstaking historical analysis, the courts never interpreted such indefinite appointments to mean permanent appointments and indeed the courts have never endorsed the concept of a professor's "property right" to his or her position. This lack of protection gave rise in the nineteenth century to scores of "at will" dismissals of professors, especially at the major public universities. A change in the political majority in the legislature could and, on occasion, did lead to the wholesale nonreappointment of the entire faculty at the University of Michigan after the Civil War (Finkelstein 1984). Nor did the situation improve in the early part of the twentieth century. During the First World War professors of German were fired for expressing pro-German sentiments (Gruber 1980), and as late as the 1950s professors were summarily fired for "communist sympathies" (Schrecker 1986). All in all, the history of academic freedom in the United States is more sordid than many of us know or would like to believe.

The concept of faculty tenure articulated in the "1940 Statement" did not provide for a permanent appointment, in the European sense of property interest or of civil service status. Rather, it provided a procedure for dismissal that guaranteed due process and peer review (Metzger 1973). Moreover, by stipulating a probationary period, the policy prescribes a timetable to ensure that campuses behave responsibly toward their employees. At the end of the probationary period the recipient cannot be dismissed at will: dismissal must be preceded by a statement of charges and an opportunity to respond (due process) and a hearing in front of peers (peer review). While the procedure may be an onerous one and not one to be undertaken lightly, that is precisely the point! Unless human nature has changed fundamentally in the past half century, the need for such protection from institutional and political caprice remains.

What is the impact of such protection on faculty? At least two kinds of evidence address the question of tenure's deleterious effects on performance. The first concerns the academic achievement of higher education during the period when the practice of tenure, as we now know it, has been in effect. How does the achievement of American higher education over the past half century compare with that of the previous three centuries? How do the academic achievements of the American system compare with those of other national systems that do not provide tenure protections? And within the United States, how does the performance of colleges and universities that employ a tenure system compare to that of those that eschew it?

By any reasonable yardstick, be it the number of Nobel laureates, the number of patents filed, or the rate of citation of scientific papers, the U.S. system of higher education has emerged as the world standard during the past 50 years (Boyer 1990). The apparent correlation between a tenure system and overall system performance is very high, whether the comparison is internal (the American system over time or the most "reputable" sectors versus the less "reputable" sectors) or external (the U.S. versus other national systems). While other factors may be at work and part of the correlation may be spurious, there is very little evidence to suggest anything but a positive linkage between tenure and academic performance of the national higher education system.

If systemwide effects are positive, what about effects at the micro level of the individual (or the individual campus)? While there is no developed literature on the changes in campus performance following the institutional decision to abandon a tenure system, there is a not inconsiderable literature on the individual performance correlates of tenure (Blackburn 1972; Finkelstein 1984; American Council on Education 1997). The findings of that literature are quite conclusive: tenure has no effect whatsoever on faculty performance. As in most areas of human behavior, past performance proves the best predictor of current and future performance. Factoring in the demonstrable ups and downs of the individual career cycle (i.e., changes attributable to human development over the life span), pretenure high performers continue to perform very well post-tenure, and vice versa. That many faculty whose performance was borderline were eventually awarded tenure and continue to exhibit problematic performance is not a defect of the tenure concept, it is a defect of human judgment and human will—and *that* no systems change can remedy.

If the evidence suggests that tenure per se does not hurt faculty performance, that does not mean that college faculty, like any other occupational group, do not experience predictable (or unpredictable) career crises requiring a variety of institutional and individual interventions. Higher education has been exceedingly late in understanding its own responsibilities for the growth and development of faculty (Rice and Finkelstein 1993). But responsibility for faculty development is now emerging as a practice that is part and parcel of our tenure systems, in the form of post-tenure review (Licata 1998).

In sum, the available evidence suggests that the tenure system does not negatively affect the academic performance of individuals, institutions, or national systems (it may even help as a recruitment incentive and as a source of employment stability). If it does not detract from academic performance, there is little doubt, however, that tenure does detract from institutional flexibility in managing personnel and academic staffing resources. The trade-offs between performance and flexibility are the proper subjects for institutional self-examination and strategic planning; and this is a much more useful exercise than playing the blame game.

Summing Up the Argument

This chapter has advanced a four-pronged argument to support an assessment of the ethics, behavior, and contributions of the American faculty to higher education and the national interest that is very different from that of the media and the general public. Let us review that argument.

—*The proper job of faculty at American research universities is as much to do research as it is to teach undergraduates.* The tensions between research and teaching were built into U.S. universities by their peculiar historical evolution—the superimposition of a continental graduate university onto an indigenous English residential college—and by the actions of the federal government in locating the national research enterprise within rather than outside the universities. In short, the tension between research and teaching is an artifact of how the system developed, aided and abetted by government policy. Faculty are behaving the way we have always expected them to and in response to incentives that the system has structured to serve the national interest.

—*The available empirical evidence suggests that faculty, especially university faculty, work hard, about 50 to 60 hours per week.* They spend as much time teaching now and are as interested in undergraduate education as at any time since 1970; and they spend less time than we think doing research. Their allocation of effort varies across institutions with different missions. The pressure to publish has increased overall, and a third of all faculty at research universities actually report being under pressure to do more research than they wish to do. Moreover, while faculty are increasingly pressured to do research, their employers are structuring their jobs (increasing teaching loads) to preclude their fully responding to these pressures. A number of recent developments beyond economic constraints, including the transition to a contingent workforce and the impact of new information technologies, are driving increases in faculty workload.

—*While faculty pay may be better in the United States than abroad, it has been declining, in real dollars, since 1970 and remains 25 to 33 percent below compensation in medicine, law, and engineering.* Academic salaries have grown more slowly than salaries in the economy as a whole. And while the decline appears to have reversed itself in the 1990s, entry-level salaries have actually declined relative to the median family income.

—*Tenure in the United States is a post–World War II practice that neither confers civil service status nor a property interest on the incumbent. It is essentially an onerous dismissal procedure that safeguards against at will termination by requiring due process and peer review.* At the macro, or systems, level the available evidence suggests that higher education systems with some form of tenure academically outperform systems without tenure, in terms of number of Nobel laureates and other forms of recognition. At the micro, or individual, level there is no evidence that receipt of tenure negatively affects faculty performance, and emerging post-tenure review systems are seeking to ensure that result. While tenure positively affects academic performance, it does negatively affect organizational staffing flexibility, and institutions need to weigh the trade-off between academic performance and organizational flexibility when considering a tenure system.

Taken together, the available empirical evidence suggests that American faculty, especially those at our research universities, are doing a remarkably good job (nay, a world-class job) of balancing a number of sometimes incompatible responsibilities (responsibilities that have largely been shaped by government policy in consideration of the national interest) despite worsening working conditions, declining research funding, and the challenges posed by information technology and reconfigured staffing.

So what accounts for the "bum rap"; or, at least, the juxtaposition of two such divergent assessments? In part, the sheer growth in participation in and public funding for higher education over the past quarter century has grossly raised the stakes, multiplying the numbers of stakeholders and the diversity of their interests. It is within such a context that higher education has created new types of institutions (community colleges and multipurpose public master's institutions) and added new functions to existing institutions (while attempting to continue unmodified faculty personnel and staffing arrangements developed for the mid-twentieth century research university). A "boutique" system focused on the scholarly role of faculty, on their autonomy to pursue research, in combination with their institutional teaching obligations has over the past quarter century been uncritically transferred (applied) to the rest of the system, where it may not fully belong. What was appropriate to promote research in a relatively narrow sector of higher education (and supported by Cold War urgency) may not be "scalable" to an expanded and diversified system. That may be the lesson we are learning from these contrasting assessments of the professoriate. And that lesson suggests that we uplift our conversation about academic staffing with a critical understanding of mission relevance and the changing mission mix in our increasingly universal system. To the extent, however, that we seek to optimize overall system performance, let us not throw the proverbial baby out with the bath water and damage an indigenous American institution that has so well served the national interest.

Future Prospects

How can the positive interpretation of academic work that we have advanced in the foregoing analysis be helpful in shaping the future of the American academic profession and ultimately American higher education? And why is the negative interpretation less helpful? And what, to be concrete, might that future look like, given current trends in the larger environment?

We have suggested that the American professoriate has, by and large, performed well and, in doing so, advanced the national interest. How assured are the prospects that contributions at so high a level will continue? To what extent will the new market for educational services and rapidly escalating college costs, aided and abetted by popular scapegoating of the academic profession, provide the pretext for the uncritical reconstituting of its roles and functions or simply vitiate any perceived national interest in maintaining the health of the academic profession? Or, to what extent will the power of inertia simply prevail by default?

The basic trend we have identified is one of increasing differentiation of roles and functions. That is, differentiation in kinds of appointments (part-time or full-time, permanent or temporary) proceeded very rapidly in the 1990s. Since 1995, full-time permanent positions have become the exception rather then the rule among new hires. Moreover, differentiation of function—that is, the establishment of new kinds of instructional roles and the increasing specialization of faculty in one role or another—is becoming increasingly tied to different types of appointments. These trends are challenging the hegemony of the trinity: the basic principle of modern academic culture that defines academic work as the combination of teaching, research, and service activities performed by a single individual.

In concrete terms, this means that most of our colleges and universities will develop at least a two-tiered faculty. The only exceptions may be a small group of affluent, elite institutions roughly equivalent to the membership of the Association of American Universities and the old Association of American Colleges. At the research universities, which are less likely than other types of institutions to employ part-timers, this two-tiered system is likely to mean varieties of full-time faculty: a "teaching only" faculty, especially in the humanities; a "research only" faculty in the natural sciences and engineering; and a shrinking core of permanent faculty playing the traditional role. Add to that a possible fourth estate consisting of a "clinical only" faculty in the professions. This will ultimately add up to a segmented or stratified faculty, one that ultimately devolves academic administrative and citizenship responsibilities onto an ever smaller and more overworked core.

How will the near-term environment of higher education, the usual demographic and financial trends, affect this scenario? The available evidence suggests several developments that will likely accelerate these trends and several that might slow them down. The most powerful trend will be demographic, the baby-boomer offspring who will be clogging traditional college classes for at least the first decade of the twenty-first century. Thus many of the research universities will have no dearth of traditional residential students. This will cut both ways. On the one hand, the presence of traditional students will support the need for traditional faculty members—at least in the short run. On the other hand, the presence of more traditional undergraduate students will increase the pressure on research universities, especially public research universities, to emphasize their teaching function and increase pressure on their faculties, especially the shrinking core, to do ever more. That in turn will encourage many promising academics, especially women who seek greater balance in their lives to accept nontraditional appointments that involve fewer and more circumscribed responsibilities.

Concurrent with demographics are the financial trends. While the economic boom of the 1990s resulted by 2000 in substantial budget surpluses in many states, there is still some question as to whether this signals the end of the state-level austerity trend of the 1980s and 1990s (note the increasing preemptiveness of the claims of corrections, Medicare, elementary education on a relatively fixed state pie). My best guess is the "boom" public higher education is experiencing will barely have repaired the damage of the previous generation before the economic cycle (if such business cycles continue into the Internet age) reverses itself. We cannot expect a substantial new infusion of public resources for vastly expanding traditional higher education at its traditional unit cost (and with its traditional staffing pattern). So, cost pressures, perhaps the biggest accelerator of the trend toward hiring mainly part-time and temporary faculty, will likely continue.

Information technology (IT) remains the greatest wildcard in all of this. Two things seem very likely, however. First, information technology will increase interinstitutional competition as all institutions gain access to a global market unconstrained by geography (no institution will retain its own geographic preserve). Thus cost competition will increasingly drive institutions in the offering of academic programs: institutions will need to offer programs at costs within the range of those offered by competitors or be unable to mount or maintain them.

Second, IT itself will transform campus budgets. It is doing so already. What we now know suggests that IT is increasingly requiring reallocation from other academic areas. Increases in the nonfaculty professional IT staff costs are putting pressure on traditional faculty budgets. This will continue to increase overall cost pressures.

Intellectual property issues will arise. To the extent that distance learning creates a new market for educational materials, professors, especially the academic stars, will likely compete in defining a new market for educational products. Professor X at Harvard will be able to offer his course material to students at other colleges. This suggests increasing differentiation within the academic market, with the "stars" becoming very big; and the little, local players being part of a different market. Of course, how this scenario will play out remains unclear. But what is obvious is the high degree of uncertainty within which higher education and its faculty are and will continue to be operating in the first decade of the twenty-first century.

Note

1. I am indebted to Carol Frances (1998) for several of the subsequent compensation-related tables and figures as well as for her assistance in furthering my understanding of faculty compensation trends.

References

Alpert, D. 1985. Performance and paralysis: The organizational context of the American research university. *Journal of Higher Education* 56 (May–June): 241–81.

American Association of University Professors. 1961. 1940 statement of principles on academic freedom and tenure. In *American higher education: A documentary history,* edited by R. Hofstadter and W. Smith. Chicago: University of Chicago Press.

American Council on Education. 1997. Senior faculty: Active and committed. *Research Notes.*

Anderson, M. 1992. *Impostors in the temple.* New York: Simon & Schuster.

Berelson, B. 1960. *Graduate education in the United States.* New York: McGraw-Hill.

Blackburn, R. T. 1972. Faculty responsiveness and faculty productivity as functions of age, rank and tenure: Some inferences from the empirical literature. *Resources in Education* 7 (June): 44.

Blackburn, R. T., and J. Lawrence. 1995. *Faculty at work: Motivations, expectations, satisfactions.* Baltimore: Johns Hopkins University Press.

Bowman, C. 1938. *The college professor in America: An analysis of articles published in the general magazines, 1890–1938.* Philadelphia: University of Pennsylvania Press.

Boyer, E. A. 1990. *Scholarship reconsidered: Priorities of the professoriate.* Princeton: Carnegie Foundation for the Advancement of Teaching.

Cowley, W. H. 1980. *Presidents, professors, and trustees,* edited by D. T. Williams. San Francisco: Jossey-Bass.

Finkelstein, M. 1984. *The American academic profession.* Columbus: Ohio State University Press.

Finkelstein, M., R. Seal, and J. Schuster. 1998. *The new academic generation.* Baltimore: Johns Hopkins University Press.

Finkelstein, M., C. Frances, F. Jewett, and B. Scholz, eds. 2000. *Dollars, distance, and online education: The new economics of college teaching and learning.* Phoenix: ACE/Oryx.

Frances, C. 1998. Higher education: Enrollment projections and staffing needs. *TIAA-CREF Research Dialogues* 55 (March).

———. 1999. Planning assumptions for instructional technology. *Change* 31 (July–August): 25.

Gappa, J., and D. Leslie. 1993. *The invisible faculty.* San Francisco: Jossey-Bass.

Green, K. C. 1999. *The campus computing survey—1999.* Encino, Calif.: Campus Computing Survey.

Gruber, M. 1980. *Mars and Minerva.* Baton Rouge: Louisiana State University Press.

Kerr, C. 1994. *The great transformation.* Albany: State University of New York Press.

———. [1963] 1998. *The uses of the university.* Rev. ed. Cambridge: Harvard University Press.

Ladd, E. C., and S. M. Lipset. 1975. *The divided academy.* New York: McGraw-Hill.

Licata, C. 1998. Post tenure review. *New Pathways Working Paper Series.* no. 12. Washington, D.C.: American Association for Higher Education.

Maitland, C., R. Hendricksen, and L. Dubeck. 2000. Faculty costs and compensation in distance education. In *Information technology: The costs for collegiate teaching and learning,* edited by M. Finkelstein, C. Frances, F. Jewett, and B. Scholz. Phoenix: ACE/Oryx.

Metzger, W. P. 1973. Tenure: An historical essay. In *Faculty tenure.* San Francisco: Jossey-Bass.

Meyer, K. A. 1998. *Faculty workload studies: Perspectives, needs and future directions.* ASHE-ERIC Higher Education Research Reports, Vol. 26, no. 1. Washington, D.C.: George Washington University.

Morison, S. E. 1956. *The intellectual life of colonial New England.* New York: New York University Press.

National Center for Education Statistics. 1995. *1993 national study of postsecondary faculty.* Washington, D.C.: U.S. Department of Education.

Pfnister, A. O. 1984. The role of the liberal arts college: A historical overview of the debates. *Journal of Higher Education* 54 (March–April): 145–70.

Rice, R. E., and M. Finkelstein. 1993. The senior faculty: A portrait and literature review. In *Developing senior faculty as teachers,* edited by M. Finkelstein and M. LaCelle, New Directions in Teaching and learning no. 55. San Franciso: Josey-Bass.

Russell, A. 1992. *Report on faculty workload.* Denver: Education Commission of the States.

Saxe, L. 1999. *The American college teacher: National norms for the 1998–1999 HERI Faculty Survey.* Los Angeles: Higher Education Research Institute, University of California, Los Angeles.

Schrecker, E. 1986. *No ivory tower: McCarthyism and the universities.* New York: Oxford University Press.

Selingo, J. 2000. How many research universities does a state need? *Chronicle of Higher Education* 96 (February 11): A-28.

Slaughter, S., and L. Leslie. 1998. *Academic capitalism: Politics, policies, and the entrepreneurial university.* Baltimore: Johns Hopkins University Press.

Sloan Foundation. 1998. *Part-time, adjunct and temporary faculty: The new majority?* Report of the Sloan Conference on Part-time and Adjunct Faculty. New York: Alfred Sloan Foundation.

Smith, P. 1990. *Killing of the spirit.* New York: Viking.

Sykes, C. 1988. *Profscam: Professors and the demise of higher education.* Washington, D.C.: Regnery Gateway.

Veysey, L. 1965. *The emergence of the American university.* Chicago: University of Chicago Press.

Wolfle, D. 1972. *The home of science.* New York: McGraw-Hill.

Yuker, H. 1984. *Faculty workload: Research, theory and interpretation.* ASHE-ERIC Higher Education Report, no. 10. Washington, D.C.: George Washington University.

Contributors 〜

Philip G. Altbach is the J. Donald Monan S.J. Professor of Higher Education and director of the Center for International Higher Education at Boston College. He has been a senior associate of the Carnegie Foundation for the Advancement of Teaching and is author of, among other books, *Comparative Higher Education: Knowledge, the University, and Development*. He is editor of the *Review of Higher Education*. He has taught at the State University of New York at Buffalo and the University of Wisconsin-Madison and has served as a Fulbright professor at the University of Bombay, India.

Robert Birnbaum is a professor of higher education at the University of Maryland, College Park, where he studies college and university organization and leadership. He previously served as vice chancellor of the University of Wisconsin-Oshkosh. Among his books are *How Colleges Work* (1988), *How Academic Leadership Works* (1992), and *Management Fads in Higher Education* (2000). Birnbaum is a former president of the Association for the Study of Higher Education and recipient of its Research Achievement Award.

Martin J. Finkelstein is a professor of higher education at Seton Hall University. He is coauthor of *The New Academic Generation*. From 1989 to 1997, he directed the New Jersey Institute for Collegiate Teaching and Learning, where he led curriculum development efforts. He also served as director of assessment for Seton Hall's online "virtual" university, Setonworldwide. His research has been supported by the U.S. Department of Education, the National Science Foundation, and other agencies.

Richard M. Freeland has been president of Northeastern University, Boston, Massachusetts, since 1996. He previously served as founding dean of the College of Professional Studies and dean of the College of Arts and Sciences at the University of Massachusetts-Boston, vice chancellor for academic affairs at the City University of New York, and as president of the CUNY Research Foundation. Dr. Freeland holds a doctorate in American civilization from the University of Pennsylvania and is the author of *Academia's Golden Age* (1992).

Patricia J. Gumport is an associate professor in the School of Education at Stanford University. She serves concurrently as the director of the Stanford Institute for Higher Education Research and as the executive director and principal investigator of the National Center for Postsecondary Improvement. She has been a member of the Stanford University faculty since 1989. Gumport's expertise extends across a range of research and policy issues in higher education— from the management of academic change and organizational restructuring to the interdependence between graduate education and knowledge production to reconciling the tensions in contemporary academic workplaces.

D. Bruce Johnstone is University Professor of Comparative and Higher Education at the State University of New York at Buffalo. He has been chancellor of the State University of New York and president of the State University College at Buffalo.

George Keller is a higher education analyst and writer and a consultant to colleges and universities. A former faculty member, college dean, presidential assistant, and chair of higher education studies at the University of Pennsylvania's Graduate School of Education, he has written many articles and reviews and has published three books, including *Academic Stategy*.

Nannerl Overholser Keohane is president of Duke University and a professor of political science. She came to Duke from the presidency of her alma mater, Wellesley College, in 1993. She attended Oxford University on a Marshall Scholarship and earned her Ph.D. at Yale University in 1967. Previously, Dr. Keohane taught at Swarthmore College, the University of Pennsylvania, and Stanford University. She has written extensively in the fields of political philosophy, feminism, and education.

George D. Kuh is a professor of higher education at Indiana University in Bloomington. He directs the College Student Experiences

Questionnaire Program and the National Survey of Student Engagement, an annual survey of first-year and senior college students, which is co-sponsored by the Pew Charitable Trusts and the Carnegie Foundation for the Advancement of Teaching. Past president of the Association for the Study of Higher Education, Kuh has written extensively and made hundreds of presentations on topics related to college and university cultures, student engagement, assessment, and institutional improvement. He has also consulted with more than 130 educational institutions and agencies in the United States and abroad.

Jules B. LaPidus was president of the Council of Graduate Schools, Washington, D.C., between 1984 and 2000. He received his bachelor's degree from the University of Illinois and M.S. and Ph.D. degrees from the University of Wisconsin. His field of specialization is medicinal chemistry. In 1958 he joined the faculty of Ohio State University as assistant professor of medicinal chemistry and was professor of medicinal chemistry from 1967 to 1984. In 1972 he was appointed dean for research in the Graduate School at Ohio State University and became dean of the Graduate School and vice provost for research in 1974.

Arthur Levine is president and a professor of education at Teachers College, Columbia University. Previously, he served as chair of the higher education program and chair of the Institute for Educational Management at the Harvard Graduate School of Education, as president of Bradford College, and as senior fellow at the Carnegie Foundation and Carnegie Council for Policy Studies in Higher Education. His most recent book is *When Hope and Fear Collide: A Portrait of Today's College Student* (with Jeanette S. Cureton), published in 1998.

Frank Shushok Jr. is a doctoral candidate in the higher education policy program at the University of Maryland, College Park. He received his M.A. in higher education from Ohio State University and his B.S. from Baylor University. He is currently studying the relationship between honors programs and student performance.

Martin Trow is professor emeritus in the Goldman School of Public Policy at the University of California, Berkeley, and a research fellow in its Center for Studies in Higher Education, of which he was founding director. Professor Trow has been a fellow of the Center for Advanced Study in the Behavioral Sciences in Palo Alto, a visiting member of the Institute for Advanced Study at Princeton, and a fellow of the Swedish Center for Advanced Study in the Social Sciences in Uppsala. He is a past vice president of the National Academy of Education, a fellow of the American Association for the Advancement of Science, and a fellow and vice president of the Society for Research in Higher Education in Great Britain. In March 1997, he was awarded the Berkeley Citation for Distinguished Achievement and Notable Service to the University.

Jack M. Wilson is the J. E. Jonsson Distinguished Professor of Physics, Engineering Science, Information Technology, and Management at Rensselaer Polytechnic Institute. He is also codirector of the Severino Center for Technological Entrepreneurship at Rensselaer. He came to Rensselaer in 1990, and has previously served as dean of undergraduate education and as acting provost and has held several other positions. He was executive officer of the American Association of Physics Teachers and a physics professor at the University of Maryland. He is also an entrepreneur who founded the LearnLinc Corporation and continues to serve as chairman of its board.

Index ◂